WATSON-GANDY ON ACCOUNTANTS
Law, Precedents, Practice and Procedure
2nd Edition

WATSON-GANDY ON ACCOUNTANTS
Law, Precedents, Practice and Procedure
2nd Edition

PROFESSOR MARK WATSON-GANDY
of the Inner Temple, Barrister
One of the Junior Counsel to the Crown
Visiting Professor to the University of Westminster

FOREWORDS BY

Lord Neubeger of Abbottsbury

Gill Ball
ACCA President

David Hunt
Institute of Financial Accountants

Philip Turnbull
Chief Executive, Association of International Accountants

© Professor Mark Watson-Gandy 2008

Produced and Distributed by   *for*

xpl publishing   Hammicks Legal Publishing
99 Hatfield Road   Ash House
St Albans AL1 4JL   Headlands Business Park
UK   Ringwood, Hants
                                        BH24 3PB, UK

www.xplpublishing.com   www.hammickslegal.com

ISBN 978 1 85811 600 6

All rights reserved. No part of this publication may be reproduced, stored in a retrieval system, or transmitted, in any form or by any means, electronic, mechanical, photocopying, recording or otherwise, without the prior permission of the publisher.

Printed and typeset in the UK

Disclaimer

This work is not a substitute for legal advice in relation to any particular case. Although the authors have attempted to produce a work which is designed to assist the practitioner, neither they or the publishers undertake any duty of care to any person or entity whatsoever, without limitation, in relation to any of the statements in, or omissions from this work, and accepts no legal liability or responsibility in respect of any statements in or omissions from this work.

With Thanks to

Ben Jowett
Institute of Chartered Accountants in England and Wales

Robin Vaughan
The Chartered Institute of Management Accountants

Jillian Smith
The Association of Chartered Certified Accountants

Steven Boakes
The Institute of Financial Accountants

CONTENTS

Foreword: Lord Neubeger of Abbottsbury	ix
Foreword: Gill Ball, ACCA President	xi
Foreword: David Hunt, Institute of Financial Accountants	xiii
Foreword: Philip Turnbull, Chief Executive, Association of International Accountants	xv
Table of Cases	xvii
Table of Statutes	xxv
Table of Regulations	xxxi

Chapters

1.	The accountant	1
2.	The accountancy practice	21
3.	The accountant and his client	47
4.	Claims against accountants	91
5.	Auditors and Reporting Accountants	103
6.	Claims against auditors	131
7.	Other Roles of the accountant	145
8.	The accountant and the courts	163
9.	Disciplinary proceedings	181
10.	International practice	201

Annexes: Checklists

1.	Checklist for a deed of partnership	207
2.	Checklist for an agreement for the sale of an accountancy practice	211
3.	Checklist for an accountant's employment contract	213
4.	Checklist for "fit and proper" enquiries of employees working for auditors or liquidators	217
5.	Checklist for Instructing an Expert Accountant	221
6.	Checklist for an expert report under the Civil Procedure Rules	223

Precedents

1.	Letter of Engagement	225
2.	Heads of Agreement – accountancy practice sale	231
3.	Claim form in an action to recover unpaid accountancy fees	233
4.	Particulars of claim in action to recover unpaid accountancy fees	236
5.	Defence to claim for unpaid fees and Counterclaim for professional negligence (late preparation of solicitors' accounts)	239
6.	Reply by accountant denying professional negligence and alleging contributory negligence	244

7.	Preliminary Letter in an action for professional negligence against an accountant (negligent tax advice/ tax return)	247
8.	Pre-action Protocol Letter in an action for professional negligence against an accountant (negligent tax advice/ tax return)	248
9.	Claim form in an action for professional negligence against an accountant (negligent tax advice/ tax return)	253
10.	Particulars of claim in an action for professional negligence against an accountant (negligent tax advice/ tax return)	256
11.	Defence in an action for professional negligence against an accountant (negligent tax advice/ tax return)	261
12.	Claim form in an action for professional negligence against an auditor (negligent audit)	263
13.	Particulars of claim in an action for professional negligence against an auditor (negligent audit)	266
14.	Defence by auditor denying professional negligence	271
15.	Application to obtain the delivery up of accountant's papers	274
16.	Claim form(delivery up of accountant's papers)	278
17.	Witness statement (delivery up of accountant's papers)	281
18.	Injunction Order (delivery up of accountant's papers)	284
19.	Claim form in an action for the dissolution of an accountancy partnership	287
20.	Particulars of Claim in an action for the dissolution of an accountancy partnership	290
21.	Grounds of appeal against the finding of a disciplinary tribunal	293
22.	Board resolution for the appointment of first auditors	297
23.	Ordinary resolution for the appointment of first auditors	298
24.	Notice of Annual General meeting	299
25.	Resolution for the reappointment of auditors	300
26.	Letter of resignation as auditors	301
27.	Ordinary resolution ending the appointment as auditors	302
28.	Letter proposing a resolution for the removal of auditors	303
29.	Resolution for the removal of auditors	304
30.	Resolution by a dormant company not to appoint an auditor	305
31.	Resolution dispensing with the laying of accounts before a general meeting	306
32.	Resolution approving auditors limited liability agreement	307

Selected Case Summaries 309

Institutes and Associations Conferring the Qualification of Accountants 326

Websites 328

Index *329*

Foreword

Lord Neuberger of Abbottsbury

There is a tendency among lawyers to approach the law by reference to legal topics, and a tendency among non-lawyers to see the law as an adjunct to their own particular fields of work. By way of example, consider a possible claim for negligence against an auditor, or the rights of partners on the dissolution of an accountants' partnership. A lawyer will see the former as raising questions on the law of tort and the latter as giving rise to questions on the law of partnership. An accountant will see the issues as throwing up problems particular to his or her profession. Such differences of approach are understandable, indeed inevitable, because they reflect the needs, interests and experience of the people concerned.

However, the consequences can be unfortunate in practice, when it comes to the need for a legal view or opinion. Legal books dealing with particular topics, such as tort or partnership law, will, no doubt, mention cases which are concerned with accountants, and may even occasionally have brief sections dealing with accountants, but particular concerns of accountants are unlikely to be addressed as such, and, where they are, the passages will often be hard to find. Many problems will involve more than one legal aspect, and there will be the additional problem of having to go from one legal book to another. On the other hand, books on accountancy, while often no doubt treating the effect of the law as important, will not see it normally as a topic of central significance, and will often deal with it in a relatively cursory manner. This is particularly unfortunate in the light of the high standards expected of professional people and in what is sometimes seen as a burgeoning climate of litigiousness, and above all for a profession which, as much as any other, is subject to ever-increasing regulation and public scrutiny.

It is for this reason that a book which concentrates on the law relating to accountancy is particularly valuable and to be welcomed. In one volume, it is possible to read about the statutory, regulatory, common law and professional rules and principles which apply to all professional aspects of the accountancy profession, and in a book which is specifically directed to accountants (and their advisers).

It is important that such a book not only sets out the law fully and accurately, but also that it is clear and practical in its structure and its contents. In that connection, this book succeeds handsomely. Consideration of the chapter headings shows that the structure is logical and easy to follow, and ensures full coverage of the issues which are likely to be of concern to accountants. This second edition also takes into account significant changes which have occurred since the first edition, such as the passing of the Companies Act 2006, the coming into force of the 2005 EC regulations relating to professional qualifications, as well as a mass of recent court decisions, new regulations, and modifications and changes to professional standards.

The volume of relevant material is very substantial indeed, and its effect and consequences are presented in a clear, logical and user-friendly way, always with supporting references, so a reader who wants to delve even more deeply into a particular aspect will know where to look.

Apart from the text and usual supporting aspects (such as index and list of cases), the author is particularly to be congratulated for including a list of precedents, and, unusually but very practically and helpfully, six checklists, each of which is designed to help accountants and their advisers through certain familiar, but very important and potentially problematic, activities.

The accountancy profession occupies a significant and responsible role in the modern commercial world, and the rule of law is self-evidently of importance to the commercial world, as well as more generally. Accordingly, we should all be very grateful to Mark Watson-Gandy for producing the second edition of Accountants: Law Practice and Procedure. It will provide invaluable assistance to accountants (as well as their legal and other advisers) on virtually all aspects of their professional lives.

Lord Neuberger of Abbottsbury
March 2008

Foreword

Gill Ball

ACCA (the Association of Chartered Certified Accountants) is the largest and fastest-growing global professional accountancy body with over 122,000 members and 325,000 students in over 170 countries. We aim to offer the first choice qualifications to people of application, ability and ambition around the world who seek a rewarding career in accountancy, finance and management.

The effective financial management of any business depends on the accurate measurement of cash flows, assets and liabilities and investment risks. Reliable accounting information also helps third parties make investment decisions and protects prospective creditors against risks associated with commercial dealings. Without thorough and professionally prepared accounting information, those risks would be altogether greater, both for the individual business and for all its varied stakeholders.

But the role of today's accountants is not just restricted to financial reporting. The law is increasingly requiring new corporate disclosures, some of which go far beyond the confines of the purely financial. All accountants need to be aware of such developments.

Accountants in business often act as directors or company secretaries and have express legal responsibilities as a result. Even where they do not act in such capacities, they are still expected to have a high awareness of how the law affects the financial management and regulatory obligations of their businesses. The scope of the auditor's work is also expanding in line with this trend. For example, practising accountants are now subject to stringent requirements regarding the detection and reporting of money laundering and financial support for terrorism.

Over and above all this, the range of services accountants now provide to clients – be they in-house or external - has today expanded far beyond what was traditionally required.

It follows that the legal environment impacts the work of accountants more today then ever before. This book is of special relevance to them addressing, as it does, the specific ways in which the law affects them and their profession. Whatever their individual roles may be, all accountants are sure to find the contents of this book invaluable.

Gill Ball
ACCA President

Foreword

Professor David Hunt

Passing the examinations for qualification as an accountant is the easy bit. It is more difficult to bring together all the knowledge that is needed to manage a business, whether in business or practice. What is needed is a handbook for the working accountant. That is something that acts as a first stop then leads, if necessary, deeper into the subject. This is that book.

As an enthusiastic reader of the first edition, I can certainly recommend this second edition. It is a very useful book to turn up to set the scene when thinking through a problem. Indeed it is so well written that I have found myself reading on and almost forgetting the original problem, being especially drawn by the precedents and case studies. So it is well researched and enjoyable – that is a rare combination.

As the President of the Institute of Financial Accountants, I have found it very useful in the administration of an accountancy institute. Therefore I would recommend for anybody in such administrative roles. In an Institute with Members specialising in the SME sector, it is particularly pleasing for me to see a book that looks at on accountants and their needs. Too often the accountant gets overlooked by emphasis on the audit role, but here the needs of both are considered. That is only right and proper, after all there are more accountants than auditors.

So read it and enjoy it – I am sure that you will do both.

Professor David Hunt
MSc FCA FCIPD CPFA FFA FMAAT FSCMA FIAB FRSA
President Institute of Financial Accountants
Past President Association of Accounting Technicians

Foreword

Philip Turnbull

It is a pleasure for me to write this foreword for Mark Watson-Gandy, who has been a valued member and friend of AIA for a number of years.

This book gives a refreshing insight into the law surrounding the accountancy profession, and highlights key aspects of the law which can affect an accountant's practice. This book is a must read for accountants, auditors and lawyers wanting to gain further understanding of the laws surrounding the accountancy profession.

The second edition of this book includes a wide range of case summaries, checklists and precedents which successfully demonstrate the authors work. The book can be used as a point of reference for practising accountants, yet also can make an interesting read for those with an interest in law.

A high level of knowledge and research is apparent in the writing of this book, and the author manages to turn the most complex issues of law into understandable reading. In addition, the case summaries make interesting reading, and help demonstrate the key issues that are raised in the book.

As with his previous works, the second edition of *Watson-Gandy on Accountants* is well structured, thoroughly researched and a delight to read.

Philip Turnbull
Chief Executive, Association of International Accountants

Table of Cases

Re Abbey Leisure [1990] BCC 69...8.3.2
Abbott v. Sullivan [1952] 1 KB 189...9.3.1
ABTA v. British Airways plc [2000] 1 Lloyd's Rep 169...3.2.3.2,3.3.5.1
Al Saudi Banque v. Clarke Pixley, The Financial Times, 4th August, 1989...6.1.3.1
Albert and le Compte v Belgium (1983) 5 EHRR 533...9.1.6,9.2.1
Alexander v. Jenkins [1842] 1 QB 797...1.4
Re Allen, Craig & Co. (London) Ltd [1934] Ch 483...5.4.3
Amalgamated Society of Carpenters v. Braithwaite [1922] 2 AC 440...9.3.1
Andreou v. ICAEW [1998] 1 All ER 14 Court of Appeal...1.2.4,9.1.1,9.3.1,9.3.2,*307*
Anglo-American Asphalt Company Ltd v. Crowley Russell & Co Ltd [1945] 2 All ER 324 Romer J...*319*
Aplin v. White [1973] 1 WLR 1311...3.5.1
Re Arctic Engineering [1986] 1 WLR 686...7.1.3
Associated Picture Houses Ltd. v Wednesbury Corporation [1948] 1 K.B. 223...9.3.2
Associated Portland Cement Manufacturers v. Price Commission [1975] ICR 27...6.2.1
The Association of Certified Public Accountants v. Secretary of State for Trade and Industry [1998] 1 WLR 164 Jacobs J...1.2.3,*307*
Attorney General for Hong Kong v. Reid [1994] 1 AC 324...3.2.3.4,3.3.5.4
AWG Group v. Morrison [2006] 1 All ER 967...9.3.2

Bank Melli Iran v. Barclays Bank [1951] TLR 1057...3.3.1
Bank of Credit and Commerce (Overseas) Limited v. Price Waterhouse (1998) The Times, 4 March...6.1.3.1
Bankole v. ACCA (1995) LTL 17 November Court of Appeal...1.5.1,9.3.1,*307,309*
Barclays Bank v. Taylor [1989] 3 All ER 563...3.2.3.7
Barings v Coopers & Lybrand [2002] Lloyds Rep PN 323...6.1.3.3
Kim Barker v. Aegon Insurance Company (UK) (1989) The Times, 9 October, Court of Appeal...8.3.2
Barry v Bradshaw [2001] ILPr 706, [2000] CLC 455 Court of Appeal...*320*
Re Bath Glass [1988] BCLC 329...3.7.3,7.3.1
Bathold v Germany (1985) 7 EHRR 383...9.2.1
Bell v Peter Browne & Co [1990] 2 QB 495...4.1.7,6.1.5
Bell v. Strathairn & Blair (1954) 104 LJ 618...4.1.2,6.1.2
Benson v Thomas Eggar & Sons, unreported, 2nd December 1977...4.1.2
Berg & Sons v. Adams (1992) Financial Times, 10th July Hobhouse J...*313*
Bernadone v. Pall Mall Services Group [1999] IRLR 617...2.4.1.6
Bevan v. Webb [1901] 2 Ch 59...3.3.2
Bolam v. Friern Hospital Management Committee [1957] 1 WLR 582....3.1.2.2.1,4.1.3.1
Bond v. Barrow [1902] 1 Ch 353...8.3.1
Bonnardet v. Taylor (1861) 1 John & H 383...3.4.7
Booth v. Arnold [1895] 1 QB 571...1.4
Bourne v. Wicker [1927] 1 Ch 667...2.5.2
Bowman v Fels [2005] EWCA Civ 226...3.6.3
Bracken Partners v. Gutteridge [2003] 2 BCLC 84...3.2.2
Briggs v. Boss LR 3 QB 268...1.1.6
Bristol Airport v Powdrill [1990] Ch 744....3.4.4
British Oxygen Co. v Minister of Technology [1971] A.C. 610...9.3.2
Brown v. IRC [1965] AC 244...3.5.1
Brown v. Smith [1895] 13 CB 596...1.4

Burchell v. Wilde [1900] 1 Ch 551...2.5.3

Campbell and Fell v UK (1984) 7 EHRR 165....9.2.1
Candler v. Crane, Christmas & Co [1951] 2 KB 164...4.1.3.1,6.1.3.1
Caparo Industries v. *Dickman* [1990] 2 AC 605 House of Lords ...4.1.3.1,4.1.6,5.2.1,6.1.3.1,6.1.4,*313*
In Re Capital Fire Assurance (1883) 24 Ch D. 408...3.4.4
Capital and Counties Bank v. George Henry & Sons (1882) App Cas 741...1.4
Re Cargo Agency [1992] BCLC 686...3.7.3
Cartledge (Widow and Administratrix of the Estate of Fred Hector Cartledge (decd)) v. E Jopling & Sons Ltd [1963] AC 758...4.1.7
Cassell v. Crutchfield (Inspector of Taxes) (1995) The Times, 8th June Blackburne J...1.2.3.1,8.1.5,*316,320*
Casson Beckman & Partners v. Papi (1990) *Financial Times*, 3 August...3.2.3.4
Cavendish Bentick v. Fenn (1887) 2 App Cas 652....3.2.3.3,3.3.5.3
Chantrey Martin v. Martin [1953] 2 QB 286...3.2.1,3.2.3.6,3.3.3,3.3.5.6,3.4.2,3.4.3,8.5.2
Chartered Accountant v Inspector of Taxes [2003] STI 885 Lloyd J...*319*
Chaudhry v.Prabhakar [1989] 1 WLR 29...3.2.3.2,3.3.5.2
Caparo Industries plc v. Dickman and Ors [1990] 2 WLR 358...4.1.3.1
Re Cargo Agency [1992] BCLC 686...7.3.3
Chauhan v. Chauhan [1997] 2 FCR 20...8.1.4
Re City Equitable Fire Insurance Co. Ltd [1925] Ch 407...5.2.5,5.4.6,6.1.2,6.1.3.1
Re Cladrose [1990] BCC 11...3.2.2,3.7.3,7.3.3
CMS Dolphin v. Simonet (23.5.01, High Court)...3.2.2
Phyllis Colgan v Kennel Club (2001) Lawtel 9th September...9.3.1
Colleen v.Wright (1857) 8 E & B 647...4.1.5
Commissioners for Revenue and Customs v. Barclays Bank plc [2007] AC 181...4.1.3.1
Continental Illinois National Bank & Trust Co. of Chicago v. Daniel Davies & Co [1987] CLY 3545...3.5.1
Conway v. Raitu [2006] 1 All ER 571...3.2.1
Cook v. Swifen [1967] 1 WLR 457...4.1.6
Cottle v. Cottle [1929] 2 All ER 535...9.3.2
Cox v. Coulson [1916] 2 KB 177...2.1.1.1
Credit Lyonnais Bank Nederland NV v. Export Credit Guarantee Department [1999] 2 WLR 540...3.3.1
Croft v. Day (1843) 7 Beav 84...2.2.3
Cruttwell v. Lyle (1810) 17 Ves 335...2.5.1
Cuff v. London and County Land and Building Co. [1912] 1 Ch 440...5.4.2

D v. S (Rights of Audience) [1997] 2 FCR 217...8.1.4
D'Arcy v. Adamson (1913) 29 TLR 367...9.3.1
Data Protection Registrar v. Griffin, (1993) *The Times*, 5 March, Divisional Court...3.4.8
de Beeche v. South American Stores [1935] AC 148...8.3.3
De Meza and Stuart v. Apple, Van Straten, Shena and Stone [1975] 1 Lloyd's Rep 498...4.1.3.1,6.1.3.2
Deloitte Haskins & Sells v. *National Mutual Nominees* [1993] AC 774 House of Lords...4.1.1,6.1.1,*313*
Derby and Co. Ltd v. Weldon (No. 9), (1990) The Times, 9th November...8.3.4
Diennert v France (1996) 21 EHRR 554...9.2.1
Dixon v. Australian Society of Accountants (1989) 95 FLR 231, Supreme Court of Australia, Capit. Territ...1.2.2
Dodd v. Amalgamated Marine Workers Union [1925] 1 Ch 116...3.3.2
Dodswell v. Jacobs (1887) 34 Ch D 278...3.2.1
Re Douglas Construction Services Ltd [1988] BCLC 3973...3.7.3,7.3.3
DTC v. Gary Sergeant [1996] 1 WLR 797 Crystal QC...3.4.4,*319*

Duchess of Argyll v. Beuselinck [1972] 2 Lloyds Rep 172, 183...4.1.2
Dunne v. English (1874) LR 18 Eq 524...2.1.1.3

Engel v Netherlands [1976] 1 EHRR 647...9.2.1
Esso Petroleum v. Mardon [1976] QB 801...4.1.6
Ewing v. Buttercup Margarine Company Ltd [1917] 2 Ch 1...2.2.3
Extrasure Travel Insurance v Scattergood [2003] 1 BCLC 598...3.2.2

Fawkes-Underwood v. Hamiltons [1997] 7 CL 456, (1997) LTL 24 March Judge Goudie QC...3.1.2.2,4.12,*321*
Flett v. Matheson [2005] IRLR 412...1.5.2
Foaminol Laboratories v. British Artid Plastics [1941] 2 All ER 393...4.1.6
Fogg v. Gaulter (1960) 110 LJ 718...3.2.3.7,3.4.3
Folkes v. Chadd (1782) 3 Doug 157...8.3.2
Fomento (Sterling Area) Ltd v. Felfdon Fountain Pen Company Limited [1958] RTC 8 House of Lords...5.4.4,*321*
Forsikringsaktieselskapet Vesta v. Butcher [1989] AC 852...4.1.3.2,6.1.3.2
Forster v. Outred & Co (a firm) [1982] 1 WLR 86...4.1.7
Fox v General Medical Council [1960] 3 All ER 225...9.1.6
Fox v Uxbridge General Commissioners [2002] STC 455 Jacob J...*318*
Franks v. Towse [2001] EWCA Civ 9...8.3.2
Friends Provident Life Office v Hillier Parker [1995] 4 All ER 26...6.1.3.3

Galoo v. Bright Grahame Murray [1994] 1 WLR 1360...4.1.6,6.1.4
Garnac Grain v. HMF Faure & Fairclough Ltd [1968] AC 1130...3.3.1
Gibbs v Guild (1882) 9 QBD 259...4.1.7,6.1.5
Gillingham v. Beddow [1900] 2 Ch 242...2.5.2
Goldstein v Levy Gee (2003) The Times 16th June Lewison J...*310*
Gorlov v Institute of Chartered Accountants in England and Wales (2002) Lawtel 19th November Stanley Burnton QC...*308*
Gray v. Haig (1855) 20 Beav 219...3.2.3.5,3.2.3.6,3.3.5.5,3.5.5.6
Green v. Howell [1910] Ch 495...2.1.1.2
Gregory v. Duke of Brunswick (1844) 6 Man & G 953...1.4
Grimm v Newman [2003] 1 All ER 67 Court of Appeal...*310*
Ginesi v. Cooker & Co. (1880) 14 Ch D 596...2.5.1,4.1.2
Gray v. Haig (1855) 20 Beav 219...3.2.1
Groom v. Crocker [1939] 1 KB 194...4.1.6
Re GSAR Realisations Ltd [1993] BCLC 409...3.7.3,7.3.3

Re H (a barrister) [1981] 3 All ER 205...9.1.6
H v Belgium (1988) 10 EHRR 339...9.1.6
Haig v. Bamford (1977) 72 DLR (3d) 68, Supreme Court...6.1.3.1
Hands v Coopers & Lybrand (2001) Lawtel 25th April Sachs J...6.1.3.1,*311*
Harmony Shipping Co v. Saudi Europe [1979] 1 WLR 1380...8.3.3
Harker v Edwards (1887) 57 LJQB 147...9.1.4
Harrington v. Sendall [1903] Ch 921...9.1.1
Harrison v. Festus Timothy [1998] 2 CL 1 Butterfield J...3.4.4,*319*
Hart v. Newspaper Publishing (1989) *The Times*, 9 November...1.4
Re Haslam [1902] 1 Ch 765...3.2.3.4,3.3.5.4
Haward v. Fawcetts [2006] 1 WLR 682...4.1.7
Heald Foods v. Hyde Dairies (1996) LTL 6 December Court of Appeal...8.4,*317*
Hedley Byrne v. Heller [1964] AC 464...4.1.3.1
Henderson v. Merrett Syndicates Ltd [1995] 2 AC 145...4.1.3,6.1.3
The Hermione [1922] P 162...3.2.3.2,3.3.5.1
Herring v Templeman (1973) 137 JP 514...9.1.4

Heywood v. Wellers [1976] QB 446, 463H-464A...4.1.6
Hiscox v. Greenwood (1802) 4 Esp 174...3.4.4
Home or Away v Customs & Excise Commissioners (2002) Lawtel 3rd May VADT (Angus Nicol, Chairman)...8.1.5,8.5.1,*315*
Hopkinsons v. Marquis of Exeter (1867) LR 5 Eq 63...9.3.1
Ex parte Horsfall 7 B & C 582...3.4.3
HRH Prince Jeffri Bolkiah v. KPMG [1999] 1 All ER 517, [1999] 2 WLR 215 House of Lords...3.2.3.7,3.4.3,p314
Hussein v Chaing Fook Kam [1970] AC 942...3.6.5.5
Re Hyams and the Public Accountants Regulation Act [1975] 2 NSWLR 854...9.1.3

In Plus Group v. Pyke [2002] 2 BCLC 201...3.2.2
Independent Advantage Insurance Company v Cook [2004] PNLR 3...6.1.1
Ingram v. Keeling (2006) Lawtel 14th November...3.4.5
Initial Services v Putterill [1967] 3 All ER 145...9.1.4
Institute of Chartered Accountants in England and Wales v Customs & Excise Commissioners (1999) *The Times*, 29 March, House of Lords...1.2.5.1
IRC V. Hamilton-Russell Executors [1943] 1 All ER 474...3.5.1
Ireland v. Livingston (1872) LR 5 HL 395...3.2.3.2,3.3.5.1

Re J [1990] F.C.R. 193...8.3.4
JEB Fasteners v Mark Bloom & Co [1983] 1 All ER 583...4.1.3.1
Johnson v. Kershaw (1847) 1 De G & Sm 260...8.3.2

K Ltd v National Westminster Bank [2006] EWCA Civ 1039...3.6.5.5
Killick v Pricewaterhouse Coopers Neuberger J [2001] 1 BCLC 65...*311*
Re Kingston Mills (No. 2) [1896] 2 Ch. 279...6.1.2,6.1.3.1
Korda v International Tennis Federation (1999) The Times 4th February...9.1.2
Kranidiotes v. Paschali [2001] EWCA Civ 357...8.3.4

Langstaff v. Birtles [2001] 1 WLR 470...3.2.1
Larchin v. North Western Deposit Bank LR 10 Ex 64...1.1.6
Law Society v KPMG Peat Marwick (2000) The Times 6th July Court of Appeal...4,1,3,1,*311*
Law Society v Sephton [2006] 3 All ER 401 House of Lords...4.1.7,*312*
Le Compte, Van Leuven and De Meyere v. Belgium (1982) 5 EHRR 18...9.2.1,9.3.2
Lee v Showmens Guild of Great Britain [1952] 2 QB 329...9.1.1,9.3.2
Lee v UK (2000) Lawtel 22nd September...9.2.1
Lee Ting Sang Chung v. Chung Chi Keung [1990] 2 WLR 1173...2.1.1.1
Leech v. Stokes [1937] IR 787...4.1.2
Leeds Estate Building Investment Co v. Shepherd (1887) 36 Ch D 787...3.3.4,5.2.3
Lees v. M Young Legal Associates [2006] 1 WLR 2652...2.1.1.1
Leicestershire County Council v. Michael Faraday & Partners Ltd [1941] 2 KB 205 216...3.4.2
LHS Holdings v. Laporte [2001] EWCA Civ 278...8.3.1
Liddell v Middleton [1996] PIQR 36...8.3.2
Lilley v. Barnsley (1844) 1 Car & Kir 344...3.4.4
Lindsay v. Gladstone (1869) LR 9 Eq 132...3.4.7
Peter Lingham v Karl Lonnkvist (2000) Lawtel 12th July Court of Appeal....*311*
Lloyd v. McMahon [1987] 1 All ER 1118...9.3.2
Lloyd Cheyham & Co. Ltd v. Littlejohn [1986] PCC 389...4.1.2,4.1.3.1,6.1.2,6.1.3.1,6.2.1
Re Lo-Line Electric Motors [1990] BCLC 677...3.7.3,7.3.1
In re London General Bank (No 2) [1895] 2 Ch 673...5.4.4,5.4.5
Luksch v Austria (2002) 35 EHRR 17 European Court of Human Rights...9.2.1,*314*

McKenzie v. McKenzie [1970] 3 All ER 1034...8.1.1
James McNaughten v. Hicks Anderson & Co [1991] 2 QB 113 Court of Appeal...6.1.3.1,*312*

Magill v. Weeks [2002] 2 WLR 37...9.3.2
Malhotra v. Dhawan (1997) LTL 28 April Court of Appeal...*316*
Marcus v Institute of Chartered Accountants (2004) EWHC 3010 (ChD) ...*308*
Markapolou v Minister for Development Case C255/01 European Court of Justice...10.2.2,*321*
Maritime Insurance Co v. Fortune (1931) 41 Lloyds Rep 16...3.1.2.1
Marsh Ferriman & Cheale v. Cutler (1998) Lawtel 24th June...2.1.1.1
Meadow v General Medical Council (2006) The Times 31 October...8.3.5
Midland Bank Co Ltd v. Hett Stubbs & Kemp [1979] Ch 384...4.12
Monarch SS v. Kalishamns Oljefabriker [1949] AC 196...4.1.6,6.1.4
Morgan Crucible Co. v. Hill Samuel Bank Ltd, The Independent, 27th July, 1990...6.1.3.1
Morton v. Arbuckle (No 2) [1919] VLR 487...3.2.3.1

Nadarajah v. Secretary of State for the Home Department [2005] EWCA Civ 1363...9.3.2
Nagle v. Fielden [1966] 2 QB 633...9.3.1
National Greyhound Racing Council v Tom Flaherty [2005] EWCA Civ 1117...1.2.4,9.1.4,9.3.1
National Justice Compania Naviera SA v. Prudential Assurance Co Ltd (The "Ikarian Reefer") [1993] 2 Lloyd's Rep. 68...8.3.4
Nationwide Building Society v. Lewis [1998] Ch 482....3.3.1
Nationwide Building Society v. Various Solicitors (1998) *The Times,* 1 May...3.2.3.7
Needham v Nursing and Midwifery Council [2003] EWHC 1141...9.1.6
Nelson Guarantee Corporation Ltd v. Hodgson [1958] NZLR 609...8.3.1
Newells v. Gillingham Corporation [1941] All ER 552...1.5.2
Newton v. Birmingham Small Arms Company Ltd [1906] 2 Ch 378...5.4.2
Nitrotrim v. Wildin (1996) LTL 29 April McKinnon J...3.2.1,*315*
Nordenfelt v. Maxim Nordenfelt Guns and Ammunition Co [1894] AC 535...2.4.1.1
Norey v. Keep [1909] 1 Ch 561...3.3.1,3.3.2
Nwabueze v GMC [2000] UKPC 16...9.1.6
Nykredit Mortgage Bank plc v. Edward Erdman Group Ltd (No 2) [1997] 1 WLR 1627...4.1.7

O'Connor & Ould v. Ralson [1920] 3 KB 451...1.1.3
Odeon Associated Theatres v. Jones [1972] 2 WLR 331...8.3.1
Sylvanus Okoye v. Leon Edgar White (1999) LTL 17 February Court of Appeal...1.1.6,3.1.2.2.2,3.1.2.2.4,8.3.1,*320*
OR v Stern [2000] 1 WLR 2230...9.2.1
Osman v. Moss [1970] 1 Lloyds Rep 313...4.1.6

Pacific Acceptance Corporation Ltd v. Forsyth (1970) 92 WN (NSW) 29...6.1.2
Re Pantone [2002] 1 BCLC 266...3.2.2
Parmar (trading as Ace Knitwear) v Woods (2002) The Times 5th June, [2002] STI 852 Lightman J...1.2.3.1,8.1.5,8.3.2,*315*
Parmiter v. Coupland [1936] 6 M & W 105...1.4
Parry-Jones v The Law Society [1968] 1 All ER 177...9.1.4
Pawsey v. Armstrong (1881) 18 Ch D 698...2.5.3
Penn v. Bristol & West Building Society [1995] 2 FLR 938...4.1.5
Peter Pan Manufacturing v. Corset Silhouette [1963] RPC 45....*318*
Phipps v. Boardman [1967] AC 46...3.2.3.3,3.3.5.3
Pinnock v. Harrison (1838) 3 M & W 532...3.4.4
Pollivitte Ltd v. Commercial Union Assurance Company Plc [1987] 1 Lloyd's Rep. 379...8.3.4
Poplar Housing and Regeneration Community Association Limited v. Donoghue, [2001] 3 W.L.R. 183, CA....9.2.1
Porter v Magill [2002] 2 A.C. 357...9.3.2
Re Press Caps [1949] Ch 434...6.2.1

Re Queens Moat Houses plc, SOS for Trade and Industry v Bairstow [2004] All ER (D) 333 (Jul)...3.7.3

R v Altrincham Justices, ex p Pennington [1975] QB 549...9.3.2
R v. Bedwelty UDC ex parte Price [1934] 1 KB 333...3.3.2,9.3.2
R v. Boal [1992] 1 QB 591...5.3.5
R. v. Brixton Prison Governor ex parte Bidwell [1937] 1 KB 305...9.1.4
R v. Callendar [1993] QB 303...1.2.3, 3.1.1
R v. Callender [1992] 3 WLR 501 Court of Appeal...*307*
R v Campbell 78 Cr App Rep 95...7.3.2
R v Da Silva [2006] EWCA 1654, K Ltd v National Westminster Bank [2006] EWCA Civ 1039...3.6.5.5
R v Deputy Industrial Injuries Commissioner ex parte Moore [1965] 1 All ER 81...9.1.5
R (Fleurose) v Financial Services Authority (2002) Times 15th January...9.2.1
R v Football Association Ltd, ex p Football League Ltd [1993] 2 All ER 833...9.3.2
R v Garvey [2001] EWCA Crim 1365...3.4.4
R v General Medical Council ex parte Nicoliades (2001) Lawtel 27th July...9.2.1
R v. Ghosh [1982] QB 1053...3.2.3.8
R v Gulbir Singh (2003) CA...3.6.1
R. v. Hull University ex parte Page [1993] AC 682...1.5.1
R v. Institute of Chartered Accountants ex parte Brindle (1994) The Times, 12th January Court of Appeal...9.3.3,*309*
R v Institute of Chartered Accountants in England and Wales ex parte Eliades (2001) Lawtel 31st January...7.1.1
R v. Institute of Chartered Accountants ex parte Nawaz [1997] 7 CL 1 Court of Appeal...9.1.4,*309*
R v. Disciplinary Committee of the Jockey Club ex parte The Aga Khan [1993] 1 WLR 909...9.3.2
R v Disciplinary Committee of the Jockey Club ex parte Massingberd-Mundy [1993] 2 All ER 207...9.3.2
R (Donoghue) v. Cork County Justices [1910] 2 IR 271...9.3.2
R v. Halifax Justices, ex p Robinson (1912) 76 JP 233...9.3.2
R v. Inland Revenue Commissioners Ex p. Unilever plc [1996] S.T.C. 681...9.3.2
R. v. Jockey Club ex Parte RAM Racecourses Ltd [1993] 2 All ER 225...9.3.1,9.3.2
R (on the application of Thompson) v The Law Society [2004] 2 All ER 113 Court of Appeal...9.1.6,9.2.1,9.3.2,*308*
R v King [1983] 1 All ER 929...8.5.2
R v Lambert [2001] HRLR 1267...9.2.1
R. v. North and East Devon Health Authority Ex p. Coughlan [2001] Q.B. 213...9.3.2
R. v North West Lancashire Health Authority Ex p. A [2000] 1 W.L.R. 977...9.3.2
R v R [1994] 4 All ER 260...8.5.2
R v Secretary of State for Transport ex parte Factortame [2002] 3 WLR 1104 Court of Appeal...8.3.4,*316*
R. v. Seelig [1991] 4 All ER 429...9.1.4
R. v. Silverlock [1894] 2 QB 766...8.3.3
R v. Southwark Crown Court ex parte Bowles [1996] 4 All ER 961 Simon Brown LJ...315,317
R. v. Sussex Justices ex parte McCarthy [1923] All ER 233...9.3.2
R v Turner [1975] QB 834...8.3.2
Raiss v Palamo (2001) PNLR 540...8.3.5
Ramrath v. Minister of Justice [1992] CL 4769 European Court of Justice...10.2.2,*322*
Ratcliffe v. Evans [1892] 2 QB 524...1.4
Regal Hastings v. Gulliver [1942] 1 All ER 378...3.2.3.4,3.3.5.4
Re Republic of Bolivia Exploration Syndicate Ltd [1914] 1 Ch 139...5.4.5,5.4.6
Re Richborough Furniture Ltd [1996] BCC 155...7.4.1
Republic of Ireland v United Kingdom (1978) 2 EHRR 25...9.2.2

Ridge v Baldwin [1963] 2 All ER 66...9.1.6,9.3.2
Roebuck v. National Union of Mineworkers (Yorkshire Area) [1977] ICR 573...9.3.2
Rommelfanger v Germany (1989) 62 DR 151...9.2.1
Ronbar Enterprises Ltd v. Green [1954] 2 All ER 266...2.4.1.1
Royal Bank of Scotland v Bannerman Johnston Maclay (2002) The Times 1st August Court of Session, Outer House (Scot)...6.1.3.1,*311*
Russell v. Duke of Norfolk [1949] 1 All ER 109...9.3.1

Same v. Stretch [1936] 2 All ER 1237...1.4
Sasea Finance v KPMG [2000] 1 BCLC 236 Court of Appeal...6.1.2,*310*
Sayers v Clarke Walker (2002) EWCA Civ 910 Court of Appeal...3.1.2.2.1,4.12,*313*
Seabrook v British Transport Commission [1959] 1 WLR 509...3.6.3
Secretary of State for Trade and Industry v Deverell [2001] Ch 340...7.3.1
Segbedzi v Segbedzi LTL 28/5/99, CA...3.5.1
Re Sevenoaks Stationers (Retail) Ltd [1990] BCLC 668...3.7.3,7.3.1
Shorrock v. Meggitt [1991] BCC 471 Court of Appeal...5.2.4,*323*
Simmons v. Pennington & Son [1955] 1 WLR 183...3.2.3.2,3.3.5.2
Slattery v Moore Stephens [2004] PNLR 241 Robert Englehart QC...p310
Smith v. Eric S Bush [1989] 2 All ER 514...6.1.3.1
Smith v UK (2000) 29 EHRR 493...9.2.1
Smith v. Wheeler (1669) 1 Mod Rep 16...3.5.1
Society of Accountants v. Lord Advocate (1924) SLT 194...1.5.2
Society of Accountants & Auditors v. Goodway [1907] 1 Ch 489, *Society of Accountants in Edinburgh v. Corporation of Accountants* (1903) 20 R 750 (Scotland)...1.2.3
Society of Incorporated Accountants v. Vincent (1954) 71 RPC 325...1.2.3
Re a Solicitor [1972] 2 All ER 81...1.2.4,9.1.2,9.1.3
Spackman v. Evans (1868) LR 3 HL 171...5.4.5
Stanton v Callaghan [2000] QB 75, Court of Appeal...8.3.5
Stekel v Ellice [1973] 1 All ER 465...2.1.1.1

Target Holdings v. Redferns [1996] 1 AC 421...4.1.6
Taylor v National Union of Seamen [1967] 1 WLR 532...9.3.1
Tehrani v United Kingdom Central Council for Nursing Midwifery and Health Visiting [2001] 1 IRLR 208...9.2.1
Thaper v. Singh [1987] FLR 369...3.4.4,3.4.5
Thlimmenos v Greece (2001) 31 EHRR 159 European Court of Human Rights...314
Re Thomas Gerrard & Sons Ltd [1967] 2 All ER 525...6.1.2
Thomson v. University of London (1864) 33 LJ Ch 625...1.5.1
Thorpe v. Dul [2004] ICR 1556...1.5.2
Three Rivers DC v Governor & Company of the Bank of England [2005] 1 AC 610...3.6.3
Tormont Holdings v. Thorne Gunn & Helliwell (1975) 62 DLR (3d) 465...4.1.6,6.1.4
Re Transplanters (Holding Co) Ltd [1958] 1 WLR 822...3.3.4,5.2.3
Trego v. Hunt [1896] AC 7...2.5.1,2.5.2
The Tzelpi [1991] 2 Lloyd's Rep 265...3.3.5

United Bank of Kuwait v. Hammoud [1989] 1 WLR 1051...3.3.1

Re Vandervell's Trusts (No. 2) [1974] Ch 269...3.5.1
Re Vickery [1931] 1 Ch 572...3.3.2

Wallace v. CA Roofing Services Ltd [1996] IRLR 435...1.5.2
Way v. Latilla [1937] 3 All ER 759...3.3.5
Re West Sussex Widows and Children Benevolent Fund Trust [1971] Ch 1...3.5.1
West Wiltshire District Council v. Garland [1995] 2 WLR 439 Court of Appeal...312
Whalley v Roberts [1990] 1 EGLR 164...8.3.3

White v. Jones [1995] 2 AC 207...4.1.3,6.1.3
Whitehouse v. Jordan [1981] 1 W.L.R. 246...8.3.4
Whiteoak v. Maxwell (1988) 4 BCC 122...6.1.2
Willingale v. International Commercial Bank Ltd [1978] AC 834 House of Lords...6.2.1,*312,323*
Wilson v. United Counties Bank [1920] AC 102...4.1.6
Woodworth v. Conroy [1976] 2 WLR 338 Court of Appeal...3.4.4,*318*

Yeong Hoi Yuen v. Secretary of State for the Home Department [1977] Imm AR 34...1.5.2
Yonge v. Toynbee [1909] 1 KB 215...4.1.5
Youssoupoff v. Metro Goldwyn-Mayer Pictures (1930) 50 TLR 581...1.4

Ziderman v General Dental Council [1976] 2 All ER 334...9.1.3

Table of Statutes

Bankruptcy Act 1978
s.101(1)...1.1.3
Bills of Exchange Acts...1.1.6
Business Names Act 1985...2.1.2.3
s1(1)...2.2.2
s1(2)...2.2.2
s4(1)...2.1.1.5
s4(4)...2.1.1.5
s8(1)...2.2.1,2.2.2

Charities Act 2006
s32...5.5.1
Civil Evidence Act 1972
s3(1)...8.3.2,8.3.3
s4(2)...8.3.3
Civil Liability (Contribution) Act 1978
s1...6.1.3.3
s2(1)...6.1.3.3
s2(3)...6.1.3.3
s6(1)...6.1.3.3
Companies Act 1947
s13(1)...5.4.3
Companies Act 1948
s149(1)...5.4.3
Companies Act 1969
s13(1)...5.1.2
Companies Act 1981...5.4.3
s188...7.1.3
Companies Act 1985
s32...1.2.3
s35...307
s144(3)...6.1.6
s144(4)...6.1.6
s221...3.4.4,3.7.3,5.1.1,7.3.1,*319*
s222...3.4.4, 3.7.3,7.3.1,*319*
s226...5.4.3
s227...5.4.3
s227(2)...5.4.3
s227(3)...5.4.3
s234ZA...5.4.2,6.1.3.3
s235...5.4.3
s235(2)...5.4.3

s235(3)...5.4.3
s236(1)...5.4.3
s236(2)...5.4.3
s236(3)...5.4.3
s236(4)...5.4.3
s237(1)...5.4.4
s237(2)...5.4.4
s237(3)...5.4.4
s237(4)...5.4.4
s238...*5.3.5*
s246...5.1.1
s249A...5.1.1.1,5.5.1
s249A(1)...5.1.1
s249A(3)...5.1.1,5.5.1
s249AA...5.1.1.1
s249B...5.1.1.1,5.5.1
s249C(1)...5.5.1
s249D...5.5.5
s249D(3)...5.5.3
s250(3)...5.1.1
s255(1)...5.1.1.2
s255(2)...5.1.1.3
s255(3)...5.1.1.2,5.1.1.3
s286...7.4.1
s288...3.7.3,7.3.1
s299...3.7.3,7.3.1
s264...3.7.4
s310...5.2.5
s310(2)...3.1.2.3,4.1.8
s310(3)(a)...6.1.6
s310(3)(b)...6.1.6
s352...3.7.3,7.3.1
s363...3.7.3,7.3.1
s364...3.7.3,7.3.1
s365...3.7.3,7.3.1
s381A...5.4.1
s384(1)...5.2.2
s385(2)...5.2.2,5.3.1
s385(3)...5.2.2,5.3.1
s385(4)...5.2.2,5.3.1
s386...5.3.2
s389...2.1.3
s389A...2.1.2.8,5.4.2,6.1.3.3

Companies Act 1985 *cont*
s389A(1)...5.4.2
s389A(2)...5.4.2
s389A(3)...5.4.2
s389A(4)...5.4.2
s389B...6.1.3.3
s390...2.1.2.8
s390(1)...5.4.1
s390(1)(a)...5.4.1
s390(1)(b)...5.4.1
s390(2)...5.4.1
s390(3)...5.4.1
s390A...2.1.2.8,5.2.2
s391...2.1.2.8,5.3.3
s391(3)...5.3.3
s391(4)...5.4.1
s392(1)...5.3.3
s392(4)...5.3.4
s392A(5)...5.3.4
s392A(6)...5.3.4
s393(1)...5.3.2
s393(2)...5.3.2
s393(3)...5.3.2
s393(4)...5.3.2
s393(5)...5.3.2
s393(6)...5.3.2
s393(7)...5.3.2
s394(1)...5.3.3,5.3.4,5.3.5
s394(3)...5.3.5
s394(4)...5.3.2,5.3.5
s394(5)...5.3.5
s394(6)...5.3.5
s394(7)(a)...5.3.5
s394(7)(b)...5.3.5
s394A...5.3.5
s394A(4)...5.3.5
s398B...5.4.2
s415...3.7.3,7.3.1
s447...9.1.5
s449(1)(L)...9.1.5
s459...8.3.1
s716(2)...2.1.1.5
s716(2)...2.1.1.5
s716(3)...2.1.1.5
s727...6.1.6
s741...7.3.1
Sch 4...3.7.4,5.1.1.2,5.4.3
Sch 4A...5.4.3
Sch 9...5.1.1.2

Sch 9A...5.1.1.3
Sch 15A...5.4.1
Companies Act 1989...2.1.2.8
s1...5.4.3
s2...3.4.4
s4(1)...5.4.3
s24(2)...10.2.1
s25(1)...5.1.2
s25(2)...5.1.4
s27(1)...5.1.5,7.4.2
s27(2)...5.1.5
s27(3)...5.1.5
s28(1)...5.1.5
s28(2)...5.1.5
s28(3)...5.1.5
s29(1)...5.1.6
s33(1)(2)...5.1.4
s34(1)...5.1.3
s34(3)...5.1.3
s35(1)...5.1.4
s35(2)...5.1.4
s41(1)...51.7
s41(2)...51.7
s41(3)...51.7
s52...5.1.5
s212...2.1.3
Sch 12...5.1.3,9.1.8
Sch 24...2.1.3
Companies Act 2006
s65...2.2.1
s113...3.7.3,7.3.1
s114...3.7.3,7.3.1
s162...3.7.3,7.3.1
s270(1)...7.4.1
s273...7.4.1
s275...3.7.3,7.3.1
ss288-297...5.4.1
s303...5.4.3
s382...5.1.1
s386...3.4.4
s387...3.4.4,3.7.3,7.3.1
s388...3.4.4
s389...3.4.4,3.7.3,7.3.1
s396...5.1.1,5.1.1.2,5.1.1.3
s404...5.4.3
s418...6.1.3.3
s477...5.1.1.1
s478...5.1.1.1
s481...5.1.1.1

Companies Act 2006 *cont*
s485...5.2.2
s485(2)...5.3.6
s485(3)...5.2.2,5.3.1
s485(5)...5.2.2,5.3.1,5.3.2
s486...5.3.2
s487(2)...5.2.2,5.3.2,5.3.6
s488...5.2.2,5.3.2,5.3.6
s489...5.2.2
s489(2)...5.3.1
s489(3)...5.2.2,5.3.1
s489(4)-(5)...5.3.2
s490...5.3.2
s492...5.2.2
s495...5.4.3
s496...5.4.3
s495(3)...5.4.3
s498...5.1.8,5.4.4
s499...5.4.2,6.1.3.3
s499(2)(c)...5.4.2
s500...5.4.2,6.1.3.3
s501...6.1.3.3
s501(2)...5.4.2
s501(3)...5.4.2
s502(1)...5.4.1
s502(2)(a)...5.4.1
s502(2)(b)...5.4.1
s502(2)(c)...5.4.1
s502(3)...5.4.1
s503...5.4.3
s503(4)...5.4.3
s504...5.1.8,6.1.8
s504(1)...5.1.8,6.1.8
s504(2)...5.1.8,6.1.8
s505(1)...5.1.8,6.1.8
s504(3)...5.1.8,6.1.8
s505...5.4.3
s505(1)...6.1.8
s506(2)...5.1.8,5.4.3
s507(2)...5.1.8
s510(1)-(2)...5.3.3
s510(3)...5.3.3
s511...5.3.3,5.3.4
s513...5.4.1
s532...3.1.2.3,4.1.8,5.2.5,6.1.7
s532(2)... 4.1.8,5.2.5,6.1.7
s534(2)(b)... 4.1.8,6.1.7
s535(1)(a)... 4.1.8,6.1.7

s535(1)(b)... 4.1.8,6.1.7
s536... 4.1.8
s537... 4.1.8,6.1.7
s538... 4.1.8,6.1.7
s854...3.7.3
s858...3.7.3
s860...3.7.3,7.3.1
s1175...5.5.5
s1212...5.1.2
s1212(2)...5.1.3
s1213(1)..5.1.5
s1213(2)..5.1.5
s1213(3)..5.1.5
s1214...7.4.2
s1214(4)..5.1.5
s1214(5)..5.1.5
s1214(6)..5.1.5
s1217...5.1.3
s1219...5.1.3,9.1.8,10.2.3
s1221(1)...10.2.3
s1239...5.1.4
s1248...5.1.6
s1250...5.1.7
s1250(1)...5.1.7
s1250(4)...5.1.7
s1260...5.1.5
Sch 16...5.5.5
Companies (Audit, Investigations and
 Community Enterprise) Act 2004
s8...5.4.2,6.1.3.3
Company Directors Disqualification
 Act 1986...2.1.2.6,9.1.3
s1...7.3.1,7.3.2
s2...7.3.1
s3...7.3.1
s4...7.3.1
s5...7.3.1
s6...3.2.2,3.7.3,7.3.1
s8...7.3.1
s9...3.7.3,7.3.1
s9A...7.3.1
s10...7.3.1
s13...7.3.1
s15...7.3.1
s17...7.3.1
s22(5)...7.3.1
Sch 1...3.7.3,7.3.1
Consumer Credit Act 1974...1.2.3.2

Copyright, Designs & Patents Act
   1988
s3(1) (a)...3.4.6
County Court Act 1984
s143...8.1.4
s143(b)...8.1.4
Courts and Legal Services Act 1990
s11...8.1.3
s17....8.1.4
s27(1)...8.1.4
s27(2)...8.1.4
s27(1)...8.1.4
s58
Criminal Law Act 1967
s64...9.1.3
Criminal Justice Act 1982
s93H...315,317

Data Protection Act 1984
s1(5)(b)...3.4.8
Defamation Act 1952
s2...1.4
Sch 1...5.4.3

Employment Rights Act 1996
s218(2)...2.4.1.6

Finance Act 1976
s159(1)...4.1.6
s159(2)...4.1.6
s159(3)...4.1.6
Sch 6...1.3.1,1.3.2
Financial Services Act 1986...5.5.1
s56...2.3.1
Sch 3...7.2.1
Financial Services & Markets Act
   2000
s16(3)...7.2.1
s19...7.2.1
s22(1)...7.2.2
s23...7.2.1
s26...7.2.1
s39...5.1.1.1
s85(1)...3.7.2
s85(2)...3.7.2
s85(3)...3.7.2
s86(1)...3.7.2
s86(3)...3.7.2
s87A(1)...3.7.2

s87A(2)...3.7.2
s87A(3)...3.7.2
s87A(5)...3.7.2
s87A(6)...3.7.2
s87A(G)...3.7.2
s87B(1)...3.7.2
s90...3.7.2
s90(12)...3.7.2
s326...7.2.1
s328...7.2.6
s329...7.2.6
s397(1)...7.2.1
s397(2)...7.2.1
s400...7.2.2
Sch 2...7.2.2,7.2.3
Sch 10
p1(2)...3.7.2
p1(3)(a)...3.7.2
p1(3)(b)...3.7.2
p1(3)(c)...3.7.2
p1(3)(d)...3.7.2
p2(1)(a)...3.7.2
p2(1)(b)...3.7.2
p2(2)(a)...3.7.2
p2(2)(b)...3.7.2
p2(3)(a)...3.7.2
p2(3)(b)...3.7.2
p2(3)(c)...3.7.2
p2(3)(d)...3.7.2
p3...3.7.2
p4...3.7.2
p8...3.7.2
Fire Precautions Act 1971
s23...5.3.5
Fraud Act 2006...3.2.3.8
s2...3.2.3.8
s3...3.2.3.8
s4...3.2.3.8

Human Rights Act 1998
s2...9.2.2
s2(1)...9.2.2
ss6-8...9.2.1,9.2.2,9.3.2
s6(1)...9.1.6
ss6(3)-21(1)...9.2.1,9.3.2
s6(3)...9.2.2
s7(1)(b)...9.2.1
s8...9.2.2

Insolvency Act 1986
s11(3)...3.4.4
s13...3.7.3,7.3.1
s22...3.7.3,7.3.1
s47...3.7.3,7.3.1
s98...3.7.3
s99...3.7.3,7.3.1
s127...3.7.3,7.3.1
s230...7.1.1
s234...3.7.3,7.3.1
s235...3.7.3,7.3.1
s238...3.7.3,7.3.1
s240...3.7.3,7.3.1
s246...3.4.4
s246(2)...3.4.4
s292(2)...7.1.1
s389(1)...7.1.1
s389A...7.1.1
s390...2.1.3,7.1.1,7.1.3
s390(2)...7.1.1
s391...7.1.2
s430...7.1.1
Sch 10...7.1.1
Sch B1...7.1.1
Insurance Brokers (Registration) Act 1977
s4...5.5.1
Insurance Companies Act 1982
s21(1)...5.1.1.3
s21A(1)...6.1.9
s21A(2)...6.1.9
s21A(5)...6.1.9

Landlord and Tenant Act 1988...2.4.1.4
Landlord and Tenant (Covenants) Act 1995...2.4.1.4
Law of Property Act 1925
s136...2.4.1.2,2.4.1.3
Law Reform (Contributory Negligence) Act 1945
s1...4.1.3.2,6.1.3.2
Legal Aid Act 1988...8.1.4
Limitation Act 1980
s2...4.1.7
s3.5.1
s5...4.1.7,6.1.5
s14A...4.1.7,6.1.5
s14A(7)...4.1.7,6.1.5

s14A(8)...4.1.7,6.1.5
s21...4.1.7
s32...4.1.7,6.1.5
Limited Liability Partnerships Act 2000
s1(2) ...2.1.2.1
s1(3) ...2.1.2.1
s1(5) ...2.1.2.1
s1(6) ...2.1.2.1
s2(1)(a)...2.1.2
s4(1) ...2.1.2.4
s4(3) ...2.1.2.4
s4(4) ...2.1.2.4
s5(1) ...2.1.2.2
s6(1) ...2.1.2.4
s6(2) ...2.1.2.4
s6(3) ...2.1.2.4
s6(4) ...2.1.2.7
s8 ...2.1.2.5
s8(2) ...2.1.2.5
s8(6) ...2.1.2.5
Sch, para 9(1)...2.1.2.1
Limited Partnership Act 1907
s3...2.1.1.6
Local Government Finance Act 1982
s15...312

Misrepresentation Act 1967
s2(1)...4.1.6

New South Wales Public Accountants Regulation Act 1945...9.1.3

Partnership Act 1890
s1(1)...2.1.1.1
s2(2)...2.1.1.1
s2(3)...2.1.1.1
s9...2.1.1.3
s24(1)...2.1.1.3
s24(5)...2.1.1.3
s24(7)...2.1.1.3
s24(8)...2.1.1.3
s24(9)...2.1.1.3
s24(2)(a)...2.1.1.3
s24(6)...2.1.1.3
s24(9)...3.3.2
s25...2.1.1.2
s26(1)...2.1.1.2
s28...2.1.1.3

Partnership Act 1890 *cont*
s29(1)...2.1.1.3
s33(1)...2.1.1.2
s44(1)...2.1.1.3
s45...2.1.1.1
Proceeds of Crime Act
    2002...3.2.3.7,3.6.1,3.6.5.5
s310...8.5.1
ss327-329...3.6.1
s328...3.6.3
s330...3.6.2,3.6.3
s330(10)...3.6.3,8.5.1
s333A...3.6.4
s333B...3.6.4
s333C...3.6.4
s333D(2)...3.6.4
s333E...3.6.4
Public Health Act 1875
s247(4)...3.3.2

Rehabilitation of Offenders Act 1974
s4(1)...9.1.3

Sale of Goods Act 1979...2.4.1.5
Sex Discrimination Act 1975
ss1-4...2.1.1.6
s7(1)...2.1.1.6
s11...2.1.1.6
s11(2)...2.1.1.6
s11(3)...2.1.1.6
s11(4)...2.1.1.6
s11(5)...2.1.1.6
Solicitors Act 1974
s20...8.1.2,8.1.4
s22...8.1.4
s25...8.1.4
Supply of Goods and Services Act 1982
s12(2)...3.1.2.2.1
s13...3.1.2.2.1
s14...3.1.2.2.2,3.1.2.2.4
s15...3.1.2.2.2,3.1.2.2.4
s18(1)...3.1.2.2.1

Taxes Management Act 1970
s20...1.3.2
s20A...1.3.1
s20B(2)...1.3.3
s20B(7)...1.3.3
s20B(9)(a)...1.3.1
s20B(9)(b)...1.3.3
s20D(2)...1.3.2
s20(3)...1.3.3,*318*
s50(5)...1.1.3,*316,320*
s88...4.1.6
s88(4)...4.16
s90...4.1.6
s98(1)...1.3.3,p318
Terrorism Act 2000...3.6.1
s14...3.6.1
s15...3.6.1
s16...3.6.1
s17...3.6.1
s18...3.6.1,3.6.5.5
s21A...3.6.2,3.6.5.5
s21D...3.6.4
s121...3.6.1
Theft Act 1968
s16...1.2.3,3.1.1
s16(1)...1.2.3,3.1.1
s16(2)(c)...1.2.3,3.1.1
Torts (Interference with Goods) Act 1977
s4...3.4.5
Trade Union and Labour Relations (Consolidation) Act 1992
s112...5.5.1
s117...5.1.1.1,5.5.1
s122...5.1.1.1
Trustee Act 1925
s22...3.3.2
s61...3.5.2.1

Unfair Contract Terms Act 1977
s2...3.1.2.3,4.18
s11...4.1.3.1

Table of Rules and Regulations

REGULATIONS AND ORDERS CITED

Accountants (Banking Act 1987) Regulations 1994...3.2.3.7

Building Societies (Auditors) Order 1994...3.2.3.7

Civil Procedure Rules 1998
35.3...8.3.4
35.5...8.3.4
35.6...8.3.4
35.6(3)...8.3.4
35.7...8.3.4
35.12...8.3.4
35.13...8.3.4
35.14...8.3.4
Companies Act 1985 (Audit Exemption) (Amendment) Regulations 1996...5.5.3
Companies Act 1989 (Register of Auditors and Information about Audit Firms) Regulations 1991
r1...5.1.4
r2...5.1.4
r3...5.1.3
r3(2)...5.1.4
r5...5.1.3
r6(4)...5.1.3
r7(2)...5.1.3
Companies (Northern Ireland) Order 1990...10.2.1

Designated Professional Body Regulations 2001
r4(2)...3.5.2

European Communities (Recognition of Professional Qualifications) (First General System) Regulations 2005
r4...10.1.2
r5(1)(a)...10.1.3
r5(1)(b)...10.1.3
r5(2)(a)...10.1.3
r5(2)(b)...10.1.3
r6...10.1.3,10.2.2
r7...10.1.3,10.2.2
r8...10.1.3,10.2.2
r11(2)...10.2.2
r11(3)...10.2.2
r11(4)...10.2.2
r11(5)...10.2.2
European Communities (Recognition of Professional Qualifications) (Second General System) (Amendment) Regulations 2005...1.1.7

Financial Institutions (Prudential Supervision) Regulations 1996...3.2.3.7
Financial Services and Markets Act 2000 (Communications by Auditors) Regulations 2001...3.2.3.7
Financial Services and Markets Act (Regulated Activities) Order 2001...7.2.3
r67...7.2.1,7.2.3
Financial Services and Markets Act 2000 (Miscellaneous Provisions) Order 2001...3.2.3.7

General and Special Commissioners (Amendment of Enactments) Regulations 1994, SI 1994/1813...1.1.33
General Commissioners (Jurisdiction and Procedure) Regulations 1994
r12(a)...8.1.5
r12(b)...8.1.5

Insolvency Practitioner Regulations
2005
r6...7.1.4
r7...7.1.4
r8...7.1.4
r10...7.1.4
r12...7.1.4
Sch 2...7.1.4
Insolvency Rules 1986
r12.3...308

Lay Representatives (Rights of
Audience) Order 1992...8.1.3
Limited Liability Partnership
Regulations 2001
r4(2)...2.1.2.7
rr7-8...2.1.2.2
r7(9)...2.1.2.5
r7(10)...2.1.2.5

Money Laundering Regulations
2007...3.6.5
r1...3.6.5
r2(1)...1.1.3
r3(7)...1.1.3,3.6.5
r3(12)...3.6.5
r5...3.6.5.1
r6(1)...3.6.5.1
r7(1)...3.6.5.1
r7(2)...3.6.5.1
r7(3)...3.6.5.1
r8...3.6.5.2
r9(2)...3.6.5.1
r9(3)...3.6.5.1
r11...3.6.5.1
r13...3.6.5.1
r14...3.6.5.1
r17...3.6.5.1
r19(1)...3.6.5.2
r19(2)...3.6.5.2
r19(3)...3.6.5.2
r20...3.6.5.2
r23(1)(d)...3.6.5
r24(1)...3.6.5
r24(2)...3.6.5
r24(3)...3.6.5
r32(4)...3.6.5
r33...3.6.5
r35...3.6.5

Sc 2, p4...3.6.5.1
Sch 3...3.6.5,3.6.5.1

Proceeds of Crime Act 2002 and
Money Laundering Regulations 2003
(Amendment) Order 2006
r2...3.6.3,8.5.1
Proceeds of Crime Act (Business in
the Regulated Sector and Supervisory
Authorities) Order 2007...3.6.5
Prospectus Regulations 2005...3.7.2

Regulatory Reform (Removal of the
20 Partner Limit in Partnerships, etc)
Order 2002...2.1.1.5
Rehabilitation of Offenders Act 1974
(Exceptions) Order 1975...9.1.3
a3(a)...9.13
a5...9.13
Sch 1...9.1.3

Special Commissioners (Jurisdiction
and Procedure) Regulations 1994
r14(a)... 1.2.3.1,8.1.5
r14(b)...8.1.5

Transfer of Undertakings
(Protection of Employment)
Regulations 2006...2.4.1.6,2.4.2

Unfair Terms in Consumer
Contracts Regulations 1994...3.1.2.3

RULES AND REGULATIONS CITED: PROFESSIONAL BODIES

AAPA Articles of Association
s14...2.2.4.3
AAPA Byelaws
b5...2.2.4.3
b6...2.2.4.3
AAPA Qualification and Audit Regulations 1991
p10(1)...1.2.5.3,5.13
p10(2)...1.2.5.3
p11...1.2.5.3
p12(1)...1.2.5.3
ACCA Code of Ethics and Conduct
s3.10, r8...3.5.3
s3.10, r9...3.5.3
s3.10, r10...3.5.3
s3.10, r13...2.3.2.2
s3.10, r14...2.3.2.2
s3.10, r15...2.3.2.2
s3.11, r13...2.2.4.2
s3.11, r14...2.2.4.2
s3.10, rr21-22...3.5.3
s3.10, rr23-24...3.5.3
s3.10, r27...3.5.3
s3.10, r28...3.5.3
s3.11, r30...2.2.4.2
s3.11, r40...2.2.4.2
s3.11, r41...2.2.4.2
s3.11, r42...2.2.4.2
s3.20, p11...9.1.3
AIA Byelaws 2003
r59G...1.2.5.7
r59M...1.2.5.7

Chartered Certified Accountants' Designated Professional Body Regulations 2001
r3(1)...7.2.4
r3(2)...7.2.4
r3(3)...7.2.4
Chartered Certified Accountants Global Practising Regulations 2003
r3(1)(a)...1.2.5.2
r4(1)(a)...1.2.5.2

r4(1)(b)...1.2.5.2
r4(1)(c)...1.2.5.2
r4(1)(d)...1.2.5.2
CIMA code of ethics
s250.2...2.3.2.7
CIMA Council Regulations
r7.1.2...12.5.4
r7.2...12.5.4
r7.3...12.5.4
r7.4...12.5.4
CIPFA Disciplinary Regulations of 19.2.07
r4.1...9.1.8
r4.3(e)...9.1.9
r6...9.1.9
r7...9.1.9
r7(2)(c)-(d)...9.1.9

Direct Professional Access Rules, Code of Conduct of the Bar of England and Wales
Annexe E, p1...8.2.1
Annexe E, p3...8.2.1
Annexe E, p4...8.2.1

ICAEW Byelaws
b1(a)...1.2.5.1
b1(b)...1.2.5.1
b11...3.1.2
b17(2)...9.1.4
b51(a)...1.2.5.1
b53(a)...1.2.5.1
ICAEW Client's Money Regulations
r9...3.5.2
r10...3.5.2
r13...3.5.2
r24...3.5.2
r29...3.5.2
ICAEW Guide to Professional Ethics
s1.209, Statement 1.0...2.1.1.4
s1.211, Statement 1.0...2.3.2.1
s1.211, Statement 3...2.3.2.1
s1.212, p1.2...2.2.4.2
s1.212, p1.3...2.2.4.2
s1.212, p2.2...2.2.4.1
ICEA Professional and Ethical Code for Members
sD...12.5.5

ICEA Professional and Ethical Code
for Members *cont*
sD(ii)...2.3.2.3
sD(iii)...2.3.2.3
sD(iv)...2.3.2.3
sE...12.5.5
sG(2)(g)...3.5.5
IFA Byelaws 2007
Sch 3...1.2.5.7
Sch 3(1)(a)...1.2.5.7
Sch 3(2)...1.2.5.7
Sch 3(2)(iii)...1.2.5.7

IFA Code of Ethics, Practice
Promotion
p1...2.3.2.6
p2...2.3.2.6
p3...2.3.2.6
p4...2.3.2.6
p6...2.3.2.6
p7...2.3.2.6

Chapter 1

THE ACCOUNTANT

1. THE ACCOUNTANT

1.1.1 Accountant – an introduction

Accountants play an increasingly important and diverse role in society today.

Traditionally in the United Kingdom accountants are the first port of call for businessmen seeking any form of professional advice or assistance.

They undertake a wide range of functions which stretch far beyond their traditional roles of preparing accounts, financial reporting, auditing and tax planning.

Today accountants also offer management consultancy, give corporate finance advice, offer company secretarial services, undertake financial management, give personal finance advice, advise on computer software and act as trustees in bankruptcy, liquidators, administrative receivers and administrators.

In numbers accountants dwarf the other professions. In the United Kingdom at the time of the first edition of this book, as a rough reckoning, there were ten qualified accountants to every solicitor and a hundred accountants to every barrister. This picture did not include the large number of "unqualified" or "part qualified" accountants who make up a significant but largely invisible part of the practising profession.

1.1.2 Accountant – a creature of common law

Whilst an accountant may in the course of his practice as an accountant undertake a variety of statutory roles (such as acting in the capacity as an auditor or liquidator), it is equally clear that his profession as an accountant is a creation of common law and not statute.

1.1.3 Accountant – a definition

The Oxford English Dictionary defines an accountant as

> one who professionally makes up or takes charge of account

Under United States law an accountant is defined as a person

> authorised under the applicable law to practice public accounting and includes professional accounting association, corporation or partnership so authorised.[1]

The definition as to what constitutes an accountant under English law is less clear. It seems that an accountant is a person who is paid to investigate accounts and certify as to their accuracy. Clearly, it is misleading for a bookmaker to describe himself as an accountant without the qualification "turf".[2]

Given the importance of the role an accountant plays, there have been a number of attempts to define what an accountant is for the purposes of provisions under individual statutes by identifying them as members of identified accountancy bodies. These cannot therefore be said to provide a definition of general application, not least since there is no common test and the lists given are contradictory.[3]

For the purposes of the Taxes Management Act 1970, an accountant has been defined as meaning a person who has been admitted as "a member of an incorporated society of accountants".[4] This section conferred an entitlement to represent and be heard on behalf of clients on issues of tax. An accountant who had been suspended or expelled from his incorporated society of accountants is not an accountant for the purposes of this definition.[5] For the purposes of the Money Laundering Regulations 2007 "external accountant" was defined as a firm or sole practitioner who by way of business provides accountancy services to other persons, when providing such services[6]. Given the draftsman's purpose, on each of these occasions,

---

[1] Bankruptcy Act 1978, s.101(1).
[2] *O'Connor & Ould v. Ralson* [1920] 3 KB 451,461.
[3] This is starkly illustrated by contrasting the definitions given to "accountant" under Part 1, Schedule 1 and Part V Rehabilitations of Offenders Act 1974 (Exceptions) Order 1975 and "accountant with appropriate qualifications" under section 685 Companies Act 1985.
[4] Section 50(5) Taxes Management Act 1970. This has been repealed by the General and Special Commissioners (Amendment of Enactments) Regulations 1994, SI 1994/1813.
[5] *Cassell v. Crutchfield* [1995] S.T.C. 663.
[6] Regulation 3(7) Money Laundering Regulations 2007. A business relationship is defined as including a profession under regulation 2(1), Money Laundering Regulations 2007.

was necessarily inclusive, that is to say to ensure that provision was to be of general applicability to all members of the accountancy profession, it is submitted that these last two statutory definitions are to be preferred.

1.1.4 A statutory test – a member of an incorporated society of accountants

There are a number of incorporated societies of accountants who confer qualifications which carry the title "accountant". The best known amongst these include:

> Institute of Chartered Accountants in England and Wales
> Institute of Chartered Accountants in Scotland
> Institute of Chartered Accountants in Ireland
> Association of Chartered Certified Accountants[7]
> Chartered Institute of Management Accountants
> Institute of Financial Accountants
> Chartered Institute of Public Finance and Accountancy
> Association of Authorised Public Accountants[8]
> Institute of Cost and Executive Accountants[9]
> Association of International Accountants.

This list used to include the Institute of Company Accountants[10] which has since been amalgamated into the Association of International Accountants.

1.1.5 History of the incorporated societies of accountants

The oldest association of accountants is the Institute of Chartered Accountants of Scotland. It received its Royal Charter in 1854.

In England and Wales, the oldest association[11] is the Institute of Chartered Accountants in England and Wales which was formed in 1880 from the merger of the Incorporated Society of Liverpool Accountants, the Institute of Accountants in London, the Manchester Institute of Accountants, the

---

[7] Formerly the Chartered Association of Certified Accountants.
[8] This association was formed in 1978 to represent those accountants who were individually authorised by the Secretary of State to conduct audits. By an extraordinary general meeting on the 24 June, 1996, members of the Association voted to become a subsidiary of the Association of Chartered Certified Accountants and its members comply with the same practising rules and regulations.
[9] Formerly the Association of Cost and Executive Accountants.
[10] Formerly the Society of Company and Commercial Accountants Limited.
[11] For a fuller analysis of the history of the accountancy profession *"Where they came from"* (2003) Accountancy June page 58, *"Six of the best"* (2002) Accountancy December p 77.

Sheffield Institute of Accountants, the Society of Accountancy and Auditors and the Society of Accountants in England.

Next in seniority is the Chartered Institute of Public Finance and Accountancy which was formed in 1885 as the Corporate Treasurers and Accountants Institute.

The Association of Chartered Certified Accountants (the association's name since 1996) was originally formed as the London Association of Accountants in 1904.

The Institute of Financial Accountants was formed in 1916 and is the oldest non chartered body of accountants.

The Chartered Institute of Management Accountants (the association's name since 1986) was originally formed as the Institute of Cost Accountants Limited in 1919.

The Association of International Accountants was formed in 1932.

1.1.6 Who is not an accountant

A person carrying on business as an agent of an accountant and who was employed as accountant by other persons could properly be described as an accountant for the purposes of The Bills of Exchange Acts.[12]

This may well mark the limit of the boundary. A clerk in the accountant's office of a railway who occasionally worked for other people after office hours is not properly described as an accountant.[13]

1.1.7 Accountants and bookkeepers

A distinction can also be drawn between the work of an accountant and a bookkeeper.[14]

A bookkeeper's work is to write up books of account and his work is considered preparatory to the involvement of the accountant. A bookkeeper is another common law profession.[15] The two main professional bodies regulating and conferring the title of "bookkeeper" are:

---

[12] *Briggs v. Boss* LR 3 QB 268.
[13] *Larchin v. North Western Deposit Bank* LR 10 Ex 64.
[14] *Sylvanus Okoye v. Leon Edgar Walker* (1999) LTL 17 February
[15] The United Kingdom government does however statutorily mutually recognise under the European Communities (Recognition of Professional Qualifications) (Second General System)

The International Association of Bookkeepers
The Institute of Certified Bookkeepers

The Association of Accounting Technicians also falls to be considered under this head although they would draw a distinction between their function and that of a bookkeeper or an accountant. They also do not consider themselves to be accountants proper although they can act as reporting accountants.[16]

1.1.8 Other uses of the term "accountant"

It is worth briefly mentioning that the law also uses the term "accountant" in two other distinct areas.

An "Accountant to the Crown" is a person who has received money for and on behalf of the Crown and is accountable therefore. This harkens back to the old legal usage of the term "an accountant" as being a reference to the defendant to an action for an account[17] rather than to any professional working in the field of accountancy.

The Accountant-General (or Clerk of the Crown) is the officer of the Supreme Court in whom funds paid into court are vested under Section 133, Judicature Act 1925.

(Amendment) Regulations 2005 the German profession of commercial bookkeeper ("Gewerblicher Buchhalter"), in accordance with the Trades, Crafts and Industry Act 1994 (Gewerbeordnung 1994) and of independent bookkeeper ("Selbständiger Buchhalter"), in accordance with the Act on Professions in the Field of Public Accountancy 1999 (Bundesgesetz über die Wirtschaftstreuhandberufe 1999).
[16] Section 249C(1) Companies Act 1985.
[17] Selden *Laws of England* II xx 98

1.2. THE BASIS UPON WHICH PROFESSIONAL BODIES REGULATE ACCOUNTANTS

1.2.1 The status of accountant is not dependent on membership of any professional body

The starting point for any consideration of the interrelationship between an accountant and his professional body is the understanding that the status of "accountant" is not dependent on his membership of any professional body.

To distinguish their members from other forms of accountant, who might be less qualified or less regulated, the professional accountancy bodies have given their members distinct professional styles – whether by designating their members say "chartered management accountants" or by giving the right to use letters after their name like "A.C.C.A".

Thus exclusion from the Institute of Chartered Accountants in England and Wales does not mean that the accountant ceases to be and be able to hold himself out as an "accountant" but will mean that he ceases to be and be able to hold himself out as a "chartered accountant".

Moreover a professional accountancy body cannot prevent an excluded member or a non-member from practising as an accountant.[18]

1.2.3 Misuse of the name or qualifications of professional bodies

A professional body may restrain any other person in a common field of activity from imitating the name or designatory letters by which a qualified person indicates their membership of it.

Thus a professional accountancy body may restrain non members from using a description which was calculated to suggest that they were members of it.[19]

The harm suffered by the professional body is represented by the pecuniary value to the society to have as many members as possible and the effect which any reduction in status might have on their membership numbers.[20]

---

[18] *Dixon v. Australian Society of Accountants* (1989) 95 FLR 231, Supreme Court of Australia, Capit. Territ.
[19] *Society of Accountants & Auditors v. Goodway* [1907] 1 Ch 489, *Society of Accountants in Edinburgh v. Corporation of Accountants* (1903) 20 R 750 (Scotland).
[20] *Society of Accountants & Auditors v. Goodway* [1907] 1 Ch 489, *Society of Accountants in Edinburgh v. Corporation of Accountants* (1903) 20 R 750 (Scotland).

An injunction may be granted by the court to a professional accountancy body to restrain the use of initials of designation likely to induce the belief that the defendant was a member or fellow of that body.[21]

The Secretary of State may also restrain the use by a company of a name which gives so misleading an indication of the nature of its activities as to be likely to cause harm to the public.[22]

Thus the Secretary of State was able to restrain the use of the word "certified" for the name of an association of unqualified accountants as the use of the word "certified" in a name suggested that there was something objectively significant in the qualification of its members' experience and training[23]. Mr Justice Jacobs ruled in that case[24] that it was likely to cause harm to the public as it raised an expectation of not only probity but expertise and they would expect more from the name than they would get and pay more accordingly; the misleading name would cost the public money and that was sufficient harm in itself.

Moreover an accountant who falsely holds himself out as a member of a professional body with a view to performing paid professional services for a client commits a criminal offence. An accountant acting for his client is "employed" by the client within the meaning of section 16 Theft Act 1968 even though no legal employment relationship exists; thus a self employed accountant who falsely represented he was a member of the Chartered Institute of Management Accountant to a prospective client was guilty of the offence of obtaining a pecuniary advantage by deception contrary to section 16(1) of the Theft Act 1968 as the services offered by him as a self-employed accountant were capable of amounting to services provided under an "office or employment" within the meaning of section 16(2)(c) of the Act.[25]

---

[21] *Society of Incorporated Accountants v. Vincent* (1954) 71 RPC 325.
[22] Section 32, Companies Act 1985.
[23] *The Association of Certified Public Accountants v. Secretary of State for Trade and Industry*; sub nomen *The Association of Certified Public Accountants in Great Britain v. Secretary of State for Trade and Industry* [1998] 1 WLR 164.
[24] *The Association of Certified Public Accountants v. Secretary of State for Trade and Industry; sub nomen, The Association of Certified Public Accountants in Great Britain v. Secretary of State for Trade and Industry* [1998] 1 WLR 164. Mr Justice Jacobs rejected the argument that there might be any confusion with this body and the US profession of "certified public accountant".
[25] *R v. Callendar* [1993] QB 303.

1.2.3 The consequences of membership of a professional body

Entry into the membership of a particular accountancy body causes significant changes in the nature and character of the accountant.

Membership may enable him to exercise new rights and privileges conferred on members of that accountancy body but it will also mean that he is bound and restricted by new rules and requirements. These privileges and obligations vary widely from body to body.

1.2.3.1 Example: Rights of audience

An unqualified accountant would not be able to represent a client as of right before the Special or General Commissioners (i.e. the Commissioners may, if they have good and sufficient reasons, decline to hear him) as he is a person who is not a member of an incorporated society of accountants.[26]

An accountant who had been suspended or expelled from his incorporated society of accountants is an accountant who is not a member of an incorporated society of accountants for the purposes of this definition.[27] An accountant appearing before the tax commissioners as an advocate cannot be treated as a witness by the tax commissioners and his submissions will not constitute evidence on his client's behalf.[28]

1.2.3.2 Example: Consumer Credit

Another illustration of this might be that a group licence under the Consumer Credit Act 1974 for Category A (consumer credit), C (credit brokerage) and D (debt adjusting and debt counselling) has been granted to:

> Institute of Chartered Accountants in England and Wales
> Institute of Chartered Accountants in Scotland
> Institute of Chartered Accountants in Ireland
> Association of Chartered Certified Accountants

The Group Licence for the Association of Chartered Certified Accountants has been extended, in principle, to Association of Authorised Public Accountants firms.[29]

---

[26] See by way of example reg. 14(a) Special Commissioners (Jurisdiction and Procedure) Regulations 1994.
[27] *Cassell v. Crutchfield* [1995] S.T.C. 663.
[28] *Parmar v. Woods* [2002] STI 852.
[29] Paragraph 8, AAPA Notes on applying for an AAPA Non Statutory Practising Certificate 1998.

1.2.4 Relationship between accountants and their professional body

The relationship between a member and his professional body is contractual. The mere fact that an institute is a public body does not prevent it from conferring private law rights on its members.[30] The act of applying for membership of a professional body will be deemed to constitute the acceptance by the applicant of an implied term that he agrees to be bound by the rules of that professional body, providing the disciplinary rules are publicly known or otherwise brought to the attention of the applicant.[31] Membership creates mutual rights and obligations between the accountants their corporate body very like the mutual contract that exist between shareholders and their limited company which can be found in the professional association's memorandum and articles of association and byelaws. It is on this basis that a professional body is entitled to discipline its members.

The contractual provisions can be wide-ranging and concern matters outside the accountant's practice. It is possible for an accountant to be answerable to his professional body not only for his own acts but for the acts and omissions of his employees or agents.[32] No term will be implied that a professional accountancy body can only exercise its power to make byelaws fairly and reasonably.[33]

The author argues that by advertising his membership of a professional body the accountant adopts a further term into his letter of engagement, namely, the implied term that he will comply with the professional rules and standards of that association or institute in his dealings with the client.

1.2.5 A professional body may licence member accountants to conduct public practice

It is possible for the professional body, on the basis of the contractual relationship with its members, to control the ability of a member to engage in public practice by the mechanism of the grant and withdrawal of licences to practise as a member. Rules may be built in over the grant of such practising certificates or prohibiting members to practise without such a practising certificate, for example, by providing in the rules that student members may not engage in public practice.[34] Conducting such regulatory

---

[30] *Andreou v. Institute of Chartered Accountants in England and Wales* [1998] 1 All ER 14.
[31] *National Greyhound Racing Council v Tom Flaherty* [2005] EWCA Civ 1117.
[32] *Re a Solicitor* [1972] 2 All ER 81. There a solicitor was liable to answer for the omissions of an accountant who had failed to write up the solicitor's books of practice.
[33] *Andreou v. ICAEW* [1998] 1 All ER 14.
[34] For example Byelaw 51, ICAEW Byelaws.

activity under a statutory regime is not an economic activity and thus does not attract Value Added Tax.[35]

1.2.5.1 Chartered Accountants

Chartered accountants are ineligible to enter into partnerships carrying on public practice without a valid current UK Practising Certificate.[36] Public practice is defined as practice as a public accountant anywhere in the world other than as an employee.[37] Practising certificates are granted for a period of one year.[38] Presently chartered accountants who are not undertaking regulated work, that is to say insolvency, audit, investment business, are not subject to any practice monitoring and inspection scheme.

It is estimated that half the chartered accountants in practice do not conduct regulated work and therefore are not subject to monitoring however the Institute of Chartered Accountants in England and Wales has from 1st November 2004 introduced a Practice Assurance Scheme to monitor all members in practice.[39] This means that all firms of chartered accountants can be subject to practice assurance visits. The Institute of Chartered Accountants of Scotland have had monitoring visits since 2000.

All chartered accountants are required to undertake continuing professional education. The Institute of Chartered Accountants in England and Wales have introduced a mandatory scheme for continuing professional education for all chartered accountants.[40]

1.2.5.2 Chartered Certified Accountants

No member of ACCA is permitted to carry on public practice in a designated territory without a valid current UK Practising Certificate authorising him to carry on the activity in question.[41] The designated territory for these purpose means the UK, Eire, Jersey, Guernsey, Isle of Man, Cyprus, Zimbabwe and such other territories as may be designated by Council from time to time.

---

[35] *Institute of Chartered Accountants in England and Wales v Customs & Excise Commissioners* (1999) *The Times,* 29 March, House of Lords.
[36] Byelaw 51(a) ICAEW Byelaws.
[37] Byelaw 1(a), ICAEW Byelaws and Byelaw 1(b) ICAEW Disciplinary Byelaws.
[38] Byelaw 53(a), ICAEW Byelaws.
[39] "*PA in practice*" (2004) Accountancy April page 32, "*Keeping up with the Jones's*" (2004) Accountancy April page 37. "*PA in practice*" (2004) Accountancy April page 32, "*Keeping up with the Jones's*" (2004) Accountancy April page 37, regulation 6.5 Practice Assurance Regulations.
[40] Section 5.2 *ICAEW Handbook.*
[41] Regulation 3(1) (a) The Chartered Certified Accountants Global Practising Regulations 2003.

Holding oneself out or allowing oneself to be held out as available to undertake audit work or signing reports, certificates or accounts on which reliance is likely to be placed constitutes public practice.[42] Using a business or partnership description incorporating the words "Accountant(s)", "Certified Accountant(s)", "Chartered Accountant(s), "Auditor(s)" is an example of holding oneself out.[43] Similarly using a business or partnership name which incorporates the words "Chartered Certified Accountant(s)" constitutes holding oneself out.

The Association of Chartered Certified Accountants conducts monitoring visits on all practising members and has, since 2005, introduced a mandatory scheme requiring all members to undertake continuing professional education.[44]

Holding oneself out, or allowing oneself to be held out, as a sole proprietor, partner or director of a firm where public practice is carried on also constitutes public practice.[45]

1.2.5.3 Authorised Public Accountants

No member is allowed to carry on public practice in the UK, Channel Islands or Isle of Man without a current practising certificate.[46] The requirements for this are that he holds a relevant qualification, is a fit and proper person, holds adequate professional indemnity insurance and has made appropriate arrangements for the continuity of his/her practice.[47] Firms are required to hold an auditing certificate to accept appointment as an auditor.[48]

Public practice includes accepting appointment as an auditor or signing any report or certificate on accounts on which reliance is likely to be placed or allowing oneself to be held out as available to undertake such work.[49] Using a business or partnership name incorporating the words "Accountant(s)", "Authorised Public Accountant(s)", "Certified Accountant(s)", "Chartered Accountant(s)", "Auditor(s)" or similar description is given as an example of

---

[42] Regulation 4(1) (a) and (b) The Chartered Certified Accountants Global Practising Regulations 2003.
[43] Regulation 4(1)(c) The Chartered Certified Accountants Global Practising Regulations 2003.
[44] "*Keeping up with the Jones's*" (2004) Accountancy April page 37, "*Knowledge Quest*" Accountancy April page 46.
[45] Regulation 4(1)(d) The Chartered Certified Accountants Global Practising Regulations 2003.
[46] Paragraph 11, AAPA Qualification and Audit Regulations 1991.
[47] Paragraph 12(1), AAPA Qualification and Audit Regulations 1991.
[48] Paragraph 11, AAPA Qualification and Audit Regulations 1991.
[49] Paragraph 10(1), AAPA Qualification and Audit Regulations 1991.

holding oneself out.[50] Special rules apply to exclude honorary audits from this definition.[51]

1.2.5.4 Chartered Management Accountants
All members in practice must register with CIMA and provisional members in practice must apply for a practising certificate after a year of practice and within 3 years of registration.[52] Each applicant for a practising certificate must satisfy a panel of assessors that he has had at least one year's experience satisfactory to the panel.[53]

Practice is widely defined and covers offering accountancy, tax, bookkeeping, company secretarial, accounting systems, business plans, forecasts or business funding advice or services to a person other than the accountant's employer.[54] Expressly excluded from this list are services regulated by the Financial Services & Markets Act 2000 or Insolvency Act 1986, honorary of *pro bono* work for clubs and associations, work in other areas unless they are peripheral to practice (such as providing training, legal, marketing, human resources or project management work).[55] Also excluded from the definition of "practice" is where the accountant is working as a subcontractor for other accountants or providing his services through an agency where the agency is invoicing direct for those services.[56]

Registration as a member in practice is renewed annually.[57] Members in practice are required on registration and on each renewal to provide evidence that they hold an appropriate level of professional indemnity insurance, provide their clients with written terms of engagement, have made continuity arrangements for the eventuality of their death or incapacity, have made provisions for internal complaints handling procedures and undertake continuing professional education.[58]

1.2.5.5 Incorporated Executive Accountants
Incorporated executive accountants may not conduct public practice either as an accountant, consultant or in any other manner for remuneration without a current ICEA practising certificate (unless the member already holds a

---

[50] Paragraph 10(1), AAPA Qualification and Audit Regulations 1991.
[51] Paragraph 10(2), AAPA Qualification and Audit Regulations 1991.
[52] Regulation 7.2, CIMA Council Regulations of 12th June 2004.
[53] Regulation 7.3, CIMA Council Regulations of 12th June 2004.
[54] Regulation 7.1, CIMA Council Regulations of 12th June 2004.
[55] Regulation 7.1.2, CIMA Council Regulations of 12th June 2004.
[56] Regulation 7.1.2, CIMA Council Regulations of 12th June 2004.
[57] Regulation 7.4, CIMA Council Regulations of 12th June 2004.
[58] Regulation 7.5, CIMA Council Regulations of 12th June 2004.

current practising certificate granted by a chartered accountancy institute).[59] Where the public practice is being conducted through a company, the Incorporated Executive Accountant will still require a current ICEA practising certificate if he holds over five per cent of the issued share capital or is a director, company secretary, shadow director or has control over the company in any other way. Publicising that one is an Incorporated Executive Accountant is forbidden if one does not hold a current practising certificate.[60]

1.2.5.6 Chartered Public Finance Accountants
Whilst practising certificates are not issued to Chartered Public Finance Accountants, special rules apply to the conduct of Chartered Public Finance Accountants in public practice.[61]

The Chartered Institute of Public Finance and Accountancy is phasing in a requirement of continuing professional education for its members.[62] The phasing in expected to be completed by the end of 2007. At this stage continuing professional education will be compulsory for all CIPFA members.

1.2.5.7 International Accountants
An international accountant is entitled to engage in public practice only if he holds a current practising certificate or a practising certificate issued by a body which is a Recognised Supervisory Body for audit purposes. Public practice for these purposes means practice as a public accountant. However the interpretation of what this means by the Council of the AIA is deemed conclusive.

Practising certificates are granted for public practice in the jurisdiction in which the international accountant obtained his post qualification experience in public accountancy and international accountants wishing to practice outside their original jurisdiction are required to pass further examinations before being issued with a certificate in another jurisdiction.[63] Ensuring adequate provision of practice in the event of death or incapacity, undertaking continuing professional education and professional indemnity insurance are pre-requisites for each certificate.[64]

---

[59] Section E, ICEA Professional and Ethical Code for Members.
[60] Section D, ICEA Professional and Ethical Code for Members.
[61] A10.1 Standards of Professional Practice on Ethics of December 2000 and Part B, IFAC Code of Ethics for Professional Accountants. The IFAC Code, which was adopted by CIPFA in May 2006, is now the principle ethical statement for CIPFA members. The Standards of Professional Practice are presently under review and a 2nd edition is expected.
[62] "*Knowledge Quest*" (2004) Accountancy April page 46.
[63] Reg 59G AIA Byelaws 2003.
[64] Reg 59M, 59N and 59O AIA Byelaws 2003.

1.2.5.8 Incorporated Financial Accountants

Any incorporated financial accountant in public practice in the UK who provides accountancy services to clients must apply for a practising certificate or a certificate of compliance or a certificate of registration.[65] Their technician grade in public practice in the UK who provides accountancy services to clients must apply for a certificate of registration.[66] Undertaking continuing professional education and professional indemnity insurance are pre-requisites for each certificate.[67]

1.3. THE CONCEPT OF A "TAX ACCOUNTANT" IN REVENUE INVESTIGATIONS

1.3.1 The Statutory Power

Where a person has been convicted of any offence in relation to tax or has had a penalty made against him under Section 99, Taxes Management Act 1970, an inspector of taxes has the right to call for such papers as are within his possession or power as relate to any client to whom he has stood as a tax accountant at any time. This overrides the normal right of auditors to withhold from Her Majesty's Revenue and Customs documents prepared for the purposes of an audit and which are their own personal property.[68]

The power is exercisable for a period of 12 months from date of conviction or penalty.[69]

1.3.2 Definition of "tax accountant" is not restricted to accountants

The provisions are not limited to accountants but apply to any person who stands in relation to other persons as a tax accountant. Standing in relation to others as a tax accountant means assisting them in preparing tax returns or accounts or other documents, which he knows are or likely to be used for a tax purpose by the other.[70] The definition of "tax accountant" may therefore extend to a client's solicitor or bookkeeper.

---

[65] Schedule 3, IFA Byelaws 2007.
[66] Schedule 3(1)(a) and 3(2)(iii), IFA Byelaws 2007.
[67] Schedule 3(2) IFA Byelaws 2007.
[68] The right arises under section 20B (9) (a) Taxes Management Act 1970 and would cover such things as the auditor's working papers. In practice Her Majesty's Revenue and Customs will afford similar protection to non statutory audit work provided it is kept separate from the work for the client on its accounts: Statement of Practice 5/90.
[69] Section 20A Taxes Management Act 1970; Finance Act 1976, Schedule 6.
[70] Section 20D (2) Taxes Management Act 1970; Finance Act 1976, Schedule 6.

1.3.3 Other powers to compel disclosure against accountants

This power is without prejudice to the power of the Her Majesty's Revenue and Customs in the course of an investigation of a specific tax payer's affairs to require the disclosure of documents within the possession or power of the taxpayer's accountant that in the tax inspector's reasonable opinion may contain information relevant to the tax payer's tax liability under section 20(3) Taxes Management Act 1970.

Failure to deliver documents required under a section 20(3) notice exposes the tax accountant to a daily fine.[71] To escape liability the accountant would need to either prove the documents had been destroyed or could not be found after a thorough search and explain the nature of the search conducted.[72]

An accountant required to produce client's documents which were of a type likely to be retained by the accountant by a notice under section 20(3) Taxes Management Act 1970, could not discharge his obligations by the bare assertion that the documents could not be found.[73]

Excluded from the scope of disclosure under s20 and 20A is information and documents relating to a pending tax appeal.[74] Excluded from the scope of disclosure under section 20(3) are documents relating to a client who has died more than six years ago[75] or the papers belonging to an auditor and which have been created in the performance of his statutory functions[76] or a tax advisor's advice to his client or other tax advisors.[77]

1.4 DEFAMATION AND THE ACCOUNTANT

A libel for which an action will lie is a defamatory statement made or conveyed by written or printed words or in some permanent form published about and concerning the claimant and published to a person other than the defendant.

The distinction between this and a claim in slander is that whilst the defamatory remark may be made in a non-permanent form (such as spoken

---

[71] The power to fine the accountant arises under section 98(1) Taxes Management Act 1970.
[72] *Fox v. Uxbridge General Commissioners* [2002] STC 455.
[73] *Fox v. Uxbridge General Commissioners* [2002] STC 455.
[74] Section 20B (2) Taxes Management Act 1970.
[75] Section 20B (7) Taxes Management Act 1970.
[76] Section 20B (9) (a), Taxes Management Act 1970.
[77] Section 20B (9) (b), Taxes Management Act 1970.

words) the claimant must show that he has suffered actual damage.[78] Damages are only awarded for such loss if the claimant can prove he has suffered as a result of the defamatory remark.[79]

With libel, the claimant does not have to prove he has suffered any particular loss or damage.[80] General damages are awarded to compensate him for his hurt feelings and the damage to his reputation. Any financial loss constitutes a separate head of claim, "special damages", and is recoverable in addition to this.

An accountant, however, need not show actual damage to bring a claim for slander against him in his professional life. Where the defamatory statement is in respect of acts in respect of an office, profession, calling, trade or business held or carried on by him at the time of publication, there is a statutory dispensation waiving the requirement on the victim to prove actual loss under section 2, Defamation Act 1952; this dispensation applies to both offices of honour and profit alike[81] although with an office of honour, the remark must suggest conduct which would lead to his removal from the office of honour.[82]

Whilst there is no clear definition of what a defamatory statement is, it is generally accepted that a statement is defamatory if:
- it tends to lower him in the estimation of right-thinking members of society generally,[83] or
- exposes him to public hatred, contempt or ridicule,[84] or
- causes him to be shunned or avoided.[85]

The test is whether in the circumstances in which the words were published an ordinary reasonable man to whom the publication was made would be likely to understand them in a defamatory sense.[86] The "ordinary reasonable man" by whose standard this is assessed is able to read between the lines, and will do so perhaps more readily than a lawyer would. He will not,

---

[78] *Gregory v. Duke of Brunswick* (1844) 6 Man & G 953 at 959, per Coltman J.
[79] *Brown v. Smith* [1895] 13 CB 596.
[80] *Ratcliffe v. Evans* [1892] 2 QB 524 at 529.
[81] *Booth v. Arnold* [1895] 1 QB 571.
[82] *Alexander v. Jenkins* [1842] 1 QB 797 (over an allegation of persistent drunkenness where drunkenness was not a ground for removal from the office of councillor).
[83] *Same v. Stretch* [1936] 2 All ER 1237.
[84] *Parmiter v. Coupland* [1936] 6 M & W 105.
[85] *Youssoupoff v. Metro Goldwyn-Mayer Pictures* (1930) 50 TLR 581.
[86] *Capital and Counties Bank v. George Henry & Sons* (1882) App Cas 741.

however, select a bad meaning where other non-defamatory meanings are available.[87]

1.5 THE STATUS OF THE TRAINEE ACCOUNTANT

1.5.1 The relationship between the institute and the trainee accountant

Many professional associations confer student membership on those seeking to pass its examinations. Quite what this entails will depend on the articles of association and byelaws of the individual professional body but usually the student is given membership albeit of a lesser kind and with fewer privileges. The purpose of this is to ensure the student has accepted the implied term that he agrees to be bound by the professional conduct rules of that professional body whilst he is studying and to empower the professional body with some means of regulating his behaviour. This may include preventing the student from using the designatory letters and professional title of the professional body inappropriately or prematurely.

The relationship between an accountancy institute and its student members is far more limited in its nature than that enjoyed by qualified accountant members. Passing the examination towards full membership of an accountancy body is purely a stepping stone and the contract with the student relates solely to internal government and administration.[88] The duty of care owed to students seeking full membership of a professional body is limited to a duty to take reasonable care in making arrangements and approving appointments for their examinations and thus there is no duty of care owed when marking the examinations.[89]

Where the professional body was incorporated under Royal Charter that was in the exclusive jurisdiction of the reader, if one has been appointed.[90] The court has no jurisdiction over such a dispute.[91] The failure to appoint a visitor does not create that jurisdiction afresh; it merely gives the student the right to complain to the Lord Chancellor over his failure to appoint a visitor.[92]

---

[87] *Hart v. Newspaper Publishing* (1989) *The Times*, 9 November.
[88] *Bankole v. ACCA* (1995) LTL 17 November.
[89] *Bankole v. ACCA* (1995) LTL 17 November.
[90] *Thomson v. University of London* (1864) 33 LJ Ch 625, 634.
[91] *R. v. Hull University ex parte* Page [1993] AC 682.
[92] *Bankole v. ACCA* (1995) LTL 17 November.

1.5.2 The relationship between a trainee accountant and his accountancy firm

A training contract with a firm of accountants is work experience and the trainee is not a student with a *bona fide* private educational institution even through the trainee has to take examinations and the work is considered a necessary part of his professional studies by his examining professional body.[93]

Indeed historically the relationship between the trainee accountant and his firm was one of apprenticeship rather than employment.[94]

Whilst it is likely that a trainee accountant these days will be employed under an employment contract (particularly since a significant percentage undertake their training in companies or in the public sector), whether an apprenticeship has been created will depending on the nature of the relationship that exists between the accountancy firm and the trainee accountant.[95]

Apprenticeship carries a different range of legal duties and obligations to employment. In a relationship of apprenticeship, the employer takes on an obligation to provide full opportunity for access to training.[96] Whilst (unlike an employee) an apprentice has no implied right to payment for his work, employers have more limited rights of dismissal and may only do so if it is impossible to teach them their trade.[97] If an apprentice is wrongly dismissed he will have an enhanced right to damage reflecting his loss of the prospect to work as an accountant.[98]

Visas may be granted for overseas trainee accountants seeking to qualify in the UK but these will be granted on the basis of the training being "work experience".[99]

To be eligible, the applicant must demonstrate:

- he holds a valid work permit from the Department of Employment
- he is not of an age which puts him outside the limits for employment

---

[93] *Yeong Hoi Yuen v. Secretary of State for the Home Department* [1977] Imm AR 34.
[94] *Society of Accountants v. Lord Advocate* (1924) SLT 194.
[95] *Thorpe v. Dul* [2004] ICR 1556.
[96] *Flett v. Matheson* [2005] IRLR 412.
[97] *Newells v. Gillingham Corporation* [1941] All ER 552.
[98] *Wallace v. CA Roofing Services Ltd* [1996] IRLR 435.
[99] Paragraphs 116-121 HC 395.

- he is capable of undertaking the training or work experience as specified in his permit
- he intends to leave the United Kingdom on the completion of his training or work experience
- he does not intend to take employment except as specified in his work permit
- he is able to maintain and accommodate himself and any dependants adequately without recourse to public funds.[100]

---

[100] Paragraphs 116 and 118 HC 395.

Chapter 2

THE ACCOUNTANCY PRACTICE

2.1 THE ACCOUNTANCY PRACTICE

2.1.1 Partnerships

Traditionally accountancy practices have elected to structure themselves as partnerships.

2.1.1.1 Creation of a partnership

Whilst partnerships are usually formulated by means of a deed, the existence of a partnership can arise by a verbal agreement or be presumed out of the nature of the relationship. A partnership is the relation which subsists between persons carrying on a business[1] in common[2] with a view to a profit.[3]

A business, for these purposes, includes a profession.[4]

The receipt of a share of the profits of the practice is, prima facie, evidence that the recipient is a partner in the practice but a payment contingent on or varying with the profits of the business does not of itself make the recipient a partner in the practice.[5] Nor would the sharing of gross returns indicate the creation of a partnership.[6]

The remuneration of an employee by a share of the profits does not of itself create a relationship of partnership.[7] Thus care should be taken to clearly identify the capacity in which employees are taken on and to confirm whether or not they are intended to be partners. Particular difficulties arise over questions whether salaried partners are in law self employed contractors

---

[1] "Business" includes "every trade, occupation or profession": Partnership Act 1890 s.45.
[2] The business must be carried on by or on behalf of all the partners.
[3] Section 1(1), Partnership Act 1890.
[4] Section 45, Partnership Act 1890.
[5] Section 2(3), Partnership Act 1890.
[6] Section 2(2), Partnership Act 1890, *Cox v. Coulson* [1916] 2 KB 177.
[7] Section 2(3), Partnership Act 1890.

or employees[8] or whether indeed they are in law full equity partners.[9] The answer to that question will turn on the facts of the individual case.[10]

2.1.1.2 Dissolution of a partnership
A partnership may last for a specified duration or only during the will of the partners.[11] Absent any agreement to the contrary, the partnership would also be dissolved by the death or bankruptcy of any partner.[12]

There is no statutory power to expel a partner whether by a majority decision of the partners or otherwise however the partners can (and often do) confer this power on themselves in the partnership deed.[13] The power to expel needs to be exercised in good faith but does not require that the expelled partner be given an opportunity to explain his conduct.[14]

2.1.1.3 Consequences flowing from the relationship of partnership
Subject to any express or implied agreement to the contrary the profits and capital of the partnership are shared equally by the partners.[15] In the absence of express agreement, no partner is separately remunerated for acting in the Partnership business.[16]

Each partner is jointly and severally liable with the other partners for all debts and obligations incurred by the firm whilst he is a partner;[17] provided the payment was made in the ordinary and proper conduct of the business of the firm, the partner is entitled to be indemnified out the firm's assets[18] and the losses of the firm are borne by the partners between themselves (subject

---

[8] The test as to whether a worker is an employee or a contractor is whether the he performed the services as a person in business on his own account. If the answer was "yes", then it was a contract for services. If the answer was "no", then he was employed under a contract of service: *Lee Ting Sang Chung v. Chung Chi Keung* [1990] 2 WLR 1173.

[9] *Lees v. M Young Legal Associates* [2006] 1 WLR 2652. There the Court of Appeal held that the payment of a fixed annual sum to the appellant to be nominal supervising partner so that a firm of solicitors could comply with rule 13 of the Solicitors Practice Rules (one principal qualified to supervise) rendered the appellant a full equity partner. Nor was this negated by the fact the appellant did not contribute to the capital of the firm.

[10] See comments in *Marsh Ferriman & Cheale v. Cutler* (1998) Lawtel 24th June (whether a salaried partner was on the facts an employee or an independent contractor) and *Stekel v Ellice* [1973] 1 All ER 465 (whether a salaried partner was on the facts an equity partner).

[11] Section 26(1) Partnership Act 1890.
[12] Section 33(1) Partnership Act 1890.
[13] Section 25 Partnership Act 1890.
[14] *Green v. Howell* [1910] Ch 495.
[15] Section 24(1) Partnership Act 1890.
[16] Section 24(6) Partnership Act 1890.
[17] Section 9 Partnership Act 1890.
[18] Section 24(2)(a) Partnership Act 1890.

to agreement to the contrary) in the same proportions as they were entitled to share the profits.[19]

Each partner is entitled to participate in the management of the partnership's business.[20] Differences as to the running of the partnership are decided upon by the vote of a simple majority of the partners. However in the absence of any agreement to the contrary, no new partner may join the partnership[21] and no change may be made to the nature of the partnership's business[22] unless all the other partners agree. Each partner however owes the others a duty to act with the utmost good faith.

Each partner is entitled to access, inspect and copy the books and records of the partnership business and these will keep at the partnership's principal place of business.[23]

Partners are bound to render true accounts and full information of all things affecting the partnership to any partner or his representative.[24] Every partner must account to the firm for any benefit derived by him with the consent of the other partners from any transaction concerning the partnership or from any use by him of the partnership property[25] name or business connections.[26]

2.1.1.4 Mixed practices
Mixed practices between members of the various professional accountancy bodies still create potential difficulties even though the former ban on mixed practices has now been lifted by all the professional accountancy bodies. Members of the Institute of Chartered Accountants in England and Wales[27] are responsible for ensuring all members of their practice abide with the ethical requirements of the ICAEW when providing services to the public.[28]

2.1.1.5 Large partnerships
The 20 partner limit on all partnerships has been abolished by the Regulatory Reform (Removal of the 20 Partner Limit in Partnerships, etc)

---

[19] Section 44(1) Partnership Act 1890.
[20] Section 24(5) Partnership Act 1890.
[21] Section 24(7) Partnership Act 1890.
[22] Section 24(8) Partnership Act 1890.
[23] Section 24(9) Partnership Act 1890.
[24] Section 28 Partnership Act 1890.
[25] Thus a partner cannot take an interest as a part purchaser in a sale of partnership property without full disclosure: *Dunne v. English* (1874) LR 18 Eq 524.
[26] Section 29(1) Partnership Act 1890.
[27] Similar provisions apply for members of the Association of International Accountants.
[28] Statement 1.0 Section 1.209, ICAEW Guide to Professional Ethics.

Order 2002.[29] There is now no longer a distinction between accountants and any other form of partnership as regards the number of partners allowed.

Names of partners where the partnership has over 20 partners need not be disclosed on the letterhead and other documents of the partnership, provided a full list of the partners is maintained for inspection at the partnership premises.[30]

There is a similar statutory exception enabling the formation of limited partnerships of accountants fulfilling the above criteria.[31]

2.1.1.6 Discrimination

It is unlawful for firms of six or more partners,[32] in relation to a position as partner in the firm, to discriminate[33] against a woman-

- a. in the arrangements they make for the purpose of determining who should be offered that position
- b. in the terms on which they offer her that position
- c. by refusing or deliberately omitting to offer her that position
- d. in any case where a woman already holds that position-
- e. in the way that they afford her access to any benefits, facilities or services, or by refusing or deliberately omitting to afford her access to them
- f. by expelling her from that position or subjecting her to any other detriment.[34]

This applies to persons proposing to form themselves into a partnership as it applies in relation to a firm.[35] There is an exception to (a) and (c) above where being a man is a genuine occupational qualification[36] for the position of partner[37] and to (b) and (d) where the provision is made in relation to death or retirement.[38]

---

[29] SI 2002/3203.
[30] Section 4(1) and 4(4), Business Names Act 1985.
[31] Companies Act 1985, Section 716(2), (3).
[32] This means a "general partner" where it is applied to limited partnerships: Sex Discrimination Act 1975, Section 11(5). "General partner" means any partner who is not a limited partner: Section 3 Limited Partnership Act 1907.
[33] See Sex Discrimination Act 1975, Sections 1 to 4.
[34] Sex Discrimination Act 1975, Section 11.
[35] Section 11(2), *ibid.*
[36] Section 7(1), *ibid.*
[37] Section 11(3), *ibid.*
[38] Section 11(4), *ibid.*

2.1.2 LLPs

Limited liability partnerships were introduced into UK law under the Limited Liability Partnerships Act 2000 on 6th April 2001. Their introduction was strongly lobbied for by the accountancy profession and they have since proven a popular form of structure. Limited Liability Partnerships are a completely new form of legal entity. They are neither a form of limited company nor a form of partnership but share some characteristics of each.

Limited Liability Partnerships are restricted to ventures for carrying on a lawful business with a view to a profit[39] however, subject to the "business with a view to a profit" proviso there is no restriction on the type of venture that a Limited Liability Partnership may embark upon and can be used as a structure for an accountancy practice.

2.1.2.1 The legal nature of Limited Liability Partnerships

Contrary to what one might infer from their name, the law relating to partnerships has no application to Limited Liability Partnerships.[40]

A Limited Liability Partnership has, once incorporated, a legal personality entirely separate from that of its members.[41] Incorporation arises on the issue of the certificate of registration rather than the creation of a limited liability partnership agreement.

A Limited Liability Partnership has unlimited legal capacity.[42] A Limited Liability Partnership can contract or own property or sue and be sued in its own name or become partner, officer or shareholder in another enterprise.

A Limited Liability Partnership needs to have a registered office;[43] the registered office is an address situated in England, Wales, or in Scotland to which communications and notices can be served.[44] All Limited Liability Partnerships must at all times have a registered office situated in England, Wales, or in Scotland to which communications and notices may be addressed.[45]

A Limited Liability Partnership must file annual returns and needs, unless exempt, to file audited accounts which are lodged at Companies House and

---

[39] S.2(1)(a) Limited Liability Partnership Act 2000.
[40] S.1(5), Limited Liability Partnerships Act 2000.
[41] S.1(2), Limited Liability Partnerships Act 2000.
[42] S.1(3), Limited Liability Partnerships Act 2000.
[43] S.1(6), Limited Liability Partnerships Act 2000.
[44] Schedule, paragraph 9(1) Limited Liability Partnerships Act 2000.
[45] Schedule, paragraph 9(1) Limited Liability Partnerships Act 2000.

are open to public inspection. Annual General Meetings to approve accounts are not required.

2.1.2.2 The Limited Liability Partnership Agreement

The Limited Liability Partnership Agreement is an agreement between the Limited Liability Partnership and its members setting out the constitution of the Limited Liability Partnership.

This is not lodged at Companies House and is private to the Limited Liability Partnership and its members.

Whilst a limited liability partnership agreement is not compulsory for the creation of a Limited Liability Partnership, it is plainly desirable that a written agreement is entered into not least because the agreement may be implied or, in the absence of such an agreement,[46] a very rudimentary "default" constitution can be derived from the Limited Liability Partnership Regulations 2001.

The default provisions include:[47]

- That all members share equally in capital and profits;[48]
- That all members be indemnified by the Limited Liability Partnership for liabilities arising from the ordinary activities of the Limited Liability Partnership;
- That all members may participate in the Limited Liability Partnership's management;
- That no members are entitled to remuneration from the Limited Liability Partnership;
- That before new members can be introduced to the Limited Liability Partnership the unanimous consent of all existing members is need;
- That a simple majority of the members can decide any resolution of the Limited Liability Partnership other than a change in the nature of the Limited Liability Partnership's business; in the latter case a unanimous decision is required;
- That the Limited Liability Partnership's books are to be kept at its place of business and that they are to be open to inspection by all members;

---

[46] S. 5(1) Limited Liability Partnership Act 2000.
[47] Reg 7-8, Limited Liability Partnership Regulations 2001.
[48] This may not always be suitable for an accountancy practice as different profit shares may be appropriate to reflect differences in seniority, earnings or capital introduced into the practice.

- That the members must render true account and full information with regard to everything affecting the Limited Liability Partnership to their fellow members.

Importantly for accountants who will have to be mindful of the "fit and proper" requirement for certain aspects of their functions, these default provisions do not allow for any power to expel members and express provisions would be required to achieve this. Moreover there is no provision under the default provisions to allow a retiring partner in an accountancy practice the opportunity to withdraw his capital from the Limited Liability Partnership.[49]

2.1.2.3 The name of a Limited Liability Partnership
A Limited Liability Partnership's name must either end with "Limited Liability Partnership" or its abbreviation "LLP". It is acceptable to substitute its Welsh equivalent, "partneriaeth atebolrwydd cyfyngedig" or its abbreviation "PAC".

Much like with a company's name, the Registrar of Companies may refuse to register a Limited Liability Partnership's name if it's the same as a name which has already been registered or includes a restricted word or phrase under the Business Names Act 1985 without permission.

2.1.2.4 Members of Limited Liability Partnerships
Any legal or natural person can become a member of a Limited Liability Partnership.

At incorporation there must be at least two members. If at any time after incorporation, the number of members reduces below two, then the continuing member will take on the liabilities of the Limited Liability Partnership (after a six-month period of grace) and the Limited Liability Partnership may be compulsorily wound up. The initial members are those stated on the formation document and subsequent members may be added by agreement. A person ceases to be a member if he dies (or if the member is a legal person, it is dissolved)[50] or otherwise with the agreement of the other members. Absent any agreement as to how a member might cease to be a member, a member may terminate his membership by giving reasonable notice to the other members.[51]

---

[49] Provisions to allow or require the purchase of a retiring member's interest in the equity can however be introduced in the Limited Liability Partnership Agreement.
[50] S. 4(1) Limited Liability Partnerships Act 2000.
[51] S. 4(3) Limited Liability Partnerships Act 2000.

Any change in the membership must be notified to Companies House.

Every member of a Limited Liability Partnership is an agent of it[52] however, unlike with a partnership, the members are not agents of each other. The Limited Liability Partnership can only avoid liability for acts done by a member in its name if both (a) the act was outside the member's authority, and, (b) the third party he dealt with was aware of the limit on the member's authority or did not know or believe him to be a member of the Limited Liability Partnership.[53]

Moreover a third party dealing with a Limited Liability Partnership is even entitled to regard a former member of the Limited Liability Partnership as having the authority to act as its agent, unless he either has notice that the person in question has ceased to be a member or notice that the person in question has ceased to be a member has been delivered to Companies House[54].

Provisions exist (subject to their being contracted out under the Limited Liability Partnership Agreement) which require members to account for secret profits; a member must account to the Limited Liability Partnership:

- For any profits made by the member in a business carried on by him, if that business is of the same nature as, and competing with, the Limited Liability Partnership, and is without the consent of the Limited Liability Partnership[55] and
- if, without the Limited Liability Partnership's consent, the member derives a benefit from any transaction which concerns the Limited Liability Partnership, or makes use of its property, name, or business connection.[56]

Members are not automatically employees of the Limited Liability Partnership[57] although there is no restriction on an employment agreement being entered with them expressly.

2.1.2.5 Designated Members of Limited Liability Partnerships
Of the members of the Limited Liability Partnership, at least two must be appointed as designated members of the Limited Liability Partnership.[58]

---

[52] S.6(1), Limited Liability Partnerships Act 2000.
[53] S.6(2), Limited Liability Partnerships Act 2000.
[54] S.6(3), Limited Liability Partnership Act 2000.
[55] Reg. 7(9) Limited Liability Partnership Regulations 2001.
[56] Reg. 7(10) Limited Liability Partnership Regulations 2001.
[57] S.4(4), Limited Liability Partnerships Act 2000.
[58] S.8, Limited Liability Partnerships Act 2000.

If two are not designated or if the number of designated members drops below two then all members automatically become designated.[59] Any member may become a designated member with the agreement of the other members.[60] Any member may cease to be a designated member with the agreement of the other members however there is no power for a designated member to unilaterally relinquish that status unless he ceases to be a member.[61]

Designated status confers responsibilities for the running of the Limited Liability Partnership; designated members take responsibility for a number of administrative and accounting functions, such as the filing of Companies House annual returns and the appointment of the auditor.

Any change in the designated membership must be notified to Companies House.

2.1.2.6 Restrictions on membership of a Limited Liability Partnership

Anyone disqualified from being a director of a limited company by the Company Directors Disqualification Act 1986 is also disqualified from being a member of a Limited Liability Partnership.

A member against whom a bankruptcy order is made may not thereafter play any part in the management or administration of the Limited Liability Partnership or its business. Further, it is an offence for a bankrupt to act as a member or directly or indirectly to take part in the promotion, management or formation of a Limited Liability Partnership.[62]

2.1.2.7 Liability for negligence

Individual members of a Limited Liability Partnership are not liable for the negligence of the Limited Liability Partnership unless they themselves were the cause of the negligent act. In cases where a member is, however, liable to any person (other than a fellow member) as a result of his own wrongful act or omission for anything done either in the course of the Limited Liability Partnership's business, or with the Limited Liability Partnership's authority, then the Limited Liability Partnership is liable to the same extent as the member.[63]

---

[59] S.8(2), Limited Liability Partnerships Act 2000.
[60] S.8, Limited Liability Partnerships Act 2000.
[61] S.8(6), Limited Liability Partnerships Act 2000.
[62] Reg 4(2) Limited Liability Partnership Regulations 2001.
[63] S.6(4) Limited Liability Partnerships Act 2000.

Thus if an accountant member was negligent in tax work undertaken by him through his Limited Liability Partnership accountancy practice claims could be brought both against the Limited Liability Partnership and against the negligent accountant member personally (but not his fellow members). The protection of limited liability is to this extent illusory and care should be taken by practices to ensure that any professional indemnity insurance they take out covers both claims against the Limited Liability Partnership and its members personally.

2.1.2.8 Audit of Limited Liability Partnerships

The Companies Act 1989 provisions on company auditors also apply to limited liability partnerships and their members as it applies to companies and their directors. The duty to appoint an auditor falls upon the designated members of the LLP, who must make the initial appointment before the end of the first financial year of the LLP. Designated members also have the power to appoint to fill casual vacancies in the office of auditor. In the event of the designated members failing to appoint an auditor, power is vested in the members generally, who may do so by passing a resolution at a meeting convened for that purpose.

Auditors of an LLP have the same rights to seek information about it as if it were a company.[64] They have the right to be notified of and to attend any meetings of the members which have been convened, if the business of the meeting concerns them as auditors.[65] There is no guidance given as to the boundaries of what an auditor is entitled to consider of his concern. The payment of auditors can be fixed either by the designated members or by any such other means as the members generally may determine.[66] The power to remove an auditor from office as auditor of a LLP is vested on the designated members.[67] If they exercise this power, they must give notice to the registrar within 14 days of their decision, and may be fined if they do not give this notice.

2.1.3 Limited Company

Accountants are free in law to constitute their practices as limited liability companies. Historically no corporate body could be appointed the auditor of

---

[64] S. 389A Companies Act 1985.
[65] S. 390 Companies Act 1985.
[66] S. 390A Companies Act 1985.
[67] S. 391 Companies Act 1985.

a company but this bar was removed in 1991.[68] Insolvency Practitioners still may not incorporate.[69]

2.2 PERMITTED NAMES FOR ACCOUNTANCY PRACTICES

2.2.1 Choice of practice name

The firm of accountants may generally be carried on under any firm name, subject to certain provisions:

- The name complies with the provisions of the Business Names Act 1985[70] and any regulations made under section 65, Companies Act 2006.
- The name must not duplicate or be colourably similar to that of any other firm or business
- The name must not contravene the professional rules governing the choice of practice name.

2.2.2 Business Names Act 1985

Compliance with the Business Names Act is necessary where the partnership[71] carries on business under a name which:

a. does not comprise of the surnames[72] of all the partners who are individuals and the corporate names of all the partners who are companies,[73] or
b. has any addition[74] other than:[75]

- the forenames of the individual partners
- the initials[76] of the forenames of the individual partners
- in the case where two or more partners have the same surname, the addition of "s" at the end of the surname
- any addition merely to indicate that the business is carried on in succession to a former owner of the business

---

[68] The bar under Section 389 Companies Act 1985 was repealed from 1st October, 1991 under Section 212 and Schedule 24 of the Companies Act 1989 as brought into force by SI 91/1996.
[69] Section 390 Insolvency Act 1986.
[70] "Business" is defined as including a profession: Business Names Act 1985, Section 8(1).
[71] "Partnership" includes a foreign partnership: Business Names Act 1985, Section 8(1).
[72] "Surname" in relation to a peer or a person usually known by a British title different from his surname means the title by which he is usually known: Business Names Act 1985, Section 8(1).
[73] Business Names Act 1985, Section 1(1).
[74] Business Names Act 1985, Section 1(1).
[75] Business Names Act 1985, Section 1(2).
[76] "Initial" includes any recognised abbreviation of the name: Business Names Act 1985, Section 8(1).

2.2.3 The name must not duplicate or be colourably similar to that of any other firm or business

An action in "passing off" may be founded where a business name used colourably resembles another business, however innocently adopted, is intended to deceive either:

    a. by diverting customers away from the other business to itself, or
    b. by creating confusion between the two businesses, e.g., by suggesting that one business is a branch, extension or agency of or somehow connected to the other.[77]

Where such an intention is apparent the court will interfere to prevent people from trading under their own names.[78]

2.2.4 Professional Restrictions on use of names

The name must not contravene the professional rules governing the choice of practice name.

2.2.4.1 Chartered Accountants

Chartered accountants must not use the words "Chartered Accountants" as part of the firm name.[79] Chartered accountants may use the description "Chartered Accountants" if more than 50 per cent of the voting rights are held by chartered accountants held and 50 percent of the partners (or directors of a company) are chartered accountants.[80]

A Chartered Accountant" for these purposes, is defined[81] as being a member of:

- The Institute of Chartered Accountants in England and Wales
- The Institute of Chartered Accountants of Scotland
- The Institute of Chartered Accountants in Ireland
- The Institute of Chartered Accountants in Australia
- The Canadian Institute of Chartered Accountants
- The South African Institute of Chartered Accountants
- The Institute of Chartered Accountants of Zimbabwe
- The Institute of Chartered Accountants of New Zealand.

---

[77] *Ewing v. Buttercup Margarine Company Ltd* [1917] 2 Ch 1.
[78] *Croft v. Day* (1843) 7 Beav 84.
[79] Paragraph 2.2, Section 1.212, ICAEW Guide to Professional Ethics.
[80] Reg 4, Regulations Relating to the Use of the Description 'Chartered Accountants' and to General Affiliates of the Institute of Chartered Accountants in England and Wales May 2000.
[81] Reg 2, Regulations Relating to the Use of the Description 'Chartered Accountants' and to General Affiliates of the Institute of Chartered Accountants in England and Wales May 2000.

The name chosen for the firm must be "consistent with the dignity of the profession in that it should not project an image inconsistent with that of a professional practice bound to high ethical and technical standards."[82] It must also not be misleading;[83] examples are given of the use of "International" by a firm with one overseas office or "& Associates" by a sole practitioner with no consultants.

2.2.4.2 Chartered Certified Accountants

The term "Chartered Certified Accountant" or "Certified Accountant" or "Registered Auditor" must not form part of the firm name.[84]

Chartered certified accountants may however use the term "Chartered Certified Accountant", "Certified Accountants" or even "an ACCA Practice" in their firm description if more than 51 per cent of the voting rights and half the members are members of ACCA.[85]

The name chosen must be "consistent with the dignity of the profession in that it should not project an image inconsistent with that of a professional practice bound to high ethical and technical standards".[86] It must not be such that it might be confused with the name of another firm.[87] It must not be misleading[88]. Sole practitioners (providing they hold the appropriate certificate) however are given the dispensation that they can use the suffix "& Co" or use the plural description "Chartered Certified Accountants" (even though there is only one of them) or use another business name which is not their own.[89]

2.2.4.3 Authorised Public Accountants

Members and firms who are members may use the description "Authorised Public Accountant".[90] Members and member firms who are on the Register of Auditors sign audits as "registered auditor".[91]

However, subject to the extraordinary power of the Council to grant permission to do this,[92] authorised public accountants must not describe their

---

[82] Paragraph 1.2, Section 1.212, ICAEW Guide to Professional Ethics.
[83] Paragraph 1.3, Section 1.212, ICAEW Guide to Professional Ethics.
[84] Rule 13, Section 3.11, ACCA Code of Ethics and Conduct.
[85] Rule 14, Section 3.11, ACCA Code of Ethics and Conduct.
[86] Rule 40, Section 3.11, ACCA Code of Ethics and Conduct.
[87] Rule 42, Section 3.11, ACCA Code of Ethics and Conduct.
[88] Rule 41, Section 3.11, ACCA Code of Ethics and Conduct.
[89] Rule 30, Section 3.11, ACCA Code of Ethics and Conduct.
[90] Byelaw 7,.
[91] Article 14, AAPA Articles of Association.
[92] Byelaw 6, AAPA Byelaws.

firm, partnership or company as "Authorised Public Accountants" if any member of the undertaking is not a member of the association,[93]

2.2.4.4 International Accountants

International accountants must choose a name consistent with the dignity of the profession in that it should not project an image inconsistent with that of a professional practice bound to high ethical and technical standards. It must not include the term "International Accountants" as part of the name or description of the firm (although individual members may be described as such). The name must comply with the local laws where the international accountants are in overseas practice and must not be misleading, e.g. using the word "international" where the firm has only one overseas office or "& Associates" for a sole practitioner.

2.2.4.5 Chartered Management Accountants

Members and not the firms they constitute are granted the description "Chartered Management Accountants". CIMA has given informal guidance that the use of the description "Chartered Management Accountants" by a firm is acceptable as long as it does not form part of the firm's name and either the sole proprietor or all the partners are chartered management accountants.[94]

2.3 MARKETING BY ACCOUNTANTS

An accountant is free to seek professional work by any means he chooses. This general freedom has been subjected to important qualifications both by statute law and by the accountants' own professional bodies.

2.3.1 Qualifications on the freedom to market under statutory law: investment business

An accountant must not make unsolicited visits or telephone calls to non clients with a view to obtaining investment business.[95]

2.3.2 Qualifications on the freedom to market by professional bodies

Outside investment business, whilst there is no special legal restriction on marketing by accountants, this is an area where many professional bodies

---

[93] Byelaw 5, AAPA Byelaws.
[94] Hayward "What's in a name" CIMAG, page 11.
[95] Formerly section 56, Financial Services Act 1986, now see *FSA Handbook of Rules and Guidance: Conduct of Business* 3.10.3R.

have adopted regulations identifying areas of potential professional misconduct.

2.3.2.1 Chartered Accountants
Chartered accountants are entitled to advertise in any way "consistent with the dignity of the profession" in that it should not project an image inconsistent with that of a professional person bound by high ethical stands.[96] Advertising should comply with the relevant advertising standards and must be legal, decent, clear honest and truthful and whilst drawing comparisons with other firms is now permitted such comparisons must be objective and not misleading, relate to the same services, be factual and verifiable and not discredit other's practice or services.[97] Marketing should never disparage others or their services and must not amount to harassment of potential clients and no fees or commissions should be paid for the introduction of work.[98]

2.3.2.2 Chartered Certified Accountants
Chartered certified accountant's advertising may contain any factual statement, the truth of which the member is able to justify however it should not unflattering references or comparisons with the services of others.[99] The promotion must not harass non clients[100] and must comply with any applicable legislation.[101]

2.3.2.3 Incorporated Executive Accountants
Incorporated Executive accountants may advertise for business without a current practising certificate.[102] Advertisements may not consist of more than an offer to provide accountancy services and may not be worded as a claim of any particular expertise.[103] There is a clearance procedure for advertisements involving the submission of the advertisement to the Secretary General for his discretionary clearance.[104]

---

[96] Statement 1.0, Chapter 1.211, *ICAEW Guide to Professional Ethics*.
[97] Statement 3, Chapter 1.211 *ICAEW Guide to Professional Ethics* Statement 3, Chapter 1.211 *ICAEW Guide to Professional Ethics*.
[98] Statement 3, Chapter 1.211 *ICAEW Guide to Professional Ethics*.
[99] Rule 13, Section 3.10, *ACCA Code of Ethics and Conduct*.
[100] Rule 15, Section 3.10 *ACCA Code of Ethics and Conduct*.
[101] Rule 14, Section 3.10 *ACCA Code of Ethics and Conduct*.
[102] Section D (ii), *ICEA Professional and Ethical Code for Members*.
[103] Section D (iii), *ICEA Professional and Ethical Code for Members*.
[104] Section D (iv), *ICEA Professional and Ethical Code for Members*.

2.3.2.4 Chartered Public Finance Accountants

Any advertising by Chartered Public Finance Accountants must be decent, honest, truthful and in good taste.[105]

Harassment or coercion of potential clients is not permitted[106]. Acceptable forms of advertising include objectively worded and factual brochures or newspaper advertisements which are limited to a bare statement of the facts (consideration in the latter case must be given to the number of insertions and the area of distribution).[107] Unacceptable forms of advertising include endorsements, any suggestion that the accountant is able to influence any court or body, comparisons with other accountants, misleading representations or anything that might create an unjustified or deceptive expectation of a favourable result.[108]

Any marketing by chartered public finance accountants whether in public practice or not should not bring the profession into disrepute, denigrate others or include exaggerated claims.[109]

2.3.2.5 International Accountants

Any advertising by International Accountants must be decent, honest, truthful and in good taste.[110]

Harassment or coercion of potential clients is not permitted.[111] Acceptable forms of advertising include objectively worded and factual brochures or newspaper advertisements which are limited to a bare statement of the facts (consideration in the latter case must be given to the number of insertions and the area of distribution).[112]

---

[105] *A10.1 Standards of Professional Practice on Ethics of December 2000* and *Section 14.2, Part B, IFAC Code of Ethics for Professional Accountants.*
[106] *A10.1 Standards of Professional Practice on Ethics of December 2000* and *Section 14.2, Part B, IFAC Code of Ethics for Professional Accountants.*
[107] *A10.1 Standards of Professional Practice on Ethics of December 2000* and *Section 14.7, Part B, IFAC Code of Ethics for Professional Accountants.* The publicity should be dignified and not give undue prominence to the name of the accountant.
[108] *A10.1 Standards of Professional Practice on Ethics of December 2000* and *Section 14.3, Part B, IFAC Code of Ethics for Professional Accountants.*
[109] *A10.1 Standards of Professional Practice on Ethics of December 2000* and *Sections 7* and, for public practice, *14, Part B, IFAC Code of Ethics for Professional Accountants.*
[110] *A10.1 Standards of Professional Practice on Ethics of December 2000* and *Section 14.2, Part B, IFAC Code of Ethics for Professional Accountants.*
[111] *A10.1 Standards of Professional Practice on Ethics of December 2000* and *Section 14.2, Part B, IFAC Code of Ethics for Professional Accountants.*
[112] *A10.1 Standards of Professional Practice on Ethics of December 2000* and *Section 14.7, Part B, IFAC Code of Ethics for Professional Accountants.* The publicity should be dignified and not give undue prominence to the name of the accountant.

Unacceptable forms of advertising include endorsements, any suggestion that the accountant is able to influence any court or body, comparisons with other accountants, misleading representations or anything that might create an unjustified or deceptive expectation of a favourable result.[113]

Any marketing by international accountants whether in public practice or not should not bring the profession into disrepute, denigrate others or include exaggerated claims.[114]

2.3.2.6 Incorporated Financial Accountants

Marketing must not bring the Institute or the profession into disrepute[115] and must show discretion and be in good taste.[116] The advertisement should be accurate[117] and not phrased in extravagant language.[118] Comparisons should not be drawn with other members or the members of other accountancy bodies.[119] Fees should not be mentioned in any advertising.[120]

2.3.2.7 Chartered Management Accountants

Chartered Management Accountants in public practice may solicit work by marketing. In doing so, he should not bring the profession into disrepute when marketing professional services. Thus the accountant in public practice should be honest and truthful and should not make exaggerated claims for services offers, qualifications possessed or experience gained, or make disparaging references to unsubstantiated comparisons to the work of another.[121]

2.4 THE SALE OF ACCOUNTANCY PRACTICES

The sale of an accountancy practice, and indeed any transfer of a business as a going concern, involves the transfer of both tangible and intangible assets.

The most important of those assets from the standpoint of an accountancy practice is the sale of the goodwill – the passage of the relationship between the practice and its clients. Often the transfer is merely the sale not of the

---

[113] *A10.1 Standards of Professional Practice on Ethics of December 2000* and *Section 14.3, Part B, IFAC Code of Ethics for Professional Accountants.*
[114] *A10.1 Standards of Professional Practice on Ethics of December 2000* and *Sections 7* and, for public practice, *14, Part B, IFAC Code of Ethics for Professional Accountants.*
[115] Paragraph 4, Practice Promotion, IFA Code of Ethics.
[116] Paragraph 1, Practice Promotion, IFA Code of Ethics.
[117] Paragraph 3, Practice Promotion, IFA Code of Ethics.
[118] Paragraph 6, Practice Promotion, IFA Code of Ethics.
[119] Paragraphs 1 and 2, Practice Promotion, IFA Code of Ethics.
[120] Paragraph 7, Practice Promotion, IFA Code of Ethics.
[121] Section 250.2, CIMA code of ethics for professional accountants.

practice but of "a block of fees" – the right to deal with certain existing clients of the practice.

Moreover the transfer of a practice may raise both liability and professional issues. Taxation issues will necessarily arise on any practice sale; these are not dealt with in this work.

2.4.1 Assets and liabilities to be considered on a practice sale

The sale may be effected by a transfer of all the assets (and possibly the liabilities) and may include the novation of the contracts entered by the practice.

If the practice is being sold as a going concern, the assets of the practice may include some or all of the following assets and liabilities:

- Premises
- Office furniture
- Debtors
- Creditors
- Employees
- Cash
- Work in progress
- Goodwill
- The Benefit (and possibly burden) of contracts
- Intellectual Property (such as the practice name, get up and trade mark)
- Hire purchase and leasing agreements
- Stationary
- Computer hardware and software
- Client records

Decisions need to be made and agreement reached as to whether the assets are to remain with the vendor or pass to the purchaser on the sale. The assets and liabilities to be retained and transferred need to be clearly identified; uncertainty of this often leads to litigation later on.

The purchase price will need to be apportioned between the assets. This is important not merely to give a pre-estimate of damages on a breach of contract but also for capital gains and stamp duty tax purposes.

2.4.1.1 Goodwill, Client list and the "Block of Fees"

The most important of the assets of any accountancy practice is the goodwill – the relationship between the practice and its clients. A transfer of the goodwill of the business normally confers on the purchaser the exclusive right to carry on the business transferred together with the exclusive right to use the name under which the business has been established.

It is important to always be mindful that selling clients is not like selling cans of baked beans. The relationship with the practice and its former owners was a personal one and clients cannot be compelled to follow the business to its new owners, who are people the clients do not know and have no reason to deal with.

Ironically therefore it is this asset above all the others which will influence the price to be set for the practice and the price for the practice is usually estimated as a multiple of gross annual fees.

Ensuring that the clients and the gross earnings remain with the practice is therefore a particularly vexed question for any counsel or solicitor facing the task of drafting a practice sale agreement.

One mechanism when fixing the price is to distinguish between recurring and non recurring fees and build in warranties that the warranted recurring fees will stay with the practice for the next twelve months.

Another mechanism is to stagger payment of the purchase price over a period of two years and to build in claw back provisions allowing the sale price to be adjusted out of the later installments if the gross fees do not match the figures previously earned by the practice.

These types of arrangements are often well suited to be combined with the vendor being given a consultancy by the purchaser. The vendor benefits from the opportunity to minimize the risk of the purchase price being clawed back from him. The purchaser benefits from the clients seeing a more seamless transition to their ownership and the vendor smoothing the introduction to his clients and giving the benefit of his insights into their needs and expectations.

It is sensible to build in express covenants against competition and the solicitation of the practice's employees. In the absence of an express covenant against competition, no covenant by the vendor against setting up a competing business nor against soliciting former customers will be implied. Thus he may set up such a competing business.

To ensure that these are enforceable against the vendor (and not void as being an unreasonable restraint of trade[122]) these should be no stricter than necessary to protect the purchaser's legitimate business interests.

Given that the purchaser has a genuine business interest to protect and given that the sale by the vendor is tantamount to his recognition of this, the courts have shown a greater readiness to enforce covenants between the vendor and purchaser of a practice than the courts have traditionally shown in cases concerning covenants between an employer and former employee.[123]

The question of reasonableness of a non-compete covenant is assessed against the geographical area of its intended operation and its duration. If the nature of the business restrained is wider than that carried on by the practice and the area of restraint wider geographically than the practice operated in, the restraint will be unreasonable and therefore void.[124]

The reasonableness of a non-solicitation covenant will depend more on an accurate yet limited identification of the former customers or clients who should not be poached.

2.4.1.2 The Contracts of the Practice
It is important to remember that whenever on a sale, there is change in the identity of the legal or natural persons who trade as the practice (which will be most cases other than where the practice sale is effected by the transfer of shares in an incorporated practice), the new owners may no longer be a party to contracts originally entered into by vendor.

The question then arises as to whether both the benefit and the burden or merely the benefit of the contract is to be transferred to the purchaser.

If the benefit of the contractual rights only is to be transferred this is best done by a statutory transfer under section 136, the Law of Property Act 1925. This provides that a legal assignment can be effected if (a) the assignment is in writing (b) it is of the entire benefit (this is usually expressed as "absolutely") and (c) written notice is given to the other contracting party. If this is effected then the purchaser will be able to sue on the assigned rights in his or her own name.

---

[122] Covenants in restraint of trade are, in the absence of special justifying circumstances, contrary to public policy and therefore void.
[123] *Nordenfelt v. Maxim Nordenfelt Guns and Ammunition Co* [1894] AC 535 at 565; *Ronbar Enterprises Ltd v. Green* [1954] 2 All ER 266 at 270.
[124] *Nordenfelt v. Maxim Nordenfelt Guns and Ammunition Co* [1894] AC 535 at 565.

If any of these preconditions is absent, the assignment will not amount to a legal assignment but may still stand as an equitable assignment. To enforce an equitable assignment, the purchaser will not be able to bring the action in his own name but must join the assignor as a party to the action and effectively enforces his rights through him.

Where it is desirable to transfer both the benefit and the burden of a contract,[125] this may be achieved by the novation of the new contract. In essence this is the rescission of the old contract and the substitution of a new contract in which the same acts are to be performed by different parties.

2.4.1.3 Work in progress, cash in hand and book debts
The approach to be taken on any sale to work in progress, book debts and cash in hand demands particular consideration.

What constitutes the book debts, work in progress and cash in hand of a practice will naturally fluctuate on a daily if not hourly basis. A clear demarcation needs to be drawn as which assets are included in the sale and which are not and when that cut off needs to be drawn.

The demarcation is also important from a liability front. A clear cut off must be identified when the purchaser's professional indemnity insurance is to take over from the vendor's.

If they are to be transferred, a schedule of debtors and amounts owed by each of them should be annexed to the agreement and to make such an assignment fully effective as against the debtors, and legally enforceable by the purchaser in his own name, the purchaser will have to give notice in writing to each of them under s. 136 Law of Property Act 1925.

Often the vendor will wish to retain the book debts for their own benefit. Even where this is the case, is often a sensible precaution for the purchaser to be mandated to collect both books debts owed to the vendor and to the purchaser. This prevents reluctant debtors from taking issue with the correct payee or clients being altered to unseemly squabbles as to who is owed their fee and protects the purchaser against any heavy-handed attempts by the vendor to collect the debts which might harm the goodwill of the business.

---

[125] As well as enabling the vendor to be freed of his historic obligations in the practice, novation would have the benefit of avoiding stamp duty that might otherwise be payable on an assignment.

Prompt payment of creditors is important to maintain the goodwill and credit terms enjoyed by the practice. Clear demarcation needs to be drawn between liabilities retained by the vendor and those (if any) to be assumed by the purchaser. Even if the liabilities are not to be assumed by the purchaser it may be in their interest to encourage the vendor to settle those historic liabilities promptly.

2.4.1.4 The Practice's premises: leases and tenancies
If the practice's premises are currently held by the vendor under the terms of a lease, a licence to assign to the new owner will normally be required from the landlord.

It should be noted that if the lease contains a covenant not to assign without the landlord's consent such consent cannot be unreasonably withheld and, since the Landlord and Tenant Act 1988, on an application for a licence to assign, the landlord must respond in writing within a reasonable time. The purchaser will usually provide references as to his creditworthiness. Where the lease has been granted after 1st January 1996 and is subject to the Landlord and Tenant (Covenants) Act 1995, it is possible that it contains an absolute prohibition against assignment; transfer of the premises is usually resolved by the grant of an underlease by the vendor.

2.4.1.5 The Office equipment, computers and furniture
Where stock and assets are transferred, vendors need to be mindful that they bear a strict liability under the Sale of Goods Act 1979 as regards the description, quality and fitness for purpose.

Key equipment of the practice, such as photocopiers, is often enjoyed through leasing agreements or hire-purchase agreements. For the purchaser to take over these agreements, the novation of the contract must been agreed with their lessor. Where this is not possible, one alternative is for the vendor to hold the lease agreement in trust for the purchaser.

The transfer of the computer equipment is often necessary to ensure that the vendor obtains both the work in progress and key correspondence and records. The transfer of the computer does not of itself transfer the benefit of the software licences and maintenance or support agreements needed to operate it and novation of those contracts needs to be considered.

2.4.1.6 The Practice's Employees
Employees represent an important consideration on the transfer of any accountancy practice. Whilst some liabilities can be refused by the purchaser, accrued rights affecting the practice's employees and any liabilities in respect of dismissal will pass to the purchaser under the Transfer of Undertakings

(Protection of Employment) Regulations 2006 and section 218(2), Employment Rights Act 1996 on the transfer of the undertaking.

At common law the sale of a business from the vendor to the purchaser, with a consequent change in the identity of the employer, meant that all contracts of employment which were current at the time of transfer would automatically terminate. Claims for redundancy pay could be made by former employees against the vendor of the practice. The purchaser was free to pick and choose which, if any, of the employees he would re-employ.

Where the Transfer of Undertakings (Protection of Employment) Regulations 2006 do apply, the rights and obligations under the original contract of employment are automatically transferred to the new purchaser of the practice. The transfer itself, therefore, does not operate as a dismissal. All the transferor's rights and liabilities (other than pension rights) under the contract of employment immediately before the transfer are automatically transferred to the purchaser unless the employee objects to becoming employed by the purchaser. Hence there will be no dismissal of the employee by virtue of the transfer of the undertaking. The purchaser of the "undertaking" will therefore be liable for anything done by the vendor in relation to an employee prior to the transfer and may be sued and liable for the vendor's breaches of his obligations as an employer.[126]

2.4.1.7 The Practice's Intellectual Property Rights

Accountancy practices will often enjoy intellectual property rights; these can range from copyright and trade marks to the existence of know-how to confidential information. Often the practice will not appreciate that this potentially valuable asset of the practice even exists. Even more often one finds that consideration is first given to the registration by a practice of the ownership of their trade name and trade marks when the sale of those rights as part of the practice is being contemplated.

Care should be taken to ensure that any intellectual property that can be registered is registered before it is assigned. Best practice is to have separate written assignments signed by the vendor for each intellectual property right being transferred on the practice sale.

Where intellectual property rights of others are used (such as with computer software or where the practice enjoys the benefit of a franchise) an assignment of those rights must be obtained.

---

[126] *Bernadone v. Pall Mall Services Group* [1999] IRLR 617.

2.4.2 Warranties and the Disclosure Letter

The concept of *caveat emptor* – "buyer beware" is well entrenched into English law. This means that each party must look out for himself and ensure that he acquires the information necessary to avoid a bad bargain. In practice, this will mean that the purchaser and his lawyers often need to undertake due diligence work before the purchase is made.

One way in which a purchaser may mitigate the risk he runs is to make enquiries and ensure that any representations made by the vendor that induce him to make his purchase are recorded as warranties under the contract of sale. Thus a purchaser should at the very least seek warranties from the vendor that:

- Assets being sold are not being transferred subject to some other person's security
- That there is no actual or contingent threat of litigation (as any litigation, even if it is only threatened, may damage the goodwill being sold)
- That the employees, the terms upon which they are employed and any disputes with them have been accurately disclosed (given that the purchaser will often find themselves taking on responsibility for these on the practice sale by virtue of the Transfer of Undertakings (Protection of Employment) Regulations 2006)
- That any pension fund that the practice has been paying for is fully disclosed and paid up to date of the date of transfer
- That the disclosure of the financial performance of the business is accurate and not caused by some one off transaction (this is because the price paid by the purchaser will often be driven by the historic income generated by the practice).

The warranties on the sale of a business are usually made subject to the contents of a disclosure letter. The object of such a letter is to record those areas where the vendor wishes to qualify the warranties.

2.5 GOODWILL OF THE ACCOUNTANCY PRACTICE

2.5.1 The nature of goodwill

Goodwill has been described as nothing more than the probability of old customers resorting to the same old place.[127] It is the connection formed by

---

[127] *Cruttwell v. Lyle* (1810) 17 Ves 335 at 346, per Lord Eldon.

years of work[128] or the advantage "whatever it may be, of the reputation and connection of the firm which may have been built up by years of honest work or gained by lavish expenditure of money".[129]

As with any professional practice, goodwill is of key importance to an accountancy practice not least because the income that the practice generates is dependent on the personal relationship built up with the practices clients.

2.5.2 Ownership and protection of the goodwill

In a partnership, goodwill is presumed to attach to the partnership rather than to the individual partners.

An injunction may therefore be obtained to restrain former partners from soliciting any customer of the old firm[130] or from holding themselves out as the old firm.[131] This will not prevent a former partner from setting up as an accountant again as a competitor firm but can be used to prevent him from using his special knowledge of the business.[132]

2.5.3 Goodwill on dissolution

On dissolution of the partnership, in the absence of agreement, the goodwill must be sold.[133] The consequences of failing to sell the goodwill or achieve an agreement over how it is to be disposed of, is that each partner would be equally entitled to use the firm's name and canvas the business's former clients.[134]

2.5.4 Sale of Goodwill

A transfer of the goodwill of the business normally confers on the purchaser the exclusive right to carry on the business transferred together with the exclusive right to use the name under which the business has been established. The sale of the goodwill is often structured as part of a sale of a "block of fees".

The reality is both are very much things "writ in sand" – the relationship the practice and its former owners will have been a personal one just as clients

---

[128] *Ginesi v. Cooker & Co.* (1880) 14 Ch D 596 at 599, per Jessel, M.R..
[129] *Trego v. Hunt* [1896] AC 7 at 24, per Lord Macnaghten.
[130] *Gillingham v. Beddow* [1900] 2 Ch 242.
[131] *Bourne v. Wicker* [1927] 1 Ch 667.
[132] *Trego v. Hunt* [1896] AC 7.
[133] *Pawsey v. Armstrong* (1881) 18 Ch D 698.
[134] *Burchell v. Wilde* [1900] 1 Ch 551.

cannot be compelled to contract with its new owners, who are people the clients do not know and have no reason to deal with.

Given the ethereal quality, practical measures need to be devised and worked into the transfer agreement to ensure the benefit of the goodwill is indeed passed. Examples of these include (a) The vendor being given a consultancy by the purchaser to create the impression amongst the clients of a more seamless transition in ownership and to smooth the introduction to his clients and guide the purchaser as to the client's needs and expectations and (b) the vendor agreeing to be bound by express covenants against competition and the solicitation of the practice's employees.

Chapter 3

THE ACCOUNTANT AND HIS CLIENTS

3.1 THE ACCOUNTANT'S CONTRACT WITH HIS CLIENT

3.1.1 The Contract with the Client

Where an accountant accepts instruction from a client to perform professional services for reward he has a contract with that client; the terms of that contract will usually be contained in the letter of engagement.

An accountant acting for his client is "employed" by the client within the meaning of section 16 Theft Act 1968 even though no legal employment relationship exists; thus a self employed accountant who falsely represented he was a member of the Chartered Institute of Management Accountant to a prospective client was guilty of the offence of obtaining a pecuniary advantage by deception contrary to section 16(1) of the Theft Act 1968 as the services offered by him as a self-employed accountant were capable of amounting to services provided under an "office or employment" within the meaning of section 16(2)(c) of the Act.[1]

3.1.2 Letter of Engagement

The contract is usually contained in the letter of engagement. The terms of an accepted engagement letter will form the express terms of the contract. Chartered Management Accountants are required to formalise their relationship with their clients by a letter of engagement. Whilst a letter of engagement is not a prerequisite for Chartered Accountants who do not undertake regulated work, it is strongly urged by the Institute of Chartered Accountants in England and Wales;[2] this has particular force since chartered accountants are under an ethical obligation to discuss and explain the basis upon which they will be charging their fees[3] and a professional obligations to notify clients in advance in writing of the name of the principal to whom any complaint can be made and their right to complain to the Institute.[4]

---

[1] *R v. Callendar* [1993] QB 303.
[2] "What if you haven't issued an engagement letter", ICAEW Help Sheet.
[3] Section 240, *ICAEW Code of Ethics.*
[4] Bye-Law 11, ICAEW Disciplinary Bye-law.

3.1.2.1 Where there is no written terms and conditions

The absence of written terms of engagement does not refute the possibility that a contract might have been created. Any formal professional relationship between an accountant and the client with the contemplation of some form of payment is, *prima facie*, enough to establish the existence of contractual relations.

If the retainer is informal, the court will look to the overall relationship and dealings between the parties to assess its scope. Low fees, the origins of the relationship and limited information are factors which have been taken into account in limiting the extent of the accountant's authority.[5]

3.1.2.2 Terms of the contract with the client

The extent of the duties of an accountant, however, goes no further than what they are requested and undertake to do - there was no such thing as a general retainer.[6]

3.1.2.2.1 Implied Terms: Reasonable care and skill

It is an implied term of an accountant's contract to provide professional services, that he will provide those professional services properly and with reasonable care and skill

Indeed in the case of any contract under which a person agrees to carry out a service (other than a contract of service or apprenticeship[7] and certain other excepted contracts) where the supplier is acting in the course of a business (a business here is deemed to include a profession[8]) there is an implied term that the supplier of those services will carry out the service with reasonable care and skill.[9]

Where the contract is for the supply of professional services, the degree of care and skill required is that which is to be expected of a professional man of ordinary competence and experience.[10]

The duty is a positive one. Simply advising a client on a share purchase to seek specialist tax advice rather than advising the client on how to maximise his tax advantages when purchasing shares in a company was not enough to absolve an accountant from his obligation to give the client competent

---

[5] *Maritime Insurance Co v. Fortune* (1931) 41 Lloyds Rep 16.
[6] *Fawkes-Underwood v. Hamiltons* [1997] 7 CL 456, Judge Goudie QC.
[7] Section 12(2) Supply of Goods and Services Act 1982.
[8] Section 18(1) Supply of Goods and Services Act 1982.
[9] Section 13 Supply of Goods and Services Act 1982.
[10] *Bolam v. Friern Hospital Management Committee* [1957] 1 WLR 582, 586.

advice; advice on how to maximise the client's tax advantages should have been within the practitioner's general competence as an accountant and the practitioner's failure to give such advice amounted to a breach of his retainer and/or negligence.[11]

If the accountant holds himself out as possessing specialist skills in the area, then the court may be willing to imply that a higher standard of care and skill was agreed to.

3.1.2.2.2 Implied Terms: Time to complete work
Where there is no express provision in the contract for the time within which the professional services are to be carried out there will be implied terms into the contract that the accountant will carry out the professional services within a reasonable time.[12]

Implicit in the term in a contract between an accountant and his client that the accountant will exercise reasonable care and skill in the performance of works under the contract is that the accountant will perform the works timeously and meet any disclosed deadlines.

It also includes not taking an excessive length of time to undertake the work.[13]

3.1.2.2.3 Implied Terms: Compliance with his professional conduct rules
As the client will employ the accountant on the basis of his holding himself out as having a particular accountancy qualification, the author suggests that the contract of engagement will contain a further implied term that the accountant will perform the works in a manner which complies with the standards of the professional association or institute that he is or holds himself out as being a member of.

That is to say, to take an example, the client buys not merely the services of a chartered accountant (the accountant will be in breach of contract if he does not hold the qualification he professes to have) but also someone who performs his services in the way a chartered accountant would. The relevant ethical code of conduct can therefore be implied into the contract of engagement as implied terms of that contract.

---

[11] *Sayers v. Clarke Walker* (2002) EWCA Civ 910.
[12] Sections 14 and 15 of the Supply of Goods and Services Act 1982. See also *Sylvanus Okoye v. Leon Edgar White* (1999) LTL 17 February.
[13] *Sylvanus Okoye v. Leon Edgar White* (1999) LTL 17 February.

3.1.2.2.4 Implied Term: Reasonable Fees

Where there is no express provision in the contract for the fee to be paid for the professional services to be carried out there will be implied terms that the client of the accountant will pay a reasonable charge.[14]

3.1.2.3 Exclusion clauses

The accountant may attempt to limit his exposure by building into the contract exclusion clauses or, in respect of third parties, by including disclaimers on the reports prepared. Exclusion clauses will only be enforceable in so far as they are deemed reasonable.[15]

Section 2 of the Unfair Contract Terms Act 1977 renders void any contractual exclusion or restriction of liability for negligence, even in a case where the client has agreed to it and where legal consideration exists, unless the person seeking to rely on that exclusion or restriction can show that it was reasonable.

The Unfair Terms in Consumer Contracts Regulations 1994 make unenforceable any "unfair term" in a contract between a supplier and a "consumer"; but if a term limiting liability has been found to be "reasonable" for the purposes of the 1977 Act it is thought unlikely that it would be held to be "unfair" for the purposes of the 1994 Regulations.

Excessive use of disclaimers is to be discouraged, not merely because they may be ineffective or inappropriate, but because excessive hedging with disclaimers may render an accountant's report meaningless to others and valueless to the client.

Accountants are unable to generally exclude liability for negligence when they act in the capacity as auditors. Any provision, whether contained in a company's article or in any contract with the company or otherwise is ineffective insofar that it exempts any officer of the company or any person (whether an officer or not) employed by the company as an auditor from or indemnifying him against any liability by virtue of any rule of law which would otherwise attach to him in respect of any negligence, default, breach of duty or breach of trust of which he may be guilty in relation to the company.[16]

---

[14] Sections 14 and 15 of the Supply of Goods and Services Act 1982. See also *Sylvanus Okoye v. Leon Edgar White* (1999) LTL 17 February.
[15] Section 2 Unfair Contract Terms Act 1977.
[16] Section 310(2) Companies Act 1985, section 532 Companies Act 2006 and see Chapter 6.17 for further discussion of this and the changes introduced by the Companies Act 2006.

3.2 FIDUCIARY DUTIES OF ACCOUNTANTS

3.2.1 The accountant owes fiduciary duties to his client

Broadly speaking there is no distinction between the fiduciary duty owed by an accountant and by a solicitor[17]. In finding a fiduciary duty to a client, the court has been prepared to pierce the corporate veil to identify the "true client" to whom the duty was owed[18] or find a relationship of trust and confidence subsisted even after the professional retainer had come to an end.[19]

An accountant owes a fiduciary duty to a client to warn his client that a conflict of interest may arise between him and his client and that the client should seek independent advice and the mere fact that the client either knows or suspects that the conflict exists does discharge the accountant's duty.[20]

It is the duty of an accountant to keep client money separate from his own and that of other people.[21]

It is the duty of an accountant when holding client money to preserve and be constantly ready with correct accounts of all his dealings and transactions with that money as his client's agent.[22]

It is the duty of the accountant when holding client's money to produce to the client, or to a proper person appointed by the client, all books and documents in his hands relating to his client's affairs and prepared by the accountant as agent for his client[23] as opposed to as a professional man.[24]

3.2.2 The accountant owes fiduciary duties to his employer

The accountant owes a similar fiduciary duty to his employer as he does a client. Thus his employer can place reliance in an employee accountant's skill and expertise. Thus a non-accountant director was able to rely on a fellow director, on the basis of his capacity as an accountant, to produce accounts and file annual returns.[25]

---

[17] *Nitrotrim Ltd v. Wildin* (1996) LTL 29 April.
[18] *Conway v. Raitu* [2006] 1 All ER 571.
[19] *Langstaff v. Birtles* [2001] 1 WLR 470.
[20] *Nitrotrim Ltd v. Wildin* (1996) LTL 29 April.
[21] *Gray v. Haig* (1855) 20 Beav 219.
[22] *Gray v. Haig* (1855) 20 Beav 219.
[23] *Dodswell v. Jacobs* (1887) 34 Ch D 278.
[24] *Chantrey Martin v. Martin* [1953] 2 QB 286.
[25] *Re Cladrose* [1990] BCC 11, Harkan J. Section 6 Company Directors Disqualification Act 1986.

Where a duty is owed to a company as a director it does not end when the company becomes insolvent or goes into liquidation. Instead the duty becomes one owed to the creditors as a whole.[26]

Mere incompetence is not a breach of fiduciary duty.[27] Fiduciary duties are fact specific.[28]

Where a fiduciary duty has been breached the remedy will be an account of the profits arising from the breach. Thus a fiduciary that passed a business opportunity from his old company to a new employer was held personally accountable for the profits earned by his new employer irrespective of the fact that he did not receive them.[29] The courts have been prepared to find trusts or a chain of trust to enable them to trace funds paid in breach of fiduciary duty.[30]

3.2.3 Nature of the fiduciary duties

The fiduciary duties of an accountant are (a) of utmost good faith to his client (b) to obey his client's instructions with reasonable care and skill (c) not to permit his interests and that of his client to conflict (d) not making secret profits (e) to keep his property separate from that of his client (f) to keep ready and make available to the client's accounts of his dealings with his client's property (g) not to disclose the confidence of his client

3.2.3.1 An accountant owes his client a duty of the utmost good faith
An accountant owes a duty of the utmost good faith and should make a complete and full disclosure to the client of all facts properly coming to his attention.[31]

3.2.3.2 An accountant owes his client a duty of obedience and must perform his duties with reasonable care and skill
An accountant has a duty to carry out the instructions of his client. The accountant needs to obey those instructions even if he reasonably believes that in departing from them he would be acting in the interests of his client.[32] An accountant however has no duty to carry out instructions which are

---

[26] *Re Pantone* [2002] 1 BCLC 266.
[27] *Extrasure Travel Insurance v Scattergood* [2003] 1 BCLC 598.
[28] *In Plus Group v. Pyke* [2002] 2 BCLC 201 (director wholly excluded from the company's business could work for a competitor as no risk of harm to the company).
[29] *CMS Dolphin v. Simonet* (23.5.01, High Court).
[30] *Bracken Partners v. Gutteridge* [2003] 2 BCLC 84, Peter Leaver QC (tracing company funds to house brought for wife - no need for wife to have a prior fiduciary relationship).
[31] *Morton v. Arbuckle* (No 2) [1919] VLR 487, 491.
[32] *The Hermione* [1922] P 162.

unlawful[33] and thus the agency relationship gives no justification to an accountant for preparing false tax accounts or returns on behalf of his client. If the instructions are capable of more than one meaning, the accountant will not be liable as an accountant for choosing incorrectly provided his interpretation was reasonable.[34]

Where an accountant is paid, he has a duty to carry out the instructions of his client with reasonable care and skill. An accountant will be judged against the standard of care and skill that might reasonably be expected from a member of his profession[35]. Where an accountant is unpaid, he has a duty to carry out the instructions of his client with the care and skill that reasonably might be expected in all the circumstances.[36]

Whilst this heading groups the duties of obedience and care and skill together, they are distinct and potentially may conflict.

Thus an accountant, when faced with instructions from a client to undertake which he considers disastrous for his client, protects himself by warning his client that he would advise against the course his client wishes to embark upon (and ideally drawing his client's attention to the nature of the risk) but, if the client persists in those instructions, obey them even though he reasonably believes that in departing from them he would be acting in the interests of his client.[37]

3.2.3.3 An accountant owes his client a duty not to allow his interest and that of his client to conflict

An accountant owes a fiduciary duty to his client not to put himself in a position where his interests and that of his client do or may conflict.[38] Thus an accountant acting as his client's accountant would be liable to account to his client for benefits he made where his and his client's interests conflicted. The conduct would only be permissible and any benefits may only be retained by the accountant if he has fully disclosed the conflict to his client and the client consents.[39]

---

[33] *ABTA v. British Airways plc* [2000] 1 Lloyd's Rep 169.
[34] *Ireland v. Livingston* (1872) LR 5 HL 395.
[35] *Simmons v. Pennington & Son* [1955] 1 WLR 183.
[36] *Chaudhry v. Prabhakar* [1989] 1 WLR 29.
[37] *The Hermione* [1922] P 162.
[38] *Phipps v. Boardman* [1967] AC 46.
[39] *Cavendish Bentick v. Fenn* (1887) 2 App Cas 652.

3.2.3.4 An accountant owes his client a duty not to make secret profits

An accountant breaches his fiduciary duty to his client if he uses his relationship with his client to make secret profits. Dishonesty is not required.

Accordingly an accountant acting as his client's accountant would be liable to account to his client for any undisclosed bribe, profit, fee or commission that he made out of his position as accountant[40] or using his client's property or any confidential information disclosed to him in his capacity as accountant by his client.[41] The secret profit may only be retained by the accountant if he has fully disclosed it and the client consents.[42]

Thus an employed accountant who obtains office of liquidator and receiver whilst in employment and because of that employment is liable to account to his employers for all sums (including fees) received in that capacity, even after he has left their employ, would be subject to an allowance for works carried out for them.[43]

3.2.3.5 An accountant owes a duty to his client to keep his property separate from that of his client

An accountant owes a fiduciary duty to his client to keep his property separate from that of his client.[44] Thus an accountant will need to pay any monies he receives from a client into a client account which is separate from his usual practice account.

3.2.3.6 An Accountant owes a duty to his client to account for his dealings with the client's property.

An accountant owes a fiduciary duty to his client to maintain and always be ready with correct accounts of his dealings with his client's property in the course of his agency.[45]

Moreover the accountant has a duty to make available to the client the accounts and books of account which set out his dealings with the client's property. Thus an accountant was liable to deliver up to his client correspondence with the then Inland Revenue as it related to the client's tax affairs and was thus prepared as its accountant.[46]

---

[40] *Attorney General for Hong Kong v. Reid* [1994] 1 AC 324.
[41] *Regal Hastings v. Gulliver* [1942] 1 All ER 378.
[42] *Re Haslam* [1902] 1 Ch 765.
[43] *Casson Beckman & Partners v. Papi* (1990) *Financial Times*, 3 August.
[44] *Gray v. Haig* (1855) 20 Beav 219.
[45] *Gray v. Haig* (1855) 20 Beav 219.
[46] *Chantrey Martin v. Martin* [1953] 2 QB 286.

3.2.3.7 An accountant must not disclose the confidence of his client

An accountant breaches his fiduciary duty to his client if he improperly discloses or misuses confidential information belonging to or relating to his client which has come to his attention out of his professional relationship with his client. The accountant will be liable in damages for any breach of his duty of confidentiality to his client.[47] The duty of confidentiality on an accountant was not greater than that on a solicitor and may well be less.[48]

It was conceded before the House of Lords in *HRH Prince Jefri Bolkiah v. KPMG* that an accountant who provides litigation support services must be treated in the same way as a solicitor. The duty on the accountant was to keep information confidential not merely to take reasonable steps to do so. A former client was entitled to prevent an accountant from exposing him to an avoidable risk of using confidential information to his prejudice - such as by accepting instructions to act for a client to which the confidential information might be relevant. Once the client had satisfied the court that there was a real and not merely fanciful or theoretical (but not necessarily substantial) risk of disclosure or misuse of confidential information, the court would restrain the accountant from acting for the second client unless the accountant could satisfy the court with clear and convincing evidence that effective measures had been taken to ensure no disclosure would occur.[49] The court would presume that unless special measures were taken, information would move within a firm and Chinese walls needed to be an established part of the organisation structure and not created *ad hoc* to be effective.[50]

He, however, will not have *locus standi* in his own right to sue to recover clients' papers which have fallen into a third party's hands.[51]

This fiduciary duty must be read subject to the statutory obligations placed on an accountant, for example, those imposed by the Financial Services and Markets Act 2000 (Communications by Auditors) Regulations 2001, Proceeds of Crime Act 2002, Financial Services and Markets Act 2000 (Miscellaneous Provisions) Order 2001, the Accountants (Banking Act 1987) Regulations 1994 and the Building Societies (Auditors) Order 1994, the Financial Institutions (Prudential Supervision) Regulations 1996. It is clearly

---

[47] *Fogg v. Gaulter* (1960) 110 LJ 718.
[48] *HRH Prince Jeffri Bolkiah v. KPMG* [1999] 1 All ER 517.
[49] *HRH Prince Jeffri Bolkiah v. KPMG* [1999] 1 All ER 517.
[50] *HRH Prince Jeffri Bolkiah v. KPMG* [1999] 1 All ER 517.
[51] By analogy, *Nationwide Building Society v. Various Solicitors* (1998) *The Times*, 1 May.

a defence to an action for breach of confidence that disclosure was made in compliance with an order of the court.[52]

3.2.3.8 Fiduciary Duties and the Fraud Act 2006

The Fraud Act 2006 provides for a general offence of fraud with three ways of committing it, which are

- by false representation,
- by failing to disclose information and
- by abuse of position.

The first of these offences is made out by making a false representation dishonestly with the intention of making a gain or causing loss or risk of loss to another.[53] The gain or loss does not actually have to take place. A representation is defined as false if it is untrue or misleading and the person making it knows that it is, or might be, untrue or misleading. The representation can be as to fact or law or even as to a person's state of mind. It may be express or implied. It can be stated in words or expressed by the way in which someone conducts themselves.

The criminal test for dishonesty[54] for these purposes is:

- Whether a defendant's behaviour would be regarded as dishonest by the ordinary standards of reasonable and honest people?
- Whether the defendant was aware that his conduct was dishonest and would be regarded as dishonest by reasonable and honest people?

The second and third of these offences have particular resonance for those, like accountants, who owe fiduciary duties towards their clients.

To commit the second of these fraud offences,[55] a person must dishonestly fail to disclose information to another person with the intention of making a gain or causing loss or risk of loss to another. To be caught by the offence you have to be under a legal duty to disclose the information. A legal duty to disclose information includes both duties under a contract but also arising out of fiduciary relationship, such as the duty owed by an accountant towards his client.

---

[52] *Barclays Bank v. Taylor* [1989] 3 All ER 563.
[53] Section 2 Fraud Act 2006.
[54] As set out in *R v. Ghosh* [1982] QB 1053.
[55] Section 3, Fraud Act 2006.

The third of these fraud offences[56] affects people who are in a position where they are expected to safeguard or not act against another's financial interests, such as accountants towards their clients. It makes it a fraud if the person then goes on to dishonestly abuse his position with the intention of making a gain or causing loss or risk of loss to another.

3.3 THE ACCOUNTANT AS HIS CLIENT'S AGENT

3.3.1 The appointment of an accountant as his client's agent

An accountant may be appointed as his client's agent[57] (a) by his client's express or implied consent (although a formal contract is not needed) or (b) retrospectively, through his client's ratification of his actions or (c) through the client being estopped from denying that the accountant is his agent.[58]

The consent can be implied if they have agreed to what in law amounts to a relationship of agency, even though neither client nor accountant recognises themselves as principal and agent and even if they disclaim it.[59] Both must consent either by words or conduct.[60]

Ratification will be inferred from an action by the client on whose behalf it was purportedly made which demonstrates an intention by the client to adopt his agent's actions. If a contract is partially adopted by the client, the client will be deemed to adopt all of it.[61]

The third category of agency through estoppel, known as the doctrine of apparent authority, can be explained thus: Where a person by words or conduct represents to a third party that another has authority to act on his behalf, he may be bound by the acts of that person whether or not he has in fact authorised them.[62] To engage this, one needs some statement or conduct by the client which makes the agent's representation of authority, such that

---

[56] Section 4 Fraud Act 2006.
[57] Although in this chapter, references to principal and agent are to the client and his accountant, it should not be forgotten that an accountant may be a person's agent without any professional or contractual relationship subsisting between them.
[58] Article 3, *Bowstead & Reynolds on Agency*.
[59] *Garnac Grain v. HMF Faure & Fairclough Ltd* [1968] AC 1130 at 1137B-C.
[60] *Garnac Grain v. HMF Faure & Fairclough Ltd* [1968] AC 1130 at 1137C-D. Lord Pearson then describes how one should approach the evidence to determine whether the relationship existed.
[61] *Bank Melli Iran v. Barclays Bank* [1951] TLR 1057. See *Bowstead & Reynolds on Agency* for further discussion on this issue.
[62] *United Bank of Kuwait v. Hammoud* [1989] 1 WLR 1051.

one might reasonably rely upon it,[63] and to show the third party's subsequent reliance on this representation.[64]

Once established, agency is not negated by the fact the agent was acting in the furtherance of his own interests so long as he was acting within the scope of his actual or apparent authority.[65]

Whilst this work does not contain a detailed examination of the law of agency, two areas of the law of agency have particular applicability to the work of an accountant. These are (a) when an accountant is asked to inspect books and records on his client's behalf and (b) when an accountant prepares tax trading accounts and tax returns on his client's behalf.

3.3.2 The accountant acting as his client's agent when inspecting books and records

Books and records may be inspected by an accountant as his client's agent. So where, for example, the rules of a trade union provide that its books are open to inspection by its members, a member may inspect the books by means of an accountant.[66] The onus would rest in such a case on the trade union to show that the member was not acting *bona fide* when requesting the inspection.[67] The company would be entitled however to require the accountant making the inspection to undertake to use the information discovered only for the purposes of the member[68] as his entitlement to access to the records is limited to those enjoyed by his client, the member.

Similarly "a person interested" under the then s. 247(4), Public Health Act 1875 was entitled to inspect the books and accounts of a local authority using an accountant[69] as his agent.

Historically this common law right derives from case law on the ability of a partner to exercise his right under s. 24(9) Partnership Act 1890 to inspect partnership accounts by means of a skilled agent.[70]

---

[63] *United Bank of Kuwait v. Hammoud* [1988] 1 WLR 1015.
[64] *Nationwide Building Society v. Lewis* [1998] Ch 482.
[65] *Credit_Lyonnais Bank Nederland NV v. Export Credit Guarantee Department* [1999] 2 WLR 540, House of Lords.
[66] *Dodd v. Amalgamated Marine Workers Union* [1925] 1 Ch 116; *Norey v. Keep* [1909] 1 Ch 561.
[67] *Dodd v. Amalgamated Marine Workers Union* [1925] 1 Ch 116.
[68] *Norey v. Keep* [1909] 1 Ch 561.
[69] *R v. Bedwelty UDC ex parte* Price [1934] 1 KB 333.
[70] *Bevan v. Webb* [1901] 2 Ch 59.

The position will, of course, be different however if personal inspection only is permitted under the empowering statute[71] or provision.

Trustees are entitled not more than once in every three years to pay accountants to conduct an examination or audit of their accounts, the cost of which is paid from the trust property.[72] It is probably also reasonable for the trustees to employ accountants, as their agents, to keep the accounting record in the meantime. The rationale for this is that a prudent man of business, particularly with the increasing complexity of the tax regime, would be justified in using an accountant in managing his own affairs.[73]

3.3.3 The accountant acting as his client's tax accountant

It is trite law that the relationship between a client and his accountant when preparing the client's tax returns is one of principal and agent.[74]

Thus the Court of Appeal held that working papers, draft and final accounts, notes and calculations and draft tax computations brought into being by chartered accountants in the course of preparing a company's accounts were the property of the accountants; however correspondence between the accountants and the Inland Revenue relating to the company's tax liability was conducted by the accountants as the company's agent so that the original and copy letters comprising such correspondence belonged to the company.[75]

There are other important consequences flowing from the fact that an accountant exercises his duties as a client's tax accountant as agent of his client and not as a principal.

This can be most graphically illustrated where a tax return contains an error or a mis-declaration. In such a case it is the client who is responsible for the mis-declaration as the accountant's acts are deemed to have been performed at the direction of his client as his principal. The accountant may be separately answerable to the client for any loss in negligence or breach of contract.

---

[71] *Dodd v. Amalgamated Marine Workers Union* [1925] 1 Ch 116; *Norey v. Keep* [1909] 1 Ch 561.
[72] Section 22, Trustee Act 1925.
[73] *Re Vickery* [1931] 1 Ch 572, 581.
[74] *Chantrey Martin v. Martin* [1953] 2 QB 286.
[75] *Chantrey Martin v. Martin* [1953] 2 QB 286.

3.3.4 An accountant acting as an auditor is not his client's agent

An auditor does not perform his statutory duties as the agent of the client company.[76] Thus any knowledge that the auditor acquires when auditing the company cannot be attributed to the members of the company, such as information over a director's unauthorised acts.[77]

3.3.5 Rights and duties of the accountant as agent

The creation of a relationship of agency at law carries with it legal consequences which necessarily also apply to accountants when they act as agent for their client.

The rights of an agent include being paid any agreed remuneration[78] and to be indemnified for any costs or liability he incurs in the execution of his agency.[79]

The duties of an agent include (a) obedience to his principal (b) perform his instructions with reasonable care and skill (c) not to permits his interests and that of his principal to conflict (d) not making secret profits (e) to keep his property separate from that of his principal (f) to keep ready and make available to the principal accounts of his dealings with the principal's property.

3.3.5.1 Obedience

An agent has a duty to carry out the instructions of his principal. The accountant needs to obey those instructions even if he reasonably believes that in departing from them he would be acting in the interests of his client.[80] An agent however has no duty to carry out instructions which are unlawful[81] and thus the agency relationship gives no justification to an accountant for preparing false tax accounts or returns on behalf of his client. If the instructions are capable of more than one meaning, the accountant will not be liable as an agent for choosing incorrectly provided his interpretation was reasonable.[82]

---

[76] *Re Transplanters (Holding Co) Ltd* [1958] 1 WLR 822.
[77] *Leeds Estate Building Investment Co v. Shepherd* (1887) 36 Ch D 787.
[78] *Way v. Latilla* [1937] 3 All ER 759.
[79] *The Tzelpi* [1991] 2 Lloyd's Rep 265.
[80] *The Hermione* [1922] P 162.
[81] *ABTA v. British Airways plc* [2000] 1 Lloyd's Rep 169.
[82] *Ireland v. Livingston* (1872) LR 5 HL 395.

3.3.5.2 Reasonable care and skill
Where an agent is paid, he has a duty to carry out the instructions of his principal with reasonable care and skill. An accountant will be judged against the standard of care and skill that might reasonably be expected from a member of his profession.[83] Where an agent is unpaid, he has a duty to carry out the instructions of his principal with the care and skill that reasonably might be expected in all the circumstances.[84]

3.3.5.3 Not to allow a conflict of interest.
An agent owes a fiduciary duty to his principal not to put himself in a position where his interests and that of his principal do or may conflict.[85] Thus an accountant acting as his client's agent would be liable to account to his client for benefits he made where his and his client's interests conflicted. The conduct would only be permissible and any benefits may only be retained by the accountant if he has fully disclosed the conflict to his client and the client consents.[86]

3.3.5.4 Not to make Secret Profits
An agent owes a fiduciary duty to his principal not to make secret profits. Thus an accountant acting as his client's agent would be liable to account to his client for any undisclosed bribe, profit, fee or commission that he made out of his position as agent[87] or using his client's property or any confidential information disclosed to him in his capacity as agent by his client.[88] The secret profit may only be retained by the accountant if he has fully disclosed it and the client consents.[89]

3.3.5.5 Keep his property separate from that of his principal
An agent owes a fiduciary duty to his principal to keep his property separate from that of his principal.[90] Thus an accountant will need to pay any monies he receives from a client into a client account which is separate from his usual practice account.

---

[83] *Simmons v. Pennington & Son* [1955] 1 WLR 183.
[84] *Chaudhry v. Prabhakar* [1989] 1 WLR 29.
[85] *Phipps v. Boardman* [1967] AC 46.
[86] *Cavendish Bentick v. Fenn* (1887) 2 App Cas 652.
[87] *Attorney General for Hong Kong v. Reid* [1994] 1 AC 324.
[88] *Regal Hastings v. Gulliver* [1942] 1 All ER 378.
[89] *Re Haslam* [1902] 1 Ch 765.
[90] *Gray v. Haig* (1855) 20 Beav 219.

3.3.5.6 Account for his dealings with the principal's property

An agent owes a fiduciary duty to his principal to maintain and always be ready with correct accounts of his dealings with his principal's property in the course of his agency.[91]

Moreover the agent has a duty to make available to the principal the accounts and books of account which set out his dealings with the principal's property. Thus an accountant was liable to deliver up to his client correspondence with the then Inland Revenue as it related to the client's tax affairs and was thus prepared as its agent.[92]

3.4 CLIENT PAPERS

3.4.1 The ownership of papers prepared by the accountant

As to the ownership of papers prepared by the accountant, much depends on whether or not the accountant prepared those papers as his client's agent.

3.4.2 Papers prepared by the accountant as his client's agent

In so far that an accountant acts as his client's agent, the papers of the accountant are the property of his principal

Correspondence with the Inland Revenue written in respect of a client's tax affairs are thus the property of the client for whom it is written.[93] This is because the accountant acts as the agent of the client when he deals with the client's tax affairs.[94]

3.4.3 Papers prepared by the accountant as his client's agent

Where an accountant is not acting as his client's agent, the papers of the accountant are the property of his accountant as papers of a professional man.

Thus the working papers and computations, the draft accounts, the draft tax computations, the final accounts brought into existence by an accountant for his clients are prepared as documents of a professional man (and do not arise out of a relationship of principal and agent) and therefore are the property of the accountant and not his client.[95]

---

[91] *Gray v. Haig* (1855) 20 Beav 219.
[92] *Chantrey Martin v. Martin* [1953] 2 QB 286.
[93] *Chantrey Martin v. Martin* [1953] 2 QB 286.
[94] *Chantrey Martin v. Martin* [1953] 2 QB 286, 294; *Leicestershire County Council v. Michael Faraday & Partners Ltd* [1941] 2 KB 205 216.
[95] *Chantrey Martin v. Martin* [1953] 2 QB 286.

This should be contrasted with the position of a solicitor, who has no title over, say, a copy of a deed for a client.[96]

Papers are relating to a client are likely to be confidential to that client and an accountant would breaches his fiduciary duty to his client if he improperly discloses or misuses confidential information belonging to or relating to his client which has come to his attention out of his professional relationship with his client. The accountant will be liable in damages for any breach of his duty of confidentiality to his client.[97] The duty of confidentiality on an accountant was not greater than that on a solicitor and may well be less.[98] The duty of confidentiality and its limits are discussed in greater detail elsewhere in this work.

3.4.4 The accountant's lien

An accountant may exercise a right to a particular lien for unpaid fees over a client's papers that come into his possession in the course of their ordinary professional work.[99]

For the lien to arise, the work must be done lawfully and with the owner's authority.[100] The work must be completed[101] unless completion is prevented by the owner when the lien arises for the work actually done.[102] No lien pending payment can arise if there was no invoice delivered or no particulars available which would enable calculation of the sum due.[103]

That right will not be exercisable when a client company is in administrative receivership or in liquidation or where a provisional liquidator has been appointed to the extent that its enforcement would deny possession of any books.[104]

Nor will this serve as a defence to an order for inspection of documents in court proceedings where the documents' production is necessary for fairly disposing the case.[105]

---

[96] *Ex parte Horsfall* 7 B & C 582 (distinguished in *Chantrey Martin v. Martin* [1953] 2 QB 286 at 293 "as turning on the nature of the services rendered by an attorney or solicitor and the system upon which he is remunerated for those services").
[97] *Fogg v. Gaulter* (1960) 110 LJ 718.
[98] *HRH Prince Jeffri Bolkiah v. KPMG* [1999] 1 All ER 517.
[99] *Woodworth v. Conroy* [1976] QB 884.
[100] *Hiscox v. Greenwood* (1802) 4 Esp 174.
[101] *Pinnock v. Harrison* (1838) 3 M & W 532 at 535, per Parke B.
[102] *Lilley v. Barnsley* (1844) 1 Car & Kir 344.
[103] *Thaper v. Singh* [1987] FLR 369.
[104] Section 246(2) Insolvency Act 1986.
[105] *Woodworth v. Conroy* [1976] QB 884.

An accountant cannot exercise a lien over accounting records of a client which are required by statute to be kept in specific places for certain periods available for inspection.[106] An example of such a statutory requirement was the duty on a company to keep accounting records under Sections 221[107] and 222[108] of the Companies Act 1985, as amended by Section 2 of the Companies Act 1989.[109] It is likely that VAT records will fall within the definition of statutory records.[110]

An accountant's lien is unenforceable so far as it would deny possession of the books, papers and records to a company's liquidator, provisional liquidator or administrator.[111] Liens affected will remain valid but will simply be unenforceable without leave of the court as against the office holder.[112] There is no equivalent statutory immunity to liens for administrative receivers or for supervisors of voluntary arrangements.

A disorganised collection of vouchers is not enough to demonstrate that a company has kept adequate accounting records for the purposes of complying with section 221 Companies Act 1985. Accounting records for these purposes need to be records which are organised enough to enable a trial balance to be constructed but it need not show the "true and fair" position.[113] It would, for example, appropriate to adduce expert accounting evidence as to whether the records show the financial position reasonably accurately and whether the records were such as would normally be kept by a company in such circumstances.[114]

3.4.5 The Court's powers to overreach an accountant's lien

The court retains a discretionary power to order the delivery up of papers subject to a lien but this will not normally be exercised if it will reduce the

---

[106] Michael Crystal QC, sitting as a Deputy High Court Judge in *DTC (CNC) Ltd v. Gary Sargent & Co* (1996) *The Times*, 25 January, rules that the principle in *In Re Capital Fire Assurance* (1883) 24 Ch D. 408 applied to accountants and solicitors equally.
[107] Section 386, 387 Companies Act 2006.
[108] Section 388, 389 Companies Act 2006.
[109] *DTC (CNC) Ltd v. Gary Sargent & Co* (1996) *The Times*, 25 January: the accounting records which the accountants were held to be unable to retain a lien over were sales invoices, purchase invoices, cheque books, paying in books and bank statements.
[110] Butterfield J. hearing argument on this point in *Harrison v. Festus* [1998] 2 CL 1 doubted, *obiter*, that an accountant's lien could arise over such records.
[111] Section 246 Insolvency Act 1986.
[112] Section 11(3) Insolvency Act 1986, *Bristol Airport v Powdrill* [1990] Ch 744 at 762.
[113] Paragraph 4, *Statement March 1992, ICAEW* approved by the Court of Appeal in *R v Garvey* [2001] EWCA Crim 1365.
[114] Paragraph 221.8 *Buckley on the Companies Acts*.

value of the lien.[115] The discretion will, however, be exercised against the accountant if he fails to prove the work which he claims the lien under was done.[116]

Where a firm of accountants had been dissolved and one partner set up a new firm, his former fellow partners could apply for an interim order for the delivery up of the files of any clients who had not signed letters of authority permitting their files to be transferred to the new practice.[117]

3.4.6 Copyright in an accountant's work?

The author submits that an accountant may be able to enforce copyright in accounts or records he compiles as long as they are substantially his own original work; these would be afforded protection as a "literary work".[118] It is already trite law that counsel has copyright in his written opinion. One possible and as yet untested route for enforcement over client papers may be the argument that the accountant withholds his licence to *use* the accounts. This is an increasingly popular debt collection tool for media companies. To argue this, the accountant would probably need to rebut any implied licence to permit the client's use by reference to terms in his letter of engagement.

3.4.7 Court's powers to order delivery of an accountant's papers

The court has a discretionary power to make an order for production for inspection of any documents if it is of the opinion that they are necessary for fairly disposing of the cause or for saving costs.[119] Inspection by a party, solicitor or agent does not, for these purposes, include an accountant[120] but it seems clear that the court does have power to permit this and will do so in a proper case.[121]

3.4.8 The accountant as data user

If a person

- collects information from clients
- where the clients do not know what information he records and
- the clients do not know what use he would make of it

---

[115] Section 4 Torts (Interference with Goods) Act 1977, RSC Order 29 r. 2A and r. 6, now Civil Procedure Rules Part 25.1(1) (e) *Thaper v. Singh* [1987] FLR 369.
[116] *Thaper v. Singh* [1987] FLR 369.
[117] *Ingram v. Keeling* (2006) Lawtel 14th November.
[118] Section 3(1) (a) Copyright, Designs & Patents Act 1988.
[119] Rules of the Supreme Court, Order 24 and, now, Civil Procedure Rules Part 31.
[120] *Bonnardet v. Taylor* (1861) 1 John & H 383.
[121] *Lindsay v. Gladstone* (1869) LR 9 Eq 132.

that person controls the contents of data within the meaning of Section 1(5)(b) Data Protection Act 1984.[122]

Accordingly an accountant who puts information onto his computer for the purpose of producing accounts for presentation to the Inland Revenue and other bodies is a data user and should be registered as such.[123]

3.5 CLIENT ACCOUNTS

3.5.1 An accountant holds client monies on trust for the client

Legally an accountant is bare trustee of any "client money" he holds. As bare trustee of the client money, the accountant has no claim to the money beyond mere legal possession[124] and can have no beneficial interest in the money held by him until he has delivered a bill.[125] Unused money must be returned to the original transferor.[126]

Interest earned on client accounts should be accounted for and apportioned between the relevant clients irrespective of the sum involved.[127]

An accountant gains no title to the money merely by reason of the trust or client money being forgotten in his client account. Section 21 Limitation Act 1980 provides that no limitation shall apply to an action by a beneficiary under a trust to recover from the trustee trust property or the proceeds of trust property in the possession of the trustee or previously received by the trustee and converted to his own use.

Where the beneficiary refuses the return of client money, the accountant as trustee should pay the money into court.[128] If ultimately, there is no beneficiary to whom the money can result, the client money will be held on trust for the Crown.[129]

The court has the power to relieve the accountant as trustee of his liability for any breach of trust, in whole or part, on the basis that he acted honestly

---

[122] *Data Protection Registrar v. Griffin*, (1993) *The Times*, 5 March, Divisional Court.
[123] *Data Protection Registrar v. Griffin*, (1993) *The Times*, 5 March, Divisional Court.
[124] *Smith v. Wheeler* (1669) 1 Mod Rep 16.
[125] *Continental Illinois National Bank & Trust Co. of Chicago v. Daniel Davies & Co* [1987] CLY 3545.
[126] *Re Vandervell's Trusts (No. 2)* [1974] Ch 269.
[127] *Brown v. IRC* [1965] AC 244, *Aplin v. White* [1973] 1 WLR 1311.
[128] *IRC V. Hamilton-Russell Executors* [1943] 1 All ER 474, 476, Court of Appeal.
[129] *Re West Sussex Widows and Children Benevolent Fund Trust* [1971] Ch 1.

and reasonably and ought fairly to be excused for the breach in the manner in which he committed that breach.[130]

The matters set out below refer to client monies which are not held as investment business money. Firms in the United Kingdom which carry on exempt regulated activities and are not authorised by Financial Services Authority to carry on regulated activities, are prohibited the holding of investment business client money.[131]

3.5.2 Client money: chartered accountants

If a chartered accountant is to hold client money he must open a separate client account giving written notice to the bank and requiring written acknowledgment from the bank that the account is designated as a client account and that the money and interest in that account belong to his clients.[132] Client money must be paid forthwith into the client account or as the client directs.[133] A client account in the client's own name must be opened where the chartered accountant holds more than £10,000 of that client's money.[134] He must maintain records for at least 6 years from the date the records were made to show the money received, how it has been dealt with and distinguishing it from his own and other clients' monies.[135] Every Principal is responsible for any breach by his firm of the Client's Money Regulations unless he is able to prove that the breach was the responsibility of some other Principal.[136]

Where the money held is investment the money is held subject in accordance with the rules set out in the Financial Services Authority Handbook[137] rather than Client Money Regulations.

3.5.3 Client money: chartered certified accountants

If a chartered certified accountant is to hold client money he must open a separate account[138] with "client" in the account title.[139] Where it is anticipated that the amount to be held by the firm exceeds £10,000 for more

---

[130] Section 61, Trustee Act 1925. This does not excuse a contractual liability however: *Segbedzi v Segbedzi* LTL 28/5/99, CA.
[131] Regulation 4(2), Designated Professional Body Regulations 2001.
[132] Regulation 9, ICAEW Client's Money Regulations of 1st January 2004.
[133] Regulation 10, ICAEW Client's Money Regulations of 1st January 2004.
[134] Regulation 13, ICAEW Client's Money Regulations of 1st January 2004. The account may also be identified by a designated numbers or letters.
[135] Regulation 24, ICAEW Client's Money Regulations of 1st January 2004.
[136] Regulation 29, ICAEW Client's Money Regulations of 1st January 2004.
[137] Regulation 2, Client Money Regulations, FSA Handbook.
[138] Paragraph 8, Section 3.10, ACCA Code of Ethics and Conduct.
[139] Paragraph 9, Section 3.10, ACCA Code of Ethics and Conduct.

than 30 days, the money should be paid into a separate bank account designated by the name of the client or number allocated to the client account[140]. Interest must be paid to client unless the sum is under £10 and the client agrees to forgo this.[141] Firms should at all times maintain accurate records and controls so as to show clearly the monies they have received, held, or paid on account of their clients, and the details of any other monies dealt with by them through a client account, clearly distinguishing the monies of each client from the monies of other clients and from the firm's monies.[142] Members should maintain such records for a period of not less than six years from the date of the last transaction recorded.[143] Fees paid in advance of professional work are not treated as client monies for these purposes but members are obliged to ensure they have sufficient liquidity to repay this money if the work is not completed.[144]

3.5.4 Chartered public finance accountant

Client accounts must be kept in credit at all times.[145] The chartered public finance accountant must at all times be ready to account for the sums held by him.[146] He must maintain records to identify each client's money and any dealings with it and provide clients with a statement at least annually.[147] Withdrawals of client funds may only be made with the client's consent.[148] Fees may not be drawn down from client funds without the client's prior consent.[149] Client money should only be placed in an interest bearing account if it is to be held for a long time and then only with the client's consent.[150] All interest must be paid to the client.[151]

---

[140] Paragraph 10, Section 3.10 ACCA Code of Ethics and Conduct.
[141] Paragraph 23-24, Section 3.10, ACCA Code of Ethics and Conduct.
[142] Paragraph 27, Section 3.10 ACCA Code of Ethics and Conduct.
[143] Paragraph 28, Section 3.10 ACCA Code of Ethics and Conduct.
[144] Paragraph 21-22, Section 3.10 ACCA Code of Ethics and Conduct.
[145] A10.1 Standards of Professional Practice on Ethics of December 2000 and Section 12.7, Part B, IFAC Code of Ethics for Professional Accountants. At least drawings should not exceed current balance.
[146] A10.1 Standards of Professional Practice on Ethics of December 2000 and Section 12.2(c), Part B, IFAC Code of Ethics for Professional Accountants.
[147] A10.1 Standards of Professional Practice on Ethics of December 2000 and Section 12.10, Part B, IFAC Code of Ethics for Professional Accountants.
[148] A10.1 Standards of Professional Practice on Ethics of December 2000 and Section 12.10, Part B, IFAC Code of Ethics for Professional Accountants.
[149] A10.1 Standards of Professional Practice on Ethics of December 2000 and Section 12.6, Part B, IFAC Code of Ethics for Professional Accountants. The client must be notified of the level of fees before the withdrawal is made.
[150] A10.1 Standards of Professional Practice on Ethics of December 2000 and Section 12.8, Part B, IFAC Code of Ethics for Professional Accountants.
[151] A10.1 Standards of Professional Practice on Ethics of December 2000 and Section 12.8, Part B, IFAC Code of Ethics for Professional Accountants.

3.5.5 Incorporated executive accountant

An incorporated executive accountant must deposit all money held for a client into a separate designated and identifiable client account and maintain reconciled accounts of the sums held and any transactions with them.[152]

3.6. MONEY LAUNDERING

3.6.1 An accountant must ensure that monies held are not the proceeds of crime

The present money laundering legislation is now enacted under the Proceeds of Crime Act 2002 and the Terrorism Act 2000.

Sections 327 to 329 of the Proceeds of Crime Act 2002 make it an offence to conceal, disguise, convert, transfer, remove, acquire, use, or possess criminal property or to help anyone else to do so if one knows or suspects that it is criminal property. This carries on conviction in the Crown Court a sentence of up to 14 years imprisonment and / or an unlimited fine. Criminal property is defined as property which is the benefit of any crime, in whole or any part, whether direct or indirect; it does not matter, for these purposes, who committed the crime or who benefited or when the crime took place. The Crown is not required to identify what crime was committed to establish the offence.[153]

Defences include "authorised disclosure" – that is to say the offender disclosed to a nominated officer (who passes it on to the Serious Organised Crime Agency - SOCA), an officer of SOCA, a customs officer or constable in the form required and either did so before he committed the offence, or, if he did so during the commission of his own initiative and as soon as practicable after he first knew or suspected that he was committing an offence or, if afterwards, he did so of his own initiative and there is good reason for failing to disclose beforehand.

If one needs to deal with the property one should ask for prior consent to do so from the person one made disclosure to. A key element of consent is the specification of time limits within which the authorities must respond to an authorised disclosure in circumstances where a consent decision is required. The law specifies that consent decisions must be made within 7 working

---

[152] Section G(2)(g) ICEA Professional and Ethical Guide for Members.
[153] *R v Gulbir Singh* (2003) CA.

days.[154] If nothing is heard within that time, then the accountant can go ahead with an otherwise prohibited act without an offence being committed. If consent is withheld within the 7 working days, then SOCA has a further 31 calendar days[155] in which to take further action such as seeking a court order to restrain the assets in question. If nothing is heard after the end of the 31 day period, then one can proceed with the transaction without committing an offence.

There are mirror offences under the Terrorism Act 2000. It is an offence to fund-raise for terrorist activity, receive property intended for terrorism and to finance terrorism.[156] It is also an offence to use money or property for terrorism or to possess money or property with the intention of using it for terrorism.[157] Similarly it is an offence to be involved in arrangements for the transfer of money or property for possible terrorist purposes.[158] Further the money laundering of terrorist property is an offence.[159] The offences also apply to persons who have either actual knowledge of the intention to apply funds for terrorist purposes or where that person had reasonable cause to suspect that the property would be used for the purposes of terrorism.

"Terrorist property" covers money and every other kind of property or possession[160] which is likely to be used for the purposes of terrorism (including any resources of a proscribed organisation) or is the proceeds of the commission of acts of terrorism or the proceeds of acts carried out for the purposes of terrorism.[161] The definition is extremely widely drawn. Thus the proceeds of an act includes any property which wholly or partly, and directly or indirectly, represents the proceeds of the act (including payments or other rewards in connection with its commission). The reference to an organisation's resources includes a reference to any money or other property which is applied or made available, or is to be applied or made available, for use by the organisation.

3.6.2 Further requirements under the Proceeds of Crime Act for members of a Regulated Profession

Members of the regulated profession commit a criminal offence under section 330 Proceeds of Crime Act 2002 if they knew or suspected or had reasonable

---

[154] This period starts the day after disclosure was made and does not count bank holidays and weekends.
[155] This period starts on the day the notice is given and includes weekends and public holidays.
[156] Section 15, Terrorism Act 2000.
[157] Section 16, Terrorism Act 2000.
[158] Section 17, Terrorism Act 2000.
[159] Section 18, Terrorism Act 2000.
[160] Section 121, Terrorism Act 2000.
[161] Section 14, Terrorism Act 2000.

grounds for suspecting that another person is committing money laundering and they discovered this from information they got from working in the regulated sector and they failed to disclose that to SOCA or their nominated money laundering officer.[162] This carries on conviction in the Crown Court a sentence of up to 5 years imprisonment and / or an unlimited fine.

The regulated sector includes insolvency practitioners, tax advisors and those providing accountancy or tax services.

The risk of imprisonment is a real one as is indicated by the sentencing of a Chester solicitor, Jonathan Duff, to 6 months imprisonment for failing to disclose knowledge or suspicions of money laundering in relation to a client.[163]

Importantly there is no *de minimis* rule for offences. This raises a difficult question for accountants in respect of whether suspicion of the offence of cheating the Revenue has arisen. Accountants often face incomplete and inaccurate records and are often relied on by their clients to spot and correct any deficiencies in the bookkeeping. Paragraph 4.7 of the CCAB Interim Guidance is that where the monetary proceeds of suspected tax fraud is small this may be explained by client error or the mistaken belief by the client that they had permission to act as they did.[164] An accountant would have reasonable grounds for suspicion where there was a pattern of behaviour or the proceeds were criminal in origin.

3.6.3 Exemption for Legal Professional Privilege

The prohibition against being "concerned in an arrangement which facilitates the acquisition, retention, use or control of criminal property" under section 328 Proceeds of Crime Act does not apply to professionals in the ordinary conduct of litigation – even where the litigation is a freezing order.[165] This principle will also apply where the case is resolved by consent.[166] The Proceeds of Crime Act requirement will not encroach a client's legal professional privilege and non disclosure will in such circumstances amount to a defence for a legal adviser provided the privilege is not relied upon with the intention of furthering some criminal purpose.[167]

---

[162] Equivalent provisions are found at section 21A, Terrorism Act 2000.
[163] "Get it wrong. Go to jail" (2004) *Accountancy* January page 46.
[164] *CCAB Interim Guidance on Money Laundering* (2004) Accountancy April page 112.
[165] *Bowman v Fels* [2005] EWCA Civ 226, paragraph 83.
[166] *Bowman v Fels* [2005] EWCA Civ 226, paragraph 101-102.
[167] Section 330(10) Proceeds of Crime Act 2002, *Bowman v Fels* [2005] EWCA Civ 226, paragraph 87.

The exemption does not apply where the services will be used in the furtherance of some criminal purpose.

This exemption from reporting knowledge and suspicions of money laundering has been extended to relevant professional advisers where the suspicion is formed in privileged circumstances.[168]

To qualify for the exemption the relevant professional adviser must be an accountant, auditor or tax adviser and be a member of a professional body which is established for accountants, auditors or tax advisers (as the case may be) and which makes provision for (a) testing the competence of those seeking admission to membership of such a body as a condition for such admission; and (b) imposing and maintaining professional and ethical standards for its members, as well as imposing sanctions for non-compliance with those standards.

Professional bodies whose membership would qualify for these purposes include:

- Institute of Chartered Accountants in England and Wales
- Institute of Chartered Accountants in Scotland
- Institute of Chartered Accountants in Ireland
- Association of Chartered Certified Accountants[169]
- Chartered Institute of Management Accountants
- Institute of Financial Accountants
- Chartered Institute of Public Finance and Accountancy
- Association of Authorised Public Accountants[170]
- Institute of Cost and Executive Accountants[171]
- Association of International Accountants.[172]

For a privileged circumstances to arise one needs to have a confidential communication between the relevant professional adviser and his client or a

---

[168] Section 310 Proceeds of Crime Act 2002 as amended by regulation 2 the Proceeds of Crime Act 2002 and Money Laundering Regulations 2003 (Amendment) Order 2006.
[169] Formerly the Chartered Association of Certified Accountants.
[170] This association was formed in 1978 to represent those accountants who were individually authorised by the Secretary of State to conduct audits. By an extraordinary general meeting on the 24 June, 1996, members of the Association voted to become a subsidiary of the Association of Chartered Certified Accountants and its members comply with the same practising rules and regulations.
[171] Formerly the Association of Cost and Executive Accountants.
[172] The Institute of Company Accountants has amalgamated into the Association of International Accountants.

third party which is made for the dominant purpose of being used in actual, pending or contemplated litigation[173] or confidential communications written for the purposes of obtaining advice or assistance to the client.[174] Examples that have been cited[175] as matters which might fall within the description of privileged communications include:

- Advice on taxation matters where the adviser is giving advice on the interpretation or application of elements of tax law and in the process of assisting a client understand his tax position
- Advice on legal aspects of a takeover bid
- Advice on the duties of directors under the Companies Acts
- Advice to directors on legal issues relating to the Insolvency Act 1986, for example, wrongful trading.

3.6.4 Further offences under the Proceeds of Crime Act for members of a Regulated Profession: Tipping Off

Disclosing information which has come to light in the course of business in the regulated sector which is likely to prejudice an investigation is an offence under section 333A of the Proceeds of Crime Act 2002.[176] The offence of "tipping off" carries on conviction in the Crown Court a sentence of up to 2 years imprisonment and / or an unlimited fine. Disclosures to SOCA, a police constable, ones money laundering reporting officer, HM Revenue and Customs,[177] within the accountant's own firm[178] and for accountants who are relevant professional advisers to other relevant professional advisers of the same kind[179] and to the client to dissuade him from committing an offence[180] fall outside the provision.

Accountants who would be relevant professional advisers (as defined by section 333E Proceeds of Crime Act 2002) are accountants, auditors or tax advisers and would be a member of a professional body which is established for accountants, auditors or tax advisers (as the case may be) and which makes provision for (a) testing the competence of those seeking admission to membership of such a body as a condition for such admission; and (b)

---

[173] *Seabrook v British Transport Commission* [1959] 1 WLR 509.
[174] *Three Rivers DC v Governor & Company of the Bank of England* [2005] 1 AC 610.
[175] Institute of Chartered Accountants in England and Wales TECH 02/06.
[176] As inserted by the Terrorism Act 2000 and Proceeds of Crime Act 2002 (Amendment) Regulations 2007.
[177] Section 333A Proceeds of Crime Act 2002 as inserted by the Terrorism Act 2000 and Proceeds of Crime Act 2002 (Amendment) Regulations 2007.
[178] Section 333B Proceeds of Crime Act 2002.
[179] Section 333C Proceeds of Crime Act 2002.
[180] Section 333D(2) Proceeds of Crime Act 2002.

imposing and maintaining professional and ethical standards for its members, as well as imposing sanctions for non-compliance with those standards.

Professional bodies whose membership would qualify for these purposes include:

- Institute of Chartered Accountants in England and Wales
- Institute of Chartered Accountants in Scotland
- Institute of Chartered Accountants in Ireland
- Association of Chartered Certified Accountants[181]
- Chartered Institute of Management Accountants
- Institute of Financial Accountants
- Chartered Institute of Public Finance and Accountancy
- Association of Authorised Public Accountants[182]
- Institute of Cost and Executive Accountants[183]
- Association of International Accountants.[184]

There is a similar offence of "tipping off" in relation to money laundering under the Terrorism Act 2000.[185]

3.6.5 Requirements under Money Laundering Regulations 2007

The Money Laundering Regulations 2007 came into force on 15th December 2007 and revoked the Money Laundering Regulations 2003.[186]

These apply to auditors, insolvency practitioners, external accountants and tax advisers as well as to credit and financial institutions, independent legal professionals, trust or company service providers, estate agents, high value dealers and casinos. An "external accountant" was defined as a firm or sole practitioner who by way of business provides accountancy services to other

---

[181] Formerly the Chartered Association of Certified Accountants.
[182] This association was formed in 1978 to represent those accountants who were individually authorised by the Secretary of State to conduct audits. By an extraordinary general meeting on the 24 June, 1996, members of the Association voted to become a subsidiary of the Association of Chartered Certified Accountants and its members comply with the same practising rules and regulations.
[183] Formerly the Association of Cost and Executive Accountants.
[184] The Institute of Company Accountants has amalgamated into the Association of International Accountants.
[185] Section 21D Terrorism Act 2000 as inserted by the Terrorism Act 2000 and Proceeds of Crime Act 2002 (Amendment) Regulations 2007.
[186] Regulation 1, Money Laundering Regulations 2007.

persons, when providing such services.[187] A high value dealer means a person or firm who trades in goods (including when acting as an auctioneer) when he receives in respect of a transaction or several linked transaction a total cash payment of 15,000 euros.[188]

Failure to comply with the regulations exposes the accountant on conviction on indictment to a potential fine and / or imprisonment for a term of up to two years.

Where an accountant has a supervisory body, the supervisory body is under a duty to effectively monitor and secure compliance by them of the Regulations.[189]

For accountants, the possible supervisory bodies include[190]

- Association of Chartered Certified Accountants
- Institute of Chartered Accountants in England and Wales
- Institute of Chartered Accountants in Ireland
- Institute of Chartered Accountants of Scotland
- Association of Accounting Technicians
- Association of International Accountants
- Association of Taxation Technicians
- Chartered Institute of Management Accountants
- Chartered Institute of Public Finance and Accountancy
- Chartered Institute of Taxation
- Insolvency Practitioners Association
- Institute of Certified Bookkeepers
- Institute of Financial Accountants
- International Association of Bookkeepers[191]

Where the accountant is not regulated by a supervisory body, they are by default subject to supervision by Her Majesty's Customs and Revenue.[192] The Commissioners may maintain a register of accountants who are not supervised by a professional body[193] and if they elect to do so, those

---

[187] Regulation 3(7) Money Laundering Regulations 2007. A business relationship is defined as including a profession under regulation 2(1), Money Laundering Regulations 2007.
[188] Regulation 3(12) Money Laundering Regulations 2007.
[189] Regulation 24(1) Money Laundering Regulations 2007.
[190] Schedule 3 Money Laundering Regulations 2007.
[191] Inserted by the Proceeds of Crime Act (Business in the Regulated Sector and Supervisory Authorities) Order 2007.
[192] Regulation 23(1)(d) Money Laundering Regulations 2007.
[193] Regulation 32(4) Money Laundering Regulations 2007.

accountants must apply to be included on that register within six months or they will be barred from carrying on their profession.[194] The Commissioners have powers to enter onto the premises of accountants regulated by them without a warrant, inspect the premises, observe the accountant carrying on his professional activities, inspect and copy his records and require him to answer questions as to his records and where they can be found. The Commissioners are also given the power to charge for the applications and monitoring of accountants regulated by them.[195]

The supervisory body is under a duty to report any suspicion they may have in the course of their monitoring that a person is engaged in money laundering to the Serious Organised Crime Agency.[196]

3.6.5.1 Customer due diligence
An accountant must undertake customer due diligence when[197] he

- establishes a business relationship
- carries out an occasional transaction
- suspects money laundering or terrorist financing
- doubts the veracity or adequacy of documents, data or information previously obtained for the purposes of identification or verification.

The customer due diligence needs to be conducted before the business relationship is established or transaction is undertaken[198] but it may be completed during the establishment of the relationship if it is necessary not to interrupt the normal course of business and there is little risk of money laundering occurring.[199]

If the accountant cannot comply with the customer due diligence requirements he must[200]

- not carry out a transaction with or for the customer through a bank account
- not establish a business relationship or carry out an occasional transaction with the customer;

---

[194] Regulation 33 Money Laundering Regulations 2007.
[195] Regulation 35 Money Laundering Regulations 2007.
[196] Regulation 24(2-3) Money Laundering Regulations 2007.
[197] Regulation 7(1) Money Laundering Regulations 2007.
[198] Regulation 9(2) Money Laundering Regulations 2007.
[199] Regulation 9(3) Money Laundering Regulations 2007.
[200] Regulation 11 Money Laundering Regulations 2007.

- terminate any existing business relationship with the customer
- consider whether he is required to make a disclosure by Part 7 of the Proceeds of Crime Act 2002 or Part 3 of the Terrorism Act 2000.

An accountant must also conduct customer due diligence measures from time to time as appropriate on a risk-sensitive basis.[201] He needs to determine the extent of the customer due diligence measures on risk sensitive basis (taking into account the type of the client, business relationship and transaction involved) and be able to demonstrate to his supervisory authority that the extent of the measures is appropriate.[202]

Customer due diligence measures involves (a) identifying the customer and verifying the customer's identity on the basis of documents, data or information obtained from a reliable and independent source (b) identifying, where there is a beneficial owner who is not the customer, the beneficial owner and taking adequate measures, on a risk-sensitive basis, to verify his identity so that the accountant is satisfied that he knows who the beneficial owner is, including, in the case of a company, trust or similar legal arrangement, measures to understand the ownership and control structure of the person, trust or arrangement; and (c) obtaining information on the purpose and intended nature of the business relationship.[203] The owner of a company is for the purposes someone who owns or controls more than 25% of the shares or voting rights.[204]

Accountants are entitled to rely on customer due diligence already conducted by members of certain professions who are already under a similar duty and are either listed under Part 1 of Schedule 3 of the Money Laundering Regulations 2007 or its EEA member state equivalent provided they agree to the accountant doing so.[205] The bodies listed under Part 1 of Schedule 3 are:

- Association of Chartered Certified Accountants
- Council for Licensed Conveyancers
- Faculty of Advocates
- General Council of the Bar
- Institute of Chartered Accountants in England and Wales
- Institute of Chartered Accountants in Ireland

---

[201] Regulation 7(2) Money Laundering Regulations 2007
[202] Regulation 7(3) Money Laundering Regulations 2007
[203] Regulation 5, Money Laundering Regulations 2007
[204] Regulation 6(1), Money Laundering Regulations 2007
[205] Regulation 17, Money Laundering Regulations 2007

- Institute of Chartered Accountants of Scotland
- The Law Society
- The Law Society in Scotland
- The Law Society of Northern Ireland

This is intended to provide limited comfort and does not exonerate the accountant from his responsibilities under the Regulations.

There are provisions for simplified due diligence in respect of certain transactions and customers such as UK and EEA credit and financial institutions, public authorities, independent legal professionals and companies whose securities are listed on a regulated market who are themselves already subject to disclosure obligations.[206]

Similarly there are provisions for enhanced due diligence by accountants if,[207] for example,

- The situation by its nature can present a higher risk of money laundering or terrorist financing
- The customer is not physically present for identification purposes
- The customer is a politically exposed person - that is to say someone who in the previous year has been entrusted with a prominent public function[208] by a state other than the UK, a community institution or international body or one of their associates[209] or immediate family[210]

---

[206] Regulation 13, Money Laundering Regulations 2007.
[207] Regulation 14, Money Laundering Regulations 2007.
[208] This includes heads of state, heads of government, ministers and deputy or assistant ministers, members of parliaments, members of supreme courts, of constitutional courts or of other high-level judicial bodies whose decisions are not generally subject to further appeal, other than in exceptional circumstances, members of courts of auditors or of the boards of central banks, ambassadors, chargés d'affaires and high-ranking officers in the armed forces, members of the administrative, management or supervisory bodies of state-owned enterprises: Schedule 2, paragraph 4, Money Laundering Regulations 2007.
[209] An associate for these purposes includes any individual who is known to have joint beneficial ownership of a legal entity or legal arrangement, or any other close business relations, with the person and any individual who has sole beneficial ownership of a legal entity or legal arrangement which is known to have been set up for the benefit of the person: Schedule 2, paragraph 4, Money Laundering Regulations 2007.
[210] This means a spouse, a partner (that is to say someone in a relationship considered under their national law to be equivalent to a spouse), children and their spouses or partners; and parents: Schedule 2, paragraph 4, Money Laundering Regulations 2007.

3.6.5.2 Ongoing monitoring

Accountants need to undertake ongoing monitoring of their professional relationships with their clients.[211] This involves scrutiny of transactions undertaken throughout the course of the relationship (including, where necessary, the source of funds) to ensure that the transactions are consistent with the relevant person's knowledge of the customer, his business and risk profile. It also involves keeping the documents, data or information obtained for the purpose of applying customer due diligence measures up-to-date.

3.6.5.3 Record keeping

Records that should be obtained include all evidence and supporting documents obtained to verify the identity of the customer and in the course of the ongoing due diligence.[212] Records should be kept for a period of five years after completion of the last activity arising out of the transaction or the end of the business relationship.[213]

3.6.5.4 Policies and procedures

The accountant must put in place policies and procedures[214] in respect of

- Customer due diligence and ongoing monitoring
- Reporting
- Internal Control
- Risk assessment and management
- The monitoring management of compliance with and the internal communication of such policies and procedures.

The policies and procedures should set out

- how to identify and examine complex or unusually large transactions, unusual patterns of transactions which have no apparent economic or visible lawful purpose and any other activity which the relevant person regards as particularly likely by its nature to be related to money laundering or terrorist financing
- which specify the taking of additional measures, where appropriate, to prevent the use for money laundering or terrorist financing of products and transactions which might favour anonymity

---

[211] Regulation 8, Money Laundering Regulations 2007
[212] Regulation 19(1),(2) Money Laundering Regulations 2007
[213] Regulation 19(3) Money Laundering Regulations 2007
[214] Regulation 20 Money Laundering Regulations 2007

- to determine whether a customer is a politically exposed person
- if the accountant is not a sole proprietor with no employees, identifying a member of staff as the "money laundering reporting officer" and requiring that staff report to him with money laundering information and vesting him with the responsibility for considering whether there are grounds for suspect money laundering or terrorist financing

3.6.5.5 Training employees

All staff of the accountant need to be trained about the Money Laundering Regulations 2007, the Proceeds of Crime Act 2002 and section 18 and 21A Terrorism Act 2000. Furthermore employers are obliged to train all employees about how to identify and deal with transactions that may involve money laundering.

Suspicion means a state of mind which more than mere speculation but falling short of proof based on firm evidence.[215] The suspicion must be of a settled nature and based on the facts as they present themselves.[216] It is however a subjective test and it does not matter that it later transpires that there were no reasonable grounds for that suspicion.[217] Factors which should raise suspicions include:

- where it is difficult to obtain evidence of the business applicant's identity
- when the business applicant is reluctant to supply evidence of identity
- where an intermediary is used for no discernible reason
- when the transaction is an unusual one whether for the business applicant or in the light of normal market transactions
- when the business applicant is introduced by a financial institution from a country with little or no money laundering regulations in place
- when the business applicant is introduced by a financial institution from a country where drug production or sales are prevalent
- when settlements are made in cash
- when settlements are made by a party unconnected with the business applicant

---

[215] *Hussein v Chaing Fook Kam* [1970] AC 942, 948.
[216] *R v Da Silva* [2006] EWCA 1654, *K Ltd v National Westminster Bank* [2006] EWCA Civ 1039 at para. 21.
[217] *K Ltd v National Westminster Bank* [2006] EWCA Civ 1039.

- when the payment is made to a party unconnected with the business applicant
- when securities are delivered to an unconnected third party

3.7. RELIANCE ON AN ACCOUNTANT'S ADVICE BY A CLIENT AS A DEFENCE

3.7.1 "The accountant defence"

The fact that misconduct by a director can be attributed to the fact of his having reasonably relied on an accountant's advice but that advice has later transpired to be erroneous has been recognised as amounting to a defence for the director or at least as giving the director grounds for substantially mitigating any penalty imposed upon him.

The rationale is threefold:

1. This passes the blame for the default elsewhere. Provided his reliance on the accountant was reasonable, the director would be entitled to substitute the accountant's perceived superior and expert views for his own.
2. The conduct of instructing an accountant is likely to be of itself considered as demonstrating a responsible reaction of a director who recognises and wishes to remedy the limitations in his own skills.
3. The views of the accountant could be viewed as a reliable and best guide as to what would have appeared at the material time to be reasonable conduct. The accountant's perception as an independent professional man provides the best evidence of how the facts would have been either known (or perceived to be) at the material time and as to what might have been seen to be a responsible or reasonable reaction to them. An expectation that a director is able to act with the benefit of hindsight has never been a touchstone for assessing the culpability of a director's conduct.

Four examples can be given where reasonable reliance on the intervention of an accountant has been given recognition as a defence. These are (a) in respect of issues of a company's shares to the public (b) in director's disqualification (c) when issuing a dividend in breach of the capital sufficiency rules (d) as a defence to a tax penalty

3.7.2 Misleading statements in a prospectus

Reliance on an accountant's statement may present a defence before the court to an allegation that a statement in a prospectus was misleading.

It is unlawful to offer transferable securities to the public without previously making available an approved prospectus to the public.[218] Similarly it is unlawful to request admission on a UK market without previously making available an approved prospectus.[219] Breach of these provisions is a criminal offence punishable on conviction on indictment by imprisonment for a term not exceeding 2 years and / or a fine.[220] Breach of these provisions also gives rise to a civil action at the instance of any person who has suffered loss as a result of the breach:[221] The defences to the tort of breach of statutory duty are expressly preserved for this action.

No prospectus is needed where (a) the offer is made to qualified persons (b) the offer is made to fewer than 100 other persons (c) the minimum subscription is at least 50,000 euros (d) the denomination of the securities are of at least 50,000 euros apiece or (e) the total price for the securities cannot exceed 10,000 euros.[222] A further exception exists where an investor engages a qualified investor to act on his behalf and gives him a discretion to make decisions about accepting offers in respect of the securities.[223]

Approval of the prospectus is by the Financial Services Authority. They will only have jurisdiction to approve the prospectus if (a) the UK is the home state of the issuer (b) the information contains the required "necessary information" and all elements of the prospectus directive are complied with.[224] The "necessary information" means the information necessary for an informed investor for the purposes of making an informed assessment of the assets and liabilities, financial position, profits and losses, and prospects of the issue of the securities and the rights attaching to those securities given the

---

[218] Section 85(1) Financial Services & Markets Act 2000 (as inserted by The Prospectus Regulations 2005).
[219] Section 85(2) Financial Services & Markets Act 2000 (as inserted by The Prospectus Regulations 2005).
[220] Section 85(3) Financial Services & Markets Act 2000 (as inserted by The Prospectus Regulations 2005).
[221] Section 85(1) Financial Services & Markets Act 2000 (as inserted by The Prospectus Regulations 2005).
[222] Section 86(1) Financial Services & Markets Act 2000 (as inserted by The Prospectus Regulations 2005).
[223] Section 86(3) Financial Services & Markets Act 2000 (as inserted by The Prospectus Regulations 2005).
[224] Section 87A(1) Financial Services & Markets Act 2000 (as inserted by The Prospectus Regulations 2005).

nature of the securities and their issuer.[225] The information must be presented in a form which is easy to understand and analyse.[226] The Financial Services Authority can authorise the omission of information which is (a) contrary to public interest (b) detrimental to the issuer (provided that its omission would be unlikely to mislead the public) and (c) that the information is of minor significance.[227] The prospectus must also contain a summary explaining in non-technical language the essential characteristics and risks associated with the issuer, any guarantor and the securities to which the prospectus relates.[228]

Furthermore, if at any time after the preparation of the prospectus for submission and before the closure of the offer or the commencement of dealings in that security, there is any new factor or a mistake or inaccuracy comes to light, which is significant enough for disclosure to have been so required if it had arisen when the prospectus was originally prepared, the issuer of the securities must submit for approval and, if approved, publish supplementary prospectus to give notice of it and correct any mistake or inaccuracy.[229]

A person responsible for any prospectus will be liable to pay compensation to any person who has acquired any of the securities in question and suffered loss in respect of them as the result of any untrue or misleading statement in the particulars or the omission from them of any matter required to be included in them.[230] No liability can however arise solely on the basis of the summary, unless the summary or its translation is misleading, inaccurate or inconsistent when read with the rest of the prospectus.[231]

A person will not incur any liability under section 90, Financial Services and Markets Act 2000 for any loss in respect of securities caused by any statements or omissions mentioned if he satisfies the court that at the time when the particulars were submitted to the competent authority he reasonably believed, having made such enquiries (if any) as were reasonable that the statement was true and not misleading or any omission was properly omitted and one of the following conditions are satisfied:[232]

---

[225] Section 87A(2) and (4) Financial Services & Markets Act 2000.
[226] Section 87A(3) Financial Services & Markets Act 2000.
[227] Section 87B(1) Financial Services & Markets Act 2000.
[228] Section 87A(5) and (6) Financial Services & Markets Act 2000.
[229] Section 87A(G) Financial Services & Markets Act 2000.
[230] Section 90, Financial Services & Markets Act 2000.
[231] Section 90(12) Financial Services & Markets Act 2000 as inserted by the Prospectus Regulations 2005.
[232] Paragraph 1(2) Schedule 10, Financial Services and Markets Act 2000.

1. that he continued in that belief until the time when the securities were acquired;[233] or
2. that they were acquired before it was reasonably practicable to bring the fact that the expert was not competent to the attention of persons likely to acquire the securities in question[234] or
3. that before the securities were acquired he had taken all such steps as it was reasonable for him to have taken to secure that that fact was brought to the attention of those persons;[235] or
4. that he continued in the belief until after the commencement of dealings in the securities following their admission to the official list that the securities were acquired after such a lapse of time that he ought in the circumstances to be reasonably excused.[236]

A person furthermore will not incur liability under section 90 Financial Services and Markets Act 2000 for any loss in respect of securities caused by any statement purporting to be made by or on the authority of another person as "an expert"[237] which is, and is stated to be, included in the particulars with that other person's consent.[238] To benefit from this protection, he will further have to satisfy the court that at the time when the particulars were submitted to the competent authority he believed on reasonable grounds that the other person was competent to make the statement and had consented to its inclusion in the form and context in which it was included and

- That the expert was competent to make that statement,[239] and,
- That he consented to its inclusion in the form and context in which it appeared.[240]

And one or more the following conditions are satisfied,

- that he continued in that belief until the time when the securities were acquired[241];
- or that they were acquired before it was reasonably practicable to bring the fact that the expert was not competent to the

---

[233] Paragraph 1(3)(a) Schedule 10, Financial Services and Markets Act 2000.
[234] Paragraph 1(3)(b) Schedule 10, Financial Services and Markets Act 2000.
[235] Paragraph 1(3)(c) Schedule 10, Financial Services and Markets Act 2000.
[236] Paragraph 1(3)(d) Schedule 10, Financial Services and Markets Act 2000.
[237] Paragraph 2(1)(a) Schedule 10, Financial Services and Markets Act 2000.
[238] Paragraph 2(1)(b) Schedule 10, Financial Services and Markets Act 2000.
[239] Paragraph 2(2)(a) Schedule 10, Financial Services and Markets Act 2000.
[240] Paragraph 2(2)(b) Schedule 10, Financial Services and Markets Act 2000.
[241] Paragraph 2(3)(a) Schedule 10, Financial Services and Markets Act 2000.

attention of persons likely to acquire the securities in question[242] or
- that before the securities were acquired he had taken all such steps as it was reasonable for him to have taken to secure that that fact was brought to the attention of those persons[243]; or
- that he continued in the belief until after the commencement of dealings in the securities following their admission to the official list that the securities were acquired after such a lapse of time that he ought in the circumstances to be reasonably excused[244].

Similarly a defence lies if a correction to the prospectus[245] or a notice that the expert was not competent (or did not consent to the inclusion of his statement)[246] was either published in a manner calculated to bring it to the attention of persons likely to acquire securities or that he took all steps that were reasonably practicable to bring a correction to the attention of persons likely to acquire them or that before the securities were acquired all reasonable steps had been taken to secure that a correction was brought to the attention of those persons.

"Expert" includes any accountant or other person whose profession, qualifications or experience give authority to a statement made by him.[247]

3.7.3 Director's disqualification

Reliance on an accountant's statement may present a defence or substantial mitigation before the court to an allegation that a director's conduct showed unfitness meriting disqualification under Section 6 Company Director's Disqualification Act 1986.

Unfitness is a question of fact.[248] The question is whether the complaints found proven against the director constitute as a matter of ordinary construction.

The objective of the legislation is the protection of the public.[249] Ordinary commercial misjudgement is not enough to justify disqualification; the BERR (formerly the DTI) must prove that the conduct displayed a lack of

---

[242] Paragraph 2(3)(b) Schedule 10, Financial Services and Markets Act 2000.
[243] Paragraph 2(3)(c) Schedule 10, Financial Services and Markets Act 2000.
[244] Paragraph 2(3)(d) Schedule 10, Financial Services and Markets Act 2000.
[245] Paragraph 3 Schedule 10, Financial Services and Markets Act 2000.
[246] Paragraph 4 Schedule 10, Financial Services and Markets Act 2000.
[247] Paragraph 8, Schedule 10, Financial Services and Markets Act 2000.
[248] *Re Lo-Line Electric Motors* [1990] BCLC 677.
[249] *Re Sevenoaks Stationers (Retail) Ltd* [1990] BCLC 668.

commercial probity or, in an extreme case, gross negligence or total incompetence would suffice to show unfitness.[250]

Factors which may be taken into account[251] in an insolvent company in determining whether a director is or was unfit set out at Schedule 1, Parts I and II, Company Directors Disqualification Act 1986 include:

- misfeasance or breach of fiduciary duty
- misapplication or retention of company money
- the extent of the director's responsibility for the company's insolvency
- whether the director entered into transactions which are liable to be set aside under the debt avoidance provisions of the Insolvency Act 1986, Part XV
- the extent of the director's responsibility for any failure by the company to:
  - keep accounting records[252]
  - retain records[253]
  - keep a register of directors and secretaries[254]
  - keep and enter up the shareholders' register[255]
  - retain the shareholders' register[256]
  - make annual returns on behalf of the company[257]
  - submit annual returns on behalf of the company in a timely fashion[258]
  - register any charges it creates[259]
- the extent of the director's responsibility for any failure by the company to supply goods or services paid for
- the extent of the director's responsibility for any transaction by the company liable to be set aside under Sections 127, 238 or 240 Insolvency Act 1986
- the extent of the director's responsibility for failing to call a creditors' meeting in a creditors' voluntary winding up under Section 98 Insolvency Act 1986

---

[250] *Re Lo-Line Electric Motors* [1990] BCLC 677, per Browne Wilkinson VC.
[251] Section 9 Company Directors Disqualification Act 1986.
[252] Section 221 Companies Act 1985, section 387 Companies Act 2006.
[253] Section 222 Companies Act 1985, section 389 Companies Act 2006.
[254] Section 288 Companies Act 1985, section 162 (directors) and 275 (secretaries) Companies Act 2006.
[255] Section 352 Companies Act 1985, section 113 Companies Act 2006.
[256] Section 352 Companies Act 1985, section 114 Companies Act 2006.
[257] Sections 363 and 364 Companies Act 1985, section 854 Companies Act 2006.
[258] Section 365 Companies Act 1985, section 858 Companies Act 2006.
[259] Sections 299 and 415 Companies Act 1985, section 860 Companies Act 2006.

- the extent to which the director failed to comply with his obligations in respect of:
  - the company's statement of affairs in administration[260]
  - the statement of affairs to the administrative receiver[261]
  - the attendance of meetings and the statement of affairs in the creditors' voluntary winding up[262]
  - the company's statement of affairs in a court winding up[263]
  - duty to deliver up the company's property[264]
  - duty to cooperate with the company's liquidator[265]

The list is not exhaustive.[266]
Reliance on an accountant that the company's statutory obligations were complied with may amount to a defence[267] or at the very least substantial mitigation.[268]

Reliance on an accountant will not amount to a blanket defence. Certainly it will not provide an excuse for matters the director should have known about or from taking steps consequent on that knowledge.[269]

The argument that a director was acting on an accountant's advice did not find favour with the Court in *Re Queens Moat Houses plc, SOS for Trade and Industry v Bairstow*[270] a listed company was found to have published misleading results prior to the suspension of the listing of its shares. The Secretary of State brought disqualification proceedings against the chairman on the grounds of gross negligence in the performance of his duties. The chairman argued that he had relied and had been entitled to rely on his fellow directors to provide financial statements, and on the fact that the company's auditors had seen no reason to qualify the company's accounts for the year ending 31st December 1991. Sir Donald Rattee (sitting as a judge of the High Court) rejected that defence. He found that, although D had not intended to mislead, he had been negligent in relying blindly on his fellow directors and auditors. Had he done his job properly, no misleading statements would have been made.

---

[260] Section 22 Insolvency Act 1986.
[261] Section 47 Insolvency Act 1986.
[262] Section 99 Insolvency Act 1986.
[263] Section 13 Insolvency Act 1986.
[264] Section 234 Insolvency Act 1986.
[265] Section 235 Insolvency Act 1986.
[266] *Re Bath Glass* [1988] BCLC 329, 332.
[267] *Re Cladrose* [1990] BCC 11, *Re Douglas Construction Services Ltd* [1988] BCLC 3973.
[268] *Re Cargo Agency* [1992] BCLC 686.
[269] *Re GSAR Realisations Ltd* [1993] BCLC 409.
[270] [2004] All ER (D) 333 (Jul).

3.7.4 Issue of dividend in breach of the capital sufficiency rules

One of the main limitations upon the powers of a company to make distributions by way of dividends is that a private company can only make a distribution out of profits legally available for that purpose.[271] The stricter rules for public limited company are set out under section 264 Companies Act 1985.[272] A "distribution" includes *"every description of distribution of a company's assets to its members"*.[273]

The profits are determined by reference to the *"relevant items"* in the *"relevant accounts"*.[274] The *"relevant items"* mean the profits, losses, assets and liabilities, provisions of any of the kinds mentioned in paragraphs 88 and 89 of Schedule 4 Companies Act 1985 (depreciation, diminution in value of assets, retentions to meet liabilities, etc) and share capital and reserves (including undistributable reserves).[275] *"Relevant accounts"* involves the directors having regard to last year's annual accounts and any interim accounts.[276] Profits available for distribution are its accumulated realised profits less its accumulated realised losses.[277] A reserve arising on the reduction of capital is realised profit even if the capital cancelled was paid up otherwise than in cash.[278]

Any unlawful distribution must be repaid by shareholders who knew or had reasonable grounds to believe there had been a breach.[279] Directors who have authorised an unlawful distribution are, *prima facie*, jointly and severally liable to repay the distribution.[280] They are able to seek an indemnity from the shareholders only if they able to demonstrate the shareholders knew or had reasonable grounds to believe there had been a breach.[281]

---

[271] Section 263(1) Companies Act 1985, section 830, Companies Act 2006.
[272] See section 831, Companies Act 2006.
[273] Section 263(2) Companies Act 1985, section 829(1) Companies Act 2006.
[274] Section 270(5) Companies Act 1985, section 836(1) Companies Act 2006.
[275] Section 270(2) Companies Act 1985, section 836(1) Companies Act 2006.
[276] Section 270(3), (4) Companies Act 1985, section 836(2), Companies Act 2006.
[277] Section 263(3) Companies Act 1985, section 830(2) Companies Act 2006.
[278] Tech 7/03 Guidance on the determination of realised profits and losses under the Companies Act 1985, March 2003.
[279] Section 277(1) Companies Act 1985, 847(2) Companies Act 2006.
[280] *Bairstow and Others v. Queens Moat House* [2002] BCC 91.
[281] *Flitcroft's Case* [1882] 21 Ch D 519.

So saying, where, after properly investigating the company's financial position, the directors make an estimate of the available profits and declare a dividend on that basis, the court will not review the decision on the ground that their estimates were erroneous, if the view taken was one which reasonable persons might take.[282]

Where, however, directors have acted without proper investigation or professional assistance, the burden lies upon them to show that the payment was fairly made out of profits available for that purpose.[283]

Advice by an accountant, who has reviewed the accounts, that sufficient distributable profits exist to allow the distribution to take place would probably constitute sufficient professional assistance for these purposes and would certainly assist a director in persuading a court to afford the director relief under section 1157 Companies Act 2006 (discretionary relief by the court where directors have acted honestly and reasonably).

3.7.5 Tax Penalties

When an accountant prepares accounts for his client his client is bound by them and any errors contained in them as they are prepared as his client's agent. Circumstances explaining the mis-declaration may however amount to a defence to the statutory penalty.

Thus where a mis-declaration of Value Added Tax was caused by the error of a bookkeeper who, unknown to his employer, was ill and acting under the influence of prescribed drugs this has been held to be a reasonable excuse and a defence to the statutory penalty.[284]

By contrast, the inaccuracy of a subordinate relied upon to prepare a return on a manual basis prior to the installation of a computer does not provide a reasonable excuse for a misdeclaration of tax.[285]

Whilst both these cases, concern bookkeepers rather than accountants, there is no reason why the same principles should not be applied to errors by accountants.

Certainly such an argument has been successfully run before the Special Commissioners in relation to direct taxation in an appeal against the

---

[282] *Re Peruvian Guano Co, ex p Kemp* [1894] 3 Ch 690.
[283] *Rance's Case* (1870) 6 Ch App 104.
[284] *Fritz Bender Metals (UK) v. Customs and Excise Commissioners* [1991] VATTR 80.
[285] *Victoria Alloys (UK) v. Customs and Excise Commissioners* [1991] VATTR 163.

imposition of a surcharge under section 59C Taxes Management Act 1970. There the taxpayer, having no specialist knowledge herself, had reasonably relied on a firm of specialist tax accountants and filed a tax return on the basis of what (unbeknownst to her) later transpired to be wrong advice from them.[286]

---

[286] *AM Rowland v. Revenue and Customs Commissioners* [2006] STC (SCD) 536.

Chapter 4

CLAIMS AGAINST ACCOUNTANTS

4.1 CLAIMS AGAINST ACCOUNTANTS

4.1.1 The basis for liability

An accountant will owe a range of different duties which may, if breached, give rise to a claim for damages.

The first is under the accountant's contract to provide professional services he has entered into with his client. Under that retainer he will owe express or implied duties to his client.

Secondly the accountant will owe tortuous duties of care to both his client and some of those third parties who are foreseeably affected by his actions.

Thirdly an accountant will owe fiduciary duties as a trustee, agent or possibly even as a director.

Finally an accountant holding himself out as acting for his client, he represents he has authority of his client. An accountant may be liable for breach of warranty of authority if he acts without authority.

To establish any claim for damages, a causal link must be proved between the breach of the duty of care and the loss suffered. The test is whether this played a real and substantial part in causing the loss even if it was not the sole cause.[1] Absence of one of the elements of the cause of action provides a defence to the claim.[2]

4.1.2 Contract

The most important area of liability is in breach of the contract to provide professional services he has entered into with his client.

---

[1] *Deloitte Haskins & Sells v. Mutual Life Nominees* [1993] 2 All ER 1015.
[2] Paragraph 2, Professional Liability of Accountants and Auditors, issued November 1993 by the Institute of Chartered Accountants in England and Wales.

It is an implied term of an accountant's contract to provide professional services, that he will provide those professional services properly and with reasonable care and skill.

Precisely how that duty of care is to be fulfilled depends very much on the nature of the contract that the accountant has with his client. The work of an accountant is very varied. Thus an accountant employed to fill in tax returns was held not liable for failing to draw his employer's attention to fraud.[3] By contrast an accountant who held himself out as able to advise, and agreed to provide "general advice and assistance" on a client's Lloyds involvement, extended his duty to the client beyond that owed by an accountant normally and assumed a responsibility to advise his client which were high risk syndicates.[4] In determining whether an accountant was negligent in his advice on tax planning the Court of Appeal has ruled that the court should determine this issue on whether or not the advice was correct in law and was not entitled examine whether or not, on the underlying substance, the transaction was vulnerable to attack by the Revenue as a sham.[5]

Nor can an accountant get out of his duty of care by advising the client to seek advice elsewhere where the advice should have been within his general competence. The Court of Appeal has held in a case concerning a share purchase that an accountant could not absolve himself by advising the client to seek tax advice elsewhere; advice on how to maximise the client's tax advantages should have been within the accountant's general competence as an accountant and the accountant's failure to give such advice was a amounted to a breach of his contract and negligent.[6]

The most common areas in which claims are brought against accountants for breach of their duty to their clients include:

- errors in preparing accounts
- failure to detect fraud
- erroneous advice relating to tax planning
- failure to comply with time limits for tax and other returns
- incorrect share valuations.

The standard of care to be applied in such a case is not absolute. One need only apply the standard expected of a reasonably careful qualified

---

[3] *Leech v. Stokes* [1937] IR 787.
[4] *Fawkes-Underwood v. Hamiltons* (1997) LTL 24 March.
[5] *Grimm v. Newman* [2003] 1 All ER 67
[6] *Sayers v. Clarke Walker* (2002) EWCA Civ 910

accountant;[7] a reasonably careful accountant may still make mistakes. Any representation that the accountant has some specialisation in the area concerned may serve to increase the level of care expected to be applied;[8] the standard of care is not reduced if the representation as to the particular skill or qualification is incorrect.

Common professional practice is strong persuasive evidence of the standard to be expected.[9] The standard is judged by the practice at the time where the conduct took place.[10]

4.1.3 Tort

It is now that clear accountants owe a concurrent duty of care in both contract and tort to their employer or client;[11] the claimant may elect which of the concurrent remedies in breach of contract or in tort at trial appears to him to provide the most advantageous remedy.

Third parties who, although not clients, were reasonably within the accountant's contemplation when performing his professional services may also be owed a duty of care;[12] whilst a negligent accountant is liable to his client both in contract and in tort,[13] a claim by a third party can be brought in tort only.

4.1.3.1 Tortious liability

In the case of accounts prepared by an accountant, third parties who would be considered to be reasonably within an accountant's contemplation (and thus to whom a duty of care might be owed by the accountant) would include any third person to whom the accountant himself shows the accounts, or to whom he himself knows that his employer or client is going to show the accounts, for example, so as to induce him to invest money or take some other action on them.[14]

---

[7] *Midland Bank Co Ltd v. Hett Stubbs & Kemp* [1979] Ch 384, 402-3.
[8] *Duchess of Argyll v. Beuselinck* [1972] 2 Lloyds Rep 172, 183, *Benson v Thomas Eggar & Sons*, unreported, 2nd December 1977.
[9] *Lloyd Cheyham & Co. Ltd v. Littlejohn* [1986] PCC 389.
[10] *Bell v. Strathairn & Blair* (1954) 104 LJ 618.
[11] *Henderson v. Merrett Syndicates Ltd* [1995] 2 AC 145.
[12] By analogy, solicitors have been held liable to the intended beneficiary of a will where the negligence resulted in the loss of an intended legacy; the duty of care was not limited to the deceased testator who was the solicitors' client: *White v. Jones* [1995] 2 AC 207.
[13] *Henderson v. Merrett Syndicates Ltd* [1994] 3 All ER 506 where a co-extensive claim in tort and breach of contract was found against a Lloyds agent.
[14] *Candler v. Crane, Christmas & Co* [1951] 2 KB 164, p. 180-181, per Denning LJ.

It is unlikely that the duty of care could be extended by the courts further to strangers of whom they have heard nothing or to whom their employer without their knowledge may choose to show their accounts. Once the accountant has handed over the accounts, he is not, by and large, responsible for what the client does with them without his knowledge or consent.[15]

The salient features of the case law where an accountant has been held liable to a non-client in negligence is that:

- the accountant giving the advice or information was fully aware of the nature of the transaction that the claimant had in contemplation, and
- knew that the advice or information would be communicated to him directly or indirectly
- knew that the claimant would rely on that advice or information in deciding whether or not to engage in the transaction in contemplation
- had voluntarily take it upon himself to provide the advice or information.[16]

In such circumstances the accountant could clearly be expected, subject always to the effect of any disclaimer of responsibility, specifically to anticipate that the claimant would rely on the advice or information given by the accountant for that very purpose.[17]

The Court of Appeal has ruled that accountants preparing reports on solicitors' accounts owe a duty of care to the Law Society, as the trustees of the solicitors' compensation fund, as the reports are relied upon by the Law Society when deciding whether or not to intervene in a solicitors' practice to protect the Compensation Fund.[18]

Action by third parties who have suffered loss as a result of relying on the accountant's advice may be brought as a claim for negligent misstatement.

As with a claim in negligence, there is no need to show the existence of a contract to found a claim in negligent misstatement[19] but the existence of a

---

[15] *Candler v. Crane, Christmas & Co* [1951] 2 KB 164, p. 180-181, per Denning LJ.
[16] *Commissioners for Revenue and Customs v. Barclays Bank plc* [2007] AC 181.
[17] *Caparo Industries plc v. Dickman and Ors* [1990] 2 WLR 358, pp. 367-8, per Lord Bridge of Harwich.
[18] *Law Society v. KPMG Peat Marwick* (2000) The Times 6th July.
[19] *Hedley Byrne v. Heller* [1964] AC 464.

contract does not prevent the use of negligence or negligent misstatement as a remedy whether on its own or pleaded in the alternative.

To establish a claim in negligent misstatement, one needs to establish:

- that there must be some form of "special relationship" between the accountant and the litigant, e.g. the relationship between an accountant and his client; and
- there is no valid disclaimer of responsibility;[20] and
- there was an untrue and misleading statement of fact; and
- the litigant placed reliance on that statement, e.g. he invested in a company on the basis of the accountant's figures; and
- the accountant owed the litigant a duty of care to represent the facts accurately; and
- there was a breach of that duty of care by the accountant's false or misleading information; and
- the litigant suffered a foreseeable loss
- The loss was caused by that breach.[21]

In advising the client who employs him, the professional man owes a duty to exercise that standard of skill and care appropriate to his professional status and will be liable both in contract and in tort for all losses which his client may suffer by reason of any breach of that duty.[22]

The standard of care to be applied in such a case is not absolute. One need only apply the standard expected of an ordinary qualified accountant exercising and professing to have the special skills of an accountant – the "Bolam test";[23] a reasonably careful accountant may still make mistakes. As with contract, any representation that the accountant has some specialisation in the area concerned may serve to increase the level of care expected to be applied; the standard of care is not reduced if the representation as to the particular skill or qualification is incorrect.

Common professional practice is strong persuasive evidence of the standard to be expected of the ordinary skilled accountant.[24]

---

[20] For the validity of such disclaimers. See, *inter alia*, Section 11 Unfair Contract Terms Act 1977.
[21] What needs to be shown is that the breach played a real and substantial part, though not necessarily a decisive part, in causing the loss: *JEB Fasteners v Mark Bloom & Co* [1983] 1 All ER 583.
[22] *Caparo Industries plc v. Dickman and Ors* [1990] 2 WLR 358, p. 366, per Lord Bridge of Harwich.
[23] *Bolam v. Friern Hospital Management Committee* [1957] 1 WLR 582, 586.
[24] *Lloyd Cheyham & Co. Ltd v. Littlejohn* [1986] PCC 389.

4.1.3.2 Contributory Negligence

It is open to the accountant[25] to offset his liability where a claim in negligence is made by arguing the contributory negligence of his client. Under section 1, the Law Reform (Contributory Negligence) Act 1945 a claimant's damages can be subjected to a pro rata reduction where he suffers damage as the result partly of his own fault.

For example, a client may be contributorily negligent if he ignores his accountant's warnings and a company director himself has a statutory duty to prepare accounts, maintain proper books of account and records and to safeguard the assets of the company.

The Act can be applied to a claim brought in contract where the defendant's liability under the contract is the same as his liability in negligence; namely one of breach of duty to apply reasonable care or skill and this applies whether or not a claim is, in fact, actually pursued in negligence.[26]

4.1.4 Breach of fiduciary duty

Claims for breaches of fiduciary duties owed by an accountant as a trustee, agent or possibly even as a director to his client are dealt with elsewhere in this work.

As with claims for contractual and tortuous liability, a claimant seeking a remedy in damages would need not merely to establish the breach of fiduciary duty but that it caused the claimant some foreseeable and recoverable head of loss or damage or there are assets or profits for which he needs to account.

4.1.5 Warranty of authority

If an accountant represents that he is acting for a client and a third party relies on this representation to his detriment, the accountant warrants that he is representing the client and may be liable in damages for loss caused by the breach of warranty of authority.[27] It does not matter that the accountant has not been negligent in making a representation of authority.[28] Nor does it matter that the representation of authority was not in express words but merely by conduct.[29]

---

[25] By way of illustration, *De Meza and Stuart v. Apple, Van Straten, Shena and Stone* [1975] 1 Lloyd's Rep 498.
[26] *Forsikringsaktieselskapet Vesta v. Butcher* [1989] AC 852.
[27] *Yonge v. Toynbee* [1909] 1 KB 215.
[28] *Colleen v. Wright* (1857) 8 E & B 647, 657.
[29] *Penn v. Bristol & West Building Society* [1995] 2 FLR 938, 953.

4.1.6 Level of damages awarded

In claims for breach of contract, the intention of the court when compensating a claimant is to put the claimant in the position that he would have been in had the contract for professional services been properly performed.

Where the claim is phrased in negligence, it is the intention of the court to place the claimant back into the position he would have been in had the accountant not acted negligently.

Where the claim is phrased in breach of fiduciary duty, the court will award equitable compensation whose intention is to put the claimant back in the position he would have been in but for the breach of trust.[30]

In either case, there is a duty on the claimant to take reasonable steps to try to mitigate his loss. The claimant cannot recover any loss he could have reasonably avoided. Nor can the claimant recover losses which he has avoided and the defendant is entitled to be credited for all benefits which the claimant has received through the steps taken to mitigate the loss.

Moreover losses are only recoverable if they can be shown to have been caused by the breach; if a breach of duty does no more than provide the occasion for loss, it is not considered to be causative and the loss cannot be recovered.[31]

The damages for losses caused by the negligently spoken or written work will normally be confined to economic loss sustained by those who rely on the accuracy of the information or advice they receive as a basis for action.[32]

In addition to that basic level of damages, "actual losses directly flowing" from the tort may also be recoverable in cases where deceit or Section 2(1) Misrepresentation Act 1967 are relied upon.

In cases of a failure to render services the basic loss is the price the claimant would have to pay in the market place in order to obtain the services

---

[30] *Target Holdings v. Redferns* [1996] 1 AC 421.
[31] *Galoo v. Bright Grahame Murray* [1994] 1 WLR 1360.
[32] *Caparo Industries plc v. Dickman and Others* [1990] 2 WLR 358, p. 366, per Lord Bridge of Harwich.

contracted for deducting the contract price, if not already paid.[33] The cost of re-doing the accountant's defective work is a recoverable head of damages.[34]

Actions based on figures produced by accountants on an over-valuation or other disadvantageous acquisition will be compensated by damages to the value of the difference between what the claimant paid and the true value at the time of the purchase, that is, unless there has been a warranty by the vendor or the accountant as to the true value of the item.[35] It is therefore the whole transaction on which compensation is based. An over-valuation of one part may be counter-balanced by an under-valuation of another and it would be incorrect to isolate these items.[36]

Where a penalty arises through the accountant acting in a way so as to induce or cause his principal to incur such a penalty (such as delays in preparing tax returns), it is possible to recover that penalty in damages for breach of contract against the accountant much as could be done against a principal's agent.[37] The tax itself is not recoverable as this would or should have been paid by the claimant in any event.

An interesting question is whether the interest element claimed by the Inland Revenue under Section 88 of the Taxes Management Act 1970 could be recovered as part of the damages as a penalty.

It has been argued that the interest cannot be recovered as part of damages as it is not imposed under the penalty provisions under Part X of that Act and merely reflects the recoupment of interest on the tax the tax payer could have earned whilst he delayed paying the money to Her Majesty's Revenue and Customs.

The author respectfully suggests that this argument is flawed and the interest is properly considered wholly as a penalty in its own right and therefore a reasonably foreseeable loss which would flow from the breach of care. Factors supporting such an interpretation are:

- the interest does not attempt to be a reflection of current commercial interest rates

---

[33] *Monarch SS v. Kalishamns Oljefabriker* [1949] AC 196.
[34] *Tormont Holdings v. Thorne Gunn & Helliwell* (1975) 62 DLR (3d) 465.
[35] *Esso Petroleum v. Mardon* [1976] QB 801: the court made no distinction in this case in assessing damages under the contractual warranty or the negligent misstatement but calculated the loss on the basis of restoring the capital that had been lost as a result.
[36] AM Dugdale & KM Stanton *Professional Negligence*, 2nd Edition, p.350.
[37] *Osman v. Moss* [1970] 1 Lloyds Rep 313.

- The historical punitive formulation of that section as "due to the fraud, wilful default or neglect of any person"[38]
- The fact that the Board has a discretion to mitigate the interest imposed and so the obligation to pay is not strict and can be influenced by external factors[39]
- No tax benefits arise out of payment of the interest under this section - it is not taken into account when assessing income, profits or losses.[40]

Damages will not lie for loss of reputation of itself on a claim for negligent accountancy work. A claim for mere loss of reputation is the proper subject of an action for defamation and cannot ordinarily be sustained by any other form of action - so saying, if pecuniary loss can be established, the mere fact that the pecuniary loss is brought about by the loss of reputation caused by a breach of contract is not sufficient to preclude the claimant from recovering in respect of that pecuniary loss.[41] However, the categories of matters where pecuniary loss was recovered that have been held to fall into this have tended to be limited to promotional contracts or, in one case, a failure to sustain the claimant's financial credit.[42] It has been argued that a nominal figure could be claimed for any difficulties the claimant might experience in the future when dealing with the Inland Revenue.[43]

A claim in damages for distress and inconvenience arising out of the investigations that necessarily arose out of the accountant's negligence is probably too remote to be recoverable.[44] Taking the analogy with solicitors in negligent litigation, it seems that a "clear distinction is drawn between mental distress which is an inevitable consequence to the client of the misconduct of litigation by his solicitor on the one hand, and mental distress which is the direct and inevitable consequence of the solicitor's failure to obtain the very relief which it was the sole purpose of the litigation to secure on the other".[45] Similarly, no claim arises in contract under this head.[46]

---

[38] This was removed by Section 159(1),(2),(4) Finance Act 1989.
[39] Section 88(4), Taxes Management Act 1970.
[40] Section 90, Taxes Management Act 1970.
[41] *Foaminol Laboratories v. British Artid Plastics* [1941] 2 All ER 393, 399-400.
[42] *Wilson v. United Counties Bank* [1920] AC 102.
[43] Dugdale Stanton, *Professional Negligence*, paragraph 20.16. The author can find no case law authority expressly supporting this proposition.
[44] *Cook v. Swifen* [1967] 1 WLR 457.
[45] *Heywood v. Wellers* [1976] QB 446, 463H-464A, per Bridge LJ.
[46] *Groom v. Crocker* [1939] 1 KB 194.

4.1.7 Limitation

Any action founded on simple contract must be brought within six years of the date upon which the cause of action accrued.[47] In contract the cause of action accrues on the date on which the breach of contract (as opposed to the loss[48]) occurred.[49] Where the breach is through a failure to act, the breach is deemed to have occurred after the accountant has been given a reasonable time to perform his duty but had failed to do so.[50]

The normal period of limitation for an action founded on tort is six years from the date on which the cause of action accrued.[51] Since a cause of action may accrue without the knowledge of the injured party[52] the six-year period may expire before he is able to bring proceedings. In actions for negligence in which the cause of action accrues before the potential claimant knows the relevant facts,[53] section 14A therefore prescribes an additional period of three years from the date on which he acquires such knowledge.

The latent damage provisions under section 14A Limitation Act 1980 apply to negligence and negligent misstatement and create an alternative limitation period of three years whose starting date is the earliest date on which the claimant had both the knowledge required for bringing an action for damages and the right to bring the action. The date of knowledge means the knowledge of the material facts about the damage as would lead a reasonable person who had suffered that damage to consider it sufficiently serious to justify his instituting proceedings against a defendant who did not dispute liability and was able to satisfy judgement[54] and that the damage was attributable to the defendant and the defendant's identity.[55]

Damage is an essential element in a cause of action for negligence and thus the Claimant has no cause of action in negligence until he has suffered damage in consequence of the accountant's negligence.[56] For the cause of action for negligence to accrue 'actual' damage must be shown – something

---

[47] Section 5, Limitation Act 1980.
[48] The breach perfects the claim because breach of itself gives rise to a claim for nominal damages.
[49] *Gibbs v Guild* (1882) 9 QBD 259.
[50] *Bell v Peter Browne & Co* [1990] 2 QB 495.
[51] S. 2, Limitation Act 1980.
[52] Cartledge (Widow and Administratrix of the Estate of Fred Hector Cartledge (decd)) v. E Jopling & Sons Ltd [1963] AC 758.
[53] *Forster v. Outred & Co (a firm)* [1982] 1 WLR 86.
[54] Section 14A(7), Limitation Act 1980.
[55] Section 14A(8), Limitation Act 1980, *Haward v. Fawcetts* [2006] 1 WLR 682.
[56] *Law Society v. Sephton* [2006] 3 All ER 401.

which is to his immediate, measurable economic disadvantage.[57] Where however the financial crystallisation of all of that damage is dependent on the happening of some other unfulfilled event, the limitation period will not start to run until that contingent event has occurred.[58]

The only occasion (other than one where the claimant is under a disability) that can suspend the operation of the limitation period in contract is where the claimant was rendered unaware of his claim through fraud, concealment or mistake.[59]

Any action for breach of fiduciary duty must be brought within six years of the date of the breach of trust.[60]

4.1.8 Exclusion clauses

A further way in which an accountant may attempt to limit his exposure is by including exclusion clauses in his contract of retainer or, in respect of third parties, by including disclaimers on the reports prepared. Exclusion clauses will only be enforceable in so far as they are deemed reasonable.[61] Moreover the author suggests it is conceivable that an excessive use of disclaimers could raise issues as to whether the accountant had performed enough to satisfy his contractual obligations at all.

Excessive use of disclaimers is to be discouraged, not merely because they may be ineffective or inappropriate, but because excessive hedging with disclaimers may render the report meaningless to others and valueless to the client.

Moreover (and whilst this a matter dealt in greater depth with elsewhere in this work) auditors are unable to exclude liability for negligence.[62] The Companies Act 2006 retains the principle that any provision, whether contained in a company's article or in any contract with the company or otherwise is void insofar that it exempts any officer of the company or any person (whether an officer or not) employed by the company as an auditor from or indemnifying him against any liability by virtue of any rule of law which would otherwise attach to him in respect of any negligence, default,

---

[57] *Forster v. Outred & Co (a firm)* [1982] 1 WLR 86 at 94 and *Nykredit Mortgage Bank plc v. Edward Erdman Group Ltd (No 2)* [1997] 1 WLR 1627 at 1630, 1631, 1632.
[58] *Law Society v. Sephton* [2006] 3 All ER 401.
[59] Section 32, Limitation Act 1980.
[60] Section 21, Limitation Act 1980.
[61] Section 2 Unfair Contract Terms Act 1977.
[62] Section 310(2) Companies Act 1985.

breach of duty or breach of trust of which he may be guilty in relation to the company.[63]

It will however permit the company to indemnify the auditor for costs incurred when successfully defending proceedings or to obtain relief in cases of honest and reasonable conduct.[64] A further exception to this rule is that the Act will also permit the company and the auditor to enter into liability limitation agreements.[65] To be effective the liability limitation agreement must be approved by the members of the company at the material time,[66] be limited to a single financial year[67] and stipulate the year it is to apply to.[68] Reference will need to be made to the agreement in the accounts and in the directors' report.[69] Even then the agreement will only be effective to limit the auditor's liability to the extent that it is fair and reasonable, having regard to the auditor's statutory responsibilities, the nature and purpose of the auditor's contractual duties to the company and his professional standards rather than the recoverability of compensation from other persons.[70]

---

[63] Section 532 Companies Act 2006
[64] Section 532(2) Companies Act 2006
[65] Section 532(2) Companies Act 2006
[66] Section 534(2)(b) and 536 Companies Act 2006
[67] Section 535(1)(a) Companies Act 2006
[68] Section 535(1)(b) Companies Act 2006
[69] Section 538 Companies Act 2006
[70] Section 537 Companies Act 2006.

Chapter 5

AUDITORS AND REPORTING ACCOUNTANTS

5.1 THE ACCOUNTANT AS AUDITOR

5.1.1 The Audit of Companies

Presently most smaller companies are now exempt from the requirement of undertaking an audit. The total exemption conditions are met by a company in respect of a financial year if:[1]

- it qualifies as a small company in relation to that year[2]
- its turnover in that year is not more than £5.6 million, and
- its balance sheet total for that year is not more than £2.8 million.

A company may by special resolution render itself exempt from the provisions of the Companies Act 1985 relating to the audits of accounts if the company has been dormant from the time of its formation or if the company has been dormant since the end of the previous financial year and

1. is entitled in respect of its individual accounts for that year to the exemptions conferred by Section 246 of a small company or would be so entitled but for being a member of an ineligible group; and

2. is not required to prepare group accounts for that year on the passing of a special resolution at a general meeting of that company.[3]

A company is "dormant" during a period in which no significant accounting transaction occurs that is to say no transaction which is required by Section 221 Companies Act 1985 to be entered in the company's accounting records

---

[1] Section 249A (1) and (3) Companies Act 1985, section 477 Companies Act 2006.
[2] It needs to satisfy the test for a "small company" under section 246 Companies Act 1985, section 382 Companies Act 2006.
[3] Section 249A Companies Act 1985, section 477 Companies Act 2006

and such a company ceases to be dormant on the occurrence of such a transaction.[4]

5.1.1.1 Where the exception does not apply

A company will not be able to be able to benefit from the exemptions from audit available to small companies[5] or dormant companies[6] if:[7]

- it was a public company,
- it was a person who had permission under Part 4 of the Financial Services and Markets Act 2000 to carry on a regulated activity,
- it carried on an insurance market activity,
- it was an appointed representative, within the meaning of section 39 of the Financial Services and Markets Act 2000 (unless its scope of appointment is limited to activities that are not regulated activities)
- it was a special register body[8] or an employers' association[9]
- it was a parent company or a subsidiary undertaking.

Under the Companies Act 2006 the dormant companies' exemption is expressed[10] as being excluded to

- Authorised insurance companies
- ISD investment firms
- Banking companies
- UCTIS management companies
- e-money issuers
- Companies which carry on insurance market activities

Under the Companies Act 2006 the small companies' exemption is expressed[11] as being excluded to

- Public companies
- Authorised insurance companies

---

[4] Section 250 (3) Companies Act 1985, 396 Companies Act 2006.
[5] Section 249A Companies Act 1985, section 477 Companies Act 2006.
[6] Section 249AA Companies Act 1985.
[7] Section 249B Companies Act 1985.
[8] Section 117, Trade Union and Labour Relations (Consolidation) Act 1992.
[9] Section 122, Trade Union and Labour Relations (Consolidation) Act 1992.
[10] Section 481 Companies Act 2006.
[11] Section 478 Companies Act 2006.

- ISD investment firms
- Banking companies
- UCTIS management companies
- e-money issuers
- Companies which carry on insurance market activities
- special register body[12] or an employers' association[13]

5.1.1.2 Special rules regarding Banking companies

A banking company must prepare its individual accounts in accordance with Schedule 9 rather than Schedule 4 of the Companies Act 1985.[14] The accounts must contain a statement that they are prepared in accordance with the special provisions relating to banking companies.[15]

5.1.1.3 Special rules regarding Insurance Companies

The accounts and balance sheet of every insurance company must be audited in the prescribed manner by a person of the prescribed description and the provisions of the Companies Act 1985 relating to audit subjects are applicable subject to such adaptation and modifications as may be necessary or expedient in the light of the special regulations relating to the audit insurance companies.[16]

An insurance company must prepare its individual accounts in accordance with Schedule 9A rather than Schedule 4 Companies Act 1985.[17] The accounts must contain a statement that they are prepared in accordance with the special provisions relating to insurance companies.[18]

5.1.2 An auditor is a creature of statute

An auditor must be an accountant, but an accountant is not necessarily an auditor. A person is not qualified for appointment as an auditor unless he is either:

a. a member of a recognised supervisory body and eligible for appointment by that body,[19] or

---

[12] Section 117, Trade Union and Labour Relations (Consolidation) Act 1992.
[13] Section 122, Trade Union and Labour Relations (Consolidation) Act 1992.
[14] Section 255 (1) Companies Act 1985, section 396 Companies Act 2006.
[15] Section 255 (3) Companies Act 1985, section 396 Companies Act 2006.
[16] Section 21 (1) Insurance Companies Act 1982.
[17] Section 255 (2) Companies Act 1985, section 396 Companies Act 2006.
[18] Section 255 (3) Companies Act 1985, section 396 Companies Act 2006.
[19] Section 25(1) Companies Act 1989, section 1212, Companies Act 2006.

b. he is for the time being authorised by the Secretary of State to be appointed either as having similar qualifications obtained outside the UK or else retains authorisation granted by the Board of Trade or the Secretary of State under earlier legislation.[20]

A person whose only appropriate qualification is that he retains authorisation granted by the Board of Trade or the Secretary of State under the old Section 13(1) of the Companies Act 1967 is eligible only for appointment as auditor of an unquoted company.[21] Such a person would not be authorised for appointment as an auditor of a company that carries on business as a promoter of a trading stamp scheme within the meaning of the Trading Stamp Act 1964.[22]

5.1.3 The Regulatory Framework

The Financial Reporting Council has assumed the functions of the Accountancy Foundation (which included the Auditing Practices Board). The Financial Reporting Council's new Auditing Practices Board has taken over responsibility for setting standards for the independence, objectivity and integrity for registered auditors from the professional bodies. The combination of the Financial Reporting Council and the Accountancy Foundation took formal effect on 1st April 2004 and during 2003 much of APB's effort was directed towards developing standards on auditor independence, objectivity and integrity. The FRC is jointly funded by the CCAB, the City and the Government. It is envisaged that the Secretary of State will in the future take steps to delegate to Financial Reporting Council the Secretary of State's statutory power to grant and revoke an institute's status as a qualifying body.[23]

The bodies of accountants who are for the time being recognised as qualifying bodies for these purposes by the Secretary of State[24] are:

- Institute of Chartered Accountants in England and Wales
- Institute of Chartered Accountants in Scotland
- Institute of Chartered Accountants in Ireland
- Association of Chartered Certified Accountants
- Association of International Accountants.

---

[20] The Association of Authorised Public Accountants was formed in 1978 to represent the interests of those statutory auditors who were individually authorised under this section.
[21] Section 34(1) Companies Act 1989, section 1212(2) Companies Act 2006.
[22] Section 34(3) Companies Act 1989, section 1212(2), Companies Act 2006.
[23] Schedule 12 Companies Act 1989, section 1219 Companies Act 2006.
[24] Schedule 12, Companies Act 1989.

Members of the Association of International Accountants are recognised for these purposes by the Secretary of State. However, the Association does not act as a supervisory body in its own right; members are currently supervised by the Institute of Chartered Accountants in England and Wales.[25]

Members of the Association of Authorised Public Accountants are entitled to apply for an ACCA auditing certificate for their firms which are issued under the ACCA Practising Regulations (which closely follow the AAPA's own Qualification and Audit Regulations). Audit work constitutes public practice for authorised public accountants and an audit certificate or practising certificate is required for members engaged in audit work.[26]

The Supervisory Bodies regulate the eligibility of persons for appointment as a statutory auditor and the conduct of statutory audit work.[27] The recognised supervisory bodies must keep and make available for the public the following information in relation to each firm eligible under its rules for appointment as company auditor:

- where the firm is a body corporate, the name and address of each person who is a director of the body and holds any shares in it
- where the firm is a partnership, the name and address of each of the partners indicating which of those persons mentioned is responsible for the company audit work on behalf of the firm.[28]

The register is to be kept at the principal office in the United Kingdom of the recognised supervisory body and must be open to inspection by any persons for a period of at least two hours between the hours 9.00 am and 5.00 pm on any business day.[29] The recognised supervisory body must ensure the register may be inspected both alphabetically and by reference to the recognised supervisory bodies. The recognised supervisory body may charge a fee for the inspection of the register or any part of it of not more than £2.50 for each hour or part of an hour conducting an inspection. The public is able to inspect the information held by the recognised supervisory body.[30]

---

[25] (1994) 8 Accountancy 12.
[26] Byelaw 10 AAPA Qualification and Audit Regulations 1991.
[27] Part II Companies Act 1989, section 1217 Companies Act 2006.
[28] Regulation 3 Companies Act 1989 (Register of Auditors and Information about Audit Firms) Regulations 1991.
[29] Regulation 5 Companies Act 1989 (Register of Auditors and Information about Audit Firms) Regulations 1991.
[30] Regulations 5 & 6(4) Companies Act 1989 (Register of Auditors and Information about Audit Firms) Regulations 1991.

The public are also entitled to make copies of any entries in the register although the recognised supervisory body may charge for copies a fee not exceeding 5p per entry.[31]

5.1.4 Who may be appointed as an auditor?

Recognised professional bodies are required to keep a register of individuals and firms eligible for appointment as company auditors and the individuals holding appropriate qualifications who are responsible for company audit work on behalf of such firms.[32] Such entries must give the name and address, and in the case of a person eligible to be appointed as a company auditor, the name of the relevant supervisory body.[33] The recognised supervisory bodies must keep a register of the individuals and firms eligible for appointment as company auditor and the individuals holding appropriate qualifications who are responsible for company audit work on behalf of such firms.[34] Each person's entry in the register gives his name and address and the name of the relevant supervisory body.[35] Each recognised supervisory body must take reasonable care to ensure that at all times the register accurately states the individuals and firms eligible for appointment as company auditor under its rules and the individuals holding an appropriate qualification who are registered for company audit work on behalf of such firms, the names and addresses shown on the register and its name as it appears on the register by virtue of Regulation 2(2) (b).[36]

The Secretary of State has power to declare that persons qualified to audit accounts under the law of a foreign country or territory outside the United Kingdom or who hold the specific foreign professional qualification recognised overseas can be regarded as holding an approved overseas qualification which will entitle them to a status equivalent of holding a recognised professional qualification to act as an auditor.[37]

A firm may be appointed as an auditor.[38]

---

[31] Regulation 7 (2).
[32] Section 35(1) Companies Act 1989, section 1239 Companies Act 2006 envisages that the Secretary of State will address this by making regulations.
[33] Section 35(2) Companies Act 1989 section 1239 Companies Act 2006 envisages that the Secretary of State will address this by making regulations.
[34] Regulation (1) Companies Act 1989 (Register of Auditors and Information about Audit Firms) Regulations 1991.
[35] Regulation (2) Companies Act 1989 (Register of Auditors and Information about Audit Firms) Regulations 1991.
[36] Regulation 3 (2) Companies Act 1989 (Register of Auditors and Information about Audit Firms) Regulations 1991.
[37] Section 33(1) (2) Companies Act 1989, section 1219 Companies act 2006.
[38] Section 25(2) Companies Act 1989, section 1216 Companies Act 2006.

5.1.5 Who may not be appointed as an auditor?

No person shall act as a company auditor if he has become ineligible for appointment to that office.[39] If, during his term of office as company auditor the auditor becomes ineligible for appointment to that office, he must immediately resign as auditor and give notice in writing to the company concerned that he has resigned because of ineligibility.[40] A person who acts as a company auditor in contravention of Section 28(1) or who fails to give notice on vacating his office as required by Sub-section 28(2), is guilty of an offence.[41]

A person is ineligible for appointment as a company auditor of a company if he is:

a. an officer or employee of the company (for this purpose, an auditor of the company is not regarded as an officer or employee of the company[42]), or

b. a partner or employee of such a person or partnership of which such a person is a partner, or

c. if he is ineligible by virtue of paras. (a) and (b) for appointment as a company auditor of an associated undertaking of the company.

The Secretary of State has powers to stipulate by regulation descriptions of connection between potential auditors or any associate of his and the company or any associated undertaking that may make him ineligible for appointment as auditor of a company.[43]

An associated undertaking in relation to a company means:

a. a parent undertaking or subsidiary undertaking of the company, or

b. a subsidiary undertaking of any parent undertaking of the company.[44]

---

[39] Section 28 (1) Companies Act 1989, section 1213(1) Companies Act 2006.
[40] Section 28 (2) Companies Act 1989, section 1213(2) Companies Act 2006
[41] Section 28 (3) Companies Act 1989, section 1213(3) Companies Act 2006.
[42] Section 27 (1) Companies Act 1989, section 1214(5) Companies Act 2006.
[43] Section 27 (2) Companies Act 1989, section 1214(4) Companies Act 2006.
[44] Section 27 (3) Companies Act 1989, section 1214(6) Companies Act 2006.

Where the auditor is a person, an associate means his spouse, child or stepchild or any body corporate of which the auditor is director and any employee or partner of his. Under the Companies Act 2006 the definition is extended to include civil partners. In relation to a corporate auditor, "associate" means any parent company or subsidiary of the auditor, or of which the auditor is a director, and any employee or partner of that body or body corporate in the same group.[45]

5.1.6 Consequences of appointing an ineligible auditor

Where a person appointed an auditor of a company was, for any part of the period during which the audit was conducted, ineligible for appointment as an auditor of the company, the Secretary of State may require the company to engage the services of somebody who is eligible for that appointment. The company has twenty one days in which to comply with that direction.[46] In those circumstances the person engaged must either audit the relevant accounts again or review the first audit and report (giving his reasons) whether a second audit is needed.

5.1.7 Misuse of the name or qualifications of auditor

It is an offence for a person whose name does not appear on the register of auditors kept by a recognised professional body to describe himself as a registered auditor or to hold himself out as such or to indicate or be reasonably understood to indicate that he is a registered auditor.[47] It is also an offence for a body which is not a recognised supervisory or qualifying body to describe itself as so recognised or to describe itself or hold itself out as or indicate or indeed be reasonably understood to indicate that it is so recognised.[48]

Furthermore an offence is committed by furnishing information when applying to become a registered auditor or comply with other requirements imposed upon him under the Companies Act 1989 in connection with becoming a registered auditor if he furnishes information which he knows to be false or misleading in a material particular or recklessly furnishes information which is false or misleading in a material particular.[49]

---

[45] Section 52 Companies Act 1989, section 1260 Companies Act 2006.
[46] Section 29 (1) Companies Act 1989, section 1248 Companies Act 2006.
[47] Section 41(2) Companies Act 1989, section 1250 Companies Act 2006.
[48] Section 41(3) Companies Act 1989, section 1250(4) Companies Act 2006.
[49] Section 41(1) Companies Act 1989, section 1250(1) Companies Act 2006.

5.1.8 Companies Act 2006

After the implementation of the Companies Act 2006, the auditor's report will need to be signed a by a Senior Statutory Auditor in his own name on behalf of the audit firm.[50]

The Senior Statutory Auditor means the person identified by the firm as the senior statutory auditor in line with the relevant standards[51] The Senior Statutory Auditor needs to be a person who is eligible for appointment as an auditor in his own right.[52]

Every copy of the auditor's report will need to disclose the name of the auditor and (where applicable) also the name of the Senior Statutory Auditor.[53] The name can be omitted if (a) there is reasonable grounds to believe that its inclusion would expose the auditor or any other person to a serious risk of violence or intimidation (b) the company resolves to remove the auditor's name from the report and (c) the notice is given to the Secretary of State of the resolution, the name and number of the company, the financial year to which this relates, the name of the auditor and of the person who signed the report as Senior Statutory Auditor.[54] The presence of the Senior Statutory Auditor's name on the audit will not of itself give rise to any personal civil liability for the audit for him.[55]

Two new offences are created. It is an offence for any person to knowingly or recklessly cause an auditor's report on annual accounts to include any matter that is misleading, false or deceptive in any material particular. It is also an offence to omit any of the statements required under section 498 Companies Act 2006.[56] These are respectively, statements that

- the company's accounts do not agree with accounting records and returns,
- that the necessary information have not been obtained and
- that the directors had wrongfully taken advantage of the exemption from the obligation to prepare group accounts

---

[50] Section 504 Companies Act 2006.
[51] Section 504(1) Companies Act 2006.
[52] Section 504(2) Companies Act 2006.
[53] Section 505(1) Companies Act 2006.
[54] Section 506(2) Companies Act 2006.
[55] Section 504(3) Companies Act 2006.
[56] Section 507 (2) Companies Act 2006.

The offences can be committed by a director, member, employee or agent of the audit firm or where the auditor is an individual by himself, his agent or his employee.

5.2 THE CONTRACT WITH THE AUDITOR

5.2.1 An auditor's office is one of supervision

The role of the auditor in law was succinctly summarised by Lord Justice Bingham in the Court of Appeal haring of *Caparo Industries plc v. Dickman and Others.*[57]

> The members, or the shareholders, of any company are its owners. But they are too numerous, and in most cases too unskilled, to undertake the day to day management of what they own. So responsibility for day to day management of the company is delegated to the directors. The shareholders, despite their overall powers of control, are for most of the time investors and little more. But it would of course be unsatisfactory and open to abuse if the shareholder received no report on the financial stewardship of their investment save from those to whom the stewardship had been entrusted. Supervision is made for the company in general meeting to appoint an auditor (Section 384 of the Companies Act 1985), whose duty is to investigate and form an opinion on the adequacy of the company's accounting records and returns and the correspondence between the company's accounting records and returns and its accounts: Section 237. The auditor then has to report to the company's members (among other things) whether in his opinion the company's accounts give a true and fair view of the company's financial position: Section 236. In carrying out his investigation and in forming his opinion the auditor necessarily works very closely with the directors and officers of the company. He receives his remuneration from the company. He naturally and rightly, regards the company as his client. But he is empowered by the company to exercise his professional skill and judgement for the purpose of giving the shareholders an independent report on the reliability of the company's accounts and thus on their investment. 'No doubt he is acting antagonistically to the directors in the sense he is appointed by the shareholders to check upon them': *In re Kingston Mill Co.* [1896] 1 Ch 6, 11 per Vaughan Williams LJ. The auditor's report must be read before the company in general meeting and must be open to inspection by any member of the company: Section 241. It is attached to and forms part of the company's accounts: Section 238(3) and 239. A copy of the company's accounts, including the auditor's report, must be sent to every member. Section 240. Any member of the company, even if not entitled to have a copy of the accounts sent to him, is entitled to be furnished with a copy of the company's last accounts on demand and without charge: Section 246.

---

[57] [1989] QB 653, pp. 680-681.

5.2.2 An auditor's contract is with the company that appoints him

The auditor's contact is with the company.[58]

The auditor is elected by the shareholders of the company at a general meeting at which accounts are laid.[59]

The only exception to this is that the first directors of the company have the power to appoint auditors who can serve up until the conclusion of the first general meeting at which accounts are laid.[60] In default, that power is exercised by the company in general meeting.[61]

Under the Companies Act 2006, the appointment of the auditors for private companies will be deemed automatically renewed at the end of each period[62] unless

- The auditor was appointed by the directors
- The company's articles require actual reappointment of the auditors
- The members resolve that the auditor should not be reappointed
- The members representing 5% (or such other percentage as the articles of association may stipulate) of the voting rights prevent reappointment by giving notice[63]
- The directors have resolved that no auditor be reappointed for the financial year in question.[64]

5.2.3 An auditor is not the agent of the company that appoints him

An auditor does not perform his statutory duties as the agent of the client company.[65] Thus any knowledge that the auditor acquires when auditing the company cannot be attributed to the members of the company, such as information over a director's unauthorised acts.[66]

---

[58] The duty is placed on the company to both to appoint the auditor: Section 384(1) Companies Act 1985 (sections 485 and 489 Companies Act 2006), and to pay the auditor: Section 390A Companies Act 1985 (section 492 Companies Act 2006).
[59] Section 385(2) Companies Act 1985; for public companies, section 489(2) Companies Act 2006.
[60] Section 385(3) Companies Act 1985; for public companies, section 489(3) Companies Act 2006, for private companies, section 485(3) Companies Act 2006.
[61] Section 385(4) Companies Act 1985; for public companies, section 489(3) Companies Act 2006, for private companies section 485(5) Companies Act 2006.
[62] Section 487(2) Companies Act 2006.
[63] Section 488 Companies Act 2006.
[64] Section 487(2)(a)-(e) Companies Act 2006.
[65] *Re Transplanters (Holding Co) Ltd* [1958] 1 WLR 822.
[66] *Leeds Estate Building Investment Co v. Shepherd* (1887) 36 Ch D 787.

5.2.4 The auditor's certificate must be certain

An auditor's certificate must be certain.[67] It should either certify a particular value or not certify at all.[68]

5.2.5 Extent of the contractual freedom in the appointment of an auditor

Outside his statutory duty and the provisions of the articles of association of the company, the role of the auditor can be extended by the terms of his engagement.[69]

There are limits on this however. An auditor's statutory duties cannot be limited or abated by the articles or a contract. An auditor moreover cannot limit his liability by an exclusion clause and any provision is ineffective to the extent that it exempts an auditor from liability in respect of any negligence, default, breach of duty or breach of trust of which he may be guilty in relation to the company.[70]

The Companies Act 2006 retains the principle that any provision, whether contained in a company's article or in any contract with the company or otherwise is void insofar that it exempts any officer of the company or any person (whether an officer or not) employed by the company as an auditor from or indemnifying him against any liability by virtue of any rule of law which would otherwise attach to him in respect of any negligence, default, breach of duty or breach of trust of which he may be guilty in relation to the company[71]. It will however permit the company to indemnify the auditor for costs incurred when successfully defending proceedings or to obtain relief in cases of honest and reasonable conduct.[72] A further exception to this rule is that the Act will also permit the company and the auditor to enter into liability limitation agreements.[73]

---

[67] *Shorrock Ltd v. Meggitt plc* [1991] BCC 471.
[68] *Shorrock Ltd v. Meggitt plc* [1991] BCC 471.
[69] *Re City Equitable Fire Insurance Co. Ltd* [1925] Ch 407, per Pollock MR
[70] Section 310 Companies Act 1985.
[71] Section 532 Companies Act 2006
[72] Section 532(2) Companies Act 2006
[73] Section 532(2) Companies Act 2006

5.3 TERMINATION OF AN AUDITOR'S APPOINTMENT

5.3.1 The Duration of the auditor's appointment

The auditor is elected by the shareholders of the company at a general meeting at which accounts are laid.[74]

The first directors of the company have the power to appoint auditors who can serve up until the conclusion of the first general meeting at which accounts are laid.[75] In default, that power is exercised by the company in general meeting.[76]

5.3.2 The office of auditor may be terminated by a failure to re-appoint

The office of auditor may be terminated by a failure to re-appoint.

If the company has elected to dispense with the annual appointment of its auditors,[77] a member may, once in any financial year, by notice deposited at the company's registered office, propose that the appointment of the company's auditors be brought to an end.[78]

Where such a notice is deposited, the directors are placed under a duty to convene a general meeting within 28 days of the notice being given and propose that the appointment of the company's auditors be brought to an end.[79] If the directors fail to convene a meeting themselves within 14 days of the deposit of the notice, the member himself may convene a meeting in the manner that the directors would have at any stage within three months of his giving the notice.[80] The member can seek reimbursement by the company for any expenses he has incurred as a result of the default and the company may in turn recoup this from the defaulting directors.[81]

If the resolution is passed, then the office of the auditors is deemed to come to an end at the next date when they would have been deemed re-appointed. Where the notice has been given after the distribution of the accounts, any

---

[74] Section 385(2) Companies Act 1985; section 489(2) Companies Act 2006.
[75] Section 385(3) Companies Act 1985; for public companies, section 489(3) Companies Act 2006, for private companies, section 485(3) Companies Act 2006.
[76] Section 385(4) Companies Act 1985; for public companies, section 489(3) Companies Act 2006, for private companies section 485(5) Companies Act 2006.
[77] Section 386 Companies Act 1985, repealed under Companies Act 2006.
[78] Section 393(1) Companies Act 1985, repealed under Companies Act 2006.
[79] Section 393(2) Companies Act 1985, repealed under Companies Act 2006.
[80] Section 393(4) and (5) Companies Act 1985, repealed under Companies Act 2006.
[81] Section 393(6) Companies Act 1985, repealed under Companies Act 2006.

deemed re-appointment for the financial year following that to which the accounts relate shall be deemed to cease to have effect.[82]

No damages may be paid for termination of an auditor's appointment in this manner.[83]

Where the resignation takes the form of a failure to seek re-appointment, the statement must be deposited not less than 14 days before the end of the time allowed for the appointment of the next auditor.[84]

Under the Companies Act 2006, the appointment of the auditors for private companies will be deemed automatically renewed at the end of each period[85] unless

- The auditor was appointed by the directors
- The company's articles require actual reappointment of the auditors
- The members resolve that the auditor should not be reappointed
- The members representing 5% (or such other percentage as the articles of association may stipulate) of the voting rights prevent reappointment by giving notice[86]
- The directors have resolved that no auditor be reappointed for the financial year in question.[87]

Both the board and the members are empowered under the Companies Act 2006 to fill vacancies for auditors if the other fails to appoint one.[88] Default provisions are built in to the Companies Act 2006 for both public[89] and private[90] limited companies to empower the Secretary of State to appoint an auditor where the company has failed to do so itself.

---

[82] Section 393(3) Companies Act 1985, repealed under Companies Act 2006.
[83] Section 393(7) Companies Act 1985, repealed under Companies Act 2006.
[84] Section 394(4) Companies Act 1985, repealed under Companies Act 2006.
[85] Section 487(2) Companies Act 2006.
[86] Section 488 Companies Act 2006.
[87] Section 487(2)(a)-(e) Companies Act 2006.
[88] For private companies section 485(4)(5) Companies Act 2006, for public companies section 489(4)(5) Companies Act 2006.
[89] Section 490 Companies Act 2006.
[90] Section 486 Companies Act 2006.

5.3.3 The office of auditor may be terminated by an ordinary resolution of the company

A company may remove an auditor from office by an ordinary resolution notwithstanding any agreement to the contrary.[91] Special notice is required for the resolution if it is to remove the auditor before the expiry of his term of office or for the appointment of a person other than a retiring auditor.[92]

This will not prevent the auditor from seeking damages for breach of contract.[93]

Within 14 days of the auditor's office terminating, the auditor must serve on the company's registered office a statement outlining the circumstances in which he ceased to hold office which he considers should be brought to the attention of the shareholders or creditors of the company, or (if there are no such circumstances) a statement to that effect.[94]

5.3.4 The office of auditor may be terminated by resignation

An auditor may resign from his office as auditor. To do so, he would need to deposit a notice of his resignation at the company's registered office.[95]

It is not effective unless[96] it is accompanied at the same time by a statement outlining the circumstances in which he ceased to hold office which he considers should be brought to the attention of the shareholders or creditors of the company, or (if there are no such circumstances) a statement to that effect.[97]

Under section 511 Companies Act 2006 the auditor must be afforded an opportunity to make representations to the shareholders and, unless representations are received too late or permission is given by the court, these must be circulated to members or failing which, read out at the meeting.

If there are circumstances that the auditor thinks should be brought to the attention of the shareholders or creditors of the company, he may

---

[91] Section 391 Companies Act 1985, section 510(1) (2) Companies Act 2006.
[92] Section 391 Companies Act 1985, section 510(2) and 511 Companies Act 2006.
[93] Section 391(3) Companies Act 1985, section 510(3) Companies Act 2006.
[94] Section 394(1) Companies Act 1985.
[95] Section 392(1) Companies Act 1985.
[96] Section 392(1) Companies Act 1985.
[97] Section 394(1) Companies Act 1985.

- by a signed requisition, require the directors to call an Extra Ordinary General Meeting so that the statement can be considered before it
- require the company to circulate to its shareholders a statement in writing of the circumstances surrounding his resignation.

The company must (unless the statement is received too late for it to comply) disclose that the statement has been made in the notice calling the meeting and circulate a copy of the notice to every member to whom notice of the meeting has been sent.[98] The directors must within 21 days of the auditor serving the requisition serve a notice convening the meeting on a date not more than 28 days from the date of that notice. Failure to take all reasonable steps to ensure that a strict timetable is complied with is a criminal offence and places the company's directors at risk of a fine.[99]

If the statement has not been disclosed, the auditor may require that the statement of circumstances be read out at the meeting.[100]

5.3.5 The statement of circumstances of the termination

It is the duty of the auditor on any termination of his office to serve on the company's registered office a statement outlining the circumstances in which he ceased to hold office which he considers should be brought to the attention of the shareholders or creditors of the company. Where he takes the view that there are no such circumstances, he must serve a statement to that effect.[101]

Failure to comply is a criminal offence.[102] It is a defence to the offence that the auditor took all reasonable steps and exercised all due diligence to avoid commission of the offence.[103] Where the auditor is a company or a partnership, the court has powers to look behind the corporate structure and bring similar proceedings against its actual or *de facto* directors, company secretary, managers,[104] partners, shareholders and shadow directors if the

---

[98] Section 392(4) Companies Act 1985.
[99] Section 392A(5) Companies Act 1985.
[100] Section 392A(6) Companies Act 1985.
[101] Section 394(1) Companies Act 1985.
[102] Section 394A Companies Act 1985: the offence carries a fine.
[103] Section 394A(2) Companies Act 1985.
[104] In *R v. Boal* [1992] 1 QB 591 the Court of Appeal quashed the conviction of an assistant general manager with day to day responsibility for running the shop for an offence under Section 23, the Fire Precautions Act 1971 where a similar expression is used. Simon Brown J said that the intention was to fix criminal liability on "only those who are in a position of real authority, the decision makers within the company who have both the power and responsibility to decide corporate policy and strategy".

court is satisfied that the offence was committed with that person's consent or connivance or was attributable to their neglect.[105]

Other than in cases of resignation or non-renewal (whose time limits are dealt with above), the statement of circumstances must be served within 14 days of the auditor's office terminating.

Where a statement of circumstances has been served, the company must send a copy of that statement to every person entitled to be served with the company's accounts.[106]

Service of the statement of circumstances can only be avoided by the company making an application to the court on the grounds that the auditor is seeking to use the statement to secure needless publicity for defamatory material.[107]

The application is made on notice to the accountant.[108]

If granted, the court can restrain publication and order the auditor to pay the costs of the application and the company need then merely serve a copy of the court's decision on all those entitled to see a copy of the accounts.[109]

If refused, the company must send a copy of the auditor's statement of circumstances to all those entitled to see a copy of the accounts[110] and notify the auditor of the court's decision.[111]

Any defaults by the company in compliance with the Act will render the company and its officers liable for a criminal offence.[112]

The auditor, unless he has received notice of the application within 21 days from his depositing the statement of circumstances, must serve a copy on the

---

[105] Sections 733, 744 Companies Act 1985.
[106] Section 394(3) Companies Act 1985.
[107] Section 394(3) and (6) Companies Act 1985.
[108] Section 394(4) Companies Act 1985.
[109] Section 394(6) Companies Act 1985; a copy of the court's order must be sent out within 14 days of the order to every person who is entitled to a copy of the accounts under Section 238 Companies Act 1985.
[110] Section 394(7)(a) Companies Act 1985; the copy of the statement of circumstances must be sent out within 14 days of the order to every person who is entitled to a copy of the accounts under Section 238 Companies Act 1985.
[111] Section 394(7)(b) Companies Act 1985; the company must notify the auditor of the court's decision within 14 days of the order.
[112] Section 394A (4) Companies Act 1985; the offence is punished by a fine and, for continued contravention, by a daily default fine.

Registrar of Companies within the next seven days.[113] If notice of the application has been received by him, the auditor must wait until he is notified of the court's decision before he sends in his statement of circumstances to the Registrar of Companies.[114]

5.3.6 Companies Act 2006

Under the Companies Act 2006, a private limited company will no longer be required to hold an annual general meeting. The auditor's term of office will run from the end of the 28 day period following circulation of the accounts until the end of the corresponding period in the following year.[115] This will apply even if the auditor is appointed at a meeting at which company accounts are laid. The auditor is now deemed to be reappointed[116] unless

- he was appointed by the directors or
- the company's articles of association expressly require reappointment or
- the members resolve he should not be reappointed.
- The members may prevent the deemed reappointment by notice to the company[117]
- The directors resolve that no auditor be appointed for the financial year in question.

5.4 THE RIGHTS AND DUTIES OF AN AUDITOR

5.4.1 The auditor's right to receive notice of, attend and be heard at any meeting of the company

An auditor has a right to

- receive all notice of and communications relating to any general meeting of the company that a member might be entitled to attend[118]
- attend at any general meeting of the company that a member might be entitled to attend[119]

---

[113] Section 394(5) Companies Act 1985.
[114] Section 394(5) Companies Act 1985.
[115] Section 485(2) Companies Act 2006
[116] Section 487(2) Companies Act 2006
[117] Section 488 Companies Act 2006
[118] Section 390(1) (a) Companies Act 1985, section 502(2) (a) Companies Act 2006.
[119] Section 390(1) (b) Companies Act 1985, section 502(2) (b) Companies Act 2006.

- be heard on issues which concern them as auditors at any general meeting of the company that a member might be entitled to attend.[120]

Where a resolution is to be passed by a written resolution signed by all its members without prior notice and without calling a meeting[121], the auditor has the right to[122]

- receive all such communication relating to the resolution as are required to be supplied to a member under Schedule 15A Companies Act 1985[123]
- to give notice of their opinion that the resolution concerns them as auditors and should be considered at general meeting or, as the case may be, by a meeting of the relevant class of members
- attend that meeting
- be heard on issues which concern them as auditors at such a meeting

Where the auditors are a partnership or a company, attendance at a meeting may be made by an individual duly authorised by it in writing.[124]

These rights are not terminated by the removal of the auditor for any meeting at which his office would otherwise have expired or at which it is proposed to fill the vacancy caused by his removal.[125]

5.4.2 The auditor's right of access to the books, records, accounts and vouchers of the company and to require information from the company's officers

An auditor has a right of access at all times to the books, records, accounts and vouchers of the company and are entitled to require from the company's officers such information as they think necessary for the performance of their duties as auditors.[126]

---

[120] Section 390(1) (c) Companies Act 1985, section 502(2)(c) Companies Act 2006.
[121] Section 381A, Companies Act 1985. Under sections 288-297 Companies Act 2006 a written resolution no longer requires the support of all the members of the company.
[122] Section 390(2) Companies Act 1985, section 502(1) Companies Act 2006.
[123] Chapter 2 of Part 13 Companies Act 2006.
[124] Section 390(3) Companies Act 1985, section 502(3) Companies Act 2006.
[125] Section 391(4) Companies Act 1985, section 513 Companies Act 2006.
[126] Section 389A (1) Companies Act 1985, section 499 Companies Act 2006.

This right cannot be limited by the company's articles of association[127]. The auditor may seek a mandatory injunction to enforce this right but the court will be reluctant to grant such an injunction if it is doubtful until after a general meeting that the company wishes the auditor to continue in his office.[128]

The duty to disclose places a similar duty on the auditor and officers of a subsidiary company registered in the United Kingdom in respect of any information required by the parent company's auditors.[129] Failure to comply is a criminal offence for the subsidiary and its officers and failure to comply without reasonable excuse is a criminal offence.[130]

Section 8, Companies (Audit, Investigations and Community Enterprise) Act 2004 inserts a new section 389A to The Companies Act 1985 which extends the rights auditors to require information and explanations from officers of a company. Under the new provisions:

- Auditors are entitled to require information and explanations from a wider group of people, including employees, and may access books, accounts and vouchers 'in whatever form they are held' (although there is a limited exception for information covered by legal professional privilege);
- It is a criminal offence to fail to provide information or explanations requested by the auditors or to fail to do so 'without delay'[131]
- Where a parent company has a subsidiary undertaking not incorporated in the United Kingdom, it is the responsibility of the parent company to ensure compliance with the auditors' request for information

The Companies (Audit, Investigations and Community Enterprise) Act 2004 also inserts a new section 234ZA CA 1985 which requires directors of companies subject to a statutory audit to make a disclosure statement in the directors' report to the effect that:

- So far as the director is aware, there is no relevant audit information of which the company's auditors are unaware; and

---

[127] *Newton v. Birmingham Small Arms Company Ltd* [1906] 2 Ch 378.
[128] *Cuff v. London and County Land and Building Co.* [1912] 1 Ch 440.
[129] Section 389A (3) Companies Act 1985, section 499(2) (c) Companies Act 2006.
[130] Section 389A (3) Companies Act 1985, section 501(3) Companies Act 2006.
[131] Section 398B, Companies Act 1985; "As soon as reasonably practicable" section 501(3) Companies Act 2006.

- He has taken all the steps that he ought to have taken as a director in order to make himself aware of any relevant audit information and to establish that the company's auditors are aware of that information.

It also creates a criminal offence which may be committed by a director, who makes a disclosure statement knowing that it is false, or is reckless as to whether it is false, and fails to take reasonable steps to prevent the report from being approved.

The new disclosure provisions apply to all directors of a company, regardless of the position or role on the board. Although the Act makes it clear that a director's duty under the new provisions does not extend beyond the duties he already owes at common law to exercise due care and skill, in practice it places a considerable burden on them to consider carefully what information is needed by the auditors of the company and to volunteer that information to them. The Act lays down a combined objective-subjective test for measuring a director's compliance with this duty:

- The knowledge, skill and experience that may reasonably be expected of a person carrying out his or her functions in relation to the company; and
- The additional knowledge, skill and experience that he or she in fact possesses (to the extent that it exceeds that of the reasonable person under the first limb of the test).

Where the subsidiary company is not registered in the United Kingdom, the duty is placed on the parent company and its officers to take such steps as are reasonably open to it to obtain from the subsidiary such information and explanations as the auditor may reasonably require to fulfil his duties.[132] The section makes the parent company and each of its officers criminally liable for any non-compliance.

It is a criminal offence for an officer of the company who knowingly or recklessly makes any statement (whether written or oral) which conveys or purports to convey any information or explanation which the auditors require or are entitled to and which is false or misleading or deceptive in any material particular.[133]

---

[132] Section 389A (4) Companies Act 1985, section 500 Companies Act 2006.
[133] Section 389A (2) Companies Act 1985, section 501(1) Companies Act 2006.

5.4.3 The auditor's duty to make a report to the company's members on all annual accounts of the company

It is the duty of the auditor to make a report to the company's members on all annual accounts of the company of which copies are to be laid before the company in general meeting during the tenure of their office.[134] This duty is fulfilled by delivering the report to the secretary of the company.[135]

It is the duty[136] of the auditor to state in his report whether in his opinion the annual accounts have been prepared in accordance with the Act and in particular whether a "true and fair view" is given:

- in the case of an individual balance sheet, of the state of the affairs of the company as at the end of the financial year
- in the case of an individual profit and loss account, of the profit and loss for the financial year
- in the case of group accounts, of the state of the affairs as at the end of the financial year and of the profit and loss for the financial year of the undertakings including the consolidation as a whole, so far as concerns the members of the company

The true and fair view was first introduced by Section 13(1) of the Companies Act 1947.[137]

In the EC 4th Directive, when assessing the true and fair view, the accounts are treated as a "composite whole" comprising a balance sheet, profit and loss account and notes.

This interpretation was first adopted in the UK in the Companies Act 1981 and is now found in Schedule 4 and 4A of the Companies Act 1985. The variations imposed by the 7th Directive were enacted by the Companies Act 1989.

The true and fair requirement for individual companies is found in Section 226[138] and in Section 227[139] Companies Act 1985 for group financial

---

[134] Section 235 Companies Act 1985, section 495 Companies Act 2006.
[135] *Re Allen, Craig & Co. (London) Ltd* [1934] Ch 483.
[136] Section 235 (2) Companies Act 1985, section 495(3) Companies Act 2006. Under the 2006, the Auditor must also state whether these have been prepared in accordance with the relevant financial reporting framework and that they have been prepared in accordance with the requirements of the Companies Act 2006 or (if applicable) Art 4 of the IAS Regulation.
[137] Re-enacted in the Companies Act 1948 as Section 149(1) and adopted into EC 4th Directive, Article 2.
[138] Section 227(2) Companies Act 1985 (as inserted by Section 1 and 4(1) Companies Act 1989 from 1st April, 1990: see SI 90/355) requires:

statements. Under the Companies Act 2006 the requirement appears at section 303.

Compliance with accepted accounting principles is *prima facie* evidence that accounts are true and fair.[140]

It is the duty[141] of the auditor to state in his report whether or not in his opinion the information given in the director's report is consistent with the accounts for the financial year for which they are prepared.

All statements by the auditors in the report arising out of the statutory duty to report enjoy qualified privilege from action in defamation if made in good faith.[142] Copies of the reports circulated to members of a UK public company by or with the auditor's authority similarly enjoy qualified privilege.[143]

The report shall state the name of the auditor and be signed by him.[144] The name can be omitted if (a) there is reasonable grounds to believe that its inclusion would expose the auditor or any other person to a serious risk of violence or intimidation (b) the company resolves to remove the auditor's name from the report and (c) the notice is given to the Secretary of State of the resolution, the name and number of the company, the financial year to which this relates, the name of the auditor and of the person who signed the report as Senior Statutory Auditor.[145]

Every copy of the report which is to be laid before the company in general meeting or otherwise circulated, published or issued must state the name of the auditors and failure to comply renders the company and each of its officers criminally liable.[146]

- the balance sheet to give a true and fair account of the company as at the end of the financial year
- the profit and loss to give a true and fair account of the company for the financial year.

[139] Section 227(3) Companies Act 1985 requires the accounts to give a true and fair view of the state of affairs as at the end of the financial year and the profit and loss of all the undertakings included in the consolidation as a whole. Section 404 Companies Act 2006.
[140] *Willingale v. International Commercial Bank Ltd* [1978] AC 834.
[141] Section 235(3) Companies Act 1985, section 496 Companies Act 2006.
[142] *Carter-Ruck on Libel and Slander*, 5th Edition, p250.
[143] Schedule 1 Defamation Act 1996.
[144] Section 236(1) Companies Act 1985, section 503 Companies Act 2006. Where the auditor is a firm the senior statutory auditor is required under the Companies Act 2006 to sign on behalf of the firm.
[145] Section 506(2) Companies Act 2006.
[146] Section 236(2), (4) Companies Act 1985, section 505 Companies Act 2006.

The copy of the report which is to be delivered to the Registrar of Companies must both state the name of the auditors and be signed by the auditors and failure to comply renders the company and each of its officers criminally liable.[147]

Where the auditor is a company or partnership, signature by the auditors is done by a person authorised by the auditors signing in their name on their behalf.[148]

5.4.4 The duty of the auditor is to form a true and fair view of the company's position as at the date of the audit

The auditor is under a statutory duty[149] to carry out such investigations as will enable them to form an opinion as to:

- whether proper accounting records have been kept by the company
- whether the proper returns, adequate for their audit, have been received from the company's branches
- whether the company's individual accounts are in agreement with the accounting records and returns

If the opinion formed is that this is not the case, the auditors must state so in their report.[150] If the auditors fail to obtain all the information which, to the best of their knowledge and belief is necessary to form that opinion, the auditors must state so in their report.[151] Similarly if the disclosure provisions under Schedule 6 of the Companies Act 1985 are not complied with then the auditors must, as far as they reasonably can do so, give a statement giving the required particulars.[152]

The auditor's responsibility under the Companies Legislation is to form an independent judgment as to whether the accounts form a "true and fair view" of the company's financial position at the time of the audit. This means that he must verify not only its arithmetical accuracy but its substantive accuracy.[153]

---

[147] Section 236(3), (4) Companies Act 1985. Under Chapter 10, Part 15 Companies Act 2006, the accounts filed must state the name of the auditor who signed the accounts.
[148] Section 236(4) Companies Act 1985, section 503(4) Companies Act 2006 requires this to be done by the firm's senior statutory auditor.
[149] Section 237(1) Companies Act 1985, section 498 Companies Act 2006.
[150] Section 237(2) Companies Act 1985, section 498 Companies Act 2006.
[151] Section 237(3) Companies Act 1985, section 498 Companies Act 2006.
[152] Section 237(4) Companies Act 1985, section 498 Companies Act 2006.
[153] *Fomento (Sterling Area) Ltd v. Selsdon Fountain Pen Co. Ltd* [1958] 1 All ER 1123.

It is no part of the auditor's duty to give advice, either to directors or shareholders as to what they ought to do.[154] An auditor has nothing to do with whether the company is being run profitably or not, indeed, even as to whether or not dividends are properly or improperly declared.[155]

5.4.5 It is the duty of the auditor to heed the powers of the audited company

The auditor must consider whether the acts of the company through its directors during the audited period were *ultra vires* the company.[156] He will potentially be liable for any *ultra vires* payments made by the director resulting from his breach of duty of care.[157]

That duty is owed to the shareholders and not to the directors and the auditor will not avoid liability by making full disclosure of his concerns only to the directors.[158]

5.4.6 The duties of the auditor may be extended by agreement or by the articles of association of the audited company

Outside the duty to form a true and fair view, the measure of the auditor's liability is dependent on the terms of his engagement and, in the absence of a specific term in a contract, reference can be made to the company's articles to elicit the extent of those duties.[159] There is accordingly a duty for an auditor to make themselves acquainted with the provisions as to their duties under each company's articles of association.[160]

So saying, it must be remembered that the auditor's statutory duties cannot be limited or abated by the articles or a contract.

5.5 REPORTING ACCOUNTANT

5.5.1 The statutory framework and the role of the reporting accountant

Reporting accountants were created to provide a less onerous level of audit for smaller companies. Under Section 249A of the Companies Act 1985 a company was exempted from the statutory provisions relating to the audit of

---

[154] *In re London General Bank (No 2)* [1895] 2 Ch 673, 682 per Lindley LJ.
[155] *In re London General Bank (No 2)* [1895] 2 Ch 673, 682 per Lindley LJ.
[156] *Re Republic of Bolivia Exploration Syndicate Ltd* [1914] 1 Ch 139.
[157] *Spackman v. Evans* (1868) LR 3 HL 171, 235-236.
[158] *Re London and General Bank (No. 2)* [1895] 2 Ch 673.
[159] *Re City Equitable Fire Insurance Co. Ltd* [1925] Ch 407, per Pollock MR.
[160] *Re Republic of Bolivia Exploration Syndicate Ltd* [1914] 1 Ch 139, 171 per Astbury J.

accounts under Part VII of the Companies Act 1985 in respect of that year when it meets the exemption conditions in respect of that financial year. Pre 15th April 1997, the conditions in which a report was required were met by a company in respect of a financial year if:

- It qualifies as a small company in relation to that year; and
- Its turnover in that year is more than £90,000 but not more than £350,000; and
- Its balance sheet total for that year is not more than 1.4 million pounds.

A company was required to conduct an audit and was not entitled[161] to take advantage of the statutory exemption from audit in respect of a financial year if at any time within that year:

- It was a public company;
- It was a banking or insurance company;
- It was enrolled on the list maintained by the Insurance Brokers Registration Council;[162]
- It was an authorised person or an appointed representative under the Financial Services Act 1986;
- It was a special register body under the Trade Union and Labour Relations (Consolidation) Act 1992, Section 117(1) or an employers association as defined under Section 112, Trade Union and Labour Relations (Consolidation) Act 1992;
- It was a parent company or a subsidiary undertaking.

Since 15th April 1997, the turnover limit under Section 249A (3) (b) has been successively increased from £90,000 to, at the date of writing, £5.6 million for all small companies except charitable companies. The effect of this is to abolish the obligation to obtain a report for all small companies except charitable companies with a turnover of between £90,000 and £500,000.[163]

The required report must be prepared by a reporting accountant who is eligible for appointment.[164]

---

[161] Section 249B, Companies Act 1985.
[162] See Insurance Brokers (Registration) Act 1977, Section 4.
[163] Section 32 Charities Act 2006 amending section 249A(4) of the Companies Act 1985
[164] Section 249C(1) Companies Act 1985.

5.5.2 Eligibility for appointment as a reporting accountant

The reporting accountant must be:

- either an individual, a body corporate or a partnership; and
- must be a member of a specified body who under the rules of the body is entitled to engage in public practice
- not for some reason be ineligible for appointment as a reporting accountant or any person whether or not a member of such a body who is subject to the rules of any such body in seeking appointment or acting as auditor and under those rules is eligible for appointment as an auditor.

5.5.3 The Specified Bodies

The bodies "specified" are:

- The Institute of Chartered Accountants in England and Wales
- The Institute of Chartered Accountants in Scotland
- The Institute of Chartered Accountants in Ireland
- The Association of Chartered Certified Accountants
- The Association of Authorised Public Accountants[165]
- The Association of International Accountants[166]
- Chartered Institute of Management Accountants
- Association of Accounting Technicians

5.5.4 The Reporting Accountant's Report

The report must state whether in the opinion of the reporting accountant making it that:

- the accounts for the company for the financial year in question are in agreement with the accounting records kept by the company
- having regard only to and on the basis of the information contained in those accounting records those accounts have been drawn up in a manner consistent with the specified statutory provisions so far as they are applicable to the company.

The report must state the name of the reporting accountant and be signed by him.

---

[165] Section 249 D(3) Companies Act 1985.
[166] The Companies Act 1985 (Audit Exemption) (Amendment) Regulations 1996, 1996 No. 3080, confers the status also of "reporting accountant on suitably qualified members of the Association of International Accountants.

5.5.5 Companies Act 2006: Abolition of the Reporting Accountant

The Companies Act 2006 effectively operates to abolish both the status of reporting accountant[167] and the last vestiges of his role with the removal the special provisions about the accounts and audits of charitable companies.[168]

---

[167] Section 249D Companies Act 1985 is repealed under Schedule 16, Companies Act 2006.
[168] Section 1175 Companies Act 2006.

Chapter 6

CLAIMS AGAINST AUDITORS

6.1 CLAIMS AGAINST AUDITORS

6.1.1 The basis for liability

An auditor will owe a range of different duties which may, if breached, give rise to a claim for damages.[1]

The first is under the auditor's contract to provide professional services he has entered into with his client. Under that retainer he will owe express or implied duties to his client.

Secondly the auditor will owe tortuous duties of care to both his client and some of those third parties who are foreseeably affected by his actions.

To establish any claim for damages, a causal link must be proved between the breach of the duty of care and the loss suffered. The test is whether this played a real and substantial part in causing the loss even if it was not the sole cause.[2] The absence of any one of the elements of the cause of action provides a defence to the claim.[3]

6.1.2 Contract

The most important area of liability is for breach of the contract to provide professional services he has entered into with his client, the company.

It is an implied term of an auditor's contract to provide professional services, that he will provide those professional services properly and with reasonable care and skill.

---

[1] The law of professional negligence for failure to provide correct advice and information is presently in a state of flux: *Independent Advantage Insurance Company v Cook* [2004] PNLR 3.
[2] *Deloitte Haskins & Sells v. Mutual Life Nominees* [1993] 2 All ER 1015.
[3] Paragraph 2, Professional Liability of Accountants and Auditors, issued November 1993 by the Institute of Chartered Accountants in England and Wales.

The standard of care is that which can be expected of a reasonably competent accountant acting as an auditor. Thus an auditor called to value a company's shares is not negligent if he falls short of the standards of a specialist valuer but not of a reasonably competent accountant acting as an auditor.[4]

It is the duty of the auditor to bring to bear on the work he has to perform that skill, care and caution which a reasonable, careful and cautious auditor would use. What is reasonable must depend on the particular circumstances of each case. An auditor is neither bound to be a detective nor approach his work with the suspicion nor with the forgone conclusion that something is wrong.[5] The auditor is a watchdog not a bloodhound. The duty is "verification not detection".[6]

The auditor is not expected to have the benefit of hindsight and it is accepted by the courts that he judges each record separately.[7] There may well be a duty to personally inspect the assets of the company in the course of an audit.[8]

If, in the course of the audit, the auditor discovers that matters are not as they ought to be (for example by finding altered invoices) the auditor is put on inquiry and if the auditor fails to make further investigations, he will be in breach of his duty of care.[9]

In *Sasea Finance v KPMG*,[10] the Court of Appeal ruled that once an auditor had discovered evidence of fraud or other serious misconduct, the auditor was under a duty to report this at once rather than waiting until the accounts were signed off so as to prevent further losses.

Common professional practice is strong persuasive evidence of the standard to be expected.[11] The standard is judged by the practice at the time where the conduct took place.[12]

---

[4] *Whiteoak v. Maxwell* (1988) 4 BCC 122, Cullen QC.
[5] *Re Kingston Mills (No. 2)* [1896] 2 Ch. 279, per Lopes LJ.
[6] *Re City Equitable Fire Insurance Co. Ltd* [1925] 1 Ch 407.
[7] *Re City Equitable Fire Insurance Co. Ltd* [1925] 1 Ch 407.
[8] *Re City Equitable Fire Insurance Co. Ltd* [1925] 1 Ch 407; in the Australian case of *Pacific Acceptance Corporation Ltd v. Forsyth* (1970) 92 WN (NSW) 29 auditors were held to be negligent when they failed to check the security of the company loans.
[9] *Re Thomas Gerrard & Sons Ltd* [1967] 2 All ER 525.
[10] *Sasea Finance v KPMG* [2000] 1 BCLC 236,
[11] *Lloyd Cheyham & Co. Ltd v. Littlejohn* [1986] PCC 389.
[12] *Bell v Strathairn & Blair* (1954) 104 LJ 618.

6.1.3 Tort

It is now that clear auditors owe a concurrent duty of care in both contract and tort to their employer or client;[13] the claimant may elect which of the concurrent remedies in breach of contract or in tort appears to him to provide the most advantageous remedy.

Third parties who, although not clients, were reasonably within the auditor's contemplation when performing his professional services may also be owed a duty of care[14]; whilst a negligent auditor is liable to his client both in contract and in tort[15] whilst a claim by a third party can only be brought in tort.

6.1.3.1 Tortious liability

Plainly auditors owe a duty of care to their clients in tort much as they do in contract.

The extent to which non-clients are owed a duty of care by auditors is far less clear cut.

The House of Lords in *Smith v. Eric S Bush*[16] set out a threefold test to assess whether a duty of care situation arose:

- Was it reasonably foreseeable that the claimant would suffer the kind of loss that occurred?
- Was there proximity between the parties?
- Was it just and reasonable the defendant auditor should owe a duty of care of the scope asserted by the claimant?

The much discussed case of *Caparo Industries v. Dickman*[17] did to a great extent clarify the type of factors which indicated that a duty of care situation existed:

- that the accountant knew the purpose of the advice, e.g., to help the would-be litigant decide whether or not to invest in the company

---

[13] *Henderson v Merrett Syndicates Ltd* [1995] 2 AC 145.
[14] By analogy, solicitors have been held liable to the intended beneficiary of a will where the negligence resulted in the loss of an intended legacy; the duty of care was not limited to the deceased testator who was the solicitors' client: *White v Jones* [1995] 2 AC 207.
[15] *Henderson v. Merrett Syndicates Ltd* [1994] 3 All ER 506 where a co-extensive claim in tort and breach of contract was found against a Lloyds agent.
[16] [1989] 2 All ER 514.
[17] [1990] 1 All ER 568.

- that the litigant was going to receive that advice with a view to using it to help him decide whether to invest in the company
- that advice was likely to be acted upon without independent inquiry
- that it would be reasonable to rely on that advice
- that the litigant acted on that advice to his detriment

The Law Lords in *Caparo* favoured a reversion to the idea of having "duty situations" rather than adopting a definite test as to whether a duty of care arose. *Caparo* dealt specifically with the situation of an audit of a large public limited company.

It seems that the same principles can be applied to statements as regards investments; in *James McNaughton Papers Group Ltd v. Hicks Anderson*[18] draft accounts were prepared by the accountants specifically for use in negotiations for a takeover. A company auditor would not owe a duty of care simply because he is aware that a potential predator has an interest in the company concerned.[19]

It seems from indications in *Caparo* and later cases that the courts may be prepared to imply a duty of care if a case arose where the auditor was aware that the litigant:

- is a small investor[20]
- was making what was for him a major investment[21]
- is probably uninsured against his loss[22]
- did not have business experience[23]
- is unlikely to have any significant level of research resources
- could not have been expected to take independent advice[24]
- received direct representations as to the accuracy of the accounts[25]

---

[18] [1991] 1 All ER 134.
[19] *James McNaughton Paper Group v. Hicks Anderson* [1991] 2 QB 113.
[20] *Morgan Crucible Co. v. Hill Samuel Bank Ltd, The Independent,* 27th July, 1990, *Smith v Eric S Bush* [1989] 2 WLR 790, HL.
[21] *Morgan Crucible, The Independent,* 27th July, 1990.
[22] *Morgan Crucible, The Independent,* 27th July, 1990.
[23] *Smith v Eric S Bush* [1989] 2 WLR 790, HL.
[24] *Smith v Eric S Bush* [1989] 2 WLR 790, HL.

- is part of a limited class of investors[26]
- risks losing property as a result of the representation rather than merely suffering pure economic loss[27]

where the auditor was actively involved in obtaining the set up finance provided by the litigant.[28]

It would be wrong to infer from this that commercially experienced clients automatically lose the possibility of being owed a duty of care. It is clearly possible, for example, for circumstances to exist where accountants auditing one bank's set of accounts could owe a duty of care to another bank, even though that bank had its own auditors[29].

Mr Justice Sachs sitting in the English High Court in *Hands v Coopers & Lybrand*[30] however indicated that auditors did not owe creditors of a company they were auditing any duty of care to advise on the prudence of making a loan.

The Scottish Outer House of the Court of Session however appeared to find no difficulty in finding a duty of care in *Royal Bank of Scotland v Bannerman Johnston Maclay*.[31] There the Court of Session ruled that for a relationship of proximity to exist between an auditor and a bank, which relied upon their financial statements when making lending decisions, it was not necessary for the bank to prove that the auditor intended that the bank should rely upon them. If the auditor did not intend that the bank should rely on such statements, it was open for the auditor to include a disclaimer.

Thus in the case of an audit undertaken by an auditor, third parties who would be considered to be reasonably within an auditor's contemplation (and thus to whom a duty of care might be owed by the auditor) would include any third person to whom the auditor himself shows the accounts, or to whom he himself knows that his employer or client is going to show the

---

[25] *Al Saudi Banque v. Clarke Pixley, The Financial Times,* 4th August, 1989.
[26] In the Canadian case of *Haig v. Bamford* (1977) 72 DLR (3d) 68, Supreme Court, a duty of care was held to exist in an audit for a private limited company due to the litigant being part of a limited class of investors.
[27] *Caparo Industries v. Dickman* [1990] 1 All ER 568, per Lord Bridge of Harwich.
[28] *Royal Bank of Scotland v Bannerman Johnstone Maclay* [2005] PNLR 43 (Scot). Lord Gill in the Outer House of the Court of Session said that the auditor did not need to intend that the claimant would rely on the accounts; it would be enough in principle to make out the claim to show that he knew it was highly likely the accounts would be relied on.
[29] *Bank of Credit and Commerce (Overseas) Limited v. Price Waterhouse* (1998) *The Times*, 4 March.
[30] *Hands v Coopers & Lybrand* (2001) Lawtel 25th April.
[31] *Royal Bank of Scotland v Bannerman Johnston Maclay* (2002) The Times 1st August.

accounts, for example, so as to induce him to invest money or take some other action on them.[32]

In such circumstances the auditor could clearly be expected, subject always to the affect of any disclaimer of responsibility, specifically to anticipate that the claimant would rely on the advice or information given by the auditor for that very purpose.[33]

The standard of care expected in tort is broadly the same as that expected under contract. The standard of care is that which can be expected of a reasonably competent accountant acting as an auditor. Common professional practice is strong persuasive evidence of the standard to be expected of the ordinary skilled auditor.[34]

Thus errors in audits do not necessarily automatically found a claim in negligence. Moreover errors in audits do not necessarily cause any loss. Audits and accounts contain a number of estimates and judgments made by the accountant preparing them. Different accountants may take a different view of the same set of facts. Provided the estimates are made with reasonable care and skill, the differences may not necessarily be either wrong or negligent. Subsequent events may demonstrate assumptions made were wrong. Hindsight is no touchstone of negligence and providing proper inquiries were made at the time of preparing the accounts, the position reflected in the accounts cannot be criticised.

It is the duty of the auditor to bring to bear on the work he has to perform that skill, care and caution which a reasonable, careful and cautious auditor would use. What is reasonable must depend on the particular circumstances of each case. An auditor is not bound to be a detective nor approach his work with the suspicion nor with the forgone conclusion that something is wrong[35]. The duty is "verification not detection".[36]

The auditor is not expected to have the benefit of hindsight and it is accepted by the courts that he judges each record separately.[37] There may well be a

---

[32] *Candler v. Crane, Christmas & Co* [1951] 2 KB 164, p. 180-181, per Denning LJ.
[33] *Caparo Industries plc v. Dickman and Ors* [1990] 2 WLR 358, pp. 367-8, per Lord Bridge of Harwich.
[34] *Lloyd Cheyham & Co. Ltd v. Littlejohn* [1986] PCC 389.
[35] *Re Kingston Mills (No. 2)* [1896] 2 Ch. 279, per Lopes LJ.
[36] *Re City Equitable Fire Insurance Co. Ltd* [1925] 1 Ch 407.
[37] *Re City Equitable Fire Insurance Co. Ltd* [1925] 1 Ch 407.

duty to personally inspect the assets of the company in the course of an audit.[38]

6.1.3.2 Contributory Negligence

It is open to the auditor[39] to offset his liability where a claim in negligence is made by arguing the contributory negligence of his client. Under section 1, The Law Reform (Contributory Negligence) Act 1945 a claimant's damages can be subjected to a *pro rata* reduction where he suffers damage as the result partly of his own fault.

For example, a client may be contributorily negligent if he ignores his auditor's warnings and a company director himself has a statutory duty to prepare accounts, maintain proper books of account and records and to safeguard the assets of the company.

The Act can be applied to a claim brought in contract where the defendant's liability under the contract is the same as his liability in negligence; namely one of breach of duty to apply reasonable care or skill and this applies whether or not a claim is, in fact, actually pursued in negligence.[40]

6.1.3.3 Contribution

Any person liable in respect of any damage suffered by another person may recover contribution from any other person liable in respect of the same damage (whether jointly with himself or otherwise).[41] This creates a statutory cause of action which allows joint wrongdoers to seek a contribution from each other where the person against whom the contribution is sought is liable to the claimant for the same damage. The basis for the liability is irrelevant[42] - thus a party liable to the claimant in breach of contract could seek a contribution from a party liable to the claimant on a restitutionary basis.[43] The court is required to apportion the liability between the parties in line with the extent of responsibility for the loss[44] however a contributory cannot be made liable for more than the sum (if any) he would be liable for if he had been sued directly (thus the court would make reductions reflecting

---

[38] *Re City Equitable Fire Insurance Co. Ltd* [1925] 1 Ch 407; in the Australian case of *Pacific Acceptance Corporation Ltd v. Forsyth* (1970) 92 WN (NSW) 29 auditors were held to be negligent when they failed to check the security of the company loans.
[39] By way of illustration, *De Meza and Stuart v Apple, Van Straten, Shena and Stone* [1975] 1 Lloyd's Rep 498.
[40] *Forsikringsaktieselskapet Vesta v Butcher* [1989] AC 852.
[41] Section 1, Civil Liability (Contribution) Act 1978.
[42] Section 6(1), Civil Liability (Contribution) Act 1978.
[43] *Friends Provident Life Office v Hillier Parker* [1995] 4 All ER 260.
[44] Section 2(1), Civil Liability (Contribution) Act 1978.

possible arguments of contributory negligence that might have been available to him if he had been sued).[45]

Any fraud on the part of the company's directors may well provide the auditors with a defence of circularity of action; if the auditors have been deceived by the directors as the company's agents, they would be entitled in turn to bring a counterclaim against the company on the basis that they are vicariously liable to the auditor for its agent's deceit.[46]

This has been given particular force given that duties have been placed on directors to make full and candid disclosure to auditors about all matters germane to the preparation of accounts. Auditors now have a right of access at all times to all the company's books accounts and vouchers and, absent legal professional privilege, may require answers from past or present directors, employees of the company or its subsidiaries or any person who has possession of such records.[47] Failure to comply is a criminal offence.[48]

Directors' reports now must include a statement concerning what steps the directors have taken to establish what information might be relevant to the auditor and have brought it to the attention of the auditors.[49]

6.1.4 Level of damages awarded

In claims for breach of contract, the intention of the court when compensating a claimant is to put the claimant in the position that he would have been in had the contract for professional services been properly performed.

Where the claim is phrased in negligence, it is the intention of the court to place the claimant back into the position he would have been in had the auditor not acted negligently.

In either case, there is a duty on the claimant to take reasonable steps to try to mitigate his loss. The claimant cannot recover any loss he could have reasonably avoided. Nor can the claimant recover losses which he has avoided and the defendant is entitled to be credited for all benefits which the claimant has received through the steps taken to mitigate the loss.

---

[45] Section 2(3), Civil Liability (Contribution) Act 1978.
[46] *Barings v Coopers & Lybrand* [2002] Lloyds Rep PN 323.
[47] Section 389A Companies Act 1985 as inserted by section 8 Companies (Audit, Investigations and Community Enterprise) Act 2004, section 499 and 500 Companies Act 2006.
[48] Section 389B Companies Act 1985 as inserted by section 8 Companies (Audit, Investigations and Community Enterprise) Act 2004, section 501 Companies Act 2006.
[49] Section 234ZA Companies Act 1985, section 418 Companies Act 2006.

Moreover losses are only recoverable if they can be shown to have been caused by the breach; if a breach of duty does no more than provide the occasion for loss, it is not considered to be causative and the loss cannot be recovered.[50]

The damages for losses caused by a negligent audit will normally be confined to economic loss sustained by those who rely on the accuracy of the information or advice they receive as a basis for action.[51] In cases of a failure to render services the basic loss is the price the claimant would have to pay in the market place in order to obtain the services contracted for deducting the contract price, if not already paid.[52] The cost of re-doing the auditor's defective work is a recoverable head of damages.[53]

6.1.5 Limitation

Any action founded on simple contract must be brought within six years of the date upon which the cause of action accrued.[54] In contract the cause of action accrues on the date on which the breach of contract (as opposed to the loss[55]) occurred.[56] Where the breach is through a failure to act, the breach is deemed to have occurred after the auditor has been given a reasonable time to perform his duty but had failed to do so.[57]

The only occasion (other than one where the claimant is under a disability) that can suspend the operation of the limitation period in contract is where the claimant was rendered unaware of his claim through fraud, concealment or mistake.[58]

The latent damage provisions under section 14A Limitation Act 1980 apply to negligence and negligent misstatement and create an alternative limitation period of three years whose starting date is the earliest date on which the claimant had both the knowledge required for bringing an action for damages and the right to bring the action. The date of knowledge means the knowledge of the material facts about the damage as would lead a

---

[50] *Galoo v Bright Grahame Murray* [1994] 1 WLR 1360.
[51] *Caparo Industries plc v. Dickman and Others* [1990] 2 WLR 358, p. 366, per Lord Bridge of Harwich.
[52] *Monarch SS v. Kalishamns Oljefabriker* [1949] AC 196.
[53] *Tormont Holdings v. Thorne Gunn & Helliwell* (1975) 62 DLR (3d) 465.
[54] Section 5, Limitation Act 1980.
[55] The breach perfects the claim because breach of itself gives rise to a claim for nominal damages.
[56] *Gibbs v Guild* (1882) 9 QBD 259.
[57] *Bell v Peter Browne & Co* [1990] 2 QB 495.
[58] Section 32, Limitation Act 1980.

reasonable person who had suffered that damage to consider it sufficiently serious to justify his instituting proceedings against a defendant who did not dispute liability and was able to satisfy judgement[59] and that the damage was attributable to the defendant and the defendant's identity.[60]

6.1.6 Exclusion clauses

Any provision, whether contained in a company's article or in any contract with the company or otherwise is ineffective insofar that it exempts any officer of the company or any person (whether an officer or not) employed by the company as an auditor from or indemnifying him against any liability by virtue of any rule of law which would otherwise attach to him in respect of any negligence, default, breach of duty or breach of trust of which he may be guilty in relation to the company.[61]

So saying, this will not prevent a company from purchasing or maintaining in force auditor insurance against such liability[62] or from indemnifying the auditor against liability incurred by him in defending any proceedings, whether civil or criminal, in which judgment is given in his favour or in which he is acquitted or in connection with any application under Sections 144(3) or 144(4) (acquisition of shares by an innocent nominee) or Section 727 (general power to grant relief in case of honest and reasonable conduct) Companies Act 1985 in which relief is granted to him by the court.[63]

6.1.7 Exclusion clauses and the Companies Act 2006

The Companies Act 2006 retains the principle that any provision, whether contained in a company's article or in any contract with the company or otherwise is void insofar that it exempts any officer of the company or any person (whether an officer or not) employed by the company as an auditor from or indemnifying him against any liability by virtue of any rule of law which would otherwise attach to him in respect of any negligence, default, breach of duty or breach of trust of which he may be guilty in relation to the company.[64]

---

[59] Section 14A(7), Limitation Act 1980.
[60] Section 14A(8), Limitation Act 1980.
[61] Section 310(1), (2) Companies Act 1985.
[62] Section 310(3)(a) Companies Act 1985.
[63] Section 310(3)(b) Companies Act 1985.
[64] Section 532 Companies Act 2006.

It however permits the company to indemnify the auditor for costs incurred when successfully defending proceedings or to obtain relief in cases of honest and reasonable conduct.[65]

A further exception to this rule is that the Act also permits the company and the auditor to enter into liability limitation agreements.[66] To be effective the liability limitation agreement must be approved by the members of the company at the material time,[67] be limited to a single financial year[68] and stipulate the year it is to apply to.[69] Reference needs to be made to the agreement in the accounts and in the directors' report.[70] Even then the agreement will only be effective to limit the auditor's liability to the extent that it is fair and reasonable, having regard to the auditor's statutory responsibilities, the nature and purpose of the auditor's contractual duties to the company and his professional standards rather than the recoverability of compensation from other persons.[71]

6.1.8 Companies Act 2006: Effect of Signature by Senior Statutory Auditor

After the Companies Act 2006 has been fully implemented, the auditor's report will need to be signed by a Senior Statutory Auditor in his own name on behalf of the audit firm.[72] The Senior Statutory Auditor means the person identified by the firm as the senior statutory auditor in line with the relevant standards[73] The Senior Statutory Auditor needs to be a person who is eligible for appointment as an auditor in his own right.[74] Every copy of the auditor's report will need to disclose the name of the auditor and (where applicable) also the name of the Senior Statutory Auditor.[75] The presence of the Senior Statutory Auditor's name on the audit will not of itself give rise to any personal civil liability for the audit.[76]

---

[65] Section 532(2) Companies Act 2006.
[66] Section 532(2) Companies Act 2006.
[67] Section 534(2)(b) and 536 Companies Act 2006.
[68] Section 535(1)(a) Companies Act 2006.
[69] Section 535(1)(b) Companies Act 2006.
[70] Section 538 Companies Act 2006.
[71] Section 537 Companies Act 2006.
[72] Section 504 Companies Act 2006.
[73] Section 504(1) Companies Act 2006.
[74] Section 504(2) Companies Act 2006.
[75] Section 505(1) Companies Act 2006.
[76] Section 504(3) Companies Act 2006.

6.1.9 Insurance Companies

No duty to which an auditor of an insurance company may be subject can be regarded as contravened by reason of his communicating in good faith to the Secretary of State whether or not in response to a request from him any information or opinion on a matter which the auditor has become aware in his capacity as auditor of that company and has relevance to any functions to the Secretary of State under the Insurance Companies Act 1982.[77] If it appears to the Secretary of State that an auditor or class of auditor to whom Sub-section 1 applies is not subject to satisfactory rules made or guidance issued by a professional body specifying circumstances in which matters are to be communicated as the Secretary of State as mentioned in that sub-section, the Secretary of State may make regulations applying to that auditor or class of auditor and specifying such circumstances in which it is the duty of the auditor, to whom the regulations made by the Secretary of State applies, to communicate a matter to the Secretary of State.[78] If it appears to the Secretary of State that an auditor has failed to comply with that duty to disclose, the Secretary of State may disqualify him from being an auditor of an insurance company or the Secretary of State may remove any disqualification imposed under the sub-section if satisfied that the person in question would in future comply with that duty.[79]

6.2 ACCOUNTING STANDARDS

6.2.1 SSAP

The Accounting Standards Board was formed in 1990. It replaced the Accounting Standards Committee. It formulates what it considers to be the generally accepted accounting principles. It adopted many of the existing Statements of Standard Accountancy Practice ("SSAP").

A SSAP has no weight in law. Compliance with a SSAP however provides strong evidence as to what was the proper standard to be adopted. It therefore provides the first bench mark against which one can assess whether the accountant was negligent by failing to follow this.[80] Mr Justice Woolf (as he then was)[81] indicated that whilst the SSAPs are not conclusive or binding, as their explanatory foreword makes clear, they are very strong evidence as to what is the proper standard which should be adopted.

---

[77] Section 21 A (1) Insurance Companies Act 1982.
[78] Section 21 A(2) Insurance Companies Act 1982.
[79] Section 21 A(5) Insurance Companies Act 1982.
[80] *Lloyd Cheyham & Co. v. Littlejohn & Co.* [1987] BCLC 303.
[81] *Lloyd Cheyham & Co. v. Littlejohn & Co.* [1987] BCLC 303 at p. 313.

So saying, any such view must take into account the fact that accounting standards are not set in stone and do change from time to time.[82]

As previously stated, compliance with accepted accounting principles is *prima facie* evidence that accounts are true and fair.[83] There is an expectation that accountants will act in conformity with it.[84]

The SSAP is, however, merely guidance as to best practice. Thus it may be that the departure from the SSAP is justified, for example, in an attempt to avoid uncertainty or to give a fairer view of the company's true position.[85]

6.2.2 FRS

The Accounting Standards Board has developed its own statement of accounting practice called Financial Reporting Standards ("FRS"). The SSAPs are gradually being replaced by FRS. These apply to Companies Act accounts.

6.2.3 SAS

The Consultative Committee of Accountancy Bodies established in 1991 the Auditing Practices Board. This issues Statements of Auditing Standards (SAS). The SAS contain the mandatory principles and procedures for audits. They also issue Practice Notes and Bulletins which are of persuasive authority.

6.2.4 IFRS and IAS

From 1st January 2005 international financial reporting standards and international accounting standards are being introduced. These are issued by the International Accounting Standards Board and apply to International Accounting Standards Accounts. Companies who are subject to these are companies incorporated in the EEC, who are listed within the EU (who have debt or equity traded on a regulated market[86]) and who prepare group accounts.[87] From 2005 all companies (other than charities) can elect to use IAS accounts.

Auditing from 2005 is undertaken in accordance with the International Auditing Standards.

---

[82] *Associated Portland Cement Manufacturers v. Price Commission* [1975] ICR 27, 45-46.
[83] *Willingale v. International Commercial Bank Ltd* [1978] AC 834.
[84] *Re Press Caps* [1949] Ch 434.
[85] *Lloyd Cheyham & Co. v. Littlejohn & Co.* [1987] BCLC 303.
[86] The Alternative Investment Market (AIM) will require the use of IAS accounts from 2007.
[87] Thus only parent companies are caught by the requirement to file IAS accounts.

Chapter 7

OTHER ROLES OF THE ACCOUNTANT

7.1 THE ACCOUNTANT AS INSOLVENCY PRACTITIONER

7.1.1 An accountant may be licensed to act as an insolvency practitioner

In so far that he is so authorised by his recognised professional body and in so far that he remains within the rules and terms of that licence, an accountant may lawfully act as an insolvency practitioner.

It is unlawful and a criminal offence for a person to act as an insolvency practitioner in relation to a company at a time when he is not qualified to do so.[1] An administrative receiver, liquidator or provisional liquidator[2] or administrator[3] or a trustee in bankruptcy[4] must be an insolvency practitioner. Whilst an insolvency practitioner may also act as a nominee of a company voluntary arrangement or a supervisor of an individual voluntary arrangement, the Secretary of State reserves the right to recognise members of other bodies as being allowed to act for these purposes.[5]

Only individuals can qualify to act as an insolvency practitioner (thus a company or partnership cannot hold the qualification in its own right).[6] Accordingly it is the licensed person who remains the individual liable for disciplinary action in respect of the conduct of his firm or staff.

To be qualified to act as an insolvency practitioner he must, at the material time:

- be authorised to act through his membership of a recognised professional body and through being permitted to act as an

---

[1] Section 389(1), Section 430 Schedule 10 Insolvency Act 1986.
[2] Section 230 Insolvency Act 1986.
[3] Paragraph 6, Schedule B1, Insolvency Act 1986
[4] Section 292(2) Insolvency Act 1986
[5] Section 389A Insolvency Act 1986
[6] Section 390 Insolvency Act 1986.

insolvency practitioner by and under the rules of that recognised professional body[7]
- be authorised under an authorisation granted by a competent authority.[8]

If a recognised professional body withdraws an accountant's licence he ceases to be qualified to act as such. A recognised professional body may withdraw the licence without prior notice and without a hearing if it is necessary to protect the public and provided the accountant is able to subsequently challenge the decision.[9] By way of example, regulation 5.14 of the ICAEW's Insolvency Licensing Regulations and Guidance Notes of January 2004 permit the relevant licensing committee to make urgent orders (including withdrawal of a licence holder's authorisation) without prior notice to the licence holder.

7.1.2 The Recognised Professional Bodies

The accountancy bodies which are currently recognised professional bodies for these purposes are:

- Institute of Chartered Accountants in England and Wales
- The Insolvency Practitioners Association
- Institute of Chartered Accountants in Scotland
- Institute of Chartered Accountants in Ireland
- Association of Chartered Certified Accountants

The Association of Chartered Certified Accountants are presently unable to licence members of its subsidiary body, the Association of Authorised Public Accountants, to conduct insolvency work and authorised public accountants seeking to conduct insolvency work must either apply direct to the Secretary of State on the basis of experience or pursue the examination route through the Insolvency Practitioners Association.[10]

The recognised professional body must maintain and enforce rules to ensure that those members authorised as insolvency practitioners are fit and proper people and meet acceptable standards of practical training and experience and to ensure that the practice of their profession is properly regulated. If the

---

[7] Section 390(2) Insolvency Act 1986.
[8] Section 390(2) Insolvency Act 1986. The competent authority is either the Secretary of State or such body as the Secretary of State may specify in directions. No directions have as yet been given: Section 392(2) Insolvency Act 1986.
[9] *R v Institute of Chartered Accountants in England and Wales ex parte Eliades* (2001) Lawtel 31st January.
[10] Notes on Applying for an AAPA Non Statutory Practising Certificate 1998.

Secretary of State considers that the recognised professional body has ceased to fulfil these requirements, the Secretary of State has the power to revoke their status.[11]

7.1.3 Disqualification from acting as an insolvency practitioner

The Secretary of State can apply to disqualify an accountant from further acting as a liquidator.[12] In exercising the power to disqualify, the court can look at acts which predate the section and matters which are not subject to a conviction.[13]

A person further ceases[14] to be qualified to act as an insolvency practitioner if at the material time:

- he has insufficient security in place
- he is adjudged bankrupt or his estate has been sequestrated and that order has not been discharged
- he is subject to a disqualification order or has given a disqualification undertaking under the Company Directors Disqualification Act 1986
- he becomes a patient under the Mental Health Act 1983.

7.1.4 Authorisation to act as an insolvency practitioner

In deciding whether or not to grant, refuse or withdraw authorisation to act as an insolvency practitioner (each authorisation lasts a maximum period of 3 years[15]), the accountant's competent authority must determine whether he is a fit and proper person[16] and satisfies the requirements for education and training that apply to him.[17]

Fitness and propriety of an applicant for authorisation by the competent authority is determined with regard to:

- Whether the applicant has been convicted of any offence of fraud, dishonesty or violence;
- Whether the applicant has contravened any provision of enactment contained in the insolvency legislation;

---

[11] Section 391 Insolvency Act 1986.
[12] Section 188 Companies Act 1981.
[13] *Re Arctic Engineering* [1986] 1 WLR 686.
[14] Section 390 Insolvency Act 1986.
[15] Regulation 10, Insolvency Practitioner Regulations 2005.
[16] Regulation 6, Insolvency Practitioner Regulations 2005.
[17] Regulations 7 and 8, Insolvency Practitioner Regulations 2005.

- Whether the applicant has engaged in any practices in the course of carrying out any trade, profession or vocation or in the course of the discharge of any functions relating to any office or employment appearing to be deceitful, oppressive or otherwise unfair or improper, whether unlawful or not, or which otherwise cast doubt upon his probity or competence for discharging the duties of an insolvency practitioner;
- Whether in respect of any insolvency practice carried on by the applicant at the date of or any time prior to the making of the application, there were established adequate systems of control of the practice and adequate records relating to the practice, including accounting records, and whether such systems of control and records have been and were maintained on an adequate basis;
- Whether the insolvency practice of the applicant is, or has been or, where the applicant is not yet carrying on such a practice, will be carried on with independence, integrity and the professional skills appropriate to the range and scale of the practice and the proper performance of the duties of an insolvency practitioner and in accordance with generally accepted professional standards, practices and principles;
- Whether the applicant, in any case where has acted as an insolvency practitioner, has failed to disclose fully to such persons as might reasonably be expected to be affected thereby circumstances where there is or appears to be a conflict of interest between his so acting and any interest of his own, whether personal, financial or otherwise, without having received such consent as might be appropriate to his acting or continuing to act despite the existence of such circumstances.[18]

Before an insolvency practitioner takes an appointment, he furthermore needs to have in force a bond in the form approved by the Secretary of State for Trade and Industry to make good any losses arising out of the fraud or dishonesty of the insolvency practitioner.[19]

---

[18] Regulation 6(a)-(f), Insolvency Practitioner Regulations 2005
[19] Regulation 12 and Part 2, Schedule 2, Insolvency Practitioner Regulations 2005

7.2 FINANCIAL SERVICES AND THE ACCOUNTANT

7.2.1 The present position

From 1st December 2002 (N2) responsibility for new investment business passed to the Financial Services Authority. Business conducted before this date remains the responsibility of the relevant Recognised Professional Body.

Under the new regime a distinction is drawn between "mainstream investment business", such as advising on public offers and direct advice on investment products and portfolio management, and those who conduct investment business which is only incidental to other professional services.

Accountants who conduct mainstream investment work are now regulated by the Financial Services Authority.

From 1st December 2002 (N2) accountants who conduct mainstream investment work are now regulated by the Financial Services Authority. Those who undertake investment activity which is only incidental to other professional services will be entitled to the status of an "exempt professional firm" under Part XX of the Financial Services and Markets Act 2000. These will continue to be regulated by their professional bodies, now known as Designated Professional Bodies.[20]

The Designated Professional Bodies for the accountancy profession are:

- The Institute of Chartered Accountants in England and Wales
- The Institute of Chartered Accountants in Ireland
- The Institute of Chartered Accountants in Scotland
- The Association of Chartered Certified Accountants.

As for business conducted before N2, membership of these bodies did not of itself confer entitlement to undertake investment activity which was only incidental to other professional services and accountants still needed to be licenced by a Designated Professional Body[21] if they wished to undertake this incidental work.

---

[20] Section 326 Financial Services and Markets Act 2000.
[21] These were described as Recognised Professional Bodies. Recognised professional bodies conferred an authorised person that status by issuing certificates (basically either to their members or concerns run by members of recognised professional bodies) in accordance with the Financial Services Act Schedule 3 Paragraph 2.

No person is allowed to carry on investment business in the United Kingdom unless he is either an authorised or an exempted person within the meaning of the Financial Services and Markets Act 2000.[22]

Unauthorised conduct of investment business, which includes investment advice and arranging deals in investments, attracts both civil and criminal penalties[23]. There is a limited exception to this where the investment advice is a necessary part of other accountancy advice.[24]

Carrying on or purporting to carry on investment business without authorisation carries criminal sanctions.[25] It is a defence if the accountant is able to prove that he took all reasonable precautions and exercised due care and diligence.[26]

It is an offence[27] for a person in order to encourage others to enter into an investment agreement

- to make a statement, promise or forecast which he knows to be misleading, false or deceptive or which dishonestly conceals any material facts
- recklessly (whether dishonestly or not) to make a statement, promise or forecast which he knows to be misleading, false or deceptive.

It is furthermore an offence[28] for a person to do any act or engage in any course of conduct which creates a misleading impression whether as to the market in, value of or price of any investments where that was done in order to encourage others to enter into any investment agreement or otherwise deal in or with any investments.

Where any offence under the Financial Services and Markets Act 2000 is committed by a limited company, every director, shadow director, secretary or manager as a result of whose neglect, connivance or consent the offence is proved to have been committed is also deemed guilty of the offence and is

---

[22] The general prohibition under the present law is now found at section 19, Financial Services and Markets Act 2000.
[23] The present law is now found at section 23 and 26, Financial Services and Markets Act 2000
[24] The present law is now found at reg 67, Financial Services and Markets Act (Regulated Activities) Order 2001. The advice must not be remunerated separately.
[25] Section 23, Financial Services and Markets Act 2000.
[26] Section 16(3), Financial Services and Markets Act 2000.
[27] Section 397(1), Financial Services and Markets Act 2000.
[28] Section 397(2), Financial Services and Markets Act 2000.

liable to be prosecuted.[29] Similarly every partner is also liable for an offence committed by the partnership where the offence was committed as a result of his neglect, connivance or consent.[30]

7.2.2 The meaning of investment

The definition of an investment is now found at Schedule 2 Part II, Financial Services and Markets Act 2000. This includes:[31]

- shares and stock in the share capital of a company
- debentures
- debenture stock
- loan stock
- bonds
- certificates of deposit
- any instruments acknowledging present or future indebtedness
- loan stock or bonds or other instrument acknowledging present or future indebtedness issued by government or a local or public authority
- warrants or other instruments entitling the holder to subscribe for other investments
- certificates or instruments allowing the holder to transfer securities held by another
- units in a collective investment scheme
- options
- futures
- contracts for differences or any contract whose purpose is to secure a profit or avoid a loss by reference to any the value of any property or of any index
- long term insurance contracts
- membership of or underwriting capacity at Lloyds of London
- deposits
- loans secured on land
- any other asset, property right or interest in respect of which business activity of a specified kind is being conducted within

---

[29] Section 400, Financial Services and Markets Act 2000. Where the offence is committed through a company, the provision catches de facto directors, the chief executive, members of committee of management or persons purporting to act as such and persons controlling the company.
[30] Section 400, Financial Services and Markets Act 2000. This provision also extends to persons holding themselves out as partners.
[31] Schedule 2 Part II, Financial Services and Markets Act 2000.

the meaning of section 22(1) Financial Services and Markets Act 2000.

7.2.3 Investment Business

The list of regulated investment activities are found in Schedule 2 Part I, Financial Services and Markets Act 2000. This includes activities relating to investment, such as:

- Buying, selling, subscribing to or underwriting investments for himself or as agent for another
- Agreeing or offering to buy, sell, subscribe to or underwrite investments
- Accepting deposits
- Offering or agreeing to make arrangements for another person to either buy, sell, subscribe to or underwrite investments or for him to participate in such a transaction
- Offering or agreeing to make arrangements to safeguard or administer assets belonging to another
- Managing or offering or agreeing to manage investments belonging to another (where these either include investments or may include investments at the manager's discretion)
- Giving or agreeing or offering to give advice in relation to buying, selling, subscribing to or underwriting investments or any rights relating to the investment
- Establishing, operating or winding up a collective investment scheme
- Sending, causing to be sent or offering or agreeing to make arrangements to send instructions on behalf of another person relating to an investment by a computer based system.

The restrictions created by this wide ranging list are qualified by the Financial Services and Markets Act (Regulated Activities) Order 2001.

Amongst other things this creates an important exception in respect of the restriction on making arrangements for another to buy, sell or subscribe for investments, administering and safeguarding investment and giving advice in relation to investments where the accountant performs this in the course of his professional work.[32] To benefit from this exception:

---

[32] Reg 67, Financial Services and Markets Act (Regulated Activities) Order 2001.

- The work should not amount to a regulated investment activity on some other basis,[33] and,
- The work needs to be reasonably regarded as a necessary part of other professional services,[34] and,
- The regulated work must not be remunerated separately from the other professional services.[35]

7.2.4 Chartered Certified Accountants

Sole practitioners will only be eligible to carry on regulated activities where he is a member of ACCA and he holds a current practicing certificate and the main business of his practice is the provision of public practice accountancy services.[36]

A partnership will only be eligible to carry on regulated activities where:

- at least one of the partners in the firm is a member and
- each partner who is not a member is
  - a member of another designated professional body and is entitled to practice accountancy and is subject to the regulations of the Association or
  - is entitled to practice accountancy and is subject to the regulations of the Association
- the partners who are members of the Association or of another designated professional body (if any) manage or control the firm and
- the main business of the partnership is the provision of public practice accountancy services
- each partner who is a member holds a practicing certificate[37]

A Company will only be eligible to carry on regulated activities where:

- at least one director and the controlling shareholder is a member and
- each director who is not a member is

---

[33] Reg 67(1)(a), Financial Services and Markets Act (Regulated Activities) Order 2001.
[34] Reg 67(1)(b), Financial Services and Markets Act (Regulated Activities) Order 2001.
[35] Reg 67(2), Financial Services and Markets Act (Regulated Activities) Order 2001.
[36] Reg 3(1), Chapter 3, The Chartered Certified Accountants' Designated Professional Body Regulations 2001 as amended.
[37] Reg 3(2), Chapter 3, The Chartered Certified Accountants' Designated Professional Body Regulations 2001 as amended.

- a member of another designated professional body and is entitled to practice accountancy and is subject to the regulations of the Association or
  - entitled to practice accountancy and is subject to the regulations of the Association
- the directors who are members of the Association or of another designated professional body manage or control the firm, and
- its main business is the provision of public practice accountancy services, and
- each director who is a member holds a practicing certificate[38]

7.2.5 Authorised Public Accountants

The special authorisation given to the Association of Chartered Certified Accountants presently does not extend to members of their subsidiary body, the Association of Authorised Public Accountants.

7.2.6 Chartered Accountants

Authorisations are limited to firms where:[39]

a. the principle business of the firm is the provision of professional services
b. at least one principal[40] must be a member of either the Institute of Chartered Accountants in England and Wales or the Institute of Chartered Accountants of Scotland or the Institute of Chartered Accountants of Ireland
c. each principal of the whose is not a member of one of the Institute must be a regulated non member[41] or an affiliate of the Institute of Chartered Accountants of Ireland or the Institute of Chartered Accountants in England and Wales
d. the firm complies with the Professional Indemnity Insurances Byelaws of the Institute of Chartered Accountants of Scotland or the Professional Indemnity Insurances Regulations of the Institute of Chartered Accountants of Ireland or the Institute of Chartered Accountants in England and Wales

---

[38] Reg 3(3), Chapter 3, The Chartered Certified Accountants' Designated Professional Body Regulations 2001 as amended.
[39] Paragraph 2.03, Designated Professional Body Handbook October 2004.
[40] A "principal" for these purposes is a sole practitioner, a partner (or salaried partner) in a partnership, a member of a limited liability partnership or a director of a company where the firm is constituted as such.
[41] With the meaning of Chapter XX of the Rules of the Institute of Chartered Accountants of Scotland.

e. There is no direction under section 328 Financial Services and Markets Act 2000 or order under section 329 Financial Services and Markets Act 2000 has been made against the firm
f. There is no reason for the Institute to believe it would not be appropriate for the firm to hold a licence.

7.3 DIRECTOR'S DISQUALIFICATION AND THE ACCOUNTANT DIRECTOR

7.3.1 Company Director's Disqualification Act 1986

A person may be disqualified from acting as a director a company:

- On his conviction for an indictable offence in connection with the promotion, formation, management, liquidation or striking off of a company, with the receivership of a company's property or with his being an administrative receiver of a company.[42]

- if he has persistently been in default in relation to provisions of the companies legislation requiring any return, account or other document to be filed with, delivered or sent, or notice of any matter to be given, to the registrar of companies.[43]

- if, in the course of the winding up of a company, it appears that he has been guilty of an offence of fraudulent trading or he has otherwise been guilty, while an officer or liquidator of the company, receiver of the company's property or administrative receiver of the company, of any fraud in relation to the company or of any breach of his duty as such officer, liquidator, receiver or administrative receiver.[44]

- On his conviction for a summary offence in consequence of a contravention of, or failure to comply with, any provision of the companies legislation requiring a return, account or other document to be filed with, delivered or sent, or notice of any matter to be given, to the registrar of companies.[45]

- if his conduct as a director of that company makes him unfit to be concerned in the management of a company.[46]

---

[42] Section 2, Company Directors Disqualification Act 1986.
[43] Section 3 Company Directors Disqualification Act 1986.
[44] Section 4 Company Directors Disqualification Act 1986.
[45] Section 5 Company Directors Disqualification Act 1986.
[46] Section 6 Company Directors Disqualification Act 1986.

- if upon an investigation, it is determined that his conduct in relation to the company makes him unfit to be concerned in the management of a company.[47]
- upon his breach of competition law if his conduct as a director makes him unfit to be concerned in the management of a company.[48]
- upon his being declared by the court to be liable to make a contribution to a company's assets for fraudulent or wrongful trading.[49]

Of these, the most common basis for instituting proceedings is the mandatory ground under section 6, namely that upon the liquidation of his company, his conduct as a director is such that it renders him unfit to be concerned in the management of a company.

A "director" includes any person occupying the position of director, by whatever name called.[50] This provision is wide enough to cover both:

- *de jure* director (the director listed at Companies House),
- *de facto* directors (a person who acts as a director although not formally appointed as such[51]), and,
- shadow directors (persons on whose instructions the directors are accustomed to act[52])

Unfitness is a question of fact.[53] The question is whether the complaints found proven against the director constitute as a matter of ordinary construction.

The objective of the legislation is the protection of the public.[54] Ordinary commercial misjudgement is not enough to justify disqualification; the Department for Business Enterprise & Regulatory Reform (formerly known as the DTI) must prove that the conduct displayed a lack of commercial

---

[47] Section 8 Company Directors Disqualification Act 1986.
[48] Section 9A Company Directors Disqualification Act 1986.
[49] Section 10 Company Directors Disqualification Act 1986.
[50] Section 741 Companies Act 1985.
[51] *Re Lo-Line Electric Motors Ltd*[1988] Ch 477, *Re Richborough Furniture Ltd* [1996] BCC 155.
[52] Section 22(5) Company Directors Disqualification Act 1986, *Secretary of State for Trade and Industry v Deverell* [2001] Ch 340.
[53] *Re Lo-Line Electric Motors* [1990] BCLC 677.
[54] *Re Sevenoaks Stationers (Retail) Ltd* [1990] BCLC 668.

probity or, in an extreme case, gross negligence or total incompetence would suffice to show unfitness.[55]

Factors which may be taken into account[56] in an insolvent company in determining whether a director is or was unfit set out at Schedule 1, Parts I and II, Company Directors Disqualification Act 1986 include:

- misfeasance or breach of fiduciary duty
- misapplication or retention of company money
- the extent of the director's responsibility for the company's insolvency
- whether the director entered into transactions which are liable to be set aside under the debt avoidance provisions of the Insolvency Act 1986, Part XV
- the extent of the director's responsibility for any failure by the company to:
    - keep accounting records[57]
    - retain records[58]
    - keep a register of directors and secretaries[59]
    - keep and enter up the shareholders' register[60]
    - retain the shareholders' register[61]
    - make annual returns on behalf of the company[62]
    - submit annual returns on behalf of the company in a timely fashion[63]
    - register any charges it creates[64]
- the extent of the director's responsibility for any failure by the company to supply goods or services paid for
- the extent of the director's responsibility for any transaction by the company liable to be set aside under Sections 127, 238 or 240 Insolvency Act 1986

---

[55] *Re Lo-Line Electric Motors* [1990] BCLC 677, per Browne Wilkinson VC.
[56] Section 9 Company Directors Disqualification Act 1986.
[57] Section 221 Companies Act 1985, section 387 Companies Act 2006.
[58] Section 222 Companies Act 1985, section 389 Companies Act 2006.
[59] Section 288 Companies Act 1985, section 162 and 275 Companies Act 2006.
[60] Section 352 Companies Act 1985, section 113 Companies Act 2006.
[61] Section 352 Companies Act 1985, section 114 Companies Act 2006.
[62] Sections 363 and 364 Companies Act 1985, section 860 Companies Act 2006.
[63] Section 365 Companies Act 1985.
[64] Sections 299 and 415 Companies Act 1985.

- the extent of the director's responsibility for failing to call a creditors' meeting in a creditors' voluntary winding up under Section 98 Insolvency Act 1986
- the extent to which the director failed to comply with his obligations in respect of:
  - the company's statement of affairs in administration[65]
  - the statement of affairs to the administrative receiver[66]
  - the attendance of meetings and the statement of affairs in the creditors' voluntary winding up[67]
  - the company's statement of affairs in a court winding up[68]
  - his duty to deliver up the company's property[69]
  - his duty to cooperate with the company's liquidator[70]

The list is not exhaustive.[71]

Upon disqualification the accountant is prohibited from being a director of a company, acting as a receiver of a company's property or in any way, directly or indirectly, being concerned in the promotion, formation or management of a company or limited liability partnership (unless he has leave of the court) or from acting as an insolvency practitioner.[72]

Breaching a disqualification order or undertaking carries serious criminal[73] and civil consequences.[74] The court's permission can be obtained by a disqualified person to undertake appointments which would otherwise breach a disqualification order or undertaking[75] if the court can be satisfied that the public can be adequately protected against a recurrence of the conduct.

7.3.2 Particular vulnerability of accountants in disqualification proceedings

Lawyers advising accountants as to the implications of conceding to a disqualification order or undertaking need to be aware that an order or

---

[65] Section 22 Insolvency Act 1986.
[66] Section 47 Insolvency Act 1986.
[67] Section 99 Insolvency Act 1986.
[68] Section 13 Insolvency Act 1986.
[69] Section 234 Insolvency Act 1986.
[70] Section 235 Insolvency Act 1986.
[71] *Re Bath Glass* [1988] BCLC 329, 332.
[72] Section 1, Company Directors Disqualification Act 1986.
[73] Section 13, Company Directors Disqualification Act 1986.
[74] Section 15 Company Directors Disqualification Act 1986.
[75] Section 17 Company Directors Disqualification Act 1986.

undertaking is likely to carry more far reaching consequences than might be apply to the ordinary director.

Most accountancy institutes now view the fact that a members is subject to a director's disqualification order as evidence of the accountant committing a serious disciplinary offence (often) justifying his exclusion from their membership. A disqualification order or undertaking is likely to result in an accountant not merely losing the possibility of acting as a director or insolvency practitioner but is also likely to result in loss of membership of his professional body. By way of illustration, Disciplinary Bye Law 7 (1) of the ICAEW's Disciplinary Bye-laws provides that such disqualifications constitute conclusive evidence of conduct bringing discredit on the member.

The disqualification order presents difficulties for an accountant seeking employment in industry. Upon disqualification the accountant is not merely prohibited from being a director of a company but also from being in any way, directly or indirectly, being concerned in the promotion, formation or management of a company.[76] Quite what amounts to "being involved in the management of a company" remains a grey area[77] and may present particular difficulties for a former financial director because any replacement post is likely to involve him entering the company at a senior level and will involve them in the central direction of their employer company. It is plainly advisable that the permission of the court is both sought and obtained as a precaution before taking any such employment.

The accountant is also likely to find it difficult to find any employment in an accountancy practice. This is because another consequence of a disqualification order or undertaking is that the accountant is likely to no longer be considered a "fit and proper" person for the purposes of his employment or engagement in work involving audit, insolvency or financial services. Engagement of a person who is not fit and proper in regulated work would expose the employer firm to regulatory action; this may include an order that the firm should cease to employ that person in so far as he is or will be engaged in any of the statutory reserved areas.

It is unlikely that the Court will be sympathetic based on the greater consequences for an accountant director. The court will expect a higher standard of conduct from him than from other directors given that he is a

---

[76] Section 1, Company Directors Disqualification Act 1986.
[77] *R v Campbell* 78 Cr App Rep 95 in which a self employed management consultant was convicted of being involved in the management of a client company in breach of his disqualification even though he was neither a director not an employee of that company.

professional; if he fails in that high standard he is viewed to bring the consequences upon himself.

7.3.3 Cut-throat defences

The accountant facing disqualification proceedings is likely to find himself blamed by other directors for the parlous state of the company. There are a number of reasons for this.

He is likely to be employed as a Financial Director and therefore the person responsible for communicating the true financial position of the company to the other directors. Directors who face allegations that they traded their company whilst insolvent or preferred trade creditors over the Crown debts have sometimes been known to suggest that their Financial Director somehow kept the company's true financial position from them.

Moreover reliance on an accountant that the company's statutory obligations were complied with may, in certain circumstances, amount to a defence[78] or at the very least substantial mitigation.[79] Reliance on an accountant will not amount to an absolute defence. Certainly it will not provide an excuse for matters the director should have known about or from taking steps consequent on that knowledge.[80]

7.4 THE ACCOUNTANT AS COMPANY SECRETARY

7.4.1 An accountant may hold the office of company secretary

An accountant may hold the office of company secretary. In the case of a public limited company, Section 286 Companies Act 1985[81] imposes a further duty upon the directors to ensure that the company secretary is a person who appears to them to have the requisite experience and knowledge to fulfil the role and who has either;

    a. on the 22nd December 1980, held the office of secretary, assistant or deputy secretary of the company, or
    b. for at least three years after the five years preceding his appointment as secretary, has held the appointment of company secretary of a company other than the private company, or

---

[78] *Re Cladrose* [1990] BCC 11, *Re Douglas Construction Services Ltd* [1988] BCLC 3973.
[79] *Re Cargo Agency* [1992] BCLC 686.
[80] *Re GSAR Realisations Ltd* [1993] BCLC 409.
[81] Section 273 Companies Act 2006

 c. is a person who by virtue of previous offices held, appears to the directors to be capable of discharging the functions required of the secretary, or
 d. is a barrister, advocate or solicitor, called or admitted in any part of the United Kingdom, or
 e. is a member of one of the following bodies:
  (i) Institute of Chartered Secretaries and Administrators
  (ii) Institute of Chartered Accountants in England and Wales
  (iii) Institute of Chartered Accountants in Scotland
  (iv) Institute of Chartered Accountants in Ireland
  (v) Chartered Institute of Management Accountants
  (vi) Association of Chartered Certified Accountants
  (vii) Chartered Institute of Public Finance and Accountancy

Under the Companies Act 2006 private limited companies will no longer be required to have a company secretary.[82]

7.4.2 Disqualification of auditors from acting as company secretary

Section 27(1), Companies Act 1989[83] however restricts appointment as company secretary to a person who is also an auditor of the company.

---

[82] Section 270(1) Companies Act 2006.
[83] Section 1214 Companies Act 2006.

Chapter 8

THE ACCOUNTANT BEFORE THE COURT

8.1 THE ACCOUNTANT AS ADVOCATE

8.1.1 General position as to rights of audience before the civil courts

Any person, whether he is a professional man or not, may attend a trial as a friend of either party and may quietly make suggestions and give advice to that party.[1] Where someone of that nature is wrongly excluded, the proceedings are not a nullity but the onus is on the other side to show that the exclusion did not cause prejudice.[2] Thus an accountant may attend a trial as a friend of either party and may quietly make suggestions and give advice to that party.

It is important to stress that this right goes far short of a right to appear and be remunerated for appearing as an advocate. Moreover a court would be slow to require a losing party to pay the costs of employing such a Mackenzie friend.

8.1.2 Professional risks of the accountant appearing as advocate

Whilst it is far from unusual for an accountant to attempt to appear as his client's advocate, such conduct in the ordinary civil courts would be redolent with risk for the accountant.

By way of illustration, such conduct may well give rise to a claim against the accountant in negligence given that:

1. there is a real risk that the court might refuse the accountant rights of audience
2. if successful at the hearing, there is a risk that the client will be financially prejudiced by difficulties in achieving recovery of the

---

[1] *McKenzie v. McKenzie* [1970] 3 All ER 1034.
[2] *McKenzie v. McKenzie* [1970] 3 All ER 1034, 1039 per Sachs LJ.

　　　　　　legal costs of employing the accountant as advocate against the other side
3. if unsuccessful, poor advice on law and procedure or indeed the very act of failing to advise a client to deploy a barrister or solicitor may show a want of professional care.

There are professional risks too. Given the wording used in court forms and attendance slips, many opportunities arise for an accountant to inadvertently mislead the court that he is appearing as a barrister or solicitor. Misleading the court as to his professional capacity is a matter of some seriousness and would almost invariably amount to an act of professional misconduct[3]. Indeed if an accountant falsely held himself out as a solicitor he would be committing a criminal offence.[4]

8.1.3 Rights of audience under the Small Claims Procedure in the County Court

An accountant does have the possibility of appearing for a client as a lay representative in proceedings at a small claims hearing on behalf of a party[5]. The right is confined to a right of audience and does not extend to the conduct of litigation (and thus excludes the preparation and filing of court documents).[6]

The right may only be exercised in the presence of the party represented;[7] thus a client would not be able to send his accountant *in his place* as his advocate as the accountant would not have rights of audience in such circumstances.

The representative must behave honestly, reasonably and responsibly and the court may refuse to hear or disqualify a lay representative if the court is not satisfied by his competence or conduct.[8]

---

[3] Having said this, the professional body is likely to take a pragmatic view and look at each case on its individual facts to assess the seriousness of the conduct; a self evidently accidental misrepresentation would be unlikely to engage any disciplinary process.
[4] Section 20, Solicitors Act 1974.
[5] Lay Representatives (Rights of Audience) Order 1992, pursuant to Section 11 Courts and Legal Services Act 1990.
[6] Paragraph 2, Lord Chancellor's Practice Direction of 22nd October, 1992 "Practice Direction: Lay Representation in County Courts.
[7] Paragraph 4, Lord Chancellor's Practice Direction of 22nd October, 1992 "Practice Direction: Lay Representation in County Courts, article 2(2) of the Lay Representative (Rights of Audience) Order 1992.
[8] Paragraphs 5, 8, 11, Lord Chancellor's Practice Direction of 22nd October, 1992 "Practice Direction: Lay Representation in County Courts, article 11 of the Lay Representative (Rights of Audience) Order 1992; see generally Notes in The County Court Practice to CCR Order 19 rule

An accountant may charge for appearing for a client as a lay representative in proceedings at a small claims hearing on behalf of a party, but if he does so a higher standard of competence will be expected from him by the court.[9]

8.1.4 Powers of the court to confer rights of audience

Section 27(1), Courts and Legal Services Act 1990 gives the court power to grant rights of audience to an accountant, as a lay person, to represent a client in a case. Section 27(2) Court and Legal Services Act provides "the person shall have rights of audience before a court in relation to any proceedings only in the following cases:

(a) Where

   (i) he has a right of audience before that court in relation to those proceedings granted by the appropriate authorised body; and

   (ii) that body's qualification regulations and rules have been approved for the purposes of this section in relation to the granting of that right.

(b) Where paragraph a) does not apply but he has a right of audience before that court in relation to those proceedings granted by or under any enactment.

(c) Where paragraph a) does not apply but he has a right of audience granted by that court in relation to those proceedings.

The court must consider the criteria set out under Section 17, Courts and Legal Services Act 1990 before granting rights of audience.[10]

Section 17, The Court and Legal Services Act 1990 sets out the following considerations when assessing whether a person should be granted a right of audience or be granted a right to conduct litigation in relation to any court proceedings:

(a) Whether he is qualified in accordance with the educational and training requirements appropriate to court or proceedings;

---

1 and para. 3.2 to the Practice Direction to Civil Procedure Rules Part 27. This last provision means that the accountant as lay representative can only represent a party who is attending unless the court gives leave.

[9] Paragraph 5, Lord Chancellor's Practice Direction of 22nd October, 1992 "Practice Direction: Lay Representation in County Courts, Section 143(b), County Court Act 1984. Outside this express and limited dispensation, it is unlawful for a person other than a legal representative to charge a fee for representation in the County Court: Section 143 County Court Act 1984.

[10] *Chauhan v. Chauhan* [1997] 2 FCR 206.

(b) Whether he is a member of a professional or other body which:

    (i) has rules of conduct (however described) governing the conduct of its members;

    (ii) has an effective mechanism for reporting the rules of conduct, and

    (iii) is likely to enforce them.

(c) Whether in the case of a body whose members are, or will be, providing advocacy services, the rules of conduct make satisfactory provision in relation to the court or proceedings in question requiring any such member not to withhold those services:

    (i) on the grounds that the nature of the case is objectionable to him or any section of the public;

    (ii) on the grounds that the conduct, opinions or beliefs of the prospective client are unacceptable to him or to any section of the public;

    (iii) on the grounds relating to the source of any financial support which may properly be given the prospective client for the proceedings in question (for example on the grounds that such support will be available under the Legal Aid Act 1988).

(d) Whether the rules of conduct are in relation to the court or proceedings, appropriate in the interests of the proper and efficient administration of justice.

The court will only exercise its discretion in favour of representation by a lay person in exceptional circumstances.[11] An accountant granted such rights has the same duty as counsel to inform the court of adverse authorities.[12]

Where the court does make such an order, special exemptions apply to the representative over the conduct of the case. Section 27(10) provides:

> Section 20 of the Solicitors Act 1974 (Unqualified Person not to act as a Solicitor). Section 22 of that Act (Unqualified Person not to prepare Certain Documents, etc) and Section 25 of that Act (Costs where an Unqualified Person acts as a Solicitor) shall not apply in relation to any act done on the exercise of a right of audience.

---

[11] *D v. S (Rights of Audience)* [1997] 2 FCR 217.
[12] *Chauhan v. Chauhan* [1997] 2 FCR 206.

Otherwise it is a criminal offence for a non-solicitor to act as a solicitor or as such issue a writ or process or defend any action or suit or proceedings.[13] It is also a criminal offence for an unqualified person to charge for the preparation of pleadings for proceedings.[14] No costs can in any event be recovered where an unqualified person acts as a solicitor.[15]

8.1.5 The accountant's rights of audience when appearing as his client's advocate before the General and Special Commissioners

An accountant who is a member of an incorporated society of accountants has rights of audience to be heard on behalf of the tax payer at any appeal before the General or Special Commissioners under the Taxes Acts.[16] The Special or General Commissioners may refuse to hear an accountant who is not a member of an incorporated society of accountants on behalf of the tax payer where there are good and sufficient reasons for doing so.[17]

Those bodies which are an incorporated society of accountants for these purposes are:

- Institute of Chartered Accountants in England and Wales
- Institute of Chartered Accountants in Scotland
- Institute of Chartered Accountants in Ireland
- Association of Chartered Certified Accountants
- Chartered Institute of Management Accountants
- Institute of Financial Accountants
- Association of Authorised Public Accountants
- Chartered Institute of Public Finance and Accountancy
- Association of Cost and Executive Accountants
- Association of International Accountants[18]

Her Majesty's Revenue and Customs may be represented by a barrister, advocate, solicitor or by one of their officers.[19]

---

[13] Section 20, Solicitors Act 1974.
[14] Section 22, Solicitors Act 1974.
[15] Section 25, Solicitors Act 1974.
[16] See Regulation 14(a) Special Commissioners (Jurisdiction and Procedure) Regulations 1994, reg 12(a) General Commissioners (Jurisdiction and Procedure) Regulations 1994.
[17] See Regulation 14(a) Special Commissioners (Jurisdiction and Procedure) Regulations 1994, reg 12(a) General Commissioners (Jurisdiction and Procedure) Regulations 1994.
[18] The Institute of Company Accountants has been amalgamated into the Association of International Accountants.
[19] See Regulation 14(b) Special Commissioners (Jurisdiction and Procedure) Regulations 1994, reg 12(b) General Commissioners (Jurisdiction and Procedure) Regulations 1994.

An accountant appearing before the tax commissioners as an advocate warrants that he has the requisite expertise and knowledge of the law, evidence and procedure required to do so and the fact he was incompetent was not enough to render the hearing unfair.[20]

Membership means full and current membership of the incorporated society. Thus the Commissioners were entitled to refuse to hear an accountant who was suspended from membership of (what was then) the Institute of Cost and Management Accountants and the Chartered Association of Certified Accountants.[21]

It would appear that even where an accountant does represent his client as advocate that legal professional privilege does not cover the relationship between an accountant and his client and thus an accountant, unlike a solicitor, was compellable as a witness against his client to give evidence on the present and previously advanced case.[22] An accountant appearing before the tax commissioners as an advocate will not be treated as a witness by the tax commissioners and his submissions will not constitute evidence on his client's behalf.[23]

8.2 THE ACCOUNTANT'S RIGHTS TO INSTRUCT COUNSEL

8.2.1 Direct Professional Access

An accountant who is a member of a body recognised by the General Council of the Bar as being entitled to have direct professional access may instruct Counsel in his own right and without recourse to a solicitor.

The bodies that have direct professional access to the Bar are:

- Institute of Chartered Accountants in England and Wales
- Institute of Chartered Accountants in Scotland
- Institute of Chartered Accountants in Ireland
- Association of Chartered Certified Accountants
- Chartered Institute of Management Accountants
- Association of Authorised Public Accountants
- Institute of Financial Accountants

---

[20] *Parmar v Woods* [2002] STI 852.
[21] *Cassell v. Crutchfield* (Inspector of Taxes) (1995) *The Times*, 5 June, Blackburne J.
[22] *Home or Away v Customs & Excise Commissioners* (2002) Lawtel 3rd May, VADT (Angus Nicol, Chairman).
[23] *Parmar v Woods* [2002] STI 852.

This entitles the accountant to brief and instruct counsel to advise in conference and by opinion, draft legal documents and negotiate.

It also entitles the accountant with direct professional access to instruct Counsel to appear in court in certain limited cases. Counsel is expressly prohibited from accepting instructions (other than through the intervention of a solicitor) to appear in the County Court, Crown Court, High Court, Employment Appeal Tribunal, Court of Appeal, House of Lords or Privy Council.[24] Counsel, however, can accept instructions from an accountant with direct professional access (and without the intervention of a solicitor) to appear in the Magistrates' Court, in any arbitration,[25] before any Tribunal, including the Employment Tribunal and before the Commissioners of the Inland Revenue.

Given that the right to instruct counsel is a right conferred on the accountant in and because of his professional capacity there can be little doubt in the fact that the accountant would be not merely entitled to pass on the cost of instructing the barrister to his client as a professional disbursement but also to charge his client professional fees for instructing counsel, attending counsel in conference and perusing documents prepared by counsel.

Barristers require separate insurance cover to accept direct professional access work. Barristers are obliged to keep a case record of all direct professional access work received and retain copies of all briefs and papers (this contrasts with instructions from a solicitor when the brief would normally be returned once the barrister has completed his instructions).[26]

A barrister is under a duty to decline the instructions if he considers that it is in the interests of his client that a solicitor be instructed.[27] Further if it becomes apparent to the barrister at any stage that it has become in the interest of the lay client that a solicitor be instructed, the barrister must decline to act further on the case.[28]

---

[24] Paragraph 3, Annexe E - The Direct Professional Access Rules, Code of Conduct of the Bar of England and Wales.
[25] Direct professional access will not extend to instructing counsel to attend a County Court "small claims track" trial.
[26] Paragraph 4, Annexe E - The Direct Professional Access Rules, Code of Conduct of the Bar of England and Wales.
[27] Paragraph 1, Annexe E - The Direct Professional Access Rules, Code of Conduct of the Bar of England and Wales.
[28] Paragraph 2, Annexe E - The Direct Professional Access Rules, Code of Conduct of the Bar of England and Wales.

8.2.2 BarDIRECT

Direct professional access now forms part of the "BarDIRECT" scheme. The rights conferred on bodies with Direct Professional Access are however distinct.

Members of the following professional organisations are now permitted under the Direct Professional Access / BarDIRECT scheme to instruct a barrister on an appeal in a tax matter to the High Court and Court of Appeal, where the member conducted that case (either representing the clients themselves or instructing a barrister) before General Commissioners' and Special Commissioners' hearings or VAT Tribunals. The scheme does not as yet extend to the House of Lords.

- The Tax Faculty of the Institute of Chartered Accountants for England and Wales
- The Association of Chartered Certified Accountants

Under the BarDIRECT terms of work, the barrister enters an enforceable contract with the accountant instructing him; this is to be contrasted with a barrister's relationship with a solicitor where by custom his instructions do not create a legally enforceable agreement.

The BarDIRECT terms of work entitle a barrister to refuse to undertake work if he feels a solicitor would better be instructed. Under clause 5(3) of the BarDIRECT Terms of Work an accountant agrees to pass on to his lay client any advice from the barrister to this effect.

Under paragraph 210 of the Bar Code of Conduct a barrister would not be able to undertake work on the instructions of an accountant which involves him handling client money, the general management of a client's affairs, litigation (including pleadings and correspondence with the other side), collecting evidence or attending a police station in the absence of a solicitor.

Under clause 6 of the BarDIRECT terms of work an accountant instructing a barrister is personally responsible for the barrister's fees. The fees are due 30 days after receipt of a fee note from the barrister and the barrister is entitled to charge interest at the judgement rate on overdue fees.[29] This does not prevent an accountant, instructing a counsel to advise one of his lay clients, to pass on the cost of counsel's fees to his lay client as a recoverable disbursement. Moreover the accountant would be entitled to charge

---

[29] Clauses 10(3) (4) and 12(7) BarDIRECT Terms of Work

professional fees to his lay client for the preparation of the barrister's brief and for attending the barrister in conference with the client (counsel will not advise a lay client in the absence of his instructing accountant).

Counsel's fees (or the basis for charging fees) for work must be negotiated in advance with counsel's clerk and agreed in writing.

Under clause 7 of the BarDIRECT Terms of Work, time for completion of the work by counsel is not of the essence and so if a short deadline is needed this should be agreed in writing.

8.3 THE ACCOUNTANT AS EXPERT WITNESS

8.3.1 The role of accountant as expert

The accountant's role in preparing expert reports to assist courts has become an increasingly important part of the fee income of accountancy practices.

Examples of the use of accountants as expert witnesses include:

- Assessing what a reasonable number of hours might be to complete accounts and distinguishing between bookkeeping work and accountancy work in disputes over accountants' fees[30]
- Valuing the shares of a company in unfair prejudice litigation[31]
- Calculating loss of past and future earnings and earnings potential in personal injury cases
- Estimating the value of damaged stock in insurance cases
- Valuing the partners' respective shares and the firm's goodwill in partnership litigation
- Showing how company profits were calculated and expenditure and loss subtracted[32]
- Expressing an opinion as to the level of competence expected of "the reasonably competent accountant" in professional negligence cases[33]
- Whether, in tax cases, payments are considered to be, under the accounting principles,[34] of a capital revenue nature

---

[30] *Sylvanus Okoye v. Leon Edgar White* (1999) LTL 17 February.
[31] Under s.459 Companies Act 1985
[32] *Bond v. Barrow* [1902] 1 Ch 353.
[33] Evidence can be given as to "matters of practice" but not as to what an accountant is bound by law to do: *Nelson Guarantee Corporation Ltd v. Hodgson* [1958] NZLR 609.
[34] *Odeon Associated Theatres v. Jones* [1972] 2 WLR 331 at 337.

- Providing in divorce cases valuations of businesses and giving advice on how tax liability might be minimised on the division of the assets.

Accountants are of particular use in fraud cases in explaining how the fraud was organised, its motive, how it was concealed, determining the extent of the fraud, identifying the weaknesses in the accounting or bookkeeping systems that facilitated the fraud or made its detection more difficult and advising on the responsibility for the recurrence of the fraud.

The Court of Appeal has however said expert evidence was not needed from an accountant on the meaning and interpretation of standard accountancy documents.[35]

The author suggests that this is a regrettable stance and does give rise to a real possibility of injustice.[36] There is a clear distinction between bookkeeping records and accounts. The courts are ill equipped, unless assisted, to interpret the latter; accounts do not mechanically record the company's figures but necessarily include the application of accounting standards and elements of judgment and interpretation which may differ according to the nature and health[37] of the business.

The importance of briefing the expert accountant at the outset cannot be underestimated (the decision to postpone his instruction by the litigation team usually proves a false economy), since often the assistance of an accountant enables the lawyers to gain at the outset a clearer overview of the case, its issues and the likely quantum of damages.

8.3.2 Privileges and limitations of the expert accountant when giving evidence

Normal witnesses of fact must confine their evidence to facts within their knowledge and may not state their opinion.[38]

The accountant is permitted, when giving evidence as an expert witness, not merely to state the facts within his knowledge but also his expert opinion. The expert accountant should explain the reasoning which led him to that

---

[35] *LHS Holdings v. Laporte* [2001] EWCA Civ 278.
[36] Whilst both the Bar and Bench do receive some training in interpreting accounts, this is of a fairly rudimentary nature.
[37] For example the approach to the valuation of assets may differ depending on whether or not the business is considered to remain a going concern.
[38] *Folkes v. Chadd* (1782) 3 Doug 157.

opinion. He may only give evidence as to the contents of books of account once those accounts have been adduced as evidence.[39]

Expert evidence is only admissible on a relevant matter on which the expert is qualified to give expert evidence.[40] Relevant matters include issues in the proceedings in question but which are outside the knowledge and experience of a layman.[41] If the matters are within the knowledge and experience of a layman, the expert is unnecessary and the judge can make up his mind without the help of an expert.[42]

An accountant appearing before the tax commissioners as an advocate will not be treated as a witness by the tax commissioners and his submissions will not constitute evidence on his client's behalf.[43] One person cannot appear both as an advocate and give expert opinion evidence.[44]

It has been said that on an application under section 726(1) Companies Act 1985[45] for an order for security for costs, a court cannot ignore the unchallenged expert evidence of an accountant over the ability of the company to pay its debts.[46]

So saying, it has been held that it is not unreasonable for a minority shareholder to reject an offer to buy his shares based on a valuation by an accountant where the accountant's valuation of the shares took into account the fact that he had a minority holding in preference to a court valuation on winding up.[47]

8.3.3 Qualification as an expert accountant

A witness is competent to give expert evidence only if in the opinion of the judge he is properly qualified in the subject calling for expertise.[48] Indeed expert evidence is only admissible on a relevant matter on which the expert is qualified to give expert evidence.[49]

---

[39] *Johnson v. Kershaw* (1847) 1 De G & Sm 260.
[40] Section 3(1), Civil Evidence Act 1972.
[41] *Liddell v Middleton* [1996] PIQR 36, 41.
[42] *R v Turner* [1975] QB 834, 841.
[43] *Parmar v Woods* [2002] STI 852.
[44] *Franks v. Towse* [2001] EWCA Civ 9.
[45] Repealed under the Companies Act 2006.
[46] *Kim Barker v. Aegon Insurance Company (UK)* (1989) *The Times*, 9 October, Court of Appeal.
[47] *Re Abbey Leisure* [1990] BCC 69.
[48] *Harmony Shipping Co v. Saudi Europe* [1979] 1 WLR 1380.
[49] Section 3(1), Civil Evidence Act 1972.

That expertise can be acquired through study, training or by experience and not necessarily through professional expertise.[50]

Thus an accountant, with many years' experience of practice in a foreign country, would be qualified to give expert evidence on issues of that foreign country's law even though his experience was not as a legal practitioner.[51]

In a professional negligence case however the expert should be qualified in the same field as the professional; only an accountant expert can speak with authority on what is to be expected of the ordinary competent accountant.[52]

8.3.4 Duties of the accountant when appearing as expert

Under Civil Procedure Rules Part 35.3, an accountant appearing as an expert witness before the civil courts is placed under a duty to help the court on the matters within his expertise and, importantly, this duty overrides any obligation to the person from whom he has received instructions or by whom he is paid. Put bluntly, however disappointing this may be for his client, the expert witness can no longer be seen as his client's "hired gun".

Mr. Justice Cresswell, in the leading authority, *The "Ikarian Reefer"*[53] set out the following principles governing the duties on an expert when giving evidence to the court:

- Expert evidence presented to the Court should be, and should be seen to be, the independent product of the expert uninfluenced as to the form or content by the exigencies of litigation[54].
- An expert witness should provide independent assistance to the court by way of objective unbiased opinion in relation to matters within his expertise.[55] An expert witness in the High Court should never assume the role of an advocate.

---

[50] Section 4(2), Civil Evidence Act 1972 and *R. v. Silverlock* [1894] 2 QB 766 (there a solicitor was able to give expert evidence as a handwriting expert although his grounding in the subject had merely been gleaned as an amateur enthusiast).
[51] *de Beeche v. South American Stores* [1935] AC 148.
[52] *Whalley v Roberts* [1990] 1 EGLR 164.
[53] *National Justice Compania Naviera SA v. Prudential Assurance Co Ltd (The "Ikarian Reefer")* [1993] 2 Lloyd's Rep. 68, 81–82.
[54] *Whitehouse v. Jordan* [1981] 1 W.L.R. 246, 256.
[55] *Pollivitte Ltd v. Commercial Union Assurance Company Plc* [1987] 1 Lloyd's Rep. 379, 386, *Re J* [1990] F.C.R. 193.

- An expert witness should state the facts or assumption on which his opinion is based. He should not omit to consider material facts which could detract from his concluded opinion.[56]
- An expert witness should make it clear when a particular question or issue falls outside his expertise.
- If an expert's opinion is not properly researched because he considers that insufficient data are available then this must be stated with an indication that the opinion is no more than a provisional one[57]. In cases where an expert witness who has prepared a report could not assert that the report contained the truth, the whole truth and nothing but the truth without some qualification that qualification should be stated in the report[58].
- If, after exchange of reports, an expert witness changes his view on the material having read the other side's expert report or for any other reason, such change of view should be communicated (though legal representative) to the other side without delay and when appropriate to the court.
- Where expert evidence refers to photographs, plans, calculations, analyses, measurements survey reports or other similar documents, these must be provided to the opposite party at the same time as the exchange of reports.

This is incorporated in the Practice Direction to Part 35 of the Civil Procedure Rules.

Indeed this change in the role of the expert is reflected in part by the increasing use by the court of the single joint expert witness who is instructed by both parties to assist the court.[59] Unless the court otherwise directs, the instructing parties are jointly and severally liable for the payment of the single joint expert's fees and expenses. Where a single joint expert receives conflicting instructions from the parties, which cannot be resolved by discussion, the expert has the right to apply to the court for directions.[60]

Any expert may file a written request for directions to assist him in carrying out his function as an expert.[61] An expert must, unless the court orders otherwise, provide a copy of any proposed request for directions to the party

---

[56] *Re J* [1990] F.C.R. 193.
[57] *Re J* [1990] F.C.R. 193.
[58] *Derby and Co. Ltd v. Weldon (No. 9)*, (1990) The Times, 9th November.
[59] Civil Procedure Rules Part 35.7.
[60] Civil Procedure Rules Part 35.14.
[61] Civil Procedure Rules Part 35.14.

instructing him, at least seven days before he files the request; and to all other parties, at least four days before he files it.

The court is given wide powers in respect of expert evidence. The court has powers to terminate instructions where the cost was disproportionate and to order that another expert be instructed.[62]

In civil court proceedings expert evidence is to be given in a written report unless the court directs otherwise.[63] Experts will not be called to give oral evidence unless and until the court has been satisfied that there is no scope for further minimising the matters in issue between the experts by discussions or written questions before lifting that limitation.

The court may, at any stage, direct a discussion between experts for the purpose of requiring the experts to identify and discuss the expert issues in the proceedings and where possible, reach an agreed opinion on those issues.[64] The court may specify the issues which the experts must discuss and will often direct that following a discussion between the experts they must prepare a statement for the court showing:-

- those issues on which they agree
- those issues on which they disagree
- a summary of their reasons for disagreeing.

It is also the general rule that, where a party wishes to use an expert's report at trial, or, having obtained the court's permission, wishes to call the expert to give evidence orally, he must disclose the report at an early stage to other parties.[65] The other side is entitled to put to an expert instructed by another party; or, to a single joint expert written questions about his report. Written questions may be put once only and within twenty-eight days of service of the expert's report; and, must be for the purpose only of clarification of the report unless either the court gives permission or the other party agrees.[66] An expert's answers to questions put by the parties in this way are treated as part of the expert's report.[67] Where the expert fails to answer a question put, the court has powers to prevent the offending party from relying on the evidence of that expert or from recovering his costs.

---

[62] *Kranidiotes v. Paschali* [2001] EWCA Civ 357.
[63] Civil Procedure Rules Part 35.5.
[64] Civil Procedure Rules Part 35.12.
[65] Civil Procedure Rules Part 35.13.
[66] Civil Procedure Rules Part 35.6.
[67] Civil Procedure Rules Part 35.6(3).

The Court of Appeal has indicated in *R v Secretary of State for Transport ex parte Factortame*[68] that, whilst legally unobjectionable, it would be very rare for the court to consent to an expert being instructed on a contingency fee basis. No such objection arose if accountants rather than being instructed as expert witnesses carefully restricted their role to the provision of accountancy support services to the experts who would be called.

8.3.5 Immunity as an expert

An expert witness cannot be sued in negligence in respect of evidence he gave in court or statements he had made for the purposes of giving such evidence. This is because expert witnesses enjoy immunity from civil suit in respect of such matters.[69]

Thus, in an extreme case, the mere fact that an expert dishonestly lied about both his expertise, experience and qualifications did not open him up to civil suit by the aggrieved party.[70]

The present position under the law now appears anomalous and legal writers have called for a review of the survival of this immunity.[71] It is now clear however that this immunity does not protect an expert from disciplinary proceedings by the professional body of which he was a member of evidence he gave in court or statements he had made for the purposes of giving such evidence.[72]

8.4 ADJUDICATION BY AN ACCOUNTANT AS EXPERT

Where an accountant is asked by both parties to adjudicate on a matter as expert but not as arbitrator, his adjudication is binding in the absence of clear proof of manifest error or that he departed from his instructions.[73]

Manifest error is limited to those errors so obvious as to admit no difference of opinion.[74] The onus of proof rests on the person challenging the accountant's determination and there is a presumption that an experienced

---

[68] [2002] 3 WLR 1104.
[69] *Stanton v Callaghan* [2000] QB 75, Court of Appeal.
[70] *Raiss v Palamo* (2001) PNLR 540.
[71] (2003) *The Times* 11, Law 5, (2003) *Counsel* July pages 17-20.
[72] *Meadow v General Medical Council* (2006) The Times 31 October.
[73] *Heald Foods v. Hyde Dairies Ltd* (1996) LTL 6 December, Court of Appeal, approving the reasoning of Potter J (1994) LTL 12 December.
[74] *Lindley on Partnership*, 16th Edition, 162.

accountant who was qualified for the task carried out the task properly and correctly.[75]

An expert is not obliged to set out his reasons and a failure to do so does not give rise to the implication of error let alone manifest error.[76]

8.5 PRIVILEGE AND ACCOUNTANTS

8.5.1 Can accountants enjoy legal professional privilege in their communications with their clients?

Whilst accountants do give legal advice in circumstances which would give rise to legal professional privilege for a solicitor or barrister, for example in tax proceedings before the General Commissioners, it now seems doubtful whether they do indeed have the benefit of legal professional privilege when advising their clients if the VAT decision in *Home or Away v Customs & Excise Commissioners*[77] is correctly decided. There it was ruled that no legal professional privilege arises in the relationship between an accountant and his client and an accountant could be a compellable witness against his client as to the previous instructions in the conduct of his case.

Parliament however has since extended to accountants the possibility of enjoying the legal professional privilege defence to the requirement to make disclosure under section 330(10) Proceeds of Crime Act 2002.[78] The exemption does not apply where the services will be used in the furtherance of some criminal purpose.

To qualify for the exemption the relevant professional adviser must be an accountant, auditor or tax adviser and be a member of a professional body which is established for accountants, auditors or tax advisers (as the case may be) and which makes provision for (a) testing the competence of those seeking admission to membership of such a body as a condition for such admission; and (b) imposing and maintaining professional and ethical standards for its members, as well as imposing sanctions for non-compliance with those standards.

---

[75] *Heald Foods v. Hyde Dairies Ltd* (1996) LTL 6 December, Court of Appeal, approving the reasoning of Potter J (1994) LTL 12 December.
[76] *Heald Foods v. Hyde Dairies Ltd* (1996) LTL 6 December, Court of Appeal.
[77] *Home or Away v Customs & Excise Commissioners* (2002) Lawtel 3rd May.
[78] Section 310 Proceeds of Crime Act 2002 as amended by regulation 2 the Proceeds of Crime Act 2002 and Money Laundering Regulations 2003 (Amendment) Order 2006.

Professional bodies whose membership would qualify for these purposes include:

- Institute of Chartered Accountants in England and Wales
- Institute of Chartered Accountants in Scotland
- Institute of Chartered Accountants in Ireland
- Association of Chartered Certified Accountants[79]
- Chartered Institute of Management Accountants
- Institute of Financial Accountants
- Chartered Institute of Public Finance and Accountancy
- Association of Authorised Public Accountants[80]
- Institute of Cost and Executive Accountants.[81]
- Association of International Accountants.[82]

8.5.2 The limits of legal professional privilege

For a privileged circumstances to arise one needs to have a confidential communication between the relevant professional adviser and his client or a third party which is made for the dominant purpose of being used in actual, pending or contemplated litigation.[83] Communications between a client and an accountant for the purposes of obtaining advice and assistance do not benefit from legal professional privilege[84] unless they arise out of threatened or contemplated litigation. Communications between an expert and a legal adviser are privileged but this privilege does not extend to the expert report or to the materials upon which the report is based.[85] Privilege may still be lost by waiver or if the communications are made for a fraudulent or illegal purpose or for the purpose of being repeated to the other party.

Examples that have been cited[86] as matters which might fall within the description of privileged communications include:

---

[79] Formerly the Chartered Association of Certified Accountants.
[80] This association was formed in 1978 to represent those accountants who were individually authorised by the Secretary of State to conduct audits. By an extraordinary general meeting on the 24 June, 1996, members of the Association voted to become a subsidiary of the Association of Chartered Certified Accountants and its members comply with the same practising rules and regulations.
[81] Formerly the Association of Cost and Executive Accountants.
[82] The Institute of Company Accountants has amalgamated into the Association of International Accountants.
[83] Institute of Chartered Accountants in England and Wales TECH 02/06.
[84] *Chantrey Martin (a firm) v. Martin* [1953] 2 All ER 691, *Halsbury's Laws of England* Vol 37, para 571.
[85] *R v King* [1983] 1 All ER 929 at 931 but c.f. *R v R* [1994] 4 All ER 260.
[86] Institute of Chartered Accountants in England and Wales TECH 02/06.

- Advice on taxation matters where the adviser is giving advice on the interpretation or application of elements of tax law and in the process of assisting a client understand his tax position
- Advice on legal aspects of a takeover bid
- Advice on the duties of directors under the Companies Acts
- Advice to directors on legal issues relating to the Insolvency Act 1986, for example, wrongful trading.

Chapter 9

DISCIPLINARY PROCEEDINGS

9.1 DISCIPLINARY PROCEEDINGS AGAINST ACCOUNTANTS

9.1.1 The relations between the members and their professional body are governed by a contract between them

The relations between the members of an association are governed by a contract between the members which may be express or implied and are usually found in the rules or byelaws of the association.[1]

The mere fact that the accountancy institute may be a public body does not prevent private rights arising between it and its members.[2]

9.1.2 An accountant contractually binds himself to abide by the decision of his professional body when sitting as a disciplinary tribunal

An accountant contractually binds himself to abide by the decision of his professional body when sitting as a disciplinary tribunal (subject to any rights of appeal, which may be specified in the professional bodies bye-laws or regulations). The act of applying for or renewing membership of a professional body will be deemed to constitute an offer to enter into a contract a term of which will require acceptance of that professional body's disciplinary rules and procedures, provided they have been brought to the attention of the applicant.[3]

It is on this basis that a professional body is entitled to discipline its members. It is possible for an accountant to be answerable to his professional body for the acts and omissions of his employees or agents.[4]

---

[1] *Harrington v. Sendall* [1903] Ch 921; *Lee v Showmens Guild of Great Britain* [1952] 2 QB 329.
[2] *Andreou v. ICAEW* [1998] 1 All ER 14.
[3] *Harris on the Law and Practice of Disciplinary & Regulatory Proceedings*, 3rd Edition, page 2, citing *Korda v International Tennis Federation* (1999) The Times 4th February. The 4th Edition does not retain this citation but makes similar comment at paragraph 1.04 to 1.07.
[4] *Re a Solicitor* [1972] 2 All ER 811 where a solicitor was liable to answer for the omissions of an accountant who had failed to write up the solicitor's books of practice.

9.1.3 Misconduct and the accountant

Misconduct may be shown by a breach of the rules or ethical code applicable to members of his institute.

One common formulation of the charge is that the accountant has performed an act "likely to bring discredit on himself, the professional body or the profession of accountancy". The author respectfully suggests that to prove a charge in this form the investigator must show not merely misconduct but also that it is likely to cause discredit - thus strong mitigation must lie in the fact that the misconduct attracted no publicity or is now an old offence[5]. Whether the conduct is discreditable is however a question of mixed fact and law for the tribunal. The use of the word "discredit" suggests the test is objective and that the misconduct must be sufficiently bad that it would be evident to the average member of the profession as being discreditable. Where the complaint is of incompetence, this is limited to cases of a very serious nature.

This is particularly a consideration where the misconduct relates to a conviction for a criminal offence. Some professional bodies[6] include a "deeming" provision, that a finding of guilt or guilty plea to an indictable offence[7] amounts to conclusive proof of misconduct and in itself renders the member liable to disciplinary action.[8] This does not offend the double jeopardy rule and an accountant is unable to rely on a plea of *autrefois convict* as an answer to a disciplinary charge; the purpose of disciplinary proceedings against a person convicted of an offence is not to punish him a second time but to protect the public and to maintain the high standards and reputation of the profession.[9]

---

[5] This view is that of the author. There is a rival view that the fact that the conduct occurred many years ago, does not make it less serious but rather affects the issue of mitigation. The argument runs that the fact that something happened a great deal of time ago and the person has moved on, would be a mitigating circumstance, similarly, if the member has had to live with the events concerned for a long time and has therefore suffered for a prolonged period, this would be taken into account.

[6] For example, the Institute of Chartered Accountants in England and Wales: para. 7(1), of the current ICAEW Disciplinary Bye-laws. The Association of International Accountants applies a similarly deeming provision. The Association of Authorised Public Accountants adopts a conclusive proof of misconduct provision for any finding of guilt or guilty plea to "*any offence discreditable to him*" or civil finding of fraud or dishonesty: Byelaw 13(c), AAPA Byelaws. An interesting contrast can be drawn with para. 11, Section 3.20, ACCA Rules of Professional Conduct where a criminal conviction is only *prima facie* evidence of misconduct.

[7] The definition of an "indictable offence" includes offences which are "triable either way" or triable only on indictment: Section 64, Criminal Law Act 1967.

[8] The validity of this provision in the New South Wales Public Accountants Regulation Act 1945 was upheld in *Re Hyams and the Public Accountants Regulation Act* [1975] 2 NSWLR 854.

[9] *Ziderman v General Dental Council* [1976] 2 All ER 334, 335B.

Whilst normally under the Rehabilitation of Offenders Act 1974, convictions must be treated as not committed if they are "spent".[10] Certain accountants are unable to benefit from this provision for disciplinary proceedings[11] and for applications for membership.[12] This applies to the

- Institute of Chartered Accountants in England and Wales
- Institute of Chartered Accountants in Scotland
- Institute of Chartered Accountants in Ireland
- Association of Chartered Certified Accountants.[13]

Other deeming provisions relate to the accountant being subject to a disqualification order or undertaking under the Company Directors Disqualification Act 1986 or being made bankrupt[14] amounting to conclusive proof of the commission of a disciplinary offence.

An accountant may be liable to disciplinary action because of the conduct of his employees[15] unless they act outside the scope of their employer's instruction or employment or in a way in which no employer could have expected.

9.1.4 Investigation of complaints against an accountant

The first stage in the disciplinary procedure is the investigation. This is to ascertain whether or not there is a *prima facie* case for disciplinary action. The test for a *prima facie* case is whether, if the evidence against the accountant was left uncontradicted, the disciplinary charge would be proven.[16] Just as an accountant contractually submits to the disciplinary rules,[17] he contractually submits to the institute's right to investigate him.

Accordingly the Court of Appeal has held that by acceptance of membership of the Institute of Chartered Accountants in England and Wales, a chartered accountant undertook, under the rules, to provide such information as the

---

[10] Section 4(1) Rehabilitation of Offenders Act 1974.
[11] Article 3(a) Rehabilitation of Offenders Act 1974 (Exceptions) Order 1975, SI 1975 No. 1023.
[12] Article 5 Rehabilitation of Offenders Act 1974 (Exceptions) Order 1975.
[13] Part 1, Schedule 1 and Part V Rehabilitation of Offenders Act 1974 (Exceptions) Order 1975.
[14] With the Institute of Chartered Accountants in England and Wales, the fact that a member is adjudicated bankrupt automatically brings membership to an end. Accordingly bankruptcy is not, in itself, a disciplinary matter.
[15] *Re a Solicitor* [1972] 2 All ER 811: A solicitor was held liable for the failures of an accountant who had been employed by him to write up the books of his practice.
[16] *R. v. Brixton Prison Governor ex parte Bidwell* [1937] 1 KB 305.
[17] *National Greyhound Racing Council v Tom Flaherty* [2005] EWCA Civ 1117.

Investigation Committee may consider necessary to discharge its functions and this acted as a waiver of the chartered accountant's privilege against self incrimination.[18]

Under the Joint Disciplinary Scheme, the investigation is conducted by the Executive Counsel. As the investigation is not conducted with a view to collating material to bring a criminal prosecution, investigators are under no duty to caution accountants they are interviewing.[19] Furthermore, it is doubtful whether accountants are able to rely on the duty of confidence that they owe their clients to avoid answering the investigator's questions.[20]

The Joint Disciplinary Scheme, whilst still in operation, is being replaced by the Accountancy Investigation and Disciplinary Board. The Accountancy Investigation & Discipline Board considers cases raising important issues affecting the public interest in the United Kingdom. Cases would normally be referred by the relevant participating accountancy institute.

Where the only question is whether there is a prima facie case against the accountant, there is no duty on the institute under natural justice to notify the accountant that the investigation is taking place or the charges likely to be levelled against him because it is a purely administrative act.[21] Having said this and whilst there is no obligation on the investigator to put all his cards on the table,[22] it is difficult to envisage, on a practical level, that an investigation would be concluded without approaching the accountant to see how he answers the allegations made against him.

The Institute of Chartered Accountants in England and Wales appoints a Reviewer of Complaints who can be asked by the complainant to refer the matter back to the Investigations Committee to reconsider a complaint where it has found there is no prima facie case for the member to answer.[23]

---

[18] *R. v. Institute of Chartered Accountants ex parte Nawaz* [1997] 7 CL 1.
[19] *R. v. Seelig* [1991] 4 All ER 429.
[20] *Harker v Edwards* (1887) 57 LJQB 147. Public interest overreaches confidentiality where it concerns the disclosure of some crime, fraud or misdeed to someone with a proper interest to receive that information: *Initial Services v Putterill* [1967] 3 All ER 145. Section 7.1 of the ICAEW Handbook advises members of their institute that they may breach client's confidence if it is necessary to defend themselves for example, in disciplinary proceedings.
[21] *Parry-Jones v The Law Society* [1968] 1 All ER 177, *Herring v Templeman* (1973) 137 JP 514
[22] This contrasts with the position once disciplinary proceedings are brought against the accountant, the accountant is entitled to know the case he must meet.
[23] Byelaw 17(2), ICAEW Disciplinary Byelaws of June 1998.

9.1.5 Admissible evidence

Unless stipulated otherwise the civil standard of proof applies in disciplinary proceedings; this test is sometimes expressed as the balance of probabilities – that the matter to be proven is more likely than not.

The strict rules of evidence do not apply to disciplinary proceedings. The tribunal may take into account any material which has some probative value in the sense that they tend to show the existence of non existence of facts relevant to the issue to be determined or show the likelihood or unlikelihood of the occurrence of some event that would be relevant.[24]

One of the exceptions to the rule that documents produced to the Secretary of State under Section 447 of the Companies Act 1985 may not, without the previous consent in writing of the company, be published or disclosed is where publication or disclosure is required with a view to the institution of or otherwise for the purposes of any disciplinary proceedings relating to exercise by an accountant or auditor of his professional duties.[25]

9.1.6 Disciplinary Hearing

The second stage in the disciplinary procedure is the disciplinary hearing.

An accountant facing disciplinary changes has a right to have notice of the charges he is facing – that is to say identifying the rule that he is said to have broken or the course of conduct giving rise to disciplinary action together with sufficient information for him to understand the nature of the disciplinary charge he is facing – in good time before the hearing.[26] Material upon which the institute seeks to rely to make out those allegations should also be disclosed in good time before the hearing.[27]

Whether a disciplinary panel was under a duty to afford an oral hearing (as opposed to one on the papers) to comply with the *audi alterem partem* rule or Article 6(1) ECHR depended on the circumstances of the particular case.[28] The disciplinary panel usually has a wide discretion in the way it chooses to regulate its own proceedings.

---

[24] *R v Deputy Industrial Injuries Commissioner ex parte Moore* [1965] 1 All ER 81.
[25] Section 449 (1) (L) Companies Act 1985.
[26] *Ridge v Baldwin* [1963] 2 All ER 66.
[27] The ICAEW Disciplinary Committee Regulations provide that written notice of the date of the hearing and of the terms of the complaint must be given not less than 42 before the hearing.
[28] *R (on the application of Thompson) v The Law Society* [2004] 2 All ER 113.

If an oral hearing is afforded, the accountant is usually entitled to be represented including legally represented. Hearings are normally recorded and all parties will be identified. Witnesses normally do not give evidence on oath although some institutes give them the choice.

The right to open rests with the Investigations / Disciplinary Committee. They will call any witnesses they seek to rely on. After they have given their evidence in chief,[29] they may be cross-examined by the Defendant. There is then an opportunity for re-examination. The Defendant then follows by calling his witnesses.

The accountant is entitled to a hearing before an independent tribunal. This is often achieved by the inclusion of lay members[30] on the disciplinary tribunal.

Often the tribunal will be advised by a legal assessor. The legal assessor's role is to advise on questions of law referred to him and to intervene to either inform the panel of any irregularity in the conduct of proceedings or to advise them when there is a possibility that, but for that advice, there is a possibility of an error of law being made.[31] Any advice of the legal assessor given to the disciplinary tribunal must be made known to the parties so that the parties so that they have an opportunity of commenting on it and correcting it.[32]

If the institute is a public body, the accountant has a right that his disciplinary hearing be in public.[33]

Hearings before the Accountancy Investigation & Discipline Board are in public. This in practice means that members of the public (including members of the press) other than witnesses, parties and representatives would be able to attend and watch the hearing subject to the constraints of space and maintaining good order. The disciplinary of private bodies are generally conducted in private and this election is justified on the basis that they are not conducting judicial proceedings.

---

[29] The procedure adopted before the ICAEW Disciplinary Tribunals is that the witnesses witness statement stands as their evidence in chief.
[30] For discussion of this in the context of Article 6 ECHR see *Albert and le Compte v Belgium* (1983) 5 EHRR 533 (requirement of independence satisfied by a mixed medical and judicial tribunal). The impartiality of each member of the tribunal is presumed until the contrary is proven.
[31] *Fox v General Medical Council* [1960] 3 All ER 225.
[32] *Nwabueze v GMC* [2000] UKPC 16.
[33] Section 6(1) Human Rights Act 1998, *H v Belgium* (1988) 10 EHRR 339.

The disciplinary tribunal should give reasons for their decision. A general explanation for the broad reasons for the determination is probably sufficient.[34] When determining the penalty, the tribunal should:[35]

- draw a distinction between the misconduct inside and outside the profession[36]
- bear in mind that an unsuccessful plea of not guilty should be weighed up but should not be the predominant factor
- bear in mind sentences in comparable cases.[37]

9.1.7 Appeals

The rules and time limits for appeals are governed by the rules of the professional body. Appeals to the Appeal Committee (a right exclusive to the member) can be against the finding that the complaint has been proven and any financial penalty or costs imposed.

The Appeal Committee will be differently constituted from the Disciplinary Committee and it is probable that any member sitting on a case on both the Disciplinary and Appeals Committee would ground an application for judicial review as a breach of natural justice.

Although the rules on appeals differ from institute to institute, the appeal hearing is usually takes the form of a re-consideration though the introduction of new evidence may be subject to a degree of restriction. Hearings are usually recorded and all parties will be identified. The right to open the case rests with the appellant member.

9.1.8 The role of the Accountancy Investigation & Discipline Board

The Financial Reporting Council has assumed the functions of the Accountancy Foundation (which included the Auditing Practices Board). The FRC is jointly funded by the CCAB, the City and the Government. It is envisaged that the Secretary of State will in the future take steps to delegate to Financial Reporting Council the Secretary of State's statutory power to

---

[34] *Needham v Nursing and Midwifery Council* [2003] EWHC 1141.
[35] *Re H (a barrister)* [1981] 3 All ER 205 per Latey J.
[36] This does not represent the ICAEW's position, because disciplinary liability can be based on work and non-work related conduct. It is, of course, correct that some non-work related conduct can be very serious e.g. conduct which may have given rise to a criminal conviction.
[37] The ICAEW publishes Sentencing Guidance, which can be viewed on its web site. In respect of other institutes, some benchmark can be gleaned from previous decisions, details of which will usually be published in the institute's journal.

grant and revoke an institute's status as a qualifying body.[38] One of the operating bodies of the FRC is the Accountancy Investigation and Disciplinary Board.

The Accountancy Investigation & Discipline Board (IDB) for the investigation and discipline of members, taking over this function from the Joint Disciplinary Scheme previously operated by ICAEW and ICAS to cover[39] all CCAB bodies. The AIDB is responsible for operating and administering an independent disciplinary scheme covering members of the following accountants' professional bodies:

- the Association of Chartered Certified Accountants
- the Chartered Institute of Management Accountants
- the Chartered Institute of Public Finance and Accountancy
- the Institute of Chartered Accountants in England and Wales
- The Institute of Chartered Accountants of Ireland
- the Institute of Chartered Accountants of Scotland.

The focus of the IDB will be on cases which raise or appear to raise important issues affecting the public interest in the UK and which need to be investigated to determine whether or not there has been any misconduct by an accountant or accountancy firm. Other disciplinary cases continue to be handled by the members own professional bodies.

Whilst most of the AIDB's cases will have been referred to it by one of the accountants' professional bodies, the AIDB may also decide of its own accord to investigate a matter.

The IDB's Executive Counsel conducts the investigation and decide whether or not any accountant or accountancy firm should be subject to disciplinary proceedings. If disciplinary proceedings are to be commenced, the Executive Counsel will file a complaint with the AIDB and the AIDB will appoint a Disciplinary Tribunal to hear the case.

Complaints are generally decided in public by a disciplinary tribunal. The Chairman of the Tribunal will always be a lawyer. In a three-person Tribunal there will also be one lay person and one accountant (or two lay

---

[38] Schedule 12 Companies Act 1989, section 1219 Companies Act 2006.
[39] Regulation 4.1, CIPFA Disciplinary Regulations of 19.2.07.

persons and two accountants in a five person Tribunal). A majority of the Tribunal will always be non-accountants. No member of a Tribunal will be an officer or employee of any of the accountants' professional bodies or of the FRC or any of its operating bodies including the AIDB.

There is a right of appeal for any accountant or accountancy firm can appeal any finding against it to an Appeal Tribunal. A retired judge or a senior barrister will first consider any appeal. If he or she gives permission to appeal, the appeal will be heard by an Appeal Tribunal

9.1.9 The Chartered Institute of Public Finance and Accountancy.

Complaints are initially passed to The Investigations Unit consists of CIPFA's in-house solicitor and external legal advisers. They carry out preliminary enquiries and collate evidence relating to the complaint.

They refer the matter to the Investigations Committee, who determines whether or not there is a case to answer and whether the matter should be referred to CIPFA's Council for a possible reference to the IDB. Members may request a review of certain decisions of the Investigations Committee by the Reviewer of Complaints, an independent lawyer, who can refer the decision back to the Investigations Committee for reconsideration.[40]

If there is sufficient evidence to justify the allegations, the Investigations committee can (with the consent of the member) impose sanctions[41] against the Member or refer the allegations for a formal hearing by the Disciplinary Committee. The Disciplinary Committee conducts formal hearings into allegations referred to it by the Investigations Committee.[42] If the allegations are proved, this committee can impose a wider range of sanctions[43] than the Investigations Committee. This committee also hears appeals by Members from certain decisions of the Investigations Committee.

The Appeals Committee considers appeals, by Members, against decisions made and sanctions imposed by the Disciplinary Committee.

---

[40] Regulation 6, CIPFA Disciplinary Regulations of 19.2.07.
[41] These are limited to an entry on the record or a reprimand: regulation 4.3(e), CIPFA Disciplinary Regulations of 19.2.07.
[42] Regulation 7, CIPFA Disciplinary Regulations of 19.2.07.
[43] These are an entry on the record, a reprimand, severe reprimand, fine, directing the member pay compensation, suspension and expulsion: regulation 7.2(c), (d), CIPFA Disciplinary Regulations.

9.2 HUMAN RIGHTS AND DISCLIPINARY PROCEEDINGS

9.2.1 Human Rights

The public nature of many accountancy institutes may mean that members are able to rely on the safeguards granted under the European Convention for the Protection of Human Rights and Fundamental Freedoms (see Article 63).

The implementation of the Human Rights Act 1998 creates an action in damages where damages are necessary to afford just satisfaction to a person who has been a victim to acts by a public authority which were incompatible with his Convention rights.[44] "Public Authority" for these purposes includes any tribunal in which legal proceedings may be brought or any person certain of whose functions are of a public nature.[45]

What is meant by a "public authority" is given a generous interpretation but the court will be influenced by whether it performs a function under an Act, whether it is controlled by a public body and the previous approach of the courts on judicial reviewability.[46] It is envisaged that hybrid bodies like the Jockey Club and the Bar Council would be open to challenge under the ECHR.[47]

The boundaries are far from clear. This is because the ECHR will protect against infringement by private law bodies by imposing an obligation on the State through its courts to positively act to ensure the freedoms protected.[48] This collateral challenge is made through section 7(1) (b), Human Rights Act 1998. Further the courts have a duty to act compatibly with the ECHR when dealing with the common law.[49]

To be a victim of an unlawful act for these purposes the accountant must point to the fact that his existing civil rights and obligations under the law have been infringed. It is suggested that rules of voluntary association are

---

[44] Sections 6-8 Human Rights Act 1998.
[45] Sections 6(3)-21(1) Human Rights Act 1998.
[46] *Poplar Housing and Regeneration Community Association Limited v. Donoghue*, [2001] 3 W.L.R. 183, CA. For a discussion of the authorities see *Carss-Frisk "Public Authorities: the Developing Definition"* [2002] E.H.R.L.R. 319.
[47] *Mulcahy on Human Rights and Civil Practice*, 2001, paragraph 8.01.
[48] *Mulcahy on Human Rights and Civil Practice*, 2001, paragraph 5.27 citing Article 1 ECHR,: *Rommelfanger v Germany* (1989) 62 DR 151 and *Diennert v France* (1996) 21 EHRR 554.
[49] *R v Lambert* [2001] HRLR 1267 paragraph 114, [2001] 2 WLR 1038, paragraph 27.

capable of being construed as "law" for these purposes as they have been construed in respect of Articles 8 and 10 as satisfying "prescribed by law".[50]

Disciplinary proceedings do not normally amount to *"a contestation over civil rights and obligations"*.[51] However the courts have been prepared to intervene where the finding excludes the victim from their business.[52] Disciplinary proceedings could give rise to a breach of Art.6 (1) if what was at stake was the right to continue to exercise a profession.[53] Thus disciplinary proceedings against an accountant, which had lasted 11 years (due to their awaiting the outcome of criminal proceedings) and were neither complex nor delayed by the accountant, were held by the European Court of Human Rights to be in breach of Article 6(1) of the European Convention of Human Rights.[54]

The European Court of Human Rights in *Le Compte, Van Leuven and De Meyere v. Belgium*[55] decided that Article 6 of The European Convention for the Protection of Human Rights and Fundamental Freedoms applies to disciplinary proceedings where the rights at issue include the right to continue professional activities or where anybody considers that interference with the exercise of one of his civil rights is unlawful and complains he has not had the possibility of submitting that claim to a tribunal meeting requirements of Article 6.

Article 6 of the European Convention provides:

> (1) in the determination of his civil rights and obligations of any criminal charge against him, everyone is entitled to a fair and public hearing within a reasonable time by an independent and impartial tribunal established by law. Judgment shall be pronounced publicly but the Press and public may be excluded in the interest of morals, Public Order or National Security in a Democratic Society, where the interest of juveniles or the protection of the private lives of the parties so require, or the extent strictly necessary in the opinion of the court in special

---

[50] *Mulcahy on Human Rights and Civil Practice*, 2001, paragraph 20.40 citing *Bathold v Germany* (1985) 7 EHRR 383 and *Smith v UK* (2000) 29 EHRR 493.
[51] *Le Compte v Belgium* (1981) 4 EHRR 1 paragraph 42 and 49.
[52] *Tehrani v United Kingdom Central Council for Nursing Midwifery and Health Visiting* [2001] 1 IRLR 208.
[53] *R (on the application of Thompson) v The Law Society* [2004] 2 All ER 113.
[54] *Luksch v Austria* (2002) 35 EHRR 17.
[55] (1982) 5 EHRR 183.

circumstances where publicity would prejudice the interests of justice;
(2) Everyone charged with a criminal offence shall be presumed innocent until proven guilty according to the law;
(3) Everyone charged with a criminal offence has the following minimum rights (a) to be informed promptly in a language he understands and in detail of the nature and cause of the accusation against him; (b) to adequate time and facilities for the preparation of his defence (c) to defend himself in person or through legal assistance of his own choosing or if he has not sufficient means to pay for legal assistance to be given it free where the interests of justice so require (d) to examine or to have examined witnesses against him and to obtain the attendance of witnesses on his behalf on the same conditions as witnesses against him (e) to have the free assistance of an interpreter if he cannot understand or speak the language used in court.

A further consideration is whether or not the disciplinary proceedings should be considered as quasi criminal. If domestic law expressly makes an offence criminal then the ECHR will accept it as such. If domestic law determines that the offence is civil, the classification of a matter under domestic law is deemed only the starting point for whether or not it is a crime under the Convention.[56] The Court has identified three factors:

- The classification under domestic law
- The nature of the offence
- The penalty.

In *Albert and Le Compte v. Belgium*[57] it was further held that the court did accept that the principles concerning a fair trial of "a criminal offence"

> are applicable, *mutatis mutandis* to disciplinary proceedings subject to paragraph 1 in the same way as in the case as a person charged with a criminal offence

The European Court of Human Rights there went on to express the view therefore that certain rights in Article 6(3) of the European Convention would be applicable to persons facing disciplinary proceedings namely (a) the right to be informed promptly in a language which he understands, and in detail, of the nature and the cause of the accusation against him (b) to have adequate time and facilities to prepare his defence and (c) to examine or have

---

[56] *Engel v Netherlands* [1976] 1 EHRR 647 paragraph 82.
[57] (1983) 5 EHRR 33.

examined witnesses against him and to obtain the attendance and examination of witnesses on his behalf under the same conditions as witnesses against him.[58]

Prison disciplinary proceedings have been held to be quasi criminal.[59] Indeed whilst the complaint in *Lee v UK*[60] that police disciplinary proceedings were criminal was rejected it was on the grounds that Lee was not at risk of a fine or deprivation of his liberty. So saying there is no sharp distinction between civil and criminal proceedings and the matter is looked at in the round.[61]

Where a barrister was not excluded from his profession but only reprimanded, the ECHR held no Article 6 rights were triggered.[62] The English court reached the same conclusion over a doctor given the "severest of reprimands".[63] A decision to reprimand, make a reference to a disciplinary tribunal did not amount to a determination of civil rights however it might do in respect to an order to pay costs.[64]

9.2.2 Enforcement by the courts

Following the implementation of the Human Rights Act 1998 the European Convention is not merely relevant to the considerations of a disciplinary tribunal but *must* be taken into account by the tribunal when reaching a decision.[65] The tribunal must also take into account judgments, decisions, declarations or advisory opinions of the European Court of Human Rights, opinions of the Commission where adopted under Article 31 of the European Convention, decisions of the Commission in connection with Articles 26 or 27 of the European Convention or decisions of the Committee of Ministers taken under Article 46 of the European Convention.[66]

The implementation of the Human Rights Act 1998 created a right of action in damages where damages are necessary to afford just satisfaction to a person who has been victim to acts by a public authority which were incompatible with his Convention Rights.[67] A "public authority" for these

---

[58] *Albert and Le Compte v. Belgium* (1983) 5 EHRR 33.
[59] *Campbell and Fell v UK* (1984) 7 EHRR 165.
[60] *Lee v UK* (2000) Lawtel 22nd September.
[61] *OR v Stern* [2000] 1 WLR 2230 (director's disqualification proceedings not quasi criminal), *R (Fleurose) v Financial Services Authority* (2002) Times 15th January (disciplinary proceedings by FSA not criminal – 2 year suspension).
[62] *Application No 10331/91* (1984) 6 EHRR 583.
[63] *R v General Medical Council ex parte Nicoliades* (2001) Lawtel 27th July.
[64] *R (on the application of Thompson) v The Law Society*: [2004] 2 All ER 113.
[65] Section 2 Human Rights Act 1998.
[66] Section 2(1) Human Rights Act 1998.
[67] Sections 6-8 Human Rights Act 1998.

purposes includes courts, tribunals or any person certain of whose functions are of a public nature.[68]

If the court finds that any act or proposed act of a public authority would amount to a breach of the European Convention it can now grant such relief as it considers just and appropriate.[69]

Whilst the Human Rights Act 1998 vests the domestic court with extensive powers, an application made be still be made to the European Court of Human Rights in Strasbourg once all domestic remedies have been exhausted.[70] The powers of the European Court of Human Rights are to make declaratory judgements and make awards of damages.[71]

9.3 DISCIPLINARY PROCEEDINGS AND THE COURTS

9.3.1 Powers of the Court to enforce the contract between institute and accountant

The court has power to intervene where a complaint is founded under its jurisdiction to protect rights under contract.[72] Indeed if the accountancy institute is a purely private law body,[73] the remedy will lie only in breach of contract. Having said this, the court will be slow to interfere with internal arrangements for the hearing of disputes and complaints.[74]

In *Phyllis Colgan v Kennel Club*[75] it was suggested that the contractual duty of an association in exercising the disciplinary functions was to act fairly, within the law and take reasonable steps to act within the rules of the association. Members have a contractual right for their cases to be dealt with fairly.[76] Fairness requires that proceedings are free of actual or apparent bias.[77] There is no contractual right to natural justice however.[78]

---

[68] Section 6(3) Human Rights Act 1998.
[69] Section 8(1) Human Rights Act 1998.
[70] Article 35(1) European Convention on Human Rights.
[71] *Republic of Ireland v United Kingdom* (1978) 2 EHRR 25.
[72] *Abbott v. Sullivan* [1952] 1 KB 189.
[73] The Institute of Cost and Executive Accountants is the clearest example of this.
[74] *Bankole v. ACCA* (1995) LTL 17 November.
[75] *Phyllis Colgan v Kennel Club* (2001) Lawtel 9th September.
[76] *National Greyhound Racing Council v Tom Flaherty* [2005] EWCA Civ 1117. The test is whether the overall end result is to be regarded as fair rather than whether or not there has been some deficiency or other in the conduct of the trial.
[77] Even where it is an association exercising disciplinary functions: *Taylor v National Union of Seamen* [1967] 1 WLR 532.
[78] *Andreou v. ICAEW* [1998] 1 All ER 14.

If a member is expelled by the association in breach of contract, the court has power to grant a declaration that their action is *ultra vires*.

The Court also has powers to grant an injunction to prevent the member's expulsion if that is necessary to protect a proprietary right of his or to protect him in his right to earn his livelihood.[79]

In the case of associations which control entry to a trade or profession it would appear that the court's powers to grant redress are not confined to cases of contract.[80] The courts will not however imply a term that the power to make byelaws would be exercised fairly and reasonably.[81]

The court will not restrain the exercise by an association of a power contained in its rules to expel members unless it is shown that it has been done contrary to the rules or it has been done in bad faith[82] or at least where there has been some sort of enquiry contemplated where the rules of natural justice have been infringed.[83] It has been said that to give one reason for expelling a member and to act upon another is evidence of bad faith.[84]

9.3.2 Judicial Review of a disciplinary decision

Judicial review will only be available where the decision determines public law rights and the accountancy institute is a public law body. The principal distinction between bodies that are subject to judicial review and those which are not is whether the body is under some public duty or exercising some public function or whether it is merely a domestic tribunal.[85] If the accountancy institute is a purely private law body, the remedy will lie only in breach of contract. By contrast, the mere fact that the accountancy institute may be a public body does not prevent private rights arising between it and its members.[86]

All routes of appeal must usually be exhausted before judicial review can be sought. The disciplinary procedure of most professional accountancy bodies includes an appeal procedure to challenge the original disciplinary finding and order.

---

[79] *Amalgamated Society of Carpenters v. Braithwaite* [1922] 2 AC 440.
[80] *Nagle v. Fielden* [1966] 2 QB 633; *R. v. Jockey Club ex Parte RAM Racecourses Ltd* [1993] 2 All ER 225, 247-248.
[81] *Andreou v. ICAEW* [1998] 1 All ER 14.
[82] *Hopkinsons v. Marquis of Exeter* (1867) LR 5 Eq 63.
[83] *Russell v. Duke of Norfolk* [1949] 1 All ER 109.
[84] *D'Arcy v. Adamson* (1913) 29 TLR 367.
[85] *R v Football Association Ltd, ex p Football League Ltd* [1993] 2 All ER 833.
[86] *Andreou v. ICAEW* [1998] 1 All ER 14.

It has been suggested that judicial review is still available where the claimant is affected by a decision made by a domestic tribunal and the claimant has no contract with the tribunal.[87] The issue was left open by Sir Thomas Bingham MR in *R v. Disciplinary Committee of the Jockey Club ex parte The Aga Khan.*[88]

There are a number of grounds upon which judicial review will lie:

- Where the decision arose out of an error of law[89]
- Where there has been a breach of the common law rules of natural justice[90] or procedural fairness[91]
- Where there has been a failure to comply with any statutory procedural obligation
- Where the decision is irrational or in breach of the Wednesbury principle (no person properly directing itself as to the relevant law could reasonably have reached that decision on the material before it[92]).
- Where the decision maker failed to take into account relevant considerations or took into account irrelevant considerations.
- Where there was an unlawfully delegation of the decision making
- Where the decision maker fettered his discretion by applying a policy unduly rigidly.[93]
- In exceptional circumstances, where a public body has created a legitimate expectation that a person would be entitled to a particular benefit, it may be so unfair as to amount to an abuse

---

[87] *R v Disciplinary Committee of the Jockey Club ex parte Massingberd-Mundy* [1993] 2 All ER 207 per Roch J, *R v Jockey Club ex parte RAM Racecourses* [1993] 2 All ER 225 per Simon Brown J and obiter remarks by the Court of Appeal in *R v Royal Life Saving Society ex parte Heather Rose Marie Howe* [1990] COD 440.

[88] *R Disciplinary Committee of the Jockey Club ex parte The Aga Khan* [1993] 1 WLR 909.

[89] The general approach of the courts at present is to regard almost every error of law by a public body as being amenable to judicial review: *R v Bedwellty Justices Ex p. Williams* [1997] A.C. 225.

[90] The rules of natural justice require that a person be given a fair hearing before a decision affecting him is taken and that the decision maker is unbiased in the sense that there is no real danger that the decision maker will unfairly favour or disfavour that person: *Porter v Magill* [2002] 2 A.C. 357.

[91] *Ridge v Baldwin* [1964] A.C. 40.

[92] *Associated Picture Houses Ltd. v Wednesbury Corporation* [1948] 1 K.B. 223.

[93] *British Oxygen Co. v Minister of Technology* [1971] A.C. 610; *R. v North West Lancashire Health Authority Ex p. A* [2000] 1 W.L.R. 977.

of power for the public body to act in a way which breached that legitimate expectation.[94]

One of the most important basis for challenge by judicial review of the disciplinary tribunal is on the grounds that it acted outside the rules of natural justice.[95] It is not possible for the professional body to exclude the rules of natural justice by agreement or under the rules.[96] Natural justice means:

- the right to be heard before an unbiased tribunal (the principle *nemo iudex in sua causa*)
- the right to have notice of the charges of misconduct (part of the principle *audi alterem partem*)
- the right to have notice of the charges of misconduct (part of the principle *audi alterem partem*)[97].

The House of Lords has determined that the correct approach to determining whether or not there is "apparent bias" is that the court must first ascertain all the circumstances which have a bearing on the suggestion that the judge was biased. It must then ask whether those circumstances would lead a fair-minded and informed observer to conclude that there was a real possibility, or a real danger, the two being the same, that the tribunal was biased.[98]

Thus the test[99] for "apparent bias" can be summarised as:

- What are the circumstances that lead to a suggestion of bias?
- Would this lead a fair-minded and informed observer to conclude that there was a real possibility or a real danger that the tribunal was biased?

Examples of situations where it has been found, on the facts, that the test for apparent bias has been satisfied, have included where a tribunal member has:-

- witnessed any facts before the tribunal[100]

---

[94] *R v. Inland Revenue Commissioners Ex p. Unilever plc* [1996] S.T.C. 681, *R. v. North and East Devon Health Authority Ex p. Coughlan* [2001] Q.B. 213; *Nadarajah v. Secretary of State for the Home Department* [2005] EWCA Civ 1363.
[95] *Lloyd v. McMahon* [1987] 1 All ER 1118, 1161.
[96] *Lee v. Showmen's Guild of Great Britain* [1952] 1 All ER 1175.
[97] *Ridge v. Baldwin* [1963] 2 All ER 66.
[98] *Magill v. Weeks* [2002] 2 WLR 37.
[99] *Magill v. Weeks* [2002] 2 WLR 37.
[100] *Roebuck v. National Union of Mineworkers (Yorkshire Area)* [1977] ICR 573.

- been friends with the Defendant [101]
- disliked the Defendant [102]
- expressed views about the parties or the issues in the case or similar issues in such a way as to suggest prejudgment [103]
- been actively associated with the body bringing the disciplinary proceedings [104]
- known a witness before the tribunal whose evidence was disputed. [105]

Justice must not only be done but be seen to be done. [106]

Since the livelihood of the individual is potentially at stake it is *likely* that the principles of the European Convention on Human Rights are also applicable to disciplinary hearings. [107] Certainly the Court of Appeal has held disciplinary proceedings could give rise to a breach of Art.6 (1) if what was at stake was the right to continue to exercise a profession. [108] A decision to reprimand, make a reference to a disciplinary tribunal did not amount to a determination of civil rights however it might do in respect to an order to pay costs. [109]

It is an abuse of process to pursue private law proceedings which rely on public law claims previously relied on in judicial review proceedings. [110]

The public nature of many accountancy institutes may mean that members are able to rely on the safeguards granted under the European Convention for the Protection of Human Rights and Fundamental Freedoms (see Article 63).

The implementation of the Human Rights Act 1998 has created an action in damages where damages are necessary to afford just satisfaction to a person who has been a victim to acts by a public authority which were incompatible

---

[101] *Cottle v. Cottle* [1929] 2 All ER 535.
[102] *R (Donoghue) v. Cork County Justices* [1910] 2 IR 271.
[103] *R v. Halifax Justices, ex p Robinson* (1912) 76 JP 233.
[104] Inactive membership of a body instituting or participating in the proceedings does not necessarily disqualify: *Hanson v Church Commissioners for England* [1978] QB 831 (Church Commissioners landlords in rent dispute; Master of Rolls and Lord Chief Justice not disqualified by ex officio, inactive membership) *R v Altrincham Justices, ex p Pennington* [1975] QB 549 (prosecution for sale of goods to schools at short weight; magistrate belonging to education committee which concluded contract disqualified).
[105] *AWG Group v. Morrison* [2006] 1 All ER 967.
[106] *R. v. Sussex Justices ex parte McCarthy* [1923] All ER 233.
[107] *Le Compte, Van Leuven & De Meyere v. Belgium* (19820 5 EHRR 183.
[108] *R (on the application of Thompson) The Law Society* [2004] 2 All ER 113.
[109] *R (on the application of Thompson) The Law Society* [2004] 2 All ER 113.
[110] *Andreou v. ICAEW* [1998] 1 All ER 14.

with his Convention rights.[111] "Public Authority" for these purposes includes any tribunal in which legal proceedings may be brought or any person certain of whose functions are of a public nature.[112]

9.3.3 The court may order a stay of proceedings if it considers that they may delay or prejudice civil or criminal proceedings

Where the continuation of proceedings risks delaying, impeding or prejudicing the accountant in the conduct of his defence of civil or criminal proceedings to an extent that could not be justified in the public interest, the court will order a stay of any disciplinary proceedings against the accountant.[113] Thus a stay granted in a case where the disciplinary inquiry would not be completed promptly, might have a distracting effect from the civil proceedings and where there were advantages for the disciplinary committee having the benefit of the findings of fact made by the court.[114]

---

[111] Sections 6-8 Human Rights Act 1998.
[112] Sections 6(3)-21(1) Human Rights Act 1998.
[113] *R. v. Institute of Chartered Accountants ex parte Brindle* (1994) *The Times* 12 January, Court of Appeal.
[114] *R. v. Institute of Chartered Accountants ex parte Brindle* (1994) *The Times* 12 January, Court of Appeal.

Chapter 10

INTERNATIONAL PRACTICE

10.1 INTERNATIONAL PRACTICE: RIGHTS OF MUTUAL RECOGNITION AS AN ACCOUNTANT

10.1.1 Mutual recognition of qualifications: European Union nationals

An accountant who is a member of a recognised profession may enjoy mutual recognition of his professional qualification in all the member states of the European Union.[1]

10.1.2 The Designated authorities enjoying mutual recognition: European Union nationals

The designated authorities[2] in the United Kingdom for the regulated professions who enjoy mutual recognition are:

- Institute of Chartered Accountants in England and Wales
- Institute of Chartered Accountants in Scotland
- Institute of Chartered Accountants in Ireland
- Association of Chartered Certified Accountants
- Chartered Institute of Public Finance and Accountancy
- Chartered Institute of Management Accountants.[3]

---

[1] Council Directive 89/48 EEC on the recognition of higher education diplomas awarded on completion of professional education and training of at least three years' duration.

[2] The designated bodies are currently only the Chartered Accountancy bodies. In an answer to a parliamentary question over the absence of the Institute of Financial Accountants from this list, Department of Trade and Industry Minister Ian McCartney said that the list was "not intended to be exhaustive". He stated that it was the Government's view that members of the Institute of Financial Accountants were not precluded from seeking mutual recognition despite their exclusion from the list: [1998] 2 *Financial Accountant* 33.

[3] Regulation 4 and Part 2, European Communities (Recognition of Professional Qualifications) (First General System) Regulations 2005.

10.1.3 The rights arising out of mutual recognition: European Union nationals

A designated authority for a regulated profession cannot refuse, on the grounds of inadequate qualification, to authorise a migrant to practise the profession on the same conditions as apply to someone who holds the diploma required of native applicants if:

- the migrant holds the diploma required by another member state of the European Union for the practice of a corresponding profession regulated by that state and the diploma having been awarded in another member state,[4] or,
- the migrant has within ten years immediately prior to his application pursued a corresponding profession for at least two years full-time in a member state which does not regulate that profession[5] subject to his proving

   i that he has completed a course of three years full time (or equivalent duration part time) post secondary education at a university or other higher education establishment in a member state,[6] or,
   ii some other education or training which is recognised as equivalent.[7]

Before authorising a migrant to practise, the regulated profession may require him to take and pass an aptitude test limited to the professional knowledge of the migrant or complete an adaptation period of not more than three years.[8] The test will take into account that he is a qualified professional elsewhere and may cover:

- topics required of native applicants but not already covered by his diploma

---

[4] Regulation 5(1) (a), European Communities (Recognition of Professional Qualifications) (First General System) Regulations 2005.
[5] Regulation 5(1) (b), European Communities (Recognition of Professional Qualifications) (First General System) Regulations 2005.
[6] Regulation 5(2) (a) European Communities (Recognition of Professional Qualifications) (First General System) Regulations 2005.
[7] Regulation 5(2) (b) European Communities (Recognition of Professional Qualifications) (First General System) Regulations 2005. The recognition must be by a competent authority in the member state and be an equivalent to the recognised professional qualification. Notification of the recognition must have been given pursuant to Article 3(b) of Council Directive 89/48/EEC.
[8] Regulation 6 European Communities (Recognition of Professional Qualifications) (First General System) Regulations 2005.

- subjects selected from those which are considered essential for the practise of the regulated profession in the United Kingdom
- the relevant rules of professional conduct.[9]

During the adaptation period the migrant may be required to undertake further training and his performance may be assessed.[10]

A supervisory body must accept as sufficient evidence certificates issued by the equivalent competent authority of another European Member State.[11]

10.2 INTERNATIONAL PRACTICE: RIGHTS OF MUTUAL RECOGNITION AS AN AUDITOR

10.2.1 Mutual recognition of qualifications: European Union Nationals

A company auditor, as defined by Section 24(2) of the Companies Act 1989 and Article 27(2) of the Companies (Northern Ireland) Order 1990, may enjoy mutual recognition of his professional qualification in all the member states of the European Union.[12]

10.2.2 The rights arising out of mutual recognition of qualifications: nationals from member states of the European Union

The right of establishment entails the right to set up and maintain more than one place of establishment within the European Community.[13]

A member state is entitled to ensure compliance with professional rules justified by the public interest concerning the good repute and independence of auditors as long as they are applicable to anyone acting as an auditor within that territory. Minimum conditions over actual presence appeared justified to ensure protection of the public interest. However if the auditor who is only temporarily in the country provides his services through a firm which is already regulated as an auditor then the national authority can ensure compliance through that firm.[14]

---

[9] Regulation 7, European Communities (Recognition of Professional Qualifications) (First General System) Regulations 2005.
[10] Regulation 8, European Communities (Recognition of Professional Qualifications) (First General System) Regulations 2005.
[11] Regulation 6, European Communities (Recognition of Professional Qualifications) (First General System) Regulations 2005.
[12] Council Directive 89/48/EEC on the recognition of higher education diplomas awarded on completion of professional education and training of at least three years' duration.
[13] *Ramrath v. Minister of Justice* [1992] CL 4769, European Court of Justice.
[14] *Ramrath v. Minister of Justice* [1992] CL 4769, European Court of Justice.

The qualifying bodies for auditors are the designated authorities for the purpose of offering the qualification as an auditor to migrants.[15] A migrant is only eligible for appointment as a company auditor if he satisfies the conditions for eligibility laid down by Part II of the Companies Act 1989.[16]

A supervisory body for auditors cannot refuse, on the grounds of inadequate education or inadequate length of training or experience or practice, membership to a migrant if he has been granted authorisation by an equivalent qualifying body in another member State of the European Union.[17] Before authorising a migrant auditor to practice, a supervisory body may however require him to take and pass an aptitude test limited to the professional knowledge of the migrant or complete an adaptation period of not more than three years.[18] The test will take into account that he is a qualified professional elsewhere and may cover:

- topics required of native applicants but not already covered by his diploma
- subjects selected from those which are considered essential for the practise of the regulated profession in the United Kingdom
- the relevant rules of professional conduct.[19]

During the adaptation period the migrant may be required to undertake further training and his performance may be assessed.[20]

A supervisory body must accept as sufficient evidence certificates issued by the equivalent competent authority of another European Member State.[21] The European Court of Justice has ruled[22] that auditors holding equivalent qualifications in a member state to the host state could be exempted from a requirement to pass an examination to practice in the host state. The host Member States had to consider whether the diplomas of the other Member

---

[15] Regulation 11(2) European Communities (Recognition of Professional Qualifications) (First General System) Regulations 2005.
[16] Regulation 11(3), European Communities (Recognition of Professional Qualifications) (First General System) Regulations 2005.
[17] Regulation 11(4) European Communities (Recognition of Professional Qualifications) (First General System) Regulations 2005.
[18] Regulation 6 European Communities (Recognition of Professional Qualifications) (First General System) Regulations 2005.
[19] Regulation 7, European Communities (Recognition of Professional Qualifications) (First General System) Regulations 2005.
[20] Regulation 8, European Communities (Recognition of Professional Qualifications) (First General System) Regulations 2005.
[21] Regulation 6 and 11(5), European Communities (Recognition of Professional Qualifications) (First General System) Regulations 2005.
[22] *Markapolou v. Minister for Development*, Case C255/01.

State certified equivalent knowledge and qualification to that in the host state. If they corresponded wholly, the host member state had to recognise the diploma as fulfilling the requirements laid down by the national provisions. If they corresponded in part, the host state had to afford the accountant the opportunity of showing that he had made up the deficiency in some other way – whether by study or experience in the host member state.

10.2.3 Companies Act 2006

Under the Companies Act 2006, an auditor who has been authorised to practice under the European Communities (Recognition of Professional Qualifications) (First General System) Regulations 2005 and satisfies any requirement imposed under regulation 6 remains deemed to hold an appropriate qualification for the purpose of undertaking audit work.[23] For countries which are not relevant states for the purposes of the European Community Regulations, the Secretary of State may declare as holding an approved overseas qualification persons who are qualified to audit accounts under the law of a specified country or persons who hold a specified professional qualification in a specified foreign country and may stipulate additional educational qualifications to ensure the foreign auditor has adequate knowledge of the law and practice in the United Kingdom relevant to the audit of accounts.[24]

---

[23] Section 1219 Companies Act 2006.
[24] Section 1221(1) Companies Act 2006.

Annex 1

CHECKLIST FOR A DEED OF PARTNERSHIP FOR A FIRM OF ACCOUNTANTS

- Who are the parties?
- What are the parties' addresses?
- What professional association are the parties members of? Will there be a mixed practice?
- Are the partners all fully qualified?
- Do all the parties hold practising certificates?
- Do all the parties hold insolvency licences?
- Will the firm carry on investment business?
- Will the practice of accountancy be its main activity?
- Has an investment business certificate been obtained from the relevant professional body?
- Will the firm include salaried partners?
- Do they hold practising certificates?
- What will the firm's name be?
- Are there any clearances required for the name?
- Who will the firm's bankers be?
- Will the firm receive money belonging to clients?
- What date will the partnership commence business upon?
- How long will the partnership last?
- Will the partnership end on the death/retirement/expulsion/bankruptcy of any one partner?
- Where will the partnership carry on its practice from?
- Will there be an obligation to pay all partnership money into the bank account?
- Will there be an obligation dealing with payments of money received on behalf of clients?
- Will there be separate provision dealing with monies received on behalf of investment business clients?
- What provisions will there be over the signing of cheques?
- Who will provide the initial capital of the partnership?
- And in what shares?
- What provisions will there be for the provision of additional capital?

- Which assets will belong to the partnership?
- Which assets will be excluded from the partnership?
- Where will the books and records of the partnership be kept?
- What provisions will there be for access by partners to the books and records of the partnership?
- What provisions will there be for the writing up of books?
- What provisions will there be for annual accounts?
- Will there be a presumption of the accuracy of the accounts?
- In what shares will the profits and losses of the partnership be shared?
- And will this include profits and losses of a capital nature?
- What drawings will each partner be entitled to draw out from the partnership bank account?
- What provisions will there be for the repayment of expenses of partners by the partnership?
- What provisions will there be for the division of the net profits of the partnership?
- What provisions will there be for provision for income tax for partners?
- Will offices, emoluments, salaries, presence money received by a partner belong to him or the partnership, e.g. directors' fees or trustees' fees?
- What provisions will there be for holiday entitlement for each partner?
- Will the partners be entitled to carry forward holiday entitlement?
- What provisions will there be over insurance policies; will there be a minimum insurance policy in force?
- What will the duties of the partners be?
- What time and attention is to be expected to be devoted by each partner?
- Will there be provisions that the partner complies with the ethical requirements of his/their professional body/bodies?
- What restrictions will there be on the authority of the partner, e.g. employing or dismissing staff, giving guarantees, dealing with his share in the partnership, compromising debts due to the partnership, endorsing bills of exchange or promissory notes on behalf of the partnership or charging assets of the partnership without consent?
- Will there be any requirement that the partners indemnify the other partners for breaches of the partnership agreements?
- How will decisions be made?
- Will there be a compulsory retirement provision?

- What provisions will there be for voluntary retirement?
- Will there be any provision built in to enable partners to compel another partner to retire, e.g. on medical grounds?
- What provisions will there be for expelling partners, e.g. in the case of flagrant or persistent breaches of the partnership agreement, if they cease to be a member of their professional body, if they neglect their professional duties, become bankrupt or insolvent, have impending bankruptcy proceedings, become incapacitated or unable to perform their duties, be in breach of any ethical or other requirement of their professional body or cease to be a "fit and proper" person?
- Will there be any arbitration provisions in the event of dispute?
- What provisions will there be to buy out an outgoing partner's share?
- How will such share be valued?
- Will there be any provision for payment in stages?
- What are the consequences of non-payment of the purchase price for a former partner's equity?
- What indemnity will be given against future debts to a partner on his being bought out?
- What provisions will there be from notification of clients and creditors, e.g. by advertisement in the *London Gazette* and by circular letter?
- Will there be any elections under the Income and Corporation Taxes Act 1988 Section 113?
- Will there be any restrictions on competition or solicitation of clients by an outgoing partner?
- Will the outgoing partner have any entitlement to examine books and records for the accounting practice?
- What provisions as regards notice will there be?
- Are gifts or bequests to be the property of the firm or of the individual partners?

Annex 2

CHECKLIST FOR AN AGREEMENT FOR THE SALE OF AN ACCOUNTANCY PRACTICE

- Who are the parties and what are their addresses?
- What are the parties' professional qualifications?
- When and where will completion take place?
- What is the name of the accountancy practice? What other trading names is it known by?
- How is it structured?
- Who owns the goodwill?
- Who owns the work in hand?
- Where does it trade from?
- Is that property included in the sale? Are there any issues that arise from taking on that property?
- What will the purchase price be?
- How will the purchase price be paid? Will there be a distinction in valuation between recurring and non-recurring fees?
- How will the purchase price be paid?
- When and in what instalments will the purchase price be paid?
- Will there be any interest due on late payments and, if so, when will it start running and at what percentage rate?
- Will there be any claw-back provision if profits do not reflect what they are warranted to be?
- What accounting period will be used?
- What formula will be used to calculate net and gross profits?
- Who are the clients? Which clients will be kept by the vendors and which sold? What other contracts are being retained or assigned?
- What provisions will be made for the transfer of clients?
- What notices and letters should be sent to the clients? Can the content be agreed now?
- Will there be any tax elections?
- Who owns the fees for work done prior to the sale and, if it is to be the vendor, how will you divide it where it relates to work in progress?

- Who will be responsible for recovering unpaid fees?
- Who will be responsible for the cost of recovering unpaid fees?
- What fittings and fitments are being bought?
- Are there any issues that need to be considered about the computer equipment and software?
- Where and how are disputes going to be resolved?
- Are there any employees of the practice? Will they be employed after the sale and, if so, by whom? Are there any issues that arise from taking on those employees?
- Will the vendor be employed under a consultancy agreement as part of the consideration?
- Will the vendor be permitted access to future books of account relating to the business of the practice and how?
- Will the purchaser be obliged to keep the books of the practice up to date?
- Will there be obligations on the vendor and/or the purchasers to use their best endeavours to promote the business of the practice?
- Will there be any non-competition provision imposed on the vendor?
- Will there be obligations on the vendor and/or the purchasers to maintain professional indemnity insurance against the risk of their respective professional negligence?
- What warranties should be given about the practice?
- What guarantees and indemnities can be given?
- Are there any stamp duty issues?
- What provisions will there be against non-solicitation of staff and/or clients?
- How will the purchase and exclusivity of the trading name of the practice be secured?
- Are there any actions or investigations current or pending which may adversely affect the value of the goodwill?
- What will happen to the office furniture?
- Who will keep the old client files?
- What responsibilities will the vendor have until completion?
- What confidentiality obligations are to be imposed on the vendor?

Annex 3

CHECKLIST FOR THE EMPLOYMENT OF AN ACCOUNTANT BY AN ACCOUNTANCY FIRM

- Who is the employer?
- What is his address?
- Who is the employee?
- What is his address?
- What is the employee's job title?
- When did the employee's employment in this position start?
- When did the employee's continuous employment start?
- Is the employment subject to a probationary period?
- Is the employment for a fixed term?
- What notice period is required of the employee to terminate the employment?
- What notice period is required of the employer to terminate the employment?[1]
- What are the duties of the employee?
- What is his job description?
- Will the employee be required to perform other duties?
- Where is the employee's usual place of work?
- Will the employee be expected to work in other places?
- Will the employee be required to work outside the UK for more than one month?[2]
- What are the employees' usual hours of work?
- Will overtime be paid?
- How much will the employee be paid and at what intervals?
- Will the pay accrue on a day to day basis or, if not, how? Is a day's wage to be calculated as $1/365^3$ of the annual salary?

---

[1] The minimum length of notice the employee is entitled to receive is:
    A.   during the first two years of continuous employment not less than one week's notice;
    B.   during the third to twelfth years of continuous employment not less than one week's notice for each year of continuous employment;
    C.   after 12 years of continuous employment not less than 12 week's notice.

[2] If so, see special added disclosure provisions under the Employment Rights Act 1996.

- When will the pay be reviewed?
- Is the employee entitled to benefit from any pension scheme?
- Is there a contracting-out certificate in force?
- Will expenses be reimbursed?
- How many days holiday can the employee take in each year?
- Must the dates be agreed in advance?
- Can holiday entitlement be carried forward to a subsequent year?
- Is the employee entitled to holiday pay and how is entitlement calculated?
- On termination of his employment, is the employee entitled to pay in lieu of outstanding holiday entitlement?
- What provisions will apply for sick pay?
- Will the employee be entitled to engage in other employments or commercial activities?
- Are there going to be any restrictions on share holding or share dealing by the employee?[4]
- When will the employee retire?
- What disciplinary rules and procedures apply to the employee and how can the employee obtain a copy of these?
- To whom should the employee go with any grievance he has relating to his employment and what grievance rules and procedures apply to the employee and how can the employee obtain a copy of these?
- How can the employer terminate the employment with immediate effect? (i.e. what will "gross misconduct" cover?[5])

---

[3] Or $1/260^{th}$ if calculated on the basis of working days.

[4] Issues that the practice will be concerned about are misuse of any un-published price sensitive information or conflicts of interest.

[5] The following are *non-exclusive* examples of gross misconduct which are particularly germane to accountants:

- theft of the firm's or client's property
- failure to disclose any criminal charge or conviction or any civil fraud judgment against him
- false disclosure or failure to disclose any or any change in the employee's circumstances which might affect the firm's view of whether the employee is a fit and proper person to carry work of a nature which the employee is or may be entrusted
- making of or permitting the making of any false or misleading statement whether in writing or otherwise in relation to any documents, files, data, accounts or records of the firm or any of their clients
- becoming bankrupt or making any arrangement or composition with his creditors or has an interim order made against him pursuant of Section 252 of the Insolvency Act 1986
- disqualification from holding office in another company in which he is concerned or interested because of wrongful trading under the Insolvency Act 1986
- conviction of an offence under the Companies Securities (Insider Dealing) Act 1985

- How can the employer terminate the employment on short notice?
- Is the employee to be required to sign a "fit and proper" form[6].[7]
- Is the employer entitled to make deductions from the employee's wages?
- Is the employee entitled to accept gifts?
- What provisions over confidentiality will apply to the employment?
- What provisions over non-solicitation of clients will apply to the employment?
- What provisions over non-solicitation of staff will apply to the employment?

❖ suspension or exclusion from membership of or being disciplined by any professional body of which the employee is or becomes a member or permitting such membership to be suspended or lapse

❖ ceasing howsoever to be a fit and proper person to carry out work of the nature with which he is or may be instructed.

[6] A "fit and proper" form means a form containing questions to elicit whether the employee is a fit and proper person to be involved in the preparation of an audit or insolvency work or in the preparation of work which may be relied on by the Company whether a set of accounts gives a true and fair view. It may contain questions as to:

❖ the employee's financial integrity and reliability, and,
❖ the employee's civil liabilities and convictions, and,
❖ the employee's good reputation and character, and
❖ any other head as may, from time to time, be required or recommended to be adopted as proper procedure for the Company's practice by any guidelines or regulations by any Accountancy or Insolvency Institute or other Regulatory Body or Institute pursuant to the Companies Act 1989 and the Insolvency Act 1986 or any supervening legislation which governs work conducted by the firm.

[7] Is the employee's work such that he is or may become involved in financial services, audit or insolvency work?

Annex 4

CHECKLIST FOR FIT AND PROPER ENQUIRIES OF EMPLOYEES WORKING FOR AUDITORS OR LIQUIDATORS

A "fit and proper" form means a form containing questions to elicit whether the employee is a fit and proper person to be involved in the preparation of an audit or in financial services work or insolvency work or in the preparation of work which may be relied on by a Company whether a set of accounts gives a true and fair view. The requirement to be "fit and proper" is an ongoing one and employers should require employees to notify them if circumstances have arisen which cause their answers to any of the questions to change.

It may contain questions as to:

- the employee's financial integrity and reliability, and,
- the employee's civil liabilities and convictions, and,
- the employee's good reputation and character, and
- any other head as may, from time to time, be required or recommended to be adopted as proper procedure for the Company's practice by any guidelines or regulations by any Accountancy or Insolvency Institute or the Financial Services Authority or other Regulatory Body or Institute pursuant to the Companies Act 1989 and the Insolvency Act 1986 or any supervening legislation which governs work conducted by the firm.

Set out below are the questions that an accountancy firm should ask to assess the individual's fit and proper status for the purposes of his or her involvement in financial services, audit or insolvency work.

The answers will be 'yes' or 'no', but a 'yes' will need further explanation.[1] The assessment of whether an applicant is "fit and proper" is not a

---

[1] Thus whilst employment by a company hit by a major scandal may trigger a "yes" on a number of heads, the employee may still be found to be "fit and proper" because on amplification it is revealed that he was perhaps a junior employee with no executive role at the

mechanical exercise but a judgement based on a review of the whole of the applicant's record and individual circumstances.

- Do you have the level of independence, integrity, skills and experience necessary to undertake the work you are to be employed to perform?[2]
- In the last ten years has a court, in the United Kingdom or elsewhere, given any judgment against you about a debt?
- In the last ten years have you made any compromise arrangement with your creditors?
- Have you ever been the subject of a bankruptcy restriction order?
- In the last ten years has any business you have been involved with made any compromise or arrangement with its creditors, or otherwise failed to satisfy creditors in full?
- Have you ever been declared bankrupt or been the subject of a bankruptcy court order in the United Kingdom or elsewhere, or has a bankruptcy petition ever been served on you?
- Has any business or practice you have been involved with been liquidated, entered a company voluntary arrangement
- Have you ever signed a trust deed for a creditor, made an assignment for the benefit of creditors, or made any arrangements for the payment of a composition to creditors?
- Have you at any time pleaded guilty to or been found guilty of any offence?[3]
- In the last five years have you, in the United Kingdom or elsewhere, been the subject of any civil action relating to your professional or business activities which has resulted in a finding against you by a court, or a settlement being agreed?
- In the last five years has any business you have been involved with, in the United Kingdom or elsewhere, been the subject of any civil action relating to professional or business activities which has resulted in an adverse finding in a court, or a settlement being agreed?

---

time or that he was not involved in the culpable activity for which his then employer was criticised.

[2] Regulation 6(e), Insolvency Practitioner Regulations 2005.

[3] Particular weight should be given to offences involving fraud, financial crime, dishonesty or violence or compliance with any legislation involving insolvency, tax, companies, banking, financial services, consumer credit, market manipulation or insider dealing. There is no need to mention offences which are spent for the purposes of the Rehabilitation of Offenders Act 1974 or offences committed before the age of 17 (unless committed within the last ten years) and road traffic offences that did not lead to a disqualification or prison sentence. It is important also to be mindful of the different treatment of members of the different professional accountancy bodies: Article 3 and 4, Rehabilitation of Offenders Act 1974 (Exceptions) Order 1975.

- Have you ever been disqualified by a court from being a director, or from acting in the management or conduct of the affairs of any company?
- Have you, in the United Kingdom or elsewhere, ever been refused the right or been restricted in the right to carry on any trade, business or profession for which a specific licence, registration or other authority is required?
- In the last ten years has any business or practice you have been involved with been refused or restricted in the right to carry on any trade, business or profession for which a specific licence, registration or other authority is required?
- In the last ten years has any business or practice you have been involved with been refused entry to any professional body or trade association, or decided not to continue with an application?
- Have you been refused entry to any professional body or trade association, or decided not to continue with an application?
- Have you, in the United Kingdom or elsewhere, ever been investigated about allegations of misconduct or malpractice in connection with your professional activities which resulted in a formal complaint being proved but no disciplinary order being made?
- In the last ten years has any business or practice you have been involved with been investigated on allegations of misconduct or malpractice in connection with its professional or business activities which resulted in a formal complaint being proved but no disciplinary order being made?
- Have you, in the United Kingdom or elsewhere, ever been the subject of disciplinary procedures by a (present or former) regulatory or professional body or employer resulting in a finding against you?
- Have you, in the United Kingdom or elsewhere, ever been reprimanded, excluded, disciplined or publicly criticised by any (present or former) regulatory or professional body which you belong to or have belonged to?
- In the last ten years has any business or practice you have been involved with been reprimanded, warned about future conduct, disciplined or publicly criticised by any profession or (present or former) regulatory body?
- In the last ten years has any business or practice you have been involved with been made the subject of a court order at the instigation of any professional or (present or former) regulatory body?
- Have you or any business you have been involved with been censured, disciplined or criticised by any court, tribunal, regulatory or professional body whether publicly or privately?

- Have you, in the United Kingdom or elsewhere, ever been refused entry to or excluded from membership of any profession or vocation?
- Have you, in the United Kingdom or elsewhere, ever been dismissed from any office (other than as auditor) or employment or requested to resign from any office, employment or partnership?
- Have you, in the United Kingdom or elsewhere, ever been reprimanded, warned about future conduct, disciplined, or publicly criticised by any regulatory body, or any officially appointed enquiry concerned with the regulation of a financial, professional or other business activity?
- Have you, in the United Kingdom or elsewhere, ever been the subject of a court order at the instigation of any regulatory body, or any officially appointed enquiry concerned with the regulation of a financial, professional or other business activity?
- Have you been the subject of any justified complaint in relation to your professional or regulated conduct?
- Have you ever been dismissed or asked to resign or resigned from any employment or from a position of trust, fiduciary appointment or similar?
- Have you ever been untruthful or less than candid in your dealings with any professional or (present or former) regulatory body or any government body or agency?
- Are you currently undergoing any investigation or criminal or disciplinary proceedings or have you been notified of any potential proceedings or investigation which might lead to those proceedings?

Annex 5

CHECKLIST FOR INSTRUCTING AN EXPERT ACCOUNTANT

It is good practice for lawyers when instructing an expert accountant to do so by letter which sets out:

- the name of the client
- the capacity in which the accountant is instructed
- the form in which his report should take
- the time limits for preparing the report
- the subject matter of the dispute, including the short facts
- the stage which the litigation has reached
- the questions that need to be addressed
- the matters the accountant should pay particular attention to
- the particular problems or arguments that the accountant needs to address or respond to
- any particular appendices the accountant should include with his report
- The address of the client and the instructing parties
- The telephone numbers
- The date of birth of the parties
- A short chronology of key dates
- The nature and extent of expertise which is called for;
- The purpose of requesting the advice or report, a description of the matter to be investigated, the principal known issues and the identity of all parties;
- The statement(s) of case (if any), those documents which form part of standard disclosure and witness statements which are relevant to the advice or report;
- Whether proceedings are being contemplated
- Where proceedings have been started, the date of any hearing and in which court and to which track they have been allocated.
- The terms of appointment including

- the basis of the expert's charges (either daily or hourly rates and an estimate of the time likely to be required, or a fee for the services);
- who is liable for any travelling expenses and other disbursements;
- rates for attendance at court and provisions for payment on late notice of cancellation of a court hearing;
- time for delivery of report;
- time for making payment; and
- whether fees are to be paid by a third party.
- How questions to experts and discussions between experts are to be dealt with, including any directions given by the court and provision should be made for the cost of this work.

The lawyer should consider whether he requires:

A preliminary view

This draft report, often in the form of a letter, sets out the accountant's preliminary views based on the available information. This is usually confidential to the client and his lawyers.

A forensic report

These report on the accountant's investigation into the facts and papers in the case from an accountant's perspective. This is usually confidential to the client and his lawyers.

An expert report

This sets out the evidence the accountant will give in court and may take the form of an affidavit. A copy of the accountant's *curriculum vitae* or a career synopsis will be included. This will usually be disclosed to the other side.

Annex 6

CHECKLIST FOR AN EXPERT REPORT UNDER THE CIVIL PROCEDURE RULES

The expert report must:

- be addressed to the court
- give details of the expert's academic and professional qualifications;
- give details of any literature or other material which the expert has relied on in making the report;
- contain a statement setting out the substance of all facts and instructions given to the expert which are material to the opinions expressed in the report or upon which those opinions are based;
- make clear which of the facts stated in the report are within the expert's own knowledge;
- Set out a chronology of the relevant events;
- Make a statement of the methodology used, in particular what tests (if any) were employed, by whom (giving their qualifications) and under whose supervision;
- Include relevant extracts of literature or any other material which might assist the court in deciding the case
- where there is a range of opinion on the matters dealt with in the report –
  - summarise the range of opinion, and
  - give reasons for his own opinion;
- In addressing questions of fact and opinion, should keep the two separate and discrete; where there are facts in dispute should not express a view in favour of one or other disputed sets of facts, unless, because of their particular learning and experience, they perceive one set of facts as being improbable or less probable, in which case they may express that view, and should give reasons;
- Should express separate opinions on every set of facts in dispute.
- if the expert is not able to give his opinion without qualification, state the qualification

- Identify (a) any question or issue which falls outside his expertise; and (b) when he is not able to reach a definite opinion, for example because he has insufficient information.
- Give a summary of conclusions reached.
- State that the expert understands his duty to the court, and has complied and will continue to comply with that duty.
- State that the report complies with the Part 35 of the Civil Procedure Rules and the Code of Guidance on Expert Evidence
- Conclude with the following signed statement of truth

> "I confirm that insofar as the facts stated in my report are within my own knowledge I have made clear which they are and I believe them to be true, and that the opinions I have expressed represent my true and complete professional opinion."

Precedent 1

LETTER OF ENGAGEMENT

Dear Mr Client

The purpose of this letter is to set out the basis upon which you have instructed us in connection with your personal and taxation affairs.

Should you require we can assist you in the preparation of the statutory accounts on your behalf. We shall finalise the accounts from your accounting records and draft accounts prepared by you and from the information supplied to us either directly by you or under your authority. We shall examine the records and make such inquiries as we consider necessary to enable us to prepare the accounts for you but shall not perform an audit unless you specifically request us to do so.

The range of supplementary accountancy services, such as investigating irregularities and fraud is available, and can be performed upon our receiving specific instructions from you. We understand people's needs vary and are happy to tailor our services to your specific identified requirements.

As to the specific tasks to be performed, you agree that:

(a) you/we be responsible for keeping the records of receipts and payments;

(b) you/we be responsible for reconciling the balances monthly of bank statements;

(c) you/we be responsible for keeping posted and balance the purchase and sales ledgers and the nominal ledger regularly;

(d) you/we be responsible for preparing a detailed list of ledger balances regularly and at the end of the year;

(e) you/we be responsible for preparing details of the annual year-end stocktaking suitably priced and extended.

Should you require further or different services we would be happy to supply them on request.

You will appreciate that the responsibility for the prevention and detection of irregularities rests with you, and our examination of the accounting records should not be relied upon to disclose irregularities which may exist. We shall discuss the accounts with you prior to their finalisation and after any adjustments arising from these discussions are made, we shall ask you to approve the accounts by asking you to sign the following statement which will be incorporated into the accounts:

> "I approve these accounts and confirm that I have made available all relevant records and information for their preparation."

Our accountant's report, which will be attached to the accounts, will take the following form:

> "In accordance with the instructions given to us we have prepared, without carrying out an audit, the attached accounts for the period ending 2009 from the accounting records of Mr Client and from the information and explanations given to us."

We have accepted responsibility for the preparation of your annual tax return which reports your income and gains for the year ended (say) 2009 and shall remain in force until cancelled by you in writing. The return will be based upon the information which is provided to us by you and third parties, such as your stockbroker, bank, and building society. We shall send you a questionnaire each April which we hope you will find helpful in collating the material which you will need to send to us. You may find it helpful to arrange with your bank, building society, and broker for them to send information directly to us on a regular basis and we shall be pleased to help establish such arrangements. The return will be sent to you to review and sign before it is submitted to the Inland Revenue on your behalf. It is essential that the return is carefully reviewed by you to check that no source of income or gain has been inadvertently omitted, since the accuracy of the return remains your legal responsibility.

We will also advise you of your tax position for the year and the likely payment date of liabilities. The late submission of a tax return, as well as the omission of a source of income or gain, will give rise to a penalty. We therefore recommend that tax returns are submitted no later than 31st January following the tax year, and to meet that timetable materials should reach us as soon as possible after 5th April each year and no later than the 31st August to ensure completion by the deadline. We will be happy to review the interim payments on account shown on the Inland Revenue statement of account, apply for any postponement which may be necessary and advise you in connection with the payment of tax due thereon. We have asked you to sign the appropriate authority which enables the Inland Revenue to send us copies of the statement of account.

We are bound by ethical guidelines of our professional institute and accept instructions to act for you on the basis that we will act in accordance therewith. You or your staff will deal with all matters required to be completed by officials of your business; for example, VAT returns and PAYE, but should be pleased to advise you and undertake these tasks on your behalf if so requested.

In addition, we shall be glad to assist you generally on tax planning related to your personal affairs and to your business, and to review and plan your income and taxation affairs. We should be pleased to discuss proposed tax transactions with you and to advise you on the most tax efficient way in which they could be structured and the tax implications or alternative courses of action.

We should also be pleased, if instructed, to review your capital assets with you and advise on tax efficient planning, both from a capital gains standpoint and from an inheritance tax standpoint, and over the use of trusts and lifetime gifts.

We should be pleased to provide general advice, financial planning and consultancy if requested. We have significant experience in helping businesses in difficulty as well as those doing well. With a well thought out strategy and business plan, the chances of success (and even survival) are improved significantly.

This letter does not instruct us to give you investment advice. Should you require such advice, which is regulated by the Financial Services and Markets Act 2000, we will deal with your instructions in a separate agreement. The firm is regulated in its conduct of investment business by the Institute of Chartered Accountants in England and Wales.

This firm will advise on pensions and life business but will not hold client monies. Any other advice must be requested in writing by the client.

If you are dissatisfied with any of the work we undertake, please contact your assignment partner or our complaints partner, Mr X. It is his duty to resolve matters to your satisfaction. It is important that we receive feedback, good or bad, to enable our service to you to continually improve. Whilst we hope and expect difficulties will not arise, we would prefer to know about them and deal with those that occur so that you remain a satisfied client.

This procedure does not affect in any way your right to contact the Institute of Chartered Accountants in England and Wales if you remain dissatisfied with the outcome of our complaints procedure.[1]

The subject of accounting fees is obviously of interest both to us and to you, as our clients. You, as the client, want to feel you are getting your monies' worth for the fee you pay, and we must have fees that are adequate to enable us to give a good service. Our fees are computed on the basis of time spent on your affairs by the partners and our staff and on the level of skill and responsibility involved. Clients are billed at agreed intervals and our settlement terms are as follows:

- All fee notes must be settled within thirty days from the fee note date.
- On the 31st day interest is chargeable at two per cent per month from the date on which they became overdue.
- Fees will be subject to the addition of disbursements and VAT will be due on presentation. Save where there has been a prior written arrangement with you, the choice of staff for any work we do for you will be at our discretion. We reserve the right to increase our current rates from time to time but will notify you in writing before we do so. Our current rates are:

    Partner £150 per hour
    Associate £120 per hour
    Bookkeeper £75 per hour

Once it has been agreed, this letter will remain effective from one year to the next until this is replaced. This agreement may be ended by either of us giving notice in writing to the other and we will cease to work from the date we become aware that this retainer has ended. Any variations to this agreement must be agreed in writing and you may be required to sign a new engagement letter to continue our instruction.

You agree to allow me to approach third parties for information where appropriate. I will treat as confidential any information you provide to me

---

[1] Chartered accountants are under a duty to identify a partner to whom complaints can be made and tell their client of their right to complain to the Institute in writing: ICAEW Disciplinary Bye-Law 11.

except where you agree otherwise or where I am required by law, an order of the court or by the professional rules that govern me or my firm to make disclosure.

All accountants and tax advisers fall within the regulated sector for the purposes of the Money Laundering Regulations 2007. As part of the client identification requirements placed upon us by the Regulations, we are obliged to ask from all our clients and retain documentary proof of client's identity (such as a passport and telephone bill) before starting work for them. Where a client acts as an intermediary, we are obliged to make this request both of the client and his principal.

This letter of engagement is governed by, and is to be construed in accordance with, the laws of England.

We hope that this letter summarises the terms under which you have asked us to act on your behalf, in which case we should be grateful if you could kindly acknowledge receipt of this letter and indicate your agreement to it by signing the enclosed copy and returning it to us. If you do not agree with our understanding of the agreement, please let us know as soon as practicable.

Yours sincerely

Minus & Co
Chartered Accountants

I agree to engage Minus & Co, Chartered Accountants, under the terms laid out under this engagement letter. I require/do not require Minus & Co, Chartered Accountants, to assist in the preparation of the statutory accounts.

Signed:

Name Mr A Client   Date 1st April 2009

Note: Formerly registered members of the Chartered Institute of Management Accountants in practice had to notify their client in their letter of engagement if they did not hold adequate profession indemnity insurance or had not made adequate arrangements for the continuity of their practice. Following changes to their Council Regulations, members in practice of the

Chartered Institute of Management Accountants are now required to hold an appropriate level of professional indemnity insurance, make continuity arrangements for the eventuality of their death or incapacity and undertake continuing professional education as a precondition of being granted a practising certificate.[2]

---

[2] Regulation 7.5, CIMA Council Regulations of 12th June 2004.

Precedent 2

HEADS OF AGREEMENT[1]
(ACCOUNTANCY PRACTICE SALE)

HEADS OF AGREEMENT - SUBJECT TO CONTRACT

BETWEEN

XAVIER MINUS A.C.A, 1 Abacus Street, London (Vendor)
ALDOUS ADDER F.C.C.A, 3 Calculator Place, London (Purchaser)

We agree that the following constitutes our present instructions in relation of the agreement to be prepared for the sale by Xavier Minus of Minus & Co to Aldous Adder. These Heads of Agreement are subject to contract and are not intended to create legal relations. The Heads of Agreement are a non-exclusive representation of the main proposed terms and may be subject to further negotiation or amendment. The Heads of Agreement are for the attention of our respective lawyers only.

1. X & Co is a sole proprietorship of Minus trading from 1 Abacus Street, London
2. Adder will buy Minus's practice, Minus & Co, for £150,000.
3. The price is paid in 2 tranches £50,000 on completion and £100,000 on the 1st anniversary of completion.
4. The price is set on at 1½ times current years earnings and is subject to a claw back pro rata to the extent that earnings after sale fail to repeat this.
5. Adder will buy on the sale
    a. The goodwill,
    b. The client list
    c. The book debts of the practice at the date of completion
    d. work in hand,
    e. office furniture
    f. the computers
    g. the client papers and records

---

[1] This does not create a binding agreement but allows the parties to record the essence of their agreement to enable their lawyers to finalise the contract.

6. Minus will retain on the sale
    a. the cash at bank at the date of completion
    b. a photocopy of any records he requires
    c. the portrait of Xavier Minus's grandfather in the entrance hall
    d. the pot plant in the reception
7. Minus will take all necessary steps to assign to Adder the commercial lease between Minus and his landlord, Grabber Snatchit, of 1 Abacus Street
8. Minus will be employed under a consultancy agreement by Adder from completion for 18 months at £10,000 per annum to facilitate the handover
9. There are two other employees of the practice who will be transferred to Adders
    a. Sophie Sums, a bookkeeper, a £18,000 per annum
    b. Betty Balance-Sheet, a bookkeeper, at £16,000 per annum

Precedent 3

CLAIM FORM
(CLAIM FOR UNPAID ACCOUNTANCY FEES)

[Royal Arms]
CLAIM FORM
N1 Claim Form (CPR Part 7)

IN THE HIGH COURT OF JUSTICE
QUEEN'S BENCH DIVISION
CLAIM HQ999999
ISSUE DATE 1ST APRIL 200X

CLAIMANT

XAVIER MINUS - trading as - Minus & Co, One Abacus Street, London

DEFENDANT

DINGLE BELL, Two Christmas Court, London

BRIEF DETAILS OF THE CLAIM

£120,000 being professional fees due for work done by the Claimant for the Defendant under a written letter of engagement dated 1st December 2005 together with interest under section 35A Supreme Court Act 1981 at a rate of 8 per cent per annum amounting to £[…………..] at the date hereof and continuing hereafter until Judgement or sooner payment at a rate of £[……….] per day

VALUE
The Claimant claims damages exceeding £100,000 but not exceeding £150,000

Amount claimed	£[....................]
Court Fee	£900
Solicitor's costs	To be assessed
Total amount	£[....................]

DEFENDANT'S NAME AND ADDRRESS

DINGLE BELL,
Two Christmas Court,
London

The Court Office at the Royal Courts of Justice, Strand, London WC2A 2LL is open between 10am and 4pm Monday to Friday. When corresponding with the court, please address forms and letters to the Court manager and quote the claim number.

Does or will your claim include any issues under the Human Rights Act 1998
Yes [ ] No [•]

CLAIM HQ999999

Particulars of claim [attached / ~~to follow~~]

STATEMENT OF TRUTH

The Claimant believes the facts stated in this Claim Form are true

* I am duly authorised by the Claimant to sign this statement

Signed:- ....

Name:- ....

Position:- ....

(if signing on behalf of a firm or company)

The Claimant's or claimant's solicitor's address to which documents or payments should be sent if different from overleaf including if appropriate details of DX, Fax or email

ADDENDUM & CO Solicitors
Wig Road
London

DX 666 LONDON CITY
Tel [...................]
Fax [..................]

Solicitors for the Claimant

Precedent 4

PARTICULARS OF CLAIMS
(CLAIM FOR UNPAID ACCOUNANCY FEES)

IN THE HIGH COURT OF JUSTICE
QUEEN'S BENCH DIVISION

CLAIM HQ999999

BETWEEN:-

XAVIER MINUS

- trading as -

Minus & Co

<u>Claimant</u>

- and -

DINGLE BELL

- formerly trading as -

DINGLE SOLICITORS

<u>Defendant</u>

PARTICULARS OF CLAIM
----

1. By an agreement in writing described as "Letter of Engagement" and dated 1st December 2005 between the Claimant and the Defendant, the Defendant agreed to instruct and the Claimant agreed to provide accountancy services at an hourly rate of £300 plus VAT ["the Contract"].

A true copy of the letter of Engagement is attached hereto at Appendix 1.

2. Pursuant to the said contract the Claimant provided the said accountancy services to the Defendant set out in the Invoices Number 001 and 002, which are attached hereto at Appendix 2 and incorporated herein by reference. Mr Minus will give evidence of this fact.

PARTICULARS

3.12.06	Invoice 001	200 hours	£ 60,000
3.12.07	Invoice 002	200 hours	£ 60,000

			£120,000

3. In the premises, the sum of £120,000 is due and owing by the Defendant to the Claimant under the said contract.

4. In breach of the said contract, the Defendant has failed and/or refused to pay to the Claimant the sum of £120,000 or any sum and the sum of £120,000 remains due and owing to the Claimant.

5. Further the Claimant claims against the Defendant interest on the said £120,000 pursuant to section 35A of the Supreme Court Act 1981 amounting to £[........] at the date hereof and accruing at a rate of £[......] per day from the date hereof until judgment or sooner payment.

AND the Claimant claims against the Defendant:-

1. £120,000 or damages
2. The aforesaid interest pursuant to section 35A of the Supreme Court Act 1981 amounting to £ [........] at the date hereof and accruing at a rate of £ [......] per day from the date hereof until judgment or sooner payment.

A BARRISTER

Dated [..............]

> **STATEMENT OF TRUTH**
>
> The Claimant believes the facts stated in this Claim Form are true
>
> * I am duly authorised by the Claimant to sign this statement
>
> Signed: - ……………………………..
>
> Name: - ……………………………..
>
> Position: - ……………………………..
>
> (if signing on behalf of a firm or company)

THE CLAIMANT'S ADDRESS FOR SERVICE IS:-

ADDENDUM & CO Solicitors
Wig Road
London

DX 666 LONDON CITY
Tel [………………]
Fax [………………]

Solicitors for the Claimant

APPENDIX

(1) The Letter of Engagement
   (2) Invoices Number 001 and 002.

Precedent 5

DEFENCE AND COUNTERCLAIM

(ALLEGING PROFESSIONAL NEGLIGENCE – LATE PREPARATION OF SOLICITOR'S ACCOUNTS)

<u>IN THE HIGH COURT OF JUSTICE</u>
<u>QUEEN'S BENCH DIVISION</u>

1999 X No 800

B E T W E E N :-

XAVIER MINUS

- trading as -

Minus & Co

<u>Claimant/Part 20 Defendant</u>

- and -

DINGLE BELL

- formerly trading as -

DINGLE SOLICITORS

<u>Defendant/Part 20 Claimant</u>

DEFENCE AND COUNTERCLAIM

DEFENCE

1. It is denied that the said or any sum is either due or payable to the Claimant and whether as professional fees or otherwise. Save as hereinafter pleaded, the Claimant's claims and every part of them are denied and the Defendant joins issue with the Particulars of Claim in its entirety.

2. The Claimant is and was, at all material times, practising as an accountant who carried on business from offices at Abacus Street, London. At all material times, the Claimant held himself out as a firm of accountants who were competent, skilled and experienced in the preparation of personal and solicitor's accounts.

3. The Defendant is and was at all material times a solicitor in private practice and, in the premises, was required as a condition of his being granted his practising certificate to promptly deliver to the Law Society each year an accountant's certificate in respect of his practice accounts.

4. By a letter dated 1st December 2005, the Defendant consulted and retained the Claimant and the Claimant agreed, in the course of his business as an accountant, to prepare the personal and professional accounts of the Defendant for reward: ["the contract"].

A true copy of the letter of Engagement is attached hereto at Appendix 1.

5. It was, *inter alia*, an express, alternatively, implied term of the contract and/or the Claimant was under a duty that the Claimant alternatively exercise such reasonable care and skill and expertise in the performance of the said contract as might be expected of a competent firm of accountants, alternatively, a firm of accountants who were competent, skilled and experience in preparing personal and solicitor's accounts.

6. It was, *inter alia*, an express, alternatively, implied term of the contract that the Claimant would for each year of the contract:

6.1 promptly draft, prepare and file and serve on the Law Society the accountant's certificate for the Defendant

6.2 record and diarise the date upon which the accountant's certificate for the Defendant needed to be delivered to the Law Society

7. It was an implied term of the contract that the Defendant would pay the Claimant's reasonable fees. It is denied that the fees claimed were agreed and/or were reasonable.

8. The Claimant acted or purported to act as accountants for the Defendant throughout the period between December 2005 and January 2008.

9. Negligently and in breach of the said express, alternatively, implied terms of the said contract, the Claimant, their servants or agents failed to take any or any appropriate action in respect of the Defendant's accounts.

PARTICULARS OF NEGLIGENCE/BREACH OF CONTRACT

The Claimant, their servants or agents were negligent, further or alternatively, were in breach of the said contract with the Defendant, in that they:

a) caused or permitted the Defendant's accounts to be sent to the Law Society late and/or conducted the audit in such a manner so as to be late;

b) failed to supply the Defendant's accounts to the Law Society within the time limit or at all;

c) failed to employ competent and/or sufficiently experienced staff to conduct the audit;

d) failed to properly supervise the staff conducting the audit;

e) in the premises, failed to exercise any or any of the reasonable care and skill and expertise in the performance of the said contract to be expected of a competent firm of accountants, alternatively, a firm of accountants who were competent, skilled and experienced in preparing solicitor's accounts

The Defendant will seek to rely on the happening of the late delivery of accounts as evidence of itself of the Claimant's negligence.

10. The Claimant is put to strict proof as to each of the professional services it is alleged to have provided

11. Further or alternatively, if which is denied, the Defendant is found liable to the Claimant in the said sum or any sum, the Defendant claims to set off so much of the sums counterclaimed herein as may extinguish his liability to the Claimant

COUNTERCLAIM

12. The Defence is repeated.

13. By reason of the Claimant's failure to provide solicitors' accounts timeously for the years 2006 and 2007 the Defendant was disciplined and struck off as a solicitor by the Law Society on 1st January 2008.

14. In the premises and by reason of the matters aforesaid, the Defendant suffered distress, inconvenience, loss and damage.

PARTICULARS

The Defendant has lost his professional qualification and livelihood as a solicitor. The Defendant is 42 years old and made a net profit of £200,000 per annum for each of his last two years trading. He has been unable to find gainful employment since his being struck off as a solicitor.

The Defendant reserves the right to provide further and better particularity of the quantum of the loss.

15. Further the Defendant counterclaims interest pursuant to Section 35A of the Supreme Court Act 1981 on the amount found due to the Defendant at such a rate and for such a period as the Court thinks fit.

AND the Defendant counterclaims:-

(1) Damages

(2) The aforesaid interest pursuant to section 35A of the Supreme Court Act 1981 to be assessed.

A COUNSEL

I believe that the facts stated in this Defence and Part 20 Statement of Case are true

Signed:- ....

DINGLE BELL, the Defendant and Part 20 Claimant

THE DEFENDANT AND PART 20 CLAIMANT'S ADDRESS FOR SERVICE IS:-

B & CO Solicitors
Law Road
London

Solicitors for the Defendant and Part 20 Claimant

Precedent 6

REPLY AND DEFENCE TO COUNTERCLAIM

(DENYING PROFESSIONAL NEGLIGENCE AND ALLEGING CONTRIBUTORY NEGLIGENCE)

IN THE HIGH COURT OF JUSTICE
QUEEN'S BENCH DIVISION
                                                  1999 X No 800

BETWEEN:-

XAVIER MINUS

- trading as -

Minus & Co
                                  Claimant/Part 20 The Defendant
- and -

DINGLE BELL

- formerly trading as -

DINGLE SOLICITORS
                                    Defendant/Part 20 Claimant

----

REPLY AND DEFENCE TO COUNTERCLAIM

----

1.   Save in so far as the same consists of admissions, the Claimant joins issue with the Defence and Counterclaim.

REPLY

2. Paragraphs 2 to 5 of the Defence and Counterclaim are admitted.

3. It is admitted under paragraph 6 of the Defence and Counterclaim that it was a term of the contract and/or the Claimant was under a duty that the Claimant alternatively exercise such reasonable care and skill and expertise in the performance of the said contract as might be expected of a competent firm of accountants. Further it is averred that the Claimant did indeed exercise such reasonable care and skill and expertise in the performance of the said contract.

4. It is denied that the Claimant was negligent and/or in breach of contract or caused or contributed to the Defendant's accounts being delayed as alleged or at all.

5. Further or in the alternative, if, which is denied, the Defendant's solicitors' accounts were delayed as alleged or at all, the same was wholly caused or contributed to by the Defendant, further or alternatively, the Defendant failed to mitigate his loss if any

PARTICULARS OF CONTRIBUTORY NEGLIGENCE/FAILURE TO MITIGATE

The Defendant was negligent and/or failed to mitigate his loss (if any) in that he

1.1 failed to answer the Claimant's calls

1.2 failed to supply to the Claimant timeously or at all the Defendant's books and records or any part of them

1.3 failed to reply to the Claimant's inquiries about his books or records timeously or at all

1.4 failed to permit the Claimant's staff to inspect the Defendant's books and records promptly or at all

1.5 delayed answering the Claimant's inquiries about his books or records by stating

    1.5.1 orally to JOE PACIOLI, one of the employees of the Claimant, on 3rd December 2005

"Can't you see I'm busy. Talk to me next month about it"

1.5.2 orally to JOE PACIOLI, one of the employees of the Claimant, on 3rd December 2006

"*Look I really don't have time to deal with it now as I am going skiing for a year*"

1.5.3 in writing to the Claimant by letter 3rd December 2007

"*Frankly this is much too boring to deal with. Talk to me about it in two years time when I'm back from my world cruise and I'll give you all the missing invoices and receipts then*"

The Defendant will rely on the evidence of JOE PACIOLI as evidence of these facts.

DEFENCE TO SET OFF AND COUNTERCLAIM

6. The Reply is repeated.

7. No admissions are made to the Defendant's loss and damage, if any, and the Defendant is put to strict proof of the same. It is denied that the Claimant caused the alleged or any loss or damage.

8. In the premises and generally, it is denied that the Defendant is entitled to the relief sought or any relief.

ARTHUR BARRISTER

I believe that the facts stated in this Reply and Defence to Counterclaim are true

Signed:- ……………………………..

XAVIER MINUS
trading as Minus & Co (a firm)
The Claimant/Part 20 Defendant

THE CLAIMANT/PART 20 DEFENDANT'S ADDRESS FOR SERVICE IS:-

ADDENDUM & CO Solicitors
Wig Road
London

Solicitors for the Claimant/Part 20 Defendant

Precedent 7

PRELIMINARY NOTICE
PROFESSIONAL NEGLIGENCE CLAIM

(NEGLIGENT TAX ADVICE/ NEGLIGENT PREPARATION OF TAX RETURN)

[Date]

Dear Sirs,

Letter of Claim
Client v yourselves

We act for George Client ("Mr Client").

This is a Preliminary Notice pursuant to paragraph B1 of the Professional Negligence Pre-action Protocol to give you notice that we are considering issuing proceedings against you on our client's behalf.

You should inform your professional indemnity insurers immediately of the contents of this letter.

The claim arises out of the conduct of yourselves as accountants and tax advisers for Mr Client for the tax years ending 30th March 2007 to 30th March 2012. Mr Client alleges that the tax planning, advice and preparation of tax returns undertaken by you for him was negligent and in breach of the contractual duty of care you owed his as his UK accountants and tax advisers.

In essence, the matters complained of are:-
- You filed incorrect tax returns for the tax years ending 30th March 2007 to 30th March 2012.
- You failed to advise on the tax effect of bringing foreign emoluments derived from overseas companies to the UK.

You are expected to acknowledge this letter of claim within 21 days.

Yours faithfully,

Precedent 8

PRE-ACTION PROTOCOL LETTER PROFESSIONAL NEGLIGENCE CLAIM

(NEGLIGENT TAX ADVICE / NEGLIGENT PREPARATION OF TAX RETURN)

[Date]

Dear Sirs,

Letter of Claim
Client v Yourselves

We act for George Client ("Mr Client").

This is an open letter of claim pursuant to paragraph B2 of the Professional Negligence Pre-action Protocol to give you notice of our intention to issue proceedings against you on our client's behalf.

You should consider the contents of this letter carefully and seek legal advice before you respond. You should inform your professional indemnity insurers immediately of the contents of this letter.

1
THE CLAIM

The claim arises out of your conduct as accountants and tax advisers for Mr Client for the tax years ending 30th March 2007 to 30th March 2012. Mr Client alleges that the tax planning and advice undertaken by you for his was negligent and in breach of the contractual duty of care you owed to his as his UK accountants and tax advisers. The allegations are set out in more detail below.

2
THE HISTORY

Mr Client is not UK domiciled. He is however resident but not ordinarily resident in the UK for tax purposes.

On 30th March 2007 Mr Minus, the principal of your firm, wrote to Mr Client confirming your engagement as his accountants and tax advisers "*to advise in all his in United Kingdom tax matters*".

Since 2007 you have acted for Mr Client as his accountants and tax advisers in all his United Kingdom tax matters.

On 1st April 2012 Her Majesty's Customs and Revenue commenced an investigation into the tax returns of Mr Client concerning the years ended 5th April 2007, 5th April 2008, 5th April 2009 and 5th April 2010 under the Taxes Management Act 1970.

You were instructed to deal with these Inland Revenue enquiries which related to tax returns you had prepared and submitted for Mr Client.

The investigation by Her Majesty's Customs and Revenue centred on foreign emoluments which had been brought into the UK from overseas but which had not been declared.

3
KEY DOCUMENTS

The key documentation relied on in this letter of claim and which appear annexed in the schedule to this letter is set out below:-

1. Letter of Engagement dated 30th March 2007
2. Report of Mr Expert
3. Tax Returns 2006- 2007
4. Tax Return 2007-2008
5. Tax Return 2008-2009
6. Tax Return 2009-2010
7. Tax return 2010-2011

4
THE ALLEGATIONS

Our client alleges that you failed to exercise the level of skill and care that may be expected of a firm of tax advisers and accountants.

The advice given and tax planning undertaken by you has created tax liabilities for Mr Client which he would not otherwise have been exposed to.

Mr Client's claim for professional negligence / breach of your contract for services against your firm arises because you failed to advise on the tax effect of bringing foreign emoluments derived from overseas companies to the UK and you failed to accurately record Mr Client's UK tax position on his returns.

Non-domiciled taxpayers who are resident but not ordinarily resident are liable to tax on UK earnings but they can mitigate their UK tax liability by keeping non-UK earnings offshore. One way of achieving this was to set up a foreign company with the view to "sheltering" foreign based income so that it would not be taxed in the UK on a non-domiciled (not ordinarily resident individual) situation.

For this to work, you should have given appropriate advice to Mr Client to ensure that no such income from the overseas companies was remitted to the UK.

You failed to advise Mr Client of the serious tax consequences of bringing income to the UK. It is now settled law that failure to give appropriate advice on this simple and well known tax mitigation step would be professionally negligent for an accountant: *Slattery v Moore Stephens* [2003] STI 1422.

5
LOSS

You were under a duty to take reasonable care when handling Mr Client's tax affairs. You failed to do so and as a result Mr Client suffered loss. Had you exercised reasonable care and skill, Mr Client would not have been subjected to the enquiry and would not be exposed to a considerable potential tax liability.

5.1 Exposure to unnecessary taxation

A mere 1% of Mr Client income derives from UK sources but for your failing to give appropriate advice on this subject the balance would have been wholly free of UK income tax liability.

The best estimate of the loss to Mr Client under this head that can be presently given is the sum of £ [....................].

5.2 Cost of Her Majesty's Customs and Revenue investigation

Through your failure to accurately record Mr Client's UK tax position on his returns, Her Majesty's Customs and Revenue commenced an investigation.

Her Majesty's Customs and Revenue will seek recovery of interest under the Taxes Management Act 1970 on sums they now assert were underpaid as a result of the matters set out above.

The best estimate of the loss to Mr Client under this head that can be presently given is the sum of £ [....................] and is accruing daily.

5.3 Cost of meeting an investigation by Her Majesty's Customs and Revenue

Had you undertaken Mr Client's tax affairs diligently and advised appropriately, Mr Client would not have been subjected to a tax investigation by Her Majesty's Customs and Revenue.

Mr Client has had to instruct professional advisers to address Her Majesty's Customs and Revenue's Investigation and to mitigate his loss and address the difficulties created by your negligence in respect of the structuring of his tax affairs.

The best estimate of the loss to Mr Client under this head that can be presently given is the sum of £ [................] and is accruing daily.

6
EXPERT

Mr Expert has been appointed by Mr Client to give expert evidence on the handling of the investigation and tax planning undertaken and advice given by your firm. A copy of his preliminary report is annexed.

7
ALTERNATIVE DISPUTE RESOLUTION

This letter should be treated as an invitation to refer this dispute to mediation or some other form of alternative dispute resolution (ADR).

8
REQUESTS FOR INFORMATION

We request that you forward to us a copy of the following documents which should be in your possession or control. We will undertake to pay your reasonable copying charges.

1. All attendance notes relating to Mr Client and his tax and accounting affairs
2. All working papers relating to Mr Client and his tax and accounting affairs
3. All correspondence relating to Mr Client and his tax and accounting affairs
4. All accounts and tax returns relating to Mr Client and his tax and accounting affairs

9
TIME LIMITS THAT APPLY TO YOU

This letter triggers certain time limits that affect you:-

You are expected to acknowledge this letter of claim within 14 days.

You are expected to respond to the invitation to refer this dispute to ADR within 14 days.

Under B4 of the Pre-action Protocol **you have 3 months from the date of this letter to investigate the claim made against you.**

Thereafter you should reply to this letter by way of open letter, responding to the claim made against you and / or setting out your proposals for settlement. You will find the requirements under B5 of the Professional Negligence Pre-Action Protocol.

If we do not hear from you within these time limits we will issue proceedings without further recourse to yourselves.

If you have any difficulty in complying with the three month time period, please explain the problem to us as soon as possible. We will usually agree to any reasonable request for an extension.

Yours faithfully,

Precedent 9

CLAIM FORM
PROFESSIONAL NEGLIGENCE CLAIM

(NEGLIGENT TAX ADVICE / NEGLIGENT PREPARATION OF TAX RETURN)

[Royal Arms]
CLAIM FORM
N1 Claim Form (CPR Part 7)

IN THE HIGH COURT OF JUSTICE
QUEEN'S BENCH DIVISION
CLAIM HQ88888888
ISSUE DATE 1ST APRIL 2007

CLAIMANT

GEORGE CLIENT, Tax Haven, Monaco

DEFENDANT

XAVIER MINUS - trading as - Minus & Co, One Abacus Street, London

BRIEF DETAILS OF THE CLAIM

The Claimant claims damages for breach of contract under a written letter of engagement dated 30th March 2007 between the Claimant for the Defendant and / or negligence and / or breach of duty arising out of advice given and work carried out by the Defendant as tax accountants for the Claimant breach of contract in the tax years ending 30th March 2007 to 30th March 2012 together with interest under section 35A Supreme Court Act 1981 to be assessed

VALUE

The Claimant claims damages exceeding £100,000 but not exceeding £150,000

Amount claimed	£[..................]
Court Fee	£900
Solicitor's costs	To be assessed
Total amount	£[..................]

DEFENDANT'S NAME AND ADDRRESS

XAVIER MINUS - trading as - Minus & Co,
One Abacus Street,
London

The Court Office at the Royal Courts of Justice, Strand, London EC2A 2LL
Is open between 10am and 4pm Monday to Friday. When corresponding with the court, please address forms and letters to the Court manager and quote the claim number.

Does or will your claim include any issues under the Human Rights Act 1998
Yes [ ]   No [•]

CLAIM HQ888888

Particulars of claim [attached / ~~to follow~~]

STATEMENT OF TRUTH

The Claimant believes the facts stated in this Claim Form are true

* I am duly authorised by the Claimant to sign this statement

Signed: - ....

Name: - ....

Position: - ....

(if signing on behalf of a firm or company)

The Claimant's or claimant's solicitor's address to which documents or payments should be sent if different from overleaf including if appropriate details of DX, Fax or email

ADDENDUM & CO Solicitors
Wig Road
London

DX 666 LONDON CITY
Tel [..................]
Fax [..................]

Solicitors for the Claimant

Precedent 10

PARTICULARS OF CLAIM
PROFESSIONAL NEGLIGENCE CLAIM

(NEGLIGENT TAX ADVICE / NEGLIGENT PREPARATION OF TAX RETURN)

IN THE HIGH COURT OF JUSTICE
QUEEN'S BENCH DIVISION

CLAIM HQ88888888

B E T W E E N:-

GEORGE CLIENT

Claimant

-and-

XAVIER MINUS
- trading as –
Minus & Co

Defendant

Particulars of Claim
----

1. At all material times the Claimant is and was domiciled in Monaco and resident but not usually resident in the United Kingdom.

2. At all material times the Defendant is and was a firm of accountants practising from 1, Abacus Street, London, holding themselves out as experienced in tax advice and planning.

3. By a letter dated 10th March 2005 the Claimants retained the Defendants for reward to act for them as their accountants in connection with United Kingdom their tax affairs ["the Contract of Retainer"].

A copy of the said Contract of Retainer is annexed hereto and is incorporated by reference

4. It was an express term under the said Contract of Retainer that the Defendant would undertake for the Claimant the computation and preparation of the Claimant's United Kingdom tax returns and to provide United Kingdom tax planning for the Claimant and to liaise on behalf of the Claimant with Her Majesty's Customs and Revenue over his United Kingdom tax affairs

5. It was, *inter alia*, an implied term of the said Contract of Retainer and / or the Defendant was under a duty that the Defendant exercise such reasonable care and skill and expertise in the performance of the said contract as might be expected of a competent firm of accountants and tax advisers

6. Further or alternatively, the Defendant owed the Claimants a duty of care at common law to exercise reasonable care and skill in acting for the Claimant

7. Pursuant to the said Contract of Retainer and for each of the years ending 30th March 2007 to 2012, the Claimant paid and the Defendant accepted £5000 plus VAT in professional fees and the Defendant prepared a "nil" tax return for the Claimant advising the Claimant by letter of like date

> "*For this year I will be preparing a nil return because even though you are working, you are domiciled overseas and therefore not subject to United Kingdom tax*"

8. Negligently and in breach of duty and of the said implied term of the said Contract of Retainer, the Defendant, their servants or agents, failed to exercise the level of skill and care that might be expected of a competent firm of accountants and taxation advisers

PARTICULARS OF NEGLIGENCE/BREACH OF CONTRACT

The Defendant, its servants or agents was negligent, further or alternatively, were in breach of duty, further or alternatively, were in breach of the said Contract of Retainer with the Claimant, in that it:

    a. Failed to advise the Claimant whether properly or at all on the tax effects for a not ordinarily resident non domiciliary of bringing foreign earned emoluments into the United Kingdom

b. Failed to provide tax planning and advice which was tailored to the Claimant's needs and circumstances;
c. Wrongly asserted in the Claimant's tax returns for each of the year 2007 to 2012 that the Claimant had no United Kingdom income
d. Failed to correctly calculate and submit correct tax returns for the Claimant's United Kingdom tax liability
e. In the premises, failed in the performance of the said contract to exercise such care and skill and expertise, alternatively, such reasonable care and skill and expertise as would be expected of a competent firm of accountants and specialist taxation advisers.

The Claimant will rely upon the principle of *res ipsa loquitur* and the principle in *Slattery v Moore Stephens* at trial.

9. By reason of the Defendant's negligence and / or breach of contract and / or breach of duty, the Her Majesty's Revenue and Customs have raised questions as part of their investigation commencing on 25th December 2013 into the tax returns of the Claimant for the years ending 30th March 2007 to 30th March 2012.
10. In the premises and by reason of the matters aforesaid, the Claimant suffered distress, inconvenience, loss and damage.

PARTICULARS

The best particulars of the Claimant's loss are as follows:

a. Both as a non domiciliary and as a person who is not ordinarily resident in the United Kingdom, the Claimant enjoys favourable treatment under the United Kingdom tax legislation and the Claimant would ordinarily only be liable to United Kingdom tax liability on his income earned in the United Kingdom or income remitted to the United Kingdom.
b. Had this advice been given the Claimant would have not remitted any income from his 2 offshore companies to the Claimant in the United Kingdom instead of sending £247,500 as the Claimant's salary
c. The Claimant then would only have incurred income tax on his United Kingdom derived earning's of £2,500 and would

have paid tax on this sum if he had been advised by the Claimant to do so

    d. The Claimant has incurred and continues to incur substantial professional fees to correct the Claimants' negligent work and address the Her Majesty's Revenue and Custom's investigation

    e. The Claimant further is exposed to a potential liability for penal interest under the Taxes Management Act 1970 in respect of any tax liability created by the Claimants' negligent handling of the Claimant's affairs and for which the Claimant is found to be liable.

A copy of the preliminary findings of Mr. Expert is annexed hereto and is incorporated by reference as further particularity of the loss and damage suffered by the Claimant.

11. Further the Claimants, and each of them, are entitled to and claim interest pursuant to section 35A, Supreme Court Act 1981 on the amount found due to the Claimants at such a rate and for such a period as the Court thinks fit.

AND THE CLAIMANT CLAIMS:-

(1)   Damages;
(2)   The aforesaid interest pursuant to section 35A, Supreme Court Act 1981 to be assessed.
(3)   Costs
(4)   Further and other relief

A BARRISTER

Statement of Truth

The Claimant believes that the facts stated in this Particulars of Claim are true.

Signed:..

THE CLAIMANT'S ADDRESS FOR SERVICE IS: -

ADDENDUM & CO Solicitors
Wig Road
London

DX 666 LONDON CITY
Tel [....................]
Fax [....................]

Solicitors for the Claimant

DEFENCE
PROFESSIONAL NEGLIGENCE CLAIM

(NEGLIGENT TAX ADVICE / NEGLIGENT PREPARATION OF TAX RETURN)

IN THE HIGH COURT OF JUSTICE
QUEEN'S BENCH DIVISION

CLAIM HQ88888888

B E T W E E N:-

GEORGE CLIENT

Claimant

-and-

XAVIER MINUS
- trading as –
Minus & Co

Defendant

Defence
----

1. Save insofar as the same is admitted or not admitted, each and every allegation in the Particulars of Claim is denied as if the same were set forth and specifically traversed.

2. Save that it is denied that the Claimant is and was resident in the United Kingdom, paragraphs 1 to 7 of the Particulars of Claim are admitted. The Claimant is and was at all material times resident and domiciled in Monaco and this was confirmed orally to the Defendant by the Claimant each year before the Defendant submitted the Claimant's tax return.

3. Paragraph 8 of the Particulars of Claim is denied. It is denied that the

Defendant or its servants or agents, or any of them were negligent, further or alternatively, were in breach of duty, further or alternatively, were in breach of the said Contract of Retainer with the Claimant whether as alleged or at all. The Defendant's advice and the tax returns were correct and / or reflected the express instructions given by the Claimant to the Defendant each year before the Defendant submitted the Claimant's tax return that (a) he was not resident in the United Kingdom and (b) he had derived no income from and remitted no income to the United Kingdom.

A copy of the Defendant's telephone attendance notes are annexed hereto and are incorporated by reference

4. Save that it is admitted that Her Majesty's Revenue and Customs have raised questions as part of their investigation commencing on 25th December 2013 into the tax returns of the Claimant for the years ending 30th March 2007 to 30th March 2012, paragraphs 9 of the Particulars of Claim are denied.

5. As to paragraph 10 of the Particulars of Claim, no admission are made as to the Claimant's loss and damage save that it is denied that the same was caused by the Defendant whether as alleged or at all. The Claimant is put to strict proof of his alleged loss and damage (if any).

6. In the premises, it is denied that the Claimant is entitled to the relief claimed or any relief.

A COUNSEL

Statement of Truth

The Defendant believes that the facts stated in this Defence are true.

Signed:..

THE DEFENDANT'S ADDRESS FOR SERVICE IS: -

Brief & Co
Gown Street
London

Solicitors for the Defendant

Precedent 12

CLAIM FORM
PROFESSIONAL NEGLIGENCE CLAIM

(CLAIM BY INVESTOR OVER NEGLIGENT AUDIT)

[Royal Arms]
CLAIM FORM
N1 Claim Form (CPR Part 7)

IN THE HIGH COURT OF JUSTICE
QUEEN'S BENCH DIVISION
CLAIM HQ88888888
ISSUE DATE 1ST APRIL 2007

CLAIMANT

IVAN INVESTOR

DEFENDANT

XAVIER MINUS - trading as - Minus & Co, One Abacus Street, London

BRIEF DETAILS OF THE CLAIM

The Claimant claims damages for negligence and / or breach of duty and / or negligent misstatement arising out of advice given and work carried out by the Defendant as auditors in respect of the Defendant's auditors report dated 1st February 2007 over the accounts of Nextbestthing Ltd together with interest under section 35A Supreme Court Act 1981 to be assessed

VALUE
The Claimant claims damages exceeding £1000,000

Amount claimed	£[..................]
Court Fee	£[................]
Solicitor's costs	To be assessed
Total amount	£[..................]

DEFENDANT'S NAME AND ADDRRESS

XAVIER MINUS - trading as - Minus & Co,
One Abacus Street,
London

The Court Office at the Royal Courts of Justice, Strand, London EC2A 2LL is open between 10am and 4pm Monday to Friday. When corresponding with the court, please address forms and letters to the Court manager and quote the claim number.

Does or will your claim include any issues under the Human Rights Act 1998
Yes [ ] No [•]

CLAIM HQ888888

Particulars of claim [attached / ~~to follow~~]

STATEMENT OF TRUTH

The Claimant believes the facts stated in this Claim Form are true

* I am duly authorised by the Claimant to sign this statement

Signed:- ……………………………..

Name:- ……………………………..

Position:- ……………………………..

(if signing on behalf of a firm or company)

The Claimant's or claimant's solicitor's address to which documents or payments should be sent if different from overleaf including if appropriate details of DX, Fax or email

ADDENDUM & CO Solicitors
Wig Road
London

DX 666 LONDON CITY
Tel [....................]
Fax [...................]

Solicitors for the Claimant

Precedent 13

PARTICULARS OF CLAIM
PROFESSIONAL NEGLIGENCE CLAIM

(CLAIM BY INVESTOR OVER NEGLIGENT AUDIT)

IN THE HIGH COURT OF JUSTICE
QUEEN'S BENCH DIVISION

CLAIM HQ88888888

B E T W E E N:-

IVAN INVESTOR

Claimant

-and-

XAVIER MINUS
- trading as –
Minus & Co

Defendant

Particulars of Claim
----

1. The Claimant is and was, at all material times, a private investor.

2. At all material times the Defendant is and was a firm of accountants practising from 1, Abacus Street, London, and were the auditors of Nextbestthing Ltd.

3. At all material times until 1st April 2007, of the 1000 issued of Nextbestthing Ltd 999 were owned by Stevie Sly and 1 share was owned by Suzie Sly.

4. The accounts of Nextbestthing Ltd for the year ending 1st January 2007 ["the accounts"] represented that the Nextbestthing Ltd's net

Particulars of Claims: Professional Negligence Claim - Audit

assets, after deduction of £1,000 by way of provision for liabilities and charges, amounted to £1,000,0000 at 1st January 2007.

5. In his auditors report dated 1st February 2007, the Defendant reported that in their opinion the said Accounts gave a true and fair view of the state of Nextbestthing Ltd as at 1st January 2007.

6. In fact, the said Accounts did not give a true and fair view of the state of Nextbestthing Ltd as at 1st January 2007 in that on 30th November 2006 proceedings had been issued against Nextbestthing Ltd in Queen's Bench Division of the High Court of Justice by Angry plc claiming damages in the sum £1 billion plus interest: ["the claim"].

7. In an opinion dated 21st December 2006, Nextbestthing plc and its then directors were advised by the counsel that the prospects of successfully defending the said claim were "poor".

8. On 15th January 2007 Angry plc issued an application for summary judgement on the said claim on the basis that the Defendant had no reasonable prospects of successfully defending the claim.

9. Negligently and in breach of duty, the Defendant, his servants or agents, failed to exercise the level of skill and care that might be expected of a competent accountant and auditor

PARTICULARS OF NEGLIGENCE

The Defendant, his servants or agents were negligent in that he:

   a. Failed to consider and / or enquire of Nextbestthing Ltd's management whether Nextbestthing Ltd's provision for liabilities and charges was or was likely to be adequate
   b. Failed to investigate whether Nextbestthing Ltd's provision for liabilities and charges was or was likely to be adequate
   c. Failed to consider and / or enquire of Nextbestthing Ltd's management whether there were or might be material post-balance sheet events such as the said Claim and the matters pleaded hereinbefore
   d. Failed to investigate whether there were or might be material post-balance sheet events such as the said Claim and the matters pleaded hereinbefore
   e. In the premises, failed in the performance of the said contract to exercise such care and skill and expertise,

alternatively, such reasonable care and skill and expertise as would be expected of a accountant and auditor

10. On 2nd February 2007 the Claimant entered negotiation with Stevie and Susie Sly for the purchase of all 1000 shares in the Nextbestthing Ltd.
11. At a meeting on 5th February 2007 at the offices of Nextbestthing Ltd, the Claimant asked the Defendant "*Do you think the accounts of Nextbestthing are right and give accurate picture of the company's position?*" and the Defendant replied "*Of course, I audited them didn't I*" ["the representation"]
12. In making the said Representation in answer to the Defendant's question at the meeting on 5th February 2007, the Defendant intended that the Claimant should rely on the answer given and knew and / or ought to have known that the Claimant would rely on the answers given for the purpose of determining whether or not to purchase the shares of Nextbestthing Ltd and whether to rely on the said accounts.

PARTICULARS OF KNOWLEDGE

a. The meeting was called as part of the negotiations for the sale of the shares of NextbestthingLtd
b. The Defendant's presence had been requested to answer questions on the accounts in connection with the sale.
c. The Claimant's question intimated his intention to rely on the Defendant's audit of the said Accounts

13. In making the said Representation in answer to the Claimant's question at the meeting on 5th February 2007, the Defendant assumed a responsibility to the Claimant for their answers and by reason of their proximity to the Claimant, owed the Claimant a duty of care at common law.
14. By reason of the matters pleaded at paragraphs 6 to 8 of the Particulars of Claim, the answer given at the meeting on 5th February 2007 was false.
15. The Defendant made the said Representation negligently and in breach of duty and failed to exercise the level of skill and care that might be expected of a competent accountant and auditor

PARTICULARS OF NEGLIGENCE

The Defendant, his servants or agents made the representation negligently in that he:

- a. Failed to consider and / or enquire of Nextbestthing Ltd's management whether Nextbestthing Ltd's provision for liabilities and charges was or was likely to be adequate
- b. Failed to investigate whether Nextbestthing Ltd's provision for liabilities and charges was or was likely to be adequate
- c. Failed to consider and / or enquire of Nextbestthing Ltd's management whether there were or might be material post-balance sheet events such as the said Claim and the matters pleaded hereinbefore
- d. Failed to investigate whether there were or might be material post-balance sheet events such as the said Claim and the matters pleaded hereinbefore
- e. In the premises, failed in the performance of the said contract to exercise such care and skill and expertise, alternatively, such reasonable care and skill and expertise as would be expected of a accountant and auditor

16. In reliance upon the said Representation and upon the Defendant's skill and care as accountant and auditor, on 6th February 2007 the Claimant entered into an agreement to purchase all 1000 issued shares of Nextbestthing Limited for £1,000,000 and paid £1,000,000 to Stevie and Susie Sly for the shares.
17. Judgement was entered against Nextbestthing Limited on 7th February 2007 for £1 billion plus interest and costs by Angry plc.
18. Since 31st March 2007, Nextbestthing Limited has been in creditors' voluntary liquidation.
19. In the premises and by reason of the matters aforesaid, the Claimant suffered loss and damage.

PARTICULARS

But for the Defendant's negligence and had the said Representation not been made by the Defendant, the Claimant would have discovered the true position and would not have purchased the shares of Nextbestthing Limited. The Claimant claims the difference between the price he paid for the shares of Nextbestthing Limited (£1,000,000) and their actual value. The shares of Nextbestthing Limited are worthless and the Claimant's loss is therefore £1,000,000.

20. Further the Claimants, and each of them, are entitled to and claim interest pursuant to section 35A, Supreme Court Act 1981 on the

amount found due to the Claimants at such a rate and for such a period as the Court thinks fit.

AND THE CLAIMANT CLAIMS:-

(1) Damages;
(2) The aforesaid interest pursuant to section 35A, Supreme Court Act 1981 to be assessed.
(3) Costs
(4) Further and other relief

A BARRISTER

Statement of Truth

The Claimant believes that the facts stated in this Particulars of Claim are true.

Signed:..

THE CLAIMANT'S ADDRESS FOR SERVICE IS: -

ADDENDUM & CO Solicitors
Wig Road
London

DX 666 LONDON CITY
Tel [...................]
Fax [...................]

Solicitors for the Claimant

Precedent 14

DEFENCE
PROFESSIONAL NEGLIGENCE CLAIM
(CLAIM BY INVESTOR OVER NEGLIGENT AUDIT)

IN THE HIGH COURT OF JUSTICE
QUEEN'S BENCH DIVISION

CLAIM HQ88888888

B E T W E E N:-

IVAN INVESTOR

Claimant

-and-

XAVIER MINUS
- trading as –
Minus & Co

Defendant

Defence
----

1. Paragraphs 1 to 5 of the Particulars of Claim are admitted.

2. Paragraphs 6 to 8 of the Particulars of Claim are not admitted.

3. It is denied that the Defendant was negligent whether as alleged at paragraph 9 of the Particulars of Claim or at all. The Defendant was assured by the directors of Nexbestthing Ltd that any claims made against Nextbestthing Ltd were spurious and that there was no material risk to Nexbestthing Ltd under the claim.

4. Save that the said Representation was made informally, paragraphs 10 and 11 of the Particulars of Claim are admitted.

5. Paragraph 13 is denied. The Defendant attended the offices on the request of the directors of Nextbestthing Limited and was at that stage unaware of the negotiations for the sale of the shares of Nextbestthing Limited.

6. Paragraph 14 of the Particulars of Claim is denied. It is denied that the Defendant intended the Claimant to rely upon the answer given by him or knew and / or ought to have known that the Claimant would rely on the answers given for the purpose of determining whether or not to purchase the shares of Nextbestthing Ltd and whether to rely on the said accounts. The Claimant is an experienced investor who had recourse to his own team of lawyers and accountants when undertaking due diligence over the purchase of the shares of Nextbestthing Ltd.

7. In the premises, it is denied that the Defendant owed the Claimant any duty of care whether as alleged in paragraph 15 of the Particulars of Claim or at all.

8. Save that no admissions are made to paragraphs 6 to 8 of the Particulars of Claim, paragraph 16 is denied.

9. It is denied that the Defendant was negligent or in breach of duty whether as alleged at paragraph 17 of the Particulars of Claim or at all.

10. Save that it is admitted that on 6th February 2007 the Claimant entered into an agreement to purchase all 1000 issued shares of Nextbestthing Limited for £1,000,000 and paid £1,000,000 to Stevie and Susie Sly for the shares, paragraph 18 is not admitted.

11. Paragraphs 19 and 20 of the Particulars of Claim are admitted.

12. As to paragraph 21, no admissions are made as to the loss and damage alleged by the Claimant save that it is denied that the loss and damage was caused by any fault on the part of the Defendant.

13. In the premises, it is denied that the Claimant is entitled to the relief claimed or any relief.

A COUNSEL

Statement of Truth

The Defendant believes that the facts stated in this Defence are true.

Signed:..

THE DEFENDANT'S ADDRESS FOR SERVICE IS: -

Brief & Co
Gown Street
London

Solicitors for the Defendant

Precedent 15

APPLICATION NOTICE

(INJUNCTION TO RELEASE ACCOUNTANCY PAPERS)

APPLICATION NOTICE
FORM N244

IN THE	HIGH COURT OF JUSTICE QUEEN'S BENCH DIVISION
CLAIM NO	HQ999999
WARRANT NO	
CLAIMANT	DINGLE BELL LIMITED Reference [................]
DEFENDANT	XAVIER MINUS - trading as - Minus & Co Reference [................]
DATE	1st April 2007

You should provide this information for listing the application
1. How do you wish to have your application dealt with?
(a) at a hearing? ☐) *Complete all questions below*
(b) at a telephone conference☐)
(c) without a hearing ☐ *Complete questions 5 and 6 below*
2. Give a time estimate for the hearing ..... hours .... minutes
3. Is this agreed by all parties? Yes ☐No☐
4. Give dates of any trial period or fixed trial date ....
5. Level of Judge ....
6. Parties served ....

Note. You must complete Parts A and B and Part C if applicable. Send any relevant fee and completed application to the court with any draft order, witness statement or other evidence and sufficient copies for service on each respondent

PART A

We Addendum & Co on behalf of the Claimant intend to apply for an order (a draft of which is attached) that the Defendant deliver up the Claimant's accounting and company papers.

Because

They are needed to defend the case of R v Dingle Bell, prosecution brought against a director of the Claimant by the Department of Trade and Industry to be heard for trial at Snaresbrook Crown Court, indictment number 1234.

CLAIM HQ999999

PART B

We wish to rely on
The attached witness statement ☐
Evidence in Part C in support of my application ☐
My statement of case ☐

Signed:
Position held (if signing on behalf of a firm or company):

The address to which documents which documents about this claim should sent (including reference if appropriate)

ADDENDUM & CO Solicitors
Wig Road
London

DX 666 LONDON CITY
Tel [..................]
Fax [..................]
Reference [...............]

Solicitors for the Claimant

The Court Office at the Royal Courts of Justice, Strand, London EC2A 2LL is open between 10am and 4pm Monday to Friday. When corresponding with the court, please address forms and letters to the Court manager and quote the claim number.

CLAIM HQ999999

PART C

We wish to rely on the following evidence in support of the application.

The witness statement of Mr Dingle Bell dated 1st April 2007

STATEMENT OF TRUTH

The Claimant believes the facts stated in Part C are true

* I am duly authorised by the Claimant to sign this statement

Signed:- ……………………………..

Name:- …………………………..

Position:- …………………………..

(if signing on behalf of a firm or company)

Date: ………………………………..

Precedent 16

CLAIM FORM

(CLAIM FOR ACCOUNTANT'S PAPERS)

[Royal Arms]
CLAIM FORM
N1 Claim Form (CPR Part 7)

IN THE HIGH COURT OF JUSTICE
QUEEN'S BENCH DIVISION
CLAIM HQ88888888
ISSUE DATE 1ST APRIL 2007

CLAIMANT

DINGLE BELL LIMITED, Two Christmas Court, London

DEFENDANT

XAVIER MINUS - trading as - Minus & Co, One Abacus Street, London

BRIEF DETAILS OF THE CLAIM

The Claimant's claim is for the delivery up of the Claimant's accounts and papers and / or the value of the said papers, and / or damages for the detention of the said papers together with interest on the same under section 35A Supreme Court Act 1981 to be assessed.

VALUE
The Claimant claims damages exceeding £50,000 but not exceeding £100,000

Amount claimed	£[...................]
Court Fee	£[.................]
Solicitor's costs	To be assessed
Total amount	£[....................]

DEFENDANT'S NAME AND ADDRRESS

XAVIER MINUS - trading as - Minus & Co,
One Abacus Street,
London

The Court Office at the Royal Courts of Justice, Strand, London EC2A 2LL is open between 10am and 4pm Monday to Friday. When corresponding with the court, please address forms and letters to the Court manager and quote the claim number.

Does or will your claim include any issues under the Human Rights Act 1998
Yes [ ] No [•]

CLAIM HQ888888

Particulars of claim [attached / ~~to follow~~]

STATEMENT OF CLAIM

1. The Claimant claims delivery up of all accounts, company documents and working papers of the Claimant prepared by the Defendant in his capacity as tax accountant and agent of the Claimant between 2004 and 2006 ["the papers"] and / or the value of the said papers, and / or damages for the detention of the said papers
2. Further the Claimant claims interest on the value of the said papers, and / or such damages under section 35A Supreme Court Act 1981 to be assessed

STATEMENT OF TRUTH

The Claimant believes the facts stated in this Claim Form are true

* I am duly authorised by the Claimant to sign this statement

Signed:- ………………………………..

Name:- ……………………………….

Position:- ……………………………….

(if signing on behalf of a firm or company)

The Claimant's or claimant's solicitor's address to which documents or payments should be sent if different from overleaf including if appropriate details of DX, Fax or email

ADDENDUM & CO Solicitors
Wig Road
London

DX 666 LONDON CITY
Tel [………………]
Fax [………………]
Solicitors for the Claimant

Precedent 17

WITNESS STATEMENT
[IN SUPPORT OF AN APPLICATION TO COMPEL THE DELIVERY UP OF AN ACCOUNTANT'S PAPERS]

Applicant: D Bell: 1st: DB1: 1 April 2007

IN THE HIGH COURT OF JUSTICE
QUEEN'S BENCH DIVISION

CASE NO HQ99999

BETWEEN

DINGLE BELL LIMITED

<u>Applicant</u>

- and –

XAVIER MINUS - trading as - Minus & Co

<u>Respondent</u>

1st WITNESS STATEMENT OF DINGLE BELL

I, DINGLE BELL, of 2 Christmas Court, London, Company Director, STATE as follows:-

1. I make this witness statement in support of the Claimant's application for an injunction against the Respondent to deliver up the Applicant's accountancy, tax and company papers so as to enable me to defend a prosecution brought against me.
2. I am a director of the Applicant in this action and I am authorised to make this affidavit on behalf of the Applicant.

3. I make this affidavit from the facts and matters within my own direct knowledge unless indicated otherwise, in which case I do so to the best of my knowledge, information and belief, stating my source.
4. There is now shown to me marked "**DB1**" a bundle consisting of the true copies of documents I will refer to in this witness statement.
5. Until 28 February 2007 both the Applicant and I personally engaged the Respondent as our accountants.
6. The terms of the Respondent's engagement by the Applicant were set out in a letter dated 19 February 2005 which terms. I refer to **pages 1 - 2** of the bundle marked "**DB1**" which is a true copy of this document.
7. The terms of the Respondent's engagement by me were set out in a letter dated 3rd May 2002. I refer to **pages 3 -4** of the bundle marked "**DB1**" which is a true copy of this document. It is clear from this that I and the Applicant were quite separate clients of the Respondent and charged on a different basis.
8. I fell out with the Respondent and there is now litigation between me and the Respondent in which the Respondent is suing me for fees which I refuse to pay. I refer to **pages 5-40** of the bundle marked "**DB1**" which is a true copy of the documents which set out the background of this litigation
9. By contrast, the Applicant has paid all the fees demanded by the Applicant. I refer to **pages 41-50** of the bundle marked "**DB1**" which is a true copy of the receipted fee notes
10. On 1st January 2007, a prosecution was brought against me under sections 221(5) and (6), Companies Act 1985 and 222 (6), Companies Act 1986 (failure to keep and retain company accounting records) relating to the affairs of the Applicant. The case is due to be tried at Snaresbrook Crown Court on 1st May 2007. I refer to **pages 51-60** of the bundle marked "**DB1**" which is a true copy of the papers relating to the prosecution.
11. I have a defence to the action. Proper books and records were indeed maintained for the Applicant.
12. Unfortunately all the statutory, company and accountancy records of the Applicant are presently held by the Respondent.
13. I understand from the Applicant's solicitors and believe that on 30th March 2007 the Applicant's solicitors wrote to Mr Minus of Minus & Co and asked for the records to enable me to defend myself at trial. I refer to **pages 61** of the bundle marked "**DB1**" which is a true copy of the facsimile sent.
14. Mr Minus telephoned me on the same day and said "I got your solicitor's letter. If you want your company's stuff, you'll have to pay me the money you owe me for your personal tax accounts. I've

got a lien". I refer to **pages 62** of the bundle marked **"DB1"** which is a true copy of my note of the conversation.
15. I understand that the Respondent asserts a lien because he says that I personally owe him money. This is however an application for the Applicant's papers however and the Applicant is up to date with its fees.
16. In any event the Respondent's conduct is depriving me of the evidence I need to clear my name. The trial is imminent and the Applicant's papers are now needed as a matter of the utmost urgency.
17. I believe that unless compelled by an order of the court the Respondent will continue to withhold the evidence I need to defend my case.
18. I have read the draft order for the injunction. I understand and am prepared to give on behalf of the Applicant the undertakings set out in the schedule to the draft order. I confirm that the Applicant has £1,000,000 in a Post Office savings account from it could meet any payment the Applicant may be obliged to make under the undertaking which they propose to make to the court. I refer to **pages 63** of the bundle marked **"DB1"** which is a true copy of the latest entries in the Applicant's Post Office savings account book showing a balance in excess of £1,000,000.
19. In all the circumstances I ask that this Honourable Court grant the Applicant an injunction in the terms of the draft minutes of order.

STATEMENT OF TRUTH
I believe that the facts stated in this witness statement are true.

Signed : -_____

Full Name of Witness: DINGLE BELL

Precedent 18

DRAFT MINUTES OF ORDER

[TO COMPEL THE DELIVERY UP OF AN ACCOUNTANT'S PAPERS]

INJUNCTION

IN THE HIGH COURT OF JUSTICE
QUEEN'S BENCH DIVISION
CASE NO HQ99999

BEFORE THE HONOURABLE MR JUSTICE……………….
DATED:-

Applicant
DINGLE BELL LIMITED

Respondent
XAVIER MINUS - trading as - Minus & Co

Name, address and reference of the Respondent:-

XAVIER MINUS - trading as - Minus & Co, One Abacus Street, London, Reference [………………..]

PENAL NOTICE

IF YOU XAVIER MINUS, DISOBEY THIS ORDER YOU MAY BE HELD IN CONTEMPT OF COURT AND MAY BE IMPRISONED, FINED OR HAVE YOUR ASSETS SEIZED

ANY PERSON WHO KNOWS OF THIS ORDER AND DOES ANYTHING WHICH HELPS OR PERMITS THE RESPONDENT TO BREACH THE TERMS OF THIS ORDER MAY ALSO BE HELD IN CONTEMPT OF COURT AND MAY BE IMPRISONED, FINED OR HAVE THEIR ASSETS SEIZED

ORDER

UPON HEARING Counsel for the Applicant without notice on
....
UPON READING the Witness Statement of Dingle Bell dated 1st April 2007 AND UPON the Judge accepting the Undertakings in the Schedule at the end of this Order.

IT IS ORDERED

1. That the Respondent deliver to the Applicant's solicitors, Addendum & Co, all the accounts, documents and papers in the Respondent's custody and power prepared for or belonging to Dingle Bell Limited as may in the opinion of the Applicant's solicitors be necessary for defending the case of R v Dingle Bell [save for such purpose such accounts and working papers to be retained subject to any lien by the Respondent for their fees]
2. The Respondent may apply on giving 24 hours notice in writing to the Applicant's legal representatives vary or discharge this order
3. Costs reserved.

Communications with the Court

All communications to the court about this order should be sent to—

Room WG08, Royal Courts of Justice, Strand, London WC2A 2LL quoting the case number. The telephone number is 0207 947 6010.

The offices are open between 10 a.m. and 4.30 p.m. Monday to Friday.

SCHEDULE 1
Undertakings given to the Court by the Applicant

1 If the Court later finds that this Order has caused loss to the Respondent and decides that the Respondent should be compensated for that loss, the Applicant will comply with any Order the Court may make; and,

[2 As soon as practicable the Applicant will issue and serve on the Respondent a Claim Form in the form of the draft Claim Form produced to the Court and initialled by the Judge claiming appropriate relief together with this Order; and,]

3 The Applicant will cause an Witness Statement to be filed confirming the substance of what was said to the Court by the Applicant's Counsel; and

4 As soon as practicable the Applicant will serve on the Respondent an application for a return date together with a copy of the Witness Statements and exhibits containing the evidence relied on by the Applicant.

5 Anyone notified of this Order will be given a copy of it by the Applicant's legal representatives.

Precedent 19

CLAIM FORM

[DISSOLUTION OF AN ACCOUNTANCY PARTNERSHIP]

[Royal Arms]
CLAIM FORM
N1 Claim Form (CPR Part 7)

IN THE HIGH COURT OF JUSTICE
CHANCERY DIVISION
CLAIM HC12345
ISSUE DATE 1ST APRIL 2008

IN THE MATTER OF THE PARTNERSHIP ACT 1890
IN THE MATTER OF A PARTNERSHIP TRADING AS "MINUS & CO"

CLAIMANT

ADOLPH ADDER, 2 The Serpentine, London

DEFENDANT

XAVIER MINUS, One Abacus Street, London

BRIEF DETAILS OF THE CLAIM

A declaration that a partnership entered into by an agreement in writing dated 1st April 2000 the Claimant on the one part and the Defendant on the other part under the style or firm name of "Minus & Co" was dissolved as from 14th March 2007 or and order that the partnership be dissolved. Further (1) An order that the affairs of the Partnership be wound up (2) an account of the benefits received by the Defendant under sections 29(1) and 29(2) of the Partnership Act 1890 (3) An order that all necessary accounts and inquiries be taken and made and an order for the payment of all sums found due thereon; (4) An order that the Defendant pay further interest on the amount of such a share at a rate of 5% per annum pursuant to section 42(1) Partnership Act 1890 (5) Interest pursuant to section 35A of the Supreme Court Act 1981 or to the equitable jurisdiction of this Court (6) Such further or other relief as may seem fit (7) Costs

VALUE
Over £15,000

Amount claimed	£[..................]
Court Fee	£900
Solicitor's costs	To be assessed
Total amount	£[..................]

DEFENDANT'S NAME AND ADDRESS

ADOLPH ADDER,
2 The Serpentine,
London

The Court Office at the Royal Courts of Justice, Strand, London WC2A 2LL is open between 10am and 4pm Monday to Friday. When corresponding with the court, please address forms and letters to the Court manager and quote the claim number.

Does or will your claim include any issues under the Human Rights Act 1998
Yes [ ] No [•]

CLAIM HC12345

Particulars of claim [attached / ~~to follow~~]

STATEMENT OF TRUTH

The Claimant believes the facts stated in this Claim Form are true

* I am duly authorised by the Claimant to sign this statement

Signed:- ……………………………..

Name:- ……………………………..

Position:- ……………………………..

(if signing on behalf of a firm or company)

The Claimant's or claimant's solicitor's address to which documents or payments should be sent if different from overleaf including if appropriate details of DX, Fax or email

Lawful & Co
Grumble Street
London

Solicitors for the Claimant

Precedent 20

PARTICULARS OF CLAIM

[DISSOLUTION OF AN ACCOUNTANCY PARTNERSHIP]

IN THE HIGH COURT OF JUSTICE
CHANCERY DIVISION

Claim No. HC 12345

IN THE MATTER OF THE PARTNERSHIP ACT 1890
IN THE MATTER OF A PARTNERSHIP TRADING AS "MINUS & CO"

B E T W E E N:

ADOLPH ADDER

Claimant

-and-

XAVIER MINUS

Defendant

PARTICULARS OF CLAIM

---

1. By an agreement in writing dated 1st April 2000 the Claimant and the Defendant and each of them ["the Partners"] agreed to carry on a partnership business as accountants under the style or firm name of "Minus & Co" ["the Partnership"]: ["the Partnership Agreement"].

The said Partnership Agreement is annexed hereto in the schedule herewith and incorporated herein by reference and the same is relied on for its full terms, true meaning and effect.

2. The Partnership carried on the Partnership business from premises at One Abacus Street, London

3. Clause 2 of the Partnership Agreement provided that:-
   a. Under sub-clause 2.1, that the initial capital of the said Partnership was £2,324.06 which belonged to the Partners equally;
   b. Under sub-clause 2.2, that the profits and losses of the Partnership would be borne by the Partners equally.

4. Clause 4 of the Partnership Agreement provided:
   a. Under clause 4.1, any Partner may terminate the Partnership at any time by giving to the others 2 weeks' notice in writing;

5. Pursuant to the said terms of the said Partnership, each of the Partners duly contributed their stated proportion of the capital to the said Partnership and carried on the Partnership business.
6. Pursuant to clause 4.1 of the Partnership Deed, by letter dated 28th February 2007 the Claimant served notice in writing of his intention to dissolve the Partnership.

7. The said letter is annexed hereto in the schedule herewith and incorporated herein by reference and the same is relied on for its full terms, true meaning and effect.

8. Since 28th February 2007 the Defendant has continued to use the name, assets and business formerly carried on by the Partnership.

AND the Claimant claims against the Defendant: -

1. A declaration that the Partnership between the Claimant and the Defendant was dissolved on 14th March 2007 or such other date
2. An order that the affairs of the Partnership be wound up
3. An order that all necessary accounts and inquiries be taken and made and an order for payment of the sums found due thereon
4. Further or alternatively, an account of the benefits received by the Defendant under sections 29(1) and 29(2) of the Partnership Act 1890
5. All necessary accounts and inquiries be taken and made of what is

due to the Claimant from the Defendant of profits made from the use of the Partnership's assets upon dissolution, alternatively, an order that the Defendant pay further interest on the amount of such a share at a rate of 5% per annum pursuant to section 42(1) Partnership Act 1890;
6. Interest pursuant to section 35A of the Supreme Court Act 1981 or to the equitable jurisdiction of this Court to be assessed;
7. Such further or other relief as may seem fit;
8. Costs

ARTHUR WIGGY

Dated ... November 2008

Statement of Truth

The Claimant believes that the facts stated in the Particulars of Claim are true.

Signed: ....
The Claimant

THE CLAIMANT'S ADDRESS FOR SERVICE IS: -

Lawful & Co
Grumble Street
London
Solicitors for the Claimant

SCHEDULE
1. Partnership Agreement dated 1st April 2000
2. Letter dated 28th February 2007 by which the Claimant served notice in writing of his intention to dissolve the Partnership

Precedent 21

MODEL GROUNDS OF APPEAL AGAINST A FINDING OF A DISCIPLINARY TRIBUNAL[1]

[APPEAL AGAINST PENALTY ONLY]

Appeal Committee Officer
The Association of Chartered Certified Accountants
29 Lincoln's Inn Fields
London WC2 3EE

1) Full Name of Appellant	*CLAUDE CARELESS*
Registration Number	*666*
2) Registered address	*12, Muddle Lane, London*
3) Representation	
Name	*Willie Wiggy*
Firm	*Addendum & Co*
Address	*1, Wig Street, London*
Telephone	*0207 123 1234*

4) Please confirm whether you intend to appear at the appeal hearing if permission is granted: Yes /~~No~~

5. The decision of the Disciplinary Committee is made up of two parts: the findings (as to what allegations are proved or not) and the orders (the sanctions imposed and any orders for costs and publicity).

i) Please confirm by ticking the box whether it is your intention to appeal against one or more of the findings of the disciplinary committee
☐

---

[1] There is no required form for the grounds of appeal however this precedent fulfils the requirements of regulation 5(1) of the Chartered Certified Accountants Appeal Regulations 2006.

If you have ticked this box, please state below which of the findings you are appealing.

ii) Please confirm by ticking the box whether it is your intention to appeal against one or more of the <u>orders</u> of the disciplinary committee
☑

If you have ticked this box, please state below which of the orders you are appealing.

The order expelling Claude Careless from membership and the order for publicity

6. Grounds of Appeal

Please confirm by ticking the relevant box which of the grounds set out below your appeal is based upon. You may tick more than one.

For each ground ticked, please state in the space provided the reasons you rely on in support of each ground. Please note that the grounds stated by you here may not be later amended without leave of the Appeal Committee

(a) The committee made an error of fact or law which would have made a material difference to the outcome of the case
☑

Reasons

The Disciplinary Committee's order is disproportionate and / or unreasonable in the light of its findings. The reasons in support are that the that the Disciplinary Committee's order to exclude the Appellant from membership was disproportionate in that:-

1. it failed to take any or adequate consideration of the previous decisions of the Disciplinary Committee in reaching

> its determination: see in particular *ACCA v Lucian Lucky (7.7.07)*
>
> 2. The Disciplinary Committee, whilst finding the matters alleged against the Appellant proved, had also found that the Appellant was contrite, had not profited from his conduct and was unlikely to ever repeat his conduct again.
>
> 3. The further mitigating factors set out in these grounds of appeal

(b) The committee misinterpreted any of the Association's byelaws or regulations or any relevant guidance or technical standards, which would have made a material difference to the outcome of the case
☐

Reasons

(c) The committee failed to take into account certain relevant evidence which would have made a material difference to the outcome of the case
☑

Reasons

> *The reasons in support are that that the Disciplinary Committee failed to take any or adequate consideration of the mitigating factors in the Appellant's case, namely*
>
> 1. that the conduct for which the Appellant was disciplined was wholly out of character and
> 2. The conduct occurred at a time when he was under great personal stress due to the ill health of his wife.

(d)   there is new evidence not previously available which would have made a material difference to the outcome of the case
☐

Reasons

7) Documents in Support

If you wish to provide further documentation or submissions in support of your application, please attach them below to this application notice and list them below:-

The following documents, evidencing the matters relied on under the grounds of appeal, are annexed hereto:

(1) medical report from Dr Laudanum on his wife's illness
(2) Letter from the Appellant's long term partner, Ernest Equal as to his prior good character.
(3) A note of the decision of the Disciplinary Committee in the present case
(4) A note of the decision of the Disciplinary Committee in the case of ACCA v Lucian Lucky (7.7.07) are annexed hereto.

Signed *Claude Clueless*

Dated *3rd August 2007*

PLEASE CHECK THAT YOU HAVE SIGNED AND DATED THIS FORM AND COMPLETED IT CORRECTLY AND IN FULL BEFORE SENDING IT TO THE APPEAL COMMITTEE OFFICER AT THE ADDRESS ON PAGE ONE. FAILURE TO COMPLETE THE FORM CORRECTLY MAY RESULT IN YOUR APPLICATION BEING REFUSED BY THE APPEAL COMMITTEE.

IF YOU HAVE ANY QUERIES ABOUT HOW TO COMPLETE THIS FORM, PLEASE CONTACT THE APPEAL COMMITTEE OFFICER ON THE FOLLOWING NUMBERS: TEL + 44 (0) 207059 5893 FAX + 44 (0) 207059 5957

Precedent 22

BOARD RESOLUTION APPOINTING FIRST AUDITORS

The Chairman proposed a resolution that Minus & Co be appointed as the Company's first auditors.

IT WAS RESOLVED THAT Minus & Co be appointed as auditors of this Company to hold office until the first General Meeting at which Accounts are laid before the shareholders.

Precedent 23

ORDINARY RESOLUTION FOR THE APPOINTMENT OF FIRST AUDITORS

NOTICE IS HEREBY GIVEN THAT THE ………………… GENERAL MEETING OF XYZ PLC WILL BE HELD AT The Jolly Roger Public House, London
ON 1st October 2007 AT 10am to consider and if deemed fit to approve the following resolutions:

ORDINARY RESOLUTION

That Minus & Co be and are hereby appointed auditors of the Company to hold office until the conclusion of the first General Meeting at which the Accounts are laid before the Company

Dated this 10th day of September 2007

BY ORDER OF THE BOARD

AND XYZ PLC at (Registered Office)

Signed……………………….
Company Secretary

Precedent 24

NOTICE OF AN
ANNUAL GENERAL MEETING

NOTICE IS HEREBY GIVEN THAT THE ANNUAL GENERAL MEETING OF XYZ PLC WILL BE HELD AT The Jolly Roger Public House, London
ON 1st October 2007 AT 10am to consider and if deemed fit to approve the following resolutions:

ORDINARY RESOLUTION

1. To receive and adopt the Directors' Report and the audited Statement of Accounts for the year period ended [say] 2006

2. To re-appoint the retiring auditors and authorise the Directors to fix their remuneration.

Dated this 10th day of September 2007

BY ORDER OF THE BOARD

AND XYZ PLC at (Registered Office)

Signed..............................
Company Secretary

Note:

A member entitled to attend and vote is entitled to appoint a proxy to attend and on a pool vote in his or her place. Such proxy need not be a member of the Company.

Precedent 25

RESOLUTION FOR RE-APPOINTMENT OF AUDITORS

NOTICE IS HEREBY GIVEN THAT THE .... GENERAL MEETING OF XYZ PLC WILL BE HELD AT The Jolly Roger Public House, London
ON 1st October 2007 AT 10am to consider and if deemed fit to approve the following resolutions:

ORDINARY RESOLUTION

That Minus & Co be and are hereby re-appointed as auditors of the Company to hold office until the conclusion of the next General Meeting at which Accounts are laid before the Company and that the Directors be and are hereby authorised to fix their remuneration.

Dated this 10th day of September 2007

BY ORDER OF THE BOARD

AND XYZ PLC at (Registered Office)

Signed............................

Company Secretary

Precedent 26

LETTER OF RESIGNATION AS AUDITORS

The Board of Directors XYZ plc
[Address of Company's Registered Office]

1st October 2007

Dear Sirs

Letter of resignation as Auditors
of XYZ plc
Registered in England and Wales Number 00000

We hereby give you notice that we are resigning as auditors of XYZ plc with effect from the date of this letter.

In accordance with Section 394(1) of the Companies Act 1985[1], we hereby state that there are no circumstances connected with our resignation which we take the view should be brought to the attention of members or creditors of XYZ plc.

Yours faithfully,

Minus & Co

---

[1] Section 519(2) Companies Act 2006.

Precedent 27

ORDINARY RESOLUTION ENDING APPOINTMENT AS AUDITORS

NOTICE IS HEREBY GIVEN THAT THE .... GENERAL MEETING OF XYZ LIMITED WILL BE HELD AT The Jolly Roger Public House, London
ON 1st October 2008 AT 10am to consider and if deemed fit to approve the following resolutions:

ORDINARY RESOLUTION

THAT Notice having been served on the company pursuant to Section 488, Companies Act 2006, the appointment of Minus & Co as auditors of this Company be brought to an end.

Dated this 10th day of September 2007

BY ORDER OF THE BOARD

AND XYZ LIMITED at (Registered Office)

Signed............................
Company Secretary

Precedent 28

NOTICE PREVENTING APPOINTMENT OF THE AUDITOR

Dear Sirs

I hereby give notice pursuant to SECTION 488 of the Companies Acts 2006 that I represent at least 5% of the total voting rights of the members who would be entitled to vote on the resolution that an auditor be reappointed and hereby prevent Minus & Co from being deemed to be reappointed. I also give you notice of and my intention to propose the following Ordinary Resolution at the next Annual General Meeting of the Company and that I require you to circulate this under section 292 Companies Act 2006.

Resolution that Messrs Minus & Co be and are hereby removed from office as auditors of the Company and that Y & Co be appointed as auditors in their place to hold office until the conclusion of the next General Meeting at which Accounts are laid before the Company at a remuneration to be fixed by the Directors.

Dated this .... day of 2008

Yours faithfully, etc..

Precedent 29

RESOLUTION FOR THE REMOVAL OF THE EXISTING AUDITORS

NOTICE IS HEREBY GIVEN THAT THE .... GENERAL MEETING OF XYZ LIMITED WILL BE HELD AT The Jolly Roger Public House, London
ON 1st October 2008 AT 10am to consider and if deemed fit to approve the following resolutions:

ORDINARY RESOLUTION

That Minus & Co be and are hereby removed as Auditors of the Company with immediate effect and that Y & Co be and are hereby appointed auditors of the Company in their stead to hold office until the conclusion of the next General Meeting at which Accounts are laid before the Company and that the Directors be and are hereby authorised to fix their remuneration.

Dated this 10th day of September 2008

BY ORDER OF THE BOARD

AND XYZ LIMITED at (Registered Office)

Signed............................
Company Secretary

Precedent 30

NON-APPOINTMENT OF AUDITORS - DORMANT COMPANY

NOTICE IS HEREBY GIVEN THAT THE .... GENERAL MEETING OF XYZ LIMITED WILL BE HELD AT The Jolly Roger Public House, London
ON 1st October 2009 AT 10am to consider and if deemed fit to approve the following resolutions:

ORDINARY RESOLUTION

That in accordance with the provisions of Section 480, Companies Act 2006, XYZ LIMITED being a dormant company within the meaning of the said section, Section 1169 of the Companies Act 2006, shall apply and accordingly no auditors shall be appointed.

Dated this 10th day of September 2009

BY ORDER OF THE BOARD

AND XYZ LIMITED at (Registered Office)

Signed............................
Company Secretary

Precedent 31

RESOLUTION DISPENSING WITH LAYING OF ACCOUNTS BEFORE A GENERAL MEETING

NOTICE IS HEREBY GIVEN THAT THE ……………. GENERAL MEETING OF XYZ LIMITED WILL BE HELD AT The Jolly Roger Public House, London
ON 1st October 2007 AT 10am to consider and if deemed fit to approve the following resolutions:

ORDINARY RESOLUTION

That in accordance with the provisions of Section 252[1] Companies Act 1985, the Company hereby dispenses with the laying of accounts and reports before the Company in General Meeting in respect of the year ending 2007 and subsequent financial years.

Dated this 10th day of September 2007

BY ORDER OF THE BOARD

AND XYZ LIMITED at (Registered Office)

Signed………………………..
Company Secretary

---

[1] Section 252 Companies Act 1985 is abolished from 1st October 2007. There is no power to waive laying accounts of a public limited company before a general meeting: section 437 Companies Act 2006. The regime of laying the accounts before the members in general meeting is replaced for private companies with one of circulating to all members.

Precedent 32

RESOLUTION APPROVING AUDITORS LIABILITY LIMITATION AGREEMENT

NOTICE IS HEREBY GIVEN THAT THE …………….. GENERAL MEETING OF XYZ PLC WILL BE HELD AT The Jolly Roger Public House, London
ON 1st October 2009 AT 10am to consider and if deemed fit to approve the following resolutions:

ORDINARY RESOLUTION

That in accordance with the provisions of Section 536 Companies Act 2006 the Directors have entered into the limitation liability agreement signed by them on behalf of the Company on the 1st August 2009 for the year 1st April 2010 to 30th March 2011 in the terms annexed hereto.

Dated this 10th day of September 2009

BY ORDER OF THE BOARD

AND XYZ PLC at (Registered Office)

Signed………………………..
Company Secretary

An Accountant's Casebook

The Accountancy Institute

The Association of Certified Public Accountants v. Secretary of State for Trade and Industry [1998] 1 WLR 164 Jacobs J	Use of "certified" in a company's name suggested that there was something objectively significant about the members' qualification, training and expertise. Adequate harm to the public for a direction to change the association's name under Section 35, Companies Act 1985 was shown by the fact that the public would expect more than they were likely to get.
Bankole v. ACCA (1995) LTL 17 November Court of Appeal	The contract between an accountancy body and its student members related solely to internal governance and administration. Where the body was incorporated under Royal Charter that was a matter over which the visitor had exclusive jurisdiction and the court could have no jurisdiction over the dispute.
R v. Callender [1992] 3 WLR 501 Court of Appeal	The provision of accounting services on a self-employed basis whilst falsely claiming to be an associate member of the Chartered Institute of Management Accountants could amount to obtaining a pecuniary advantage by deception by obtaining the opportunity to earn remuneration in an "office or employment" within the meaning of Section 16(2)(c) Theft Act 1968.
Andreou v. ICAEW [1998] 1 All ER 14 Court of Appeal	The mere fact that an association is a public body did not prevent private rights from arising. No term would be implied by the courts that an association would exercise its powers to make byelaws fairly or reasonably.

Discipline and regulation

Marcus v Institute of Chartered Accountants (2004) EWHC 3010 (ChD)	Unlike fines imposed in criminal proceedings, a fine imposed by a disciplinary hearing falls outside rule 12.3 Insolvency Rules 1986 is provable in bankruptcy and can found a statutory demand.
Gorlov v Institute of Chartered Accountants in England and Wales (2002) Lawtel 19th November Stanley Burnton QC	Where a disciplinary tribunal was required to hear charges referred by the investigation committee of the Institute of Chartered Accountants in England and Wales, the jurisdiction of the disciplinary tribunal was not necessarily restricted to identical charges but could also hear charges substantially identical to those referred by the investigation committee.
R (on the application of Thompson) v. The Law Society [2004] 2 All ER 113 Court of Appeal	Whether a disciplinary panel was under a duty to afford an oral hearing (as opposed to one on the papers) to comply with the *audi alterem partem* rule or Article 6(1) ECHR depended on the circumstances of the particular case. The applicant could not complain after the event if he had not asked for an oral hearing at the time. Disciplinary proceedings could give rise to a breach of Art.6 (1) if what was at stake was the right to continue to exercise a profession. A decision to reprimand, make a reference to a disciplinary tribunal did not amount to a determination of civil rights however it might do in respect to an order to pay costs

R v. Institute of Chartered Accountants ex parte Brindle (1994) The Times, 12th January Court of Appeal	Where the continuation of proceedings risks delaying, impeding or prejudicing the accountant in the conduct of his defence of civil or criminal proceedings to an extent that could not be justified in the public interest, the court will order a stay of any disciplinary proceedings against the accountant. The Court of Appeal ruled that a stay should be granted where the disciplinary inquiry would not be completed promptly, might have a distracting effect from the civil proceedings and where there were advantages for the disciplinary committee having the benefit of the findings of fact made by the court.
Bankole v. ACCA (1995) LTL 17 November Court of Appeal	The contract between an accountancy body and its student members related solely to internal governance and administration. Where the body was incorporated under Royal Charter that was a matter over which the visitor had exclusive jurisdiction and the court could have no jurisdiction over the dispute.
R. v. Institute of Chartered Accountants ex parte Nawaz [1997] 7 CL 1 Court of Appeal	By acceptance of membership of the ICAEW a chartered accountant undertook, under the rules, to provide such information as the Investigation Committee may consider necessary to discharge its functions and this acted as a waiver of the chartered accountant's privilege against self incrimination.

Professional Negligence

Slattery v Moore Stephens [2004] PNLR 241 Robert Englehart QC	Failure to advise a client who was resident but not ordinarily resident in the UK for tax purposes to pay his foreign earnings into an offshore bank account was a breach of the duty of care owed by a reasonably competent and careful accountant to advise on tax mitigation.
Goldstein v Levy Gee (2003) The Times 16th June Lewison J	Valuation of shares was a matter of judgement to be exercised by the accountant with reasonable care and skill and in determining whether or not liability arose a judge must determine whether the figures fell outside the bracket of a permissible margin of error.
Sasea Finance v KPMG [2000] 1 BCLC 236 Court of Appeal	Once an auditor had discovered evidence of fraud or other serious misconduct, the auditor was under a duty to report this at once rather than waiting until the accounts were signed off.
Grimm v Newman [2003] 1 All ER 67 Court of Appeal	In determining whether an accountant was negligent in his advice on tax planning the court would determine the issue on whether or not the advice was correct in law and was not entitled examine whether or not, on the underlying substance, the transaction was vulnerable to attack by the Revenue as a sham.

Law Society v KPMG Peat Marwick (2000) The Times 6th July Court of Appeal	Accountants preparing reports on solicitors accounts owe a duty of care to the Law Society as the trustees of the solicitors' compensation fund as the reports are relied upon by the Law Society when deciding whether or not to intervene in a solicitors' practice or not.
Peter Lingham v Karl Lonnkvist (2000) Lawtel 12th July Court of Appeal	The nexus was too remote between the negligent preparation of figures on behalf of a client to raise finance from a potential lender to buy a business to recover losses suffered by his client flowing from the client's decision to purchase the business.
Hands v Coopers & Lybrand (2001) Lawtel 25th April Sachs J	Auditors did not owe creditors of a company they were auditing any duty of care to advise on the prudence of making a loan.
Royal Bank of Scotland v Bannerman Johnston Maclay (2002) The Times 1st August Court of Session, Outer House (Scot)	For a relationship of proximity to exist between an auditor and a bank that relied upon their financial statements when making lending decisions, it was not necessary for the bank to prove that the auditor intended that the bank should rely upon them. It was open for the auditor to include a disclaimer and they had not done so.
Killick v Pricewaterhouse Coopers Neuberger J [2001] 1 BCLC 65	An accountant owed a duty of care to the executors under the will of a shareholder when valuing the shareholder's shares even though the executors were not party to the contract for the valuation.

West Wiltshire District Council v. Garland [1995] 2 WLR 439 Court of Appeal	Whilst local authorities were able to bring an action against a district auditor for breach of statutory duty under Section 15, Local Government Finance Act 1982 or in negligence, no such duty of care was owed to council officers.
Willingale v. International Commercial Bank Ltd [1978] AC 834 House of Lords	Whilst a SSAP has no weight in law, compliance with its accounting principles is *prima facie* evidence that accounts are true and fair.
Law Society v Sephton [2006] 3 All ER 401 House of Lords	The Law Society's cause of action against a negligent accountant arose not when he negligently certified that solicitor had complied with the Solicitors Accounts Rules but when the Law Society's Solicitors Compensation Fund faced a claim for compensation. By virtue of the terms of the compensation fund rules, the solicitor's misappropriations gave rise to the possibility of a liability to pay a grant out of the fund, contingent upon the misappropriation not otherwise being made good and a claim in the proper form being made. Such a contingent liability was only actionable damage when the contingency occurred and until then the claim was hypothetical.
James McNaughten v. Hicks Anderson & Co [1991] 2 QB 113 Court of Appeal	Group's accountants were held to be insufficiently proximate to owe a duty of care in a case where their draft accounts were shown to a company seeking to take over the group.

Deloitte Haskins & Sells v. National Mutual Nominees [1993] AC 774 House of Lords	Auditors were insufficiently proximate to the trustees of a company to owe a duty of care to report of the company's probable insolvency. Note also, here no loss was proven.
Caparo Industries v. Dickman [1990] 2 AC 605 House of Lords	Audited accounts were not supplied to shareholders to assist them in their decision as to whether or not to invest in the company and therefore the auditors owed them no duty of care in the preparation of the audit whether as members of the public or as shareholders.
Berg & Sons v. Adams (1992) *Financial Times*, 10th July Hobhouse J	Auditors were not liable in negligence to the company for failing to qualify their certification of accounts for uncertainty over information provided by the effective sole proprietor of the company as the company neither relied on the accounts nor was it misled by them.
Sayers v Clarke Walker (2002) EWCA Civ 910 Court of Appeal	A practitioner who had failed to advise a client on how to maximise his tax advantages when purchasing shares in a company but instead suggested to the client that specialist tax advice be sought, did not do enough to absolve him from his obligation to give the client competent advice. Advice on how to maximise the client's tax advantages should have been within the practitioner's general competence as an accountant and the practitioner's failure to give such advice amounted to a breach of his retainer and/or negligence.

Human Rights

Thlimmenos v Greece (2001) 31 EHRR 159 European Court of Human Rights	Where a Greek Jehovah's witness had been refused admission as an accountant on the grounds that he had a military tribunal conviction for refusing to wear a military uniform, the refusal to admit him to his chosen profession was in breach of his human rights (Articles 9 and 14 ECHRR) as it was disproportionate given that the underlying reason for his conviction was his religious beliefs.
Luksch v Austria (2002) 35 EHRR 17 European Court of Human Rights	Disciplinary proceedings against an accountant, which had lasted 11 years (due to their awaiting the outcome of criminal proceedings) and were neither complex nor delayed by the accountant, were in breach of Article 6(1) of the European Convention of Human Rights.

Fiduciary Duties

HRH Prince Jeffri Bolkiah v. KPMG [1999] 1 All ER 517, [1999] 2 WLR 215 House of Lords	The court would restrain an accountant from taking on a client where there was a real and not merely fanciful or theoretical but not substantial risk of disclosure or misuse of confidential information of a former client unless the accountant could satisfy the court by clear and convincing evidence that effective measures had been taken to ensure no disclosure would occur.

Nitrotrim v. Wildin (1996) LTL 29 April McKinnon J	An accountant has a fiduciary duty to warn a client that a conflict of interest might arise and that he should seek independent advice. The fiduciary duty of accountants is the same as that of solicitors.
R. v. Southwark Crown Court ex parte Bowles [1996] 4 All ER 961 Simon Brown LJ	Breach of client confidentiality exposing an accountant to possible disciplinary action may amount to grounds to challenge a production order under Section 93H, Criminal Justice Act 1982.

Accountants and the courts

Home or Away v Customs & Excise Commissioners (2002) Lawtel 3rd May VADT (Angus Nicol, Chairman)	Legal professional privilege did not cover the relationship between an accountant and his client and thus an accountant, unlike a solicitor, was compellable as a witness against his client to give evidence on the present and previously advanced case.
Parmar (trading as Ace Knitwear) v Woods (2002) The Times 5th June, [2002] STI 852 Lightman J	The mere fact that the chartered accountant, appearing as advocate for a tax payer before the tax commissioners, was incompetent or had misunderstood that his submissions could not be treated as evidence by the commissioners was not enough to render the hearing unfair. An accountant appearing before the tax commissioners as an advocate warrants that he had the requisite expertise and legal knowledge required to do so.

R v Secretary of State for Transport ex parte Factortame [2002] 3 WLR 1104 Court of Appeal	An arrangement under which accountants provided forensic accountancy services to litigants on a contingency fee basis was not one to which s.58 Courts and Legal Services Act 1990 had any application and was not void for champerty. Section 58 applied only to conditional fee agreements between clients and "litigators", i.e. in relation to the provision of advocacy and litigation services. To allow an expert to have a financial interest in the outcome of the case carried great dangers for his objectivity and the proper administration of justice and it would be very rare for the court to consent to an expert being instructed on a contingency fee basis. Here the accountants were not instructed as expert witnesses but had carefully restricted their role to the provision of accountancy support services to the experts who would be called for the claimants.
Cassell v. Crutchfield (Inspector of Taxes) (1995) The Times, 8th June Blackburne J	Suspension from membership of the Institute of Cost and Management Accountants and the Chartered Association of Certified Accountants deprived an accountant of his right of audience under Section 50(5), Taxes Management Act 1970 before the General Commissioners.
Malhotra v. Dhawan (1997) LTL 28 April Court of Appeal.	Where accounting records had been destroyed the principle in *Gray v. Haig - omnia praesumuntur contra spoiliatorem* - should be applied in the following way:

	• if the destruction was deliberate so as to hinder the proof of the claimant's claim, then there would be an inference as to the credibility as to the destroyer enabling the court to disregard his evidence • if the court was undecided as to which of the two parties' evidence to accept, then it should decide in favour of the party who had not destroyed the documents • if the court had a clear view as to the truth, the Judge was not bound to follow the principle
R. v. Southwark Crown Court ex parte Bowles [1996] 4 All ER 961 Simon Brown LJ	Breach of client confidentiality exposing an accountant to possible disciplinary action may amount to grounds to challenge a production order under Section 93H, Criminal Justice Act 1982.
Heald Foods v. *Hyde Dairies* (1996) LTL 6 December Court of Appeal	The determination of an accountant sitting as expert and not arbitrator is only challengeable by proof by the person challenging his determination of manifest error or that the expert had departed from his instructions. There was a presumption that an experienced accountant qualified for the task has carried out the task properly and correctly. There was no obligation on the expert to set out his reasons and the failure to do so did not give rise to an implication of error.

Client's papers

Fox v Uxbridge General Commissioners [2002] STC 455 Jacob J	An accountant required to produce client's documents which were of a type likely to be retained by the accountant by a notice under section 20(3) Taxes Management Act 1970, could not discharge his obligations by the bare assertion that the documents could not be found. To escape from a penalty under section 98(1) Taxes Management Act 1970, the account needed to either prove the documents had been destroyed or could not be found after a thorough search and explain the nature of the search conducted.
Woodworth* v. *Conroy [1976] 2 WLR 338 Court of Appeal	Accountants in the course of their ordinary business had at least a particular lien over books of accounts, files and papers which had come into their possession in the course of that work for unpaid fees. In considering whether to refuse inspection under RSC Order 24 rule 13 the court would consider whether disclosure was necessary for fairly disposing of the action or for saving costs.
Peter Pan Manufacturing* v. *Corset Silhouette [1963] RPC 45	An obligation to examine books enables the examining accountant to query whether the books offered for inspection are the only relevant ones and may demand, on behalf of his principal, that other books be produced which he has reason to believe contain relevant information.

DTC v. ***Gary Sergeant*** [1996] 1 WLR 797 Crystal QC	No accountant's lien can arise over a company's statutory accounting records within the meaning of Sections 221 and 222 Companies Act 1985.
Anglo-American Asphalt Company Ltd v. ***Crowley Russell & Co Ltd*** [1945] 2 All ER 324 Romer J	A contractual obligation to permit the grantor to inspect accounts would ordinarily continue in force even if the agreement is terminated.
Harrison v. ***Festus Timothy*** [1998] 2 CL 1 Butterfield J	An accountant's lien over papers is sufficiently preserved by a solicitor's undertaking to preserve the lien where the papers are needed for litigation. *Obiter*, it was doubted whether an accountant's lien could arise over VAT returns.

Accountants and Tax

Chartered Accountant v ***Inspector of Taxes*** [2003] STI 885 Lloyd J	In determining whether or not an accountant had made fraudulent claims for interest relief, the standard of proof before the Special Commissioners was the balance of probabilities. In weighing the evidence the Special Commissioners should however take into account that it was inherently unlikely that a professional accountant of good standing would have acted fraudulently in the absence of strong evidence to the contrary.

Cassell v. Crutchfield (Inspector of Taxes) (1995) The Times, 8th June Blackburne J	Suspension from membership of the Institute of Cost and Management Accountants and the Chartered Association of Certified Accountants deprived an accountant of his right of audience under Section 50(5), Taxes Management Act 1970 before the General Commissioners.

Contract

Barry v Bradshaw [2001] ILPr 706, [2000] CLC 455 Court of Appeal	Where an Irish accountant was sued by Irish domiciled clients in relation to an alleged breach of contract and negligence by failing to make representations in respect of the clients' English tax affairs, the Irish accountant was held to have submitted to the English court's jurisdiction. The Court of Appeal reasoned that the place of performance of the contract was England as this was the place where the Inland Revenue and any communication by the accountant with the Inland Revenue would therefore have been performed in England.
Sylvanus Okoye v. Leon Edgar White (1999) LTL 17 February Court of Appeal	The implied term that an accountant would use reasonable care and skill in preparing accounts included a duty not to take an excessive length of time. It was therefore open to a trial Judge to adjust the recoverable hours claimed to a figure he found reasonable for the work done and to

	adjust billing rate down where the work reflected bookkeeping services done by the accountant as opposed to accounting work.
Fomento (Sterling Area) Ltd v. Felfdon Fountain Pen Company Limited [1958] RTC 8 House of Lords	Breach of an obligation to allow an examining accountant to examine their books was a breach entitling rescission of the contract.
Fawkes-Underwood v. *Hamiltons* [1997] 7 CL 456, (1997) LTL 24 March Judge Goudie QC	The extent of the duties of an accountant went no further than what they are requested and undertake to do - there was no such thing as a general retainer. By offering and agreeing to provide "general advice and assistance" as regards Lloyds' membership, the accountants took themselves beyond the normal duties of an accountant and took on a duty to identify which were high risk syndicates.

Freedom to provide accountancy services

| *Markapolou v Minister for Development* Case C255/01 European Court of Justice | The 8th Council Directive 84/253 EEC on the approval of persons to carry out statutory audits of accounting documents had to be transposed into national law before 1st January 1998. Accountants holding equivalent qualifications in a member state to the host state could be exempted from a requirement to pass an examination to practice in the host state. The host Member States had to consider whether the |

	diplomas of the other Member State certified equivalent knowledge and qualification to that in the host state. If they corresponded wholly, the host member state had to recognise the diploma as fulfilling the requirements laid down by the national provisions. If they corresponded in part, the host state had to afford the accountant the opportunity of showing that he had made up the deficiency in some other way – whether by study or experience in the host member state.
Ramrath* v. *Minister of Justice [1992] CL 4769 European Court of Justice	The right of establishment entailed the right to set up and maintain more than one place of establishment within the European Community. A member state was entitled to ensure compliance with professional rules justified by the public interest concerning the good repute and independence of auditors as long as they were applicable to anyone acting as an auditor within that territory. Minimum conditions over actual presence appeared justified to ensure protection of the public interest. However, if the auditor, who was only temporarily in the country, provided his services through a firm who was already regulated as an auditor then the national authority could ensure compliance through that firm.

Accounts

Shorrock* v. *Meggitt [1991] BCC 471 Court of Appeal	A certificate of net deficit was not valid where the auditors, as they were uncertain, declined either to certify the deficit or refuse to do so.
Willingale* v. *International Commercial Bank Ltd [1978] AC 834 House of Lords	Whilst a SSAP has no weight in law, compliance with its accounting principles is *prima facie* evidence that accounts are true and fair.

Qualifications

INSTITUTES AND ASSOCIATIONS IN ENGLAND CONFERRING THE QUALIFICATION OF ACCOUNTANT

Title conferred:

Chartered Accountant

The Institute of Chartered Accountants in England and Wales
Moorgate Place
London EC2P 2BJ

(Member of the Consultative Committee of Accounting Bodies)

Chartered Certified Accountant

The Association of Chartered Certified Accountants
29 Lincoln's Inn Fields
London WC2 3EE

(Member of the Consultative Committee of Accounting Bodies)

Chartered Management Accountant

The Chartered Institute of Management Accountants
26 Chapter Street
London SW1P 4NP

(Member of the Consultative Committee of Accounting Bodies)

Chartered Public Finance Accountant

The Chartered Institute of Public Finance and Accountancy
3 Robert Street
London WC2N 6RL

(Member of the Consultative Committee of Accounting Bodies)

Incorporated Executive Accountant

The Institute of Cost and Executive Accountants
Akhtar House
2 Shepherds Bush Road
London W6 7PJ

Incorporated Financial Accountant

The Institute of Financial Accountants
Burford House
44 London Road
Sevenoaks
Kent TN13 1AS

Incorporated International Accountant[1]

The Association of International Accountants
Staithes 3,
The Watermark
Metro Riverside
Newcastle upon Tyne
NE11 9SN

Authorised Public Accountant/Registered Auditor

Association of Authorised Public Accountants
29 Lincoln's Inn Fields
London WC2 3EE

---

[1] The Institute of Company Accountants has been amalgamated into the Association of International Accountants and their members (Incorporated Commercial Accountants) are now entitled to style themselves "International Accountants".

Useful Websites

www.ccab.org.uk	Consultative Committee of Accountancy Bodies
www.icaew.co.uk	Institute of Chartered Accountants in England and Wales
www.icai.ie	Institute of Chartered Accountants in Ireland
www.icas.org	Institute of Chartered Accountants in Scotland
www.accaglobal.com	Association of Chartered Certified Accountants
www.cimaglobal.com	Chartered Institute of Management Accountants
www.cipfa.org.uk	Chartered Institute of Public Finance and Accountancy
www.icea.enta.net	Institute of Cost and Executive Accountants
www.ifa.org.uk	Institute of Financial Accountants
www.aia.org.uk	The Association of International Accountants[1]
www.accaglobal.com/aapa/	The Association of Authorised Public Accountants
www.frc.org.uk	Financial Reporting Council
www.frc.org.uk/aidb	Accountancy Investigations and Discipline Board
www.frc.org.uk/apb	Auditing Practices Board
www.frc.org.uk/asb	Auditing Standards Board
www.frc.org.uk/frrp	Financial Reporting Review Panel
www.frc.org.uk/pob	Professional Oversight Board
www.efrag.org	European Financial Reporting Advisory Group
www.fee.be	European Federation of Accountants
www.fasb.org	Financial Accounting Standards Board

---

[1] The Institute of Company Accountants has been amalgamated into the Association of International Accountants and their members are now entitled to style themselves "International Accountants".

Index

All references are to Paragraph number

Accountancy Investigation and Discipline Board
  disciplinary proceedings, and, 9.1.8
Accountancy practices
  companies, 2.1.3
  forms
    companies, 2.1.3
    limited liability partnerships, 2.1.2
    partnerships, 2.1.1
  goodwill
    dissolution, on, 2.5.3
    nature, 3.5.1
    ownership, 2.5.2
    protection, 2.5.2
    sale, 2.5.4
  limited companies, 2.1.3
  limited liability partnerships
    agreements, 2.1.2.2
    audit, 2.1.2.8
    bankruptcy, and, 2.1.2.6
    designated members, 2.1.2.5
    disqualification of directors, and, 2.1.2.6
    introduction, 2.1.2
    legal nature, 2.1.2.1
    liability for negligence, 2.1.2.7
    membership, 2.1.2.4—2.1.2.6
    name, 2.1.2.3
    restrictions on membership, 2.1.2.6
  marketing
    general freedom, 2.3
    investment business, 2.3.1
    qualifications on freedom, 2.3.1—2.3.2
  name
    common law restrictions, 2.2.3
    generally, 2.2.1
    passing off, and, 2.2.3
    professional restrictions, 2.2.4—2.2.4.5
    statutory restrictions, 2.2.2
  partnerships
    checklist for deed, Annex 1
    consequences of relationship, 2.1.1.3
    creation, 2.1.1.1
    discrimination, 2.1.1.6
    dissolution, 2.1.1.2
    introduction, 2.1.1
    large partnerships, 2.1.1.5
    mixed practices, 2.1.1.4
    remuneration, 2.1.1.1
    sex discrimination, 2.1.1.6
  permitted name
    common law restrictions, 2.2.3
    generally, 2.2.1
    passing off, and, 2.2.3
    professional restrictions, 2.2.4—2.2.4.5
    statutory restrictions, 2.2.2
  sale
    assets and liabilities, 2.4.1
    "block of fees", 2.4.1.1
    book debts, 2.4.1.3
    cash in hand, 2.4.1.3
    caveat emptor, and, 2.4.2
    checklist for agreement, Annex 2
    client list, 2.4.1.1
    computers, 24.1.5
    contracts, 2.4.1.2
    disclosure letter, 2.4.2
    employees, 2.4.1.6
    furniture, 2.4.1.5
    goodwill, 2.4.1.1
    heads of agreement, Precedent 2
    intellectual property rights, 2.4.1.7
    introduction, 2.4
    leases, 2.4.1.4

office equipment, 2.4.1.5
premises, 2.4.1.4
tenancies, 2.4.1.4
warranties, 2.4.2
work in progress, 2.4.1.3
Accountants
common law, and, 1.1.2
defamation, 1.4
definition
generally, 1.1.3
membership of incorporated society, 1.1.4—1.1.5
statutory test, 1.1.4
distinction from bookkeepers, 1.1.7
excluded persons, 1.1.6
introduction, 1.1.1
other uses of term, 1.1.8
status, 1.2.1
Accounting standards
FRS, 6.2.2
IAS, 6.2.4
IFRS, 6.2.4
SAS, 6.2.3
SSAP, 6.2.1
Advocacy
Commissioners, before, 8.1.5
general position, 8.1.1
powers of court, 8.1.4
professional risks, 8.1.2
small claims, 8.1.3
Assets and liabilities
sale of accountancy practices, and, 2.4.1
Association of Authorised Public Accountants (AAPA)
And see Professional bodies
generally, 1.1.4
investment business, 7.2.5
licensing, 1.2.5.3
name of accountancy practices, 2.2.4.3
Association of Chartered Certified Accountants (ACCA)
And see Professional bodies
generally, 1.1.4
history, 1.1.5
investment business, 7.2.4
licensing, 1.2.5.2

marketing, 2.3.2.2
misuse of name, 1.2.3
mutual recognition of qualifications, 10.1.2
name of accountancy practices, 2.2.4.2
status of membership, 1.2.1
Association of International Accountants (AIA)
And see Professional bodies
generally, 1.1.4
history, 1.1.5
licensing, 1.2.5.7
marketing, 2.3.2.5
misuse of name, 1.2.3
name of accountancy practices, 2.2.4.4
status of membership, 1.2.1
Auditors
See also Audits
agency, and, 5.2.3
appointees, 5.1.4
appointment
appointees, 5.1.4
consequences, 5.1.6
duration, 5.3.1
eligible persons, 5.1.3
excluded persons, 5.1.5
termination, 5.3.2—5.3.5
certainty of certificate, 5.2.4
claims against
See also Claims against auditors
auditor's reports, 6.1.8
basis of liability, 6.1.1
breach of contract, 6.1.2
damages, 6.1.4
exclusion clauses, 6.1.6—6.1.7
insurance companies, 6.1.9
limitation period, 6.1.5
tortious liability, 6.1.3
consequences of appointment, 5.1.6
contracts with, 5.2.2
duties
extension of, 5.4.6
form true and fair view of company's position, 5.4.4

heed powers of audited
  company, 5.4.5
 report to members on annual
  accounts, 5.4.3
eligible persons, 5.1.3
excluded persons, 5.1.5
failure to re-appoint, 5.3.2
freedom to appoint, 5.2.5
generally, 5.1.2
misuse of name or qualifications,
  5.1.7
mutual recognition
 Companies Act 2006, and,
  10.2.3
 generally, 10.21
 rights arising, 10.2.2
reappointment, 5.3.5
regulatory framework, 5.1.3
resignation, 5.3.4
rights
 access to books, records and
  accounts, 5.4.2
 receipt of notice of meetings,
  5.4.1
 require information from
directors, 5.4.2
role, 5.2.1
supervisory function, 5.2.1
termination of appointment
 failure to re-appoint, 5.3.2
 introduction, 5.3.1
 ordinary resolution of
  company, 5.3.3
 resignation, 5.3.4
 statement of circumstances,
  5.3.5
Auditors' report
 claims against auditors, and, 6.1.8
 generally, 5.1.8
Audits
 auditors
  And see **Auditors**
  agency, and, 5.2.3
  appointees, 5.1.4
  certainty of certificate, 5.2.4
  consequences of appointment,
   5.1.6
  contracts with, 5.2.2
  eligible persons, 5.1.3

excluded persons, 5.1.5
freedom to appoint, 5.2.5
generally, 5.1.2
misuse of name or
 qualifications, 5.1.7
regulatory framework, 5.1.3
rights and duties, 5.4.1—5.4.6
role, 5.2.1
supervisory function, 5.2.1
termination of appointment,
 5.3.1—5.3.6
auditors' report, 5.1.8
banking companies, 5.1.1.2
dormant companies exemption
 exceptions, 5.1.2
 generally, 5.1.1
exemptions
 exceptions, 5.1.2
 generally, 5.1.1
 insurance companies, 5.1.1.3
limited liability partnerships, and,
 2.1.2.8
reporting accountants
 abolition, 5.5.5
 eligibility for appointment,
  5.5.2
 membership of specified
  bodies, 5.5.2—5.5.3
 report, 5.5.4
 role, 5.5.1
 statutory framework, 5.5.1
small companies
 exceptions, 5.1.2
 generally, 5.1.1
statutory auditor, 5.1.8
Authorised public accountants
 investment business, 7.2.5
 licensing, 1.2.5.3
 name of accountancy practices,
  2.2.4.3

Banking companies
 audits, and, 5.1.1.2
Bankruptcy
 limited liability partnerships, and,
  2.1.2.6
BarDIRECT scheme
 instruction of counsel, and, 8.2.2

"Block of fees"
  sale of accountancy practices, and, 2.4.1.1
"Bolam" test
  claims against accountants, and, 4.1.3.1
Book debts
  sale of accountancy practices, and, 2.4.1.3
Bookkeepers
  distinction from accountants, 1.1.7
Breach of contract
  claims against accountants, and, 4.1.2
  claims against auditors, and, 6.1.2
Breach of fiduciary duty
  claims against accountants, and, 4.1.4

Cash in hand
  sale of accountancy practices, and, 2.4.1.3
Caveat emptor
  sale of accountancy practices, and, 2.4.2
Chartered accountants
  investment business, 7.2.6
  licensing, 1.2.5.1
  marketing, 2.3.2.1
  name of accountancy practices, 2.2.4.1
Chartered certified accountants
  investment business, 7.2.4
  licensing, 1.2.5.2
  marketing by accountants, 2.3.2.2
  name of accountancy practices, 2.2.4.2
Chartered Institute of Management Accountants (CIMA)
  And see Professional bodies
  generally, 1.1.4
  history, 1.1.5
  licensing, 1.2.5.4
  marketing, 2.3.2.7
  misuse of name, 1.2.3
  mutual recognition of qualifications, 10.1.2
  name of accountancy practices, 2.2.4.5
  status of membership, 1.2.1
Chartered Institute of Public Finance and Accountancy (CIPFA)
  And see Professional bodies
  disciplinary proceedings, 9.1.9
  generally, 1.1.4
  history, 1.1.5
  licensing, 1.2.5.6
  marketing, 2.3.2.4
  misuse of name, 1.2.3
  mutual recognition of qualifications, 10.1.2
  status of membership, 1.2.1
Chartered management accountants
  licensing, 1.2.5.4
  marketing, 2.3.2.7
  name of accountancy practices, 2.2.4.5
Chartered public finance accountants
  licensing, 1.2.5.6
  marketing, 2.3.2.4
Civil litigation
  claims against accountants
    See also Claims against accountants
    basis of liability, 4.1.1—4.1.5
    breach of contract, 4.1.2
    breach of fiduciary duty, 4.1.4
    contractual liability, 4.1.2
    damages, 4.1.6
    exclusion clauses, 4.1.8
    limitation period, 4.1.7
    tortious liability, 4.1.3
    warranty of authority, 4.1.5
  claims against auditors
    See also Claims against auditors
    auditor's reports, 6.1.8
    basis of liability, 6.1.1
    breach of contract, 6.1.2
    damages, 6.1.4
    exclusion clauses, 6.1.6—6.1.7
    insurance companies, 6.1.9
    limitation period, 6.1.5
    tortious liability, 6.1.3
  expert adjudicators, 8.4
  expert witnesses

duties, 8.3.4
generally, 8.3.1
immunity from suit, 8.3.5
privileges and limitations, 8.3.2
qualification, 8.3.3
instruction of Counsel
  BarDIRECT scheme, 8.2.2
  generally, 8.2.1
legal professional privilege
  generally, 8.5.1
  limits, 8.5.2
rights of audience
  Commissioners, before, 8.1.5
  general position, 8.1.1
  membership of professional bodies, and, 1.2.3.1
  powers of court, 8.1.4
  professional risks, 8.1.2
  small claims, 8.1.3
Claims against accountants
  basis of liability
    contract, 4.1.2
    fiduciary duty, 4.1.4
    introduction, 4.1.1
    tort, 4.1.3
    warranty of authority, 4.1.5
  breach of contract, 4.1.2
  breach of fiduciary duty, 4.1.4
  contractual liability, 4.1.2
  damages, 4.1.6
  exclusion clauses, 4.1.8
  limitation period, 4.1.7
  tortious liability
    "Bolam" test, 4.1.3.1
    contributory negligence, 4.1.3.2
    generally, 4.1.3.1
    introduction, 4.1.3
    negligent misstatements, 4.1.3.1
  warranty of authority, 4.1.5
Claims against auditors
  auditor's reports, 6.1.8
  basis of liability
    breach of contract, 6.1.2
    introduction, 6.1.1
    tort, 6.1.3
  breach of contract, 6.1.2

damages, 6.1.4
exclusion clauses, 6.1.6—6.1.7
insurance companies, 6.1.9
limitation period, 6.1.5
tortious liability
  contribution, 6.1.3.3
  contributory negligence, 6.1.3.2
  generally, 6.1.3.1
  introduction, 6.1.3
Client list
  sale of accountancy practices, and, 2.4.1.1
Client-accountant relationship
  contracts of engagement
    absence of written terms of engagement, 3.1.2.1
    compliance with professional conduct rules, 3.1.2.2.3
    exclusion clauses, 3.1.2.3
    implied terms, 3.1.2.2
    introduction, 3.1.1
    letter of engagement, 3.1.2
    reasonable care and skill, 3.1.2.2.1
    sample, Precedent 1
    terms, 3.1.2.2
    time to complete work, 3.1.2.2.2
    unfair contract terms, 3.1.2.3
  fiduciary duties
    client, to, 3.2.1
    conflicts of interest, 3.2.3.3
    employer, to, 3.2.2
    nature, 3.2.3
    obedience, 3.2.3.2
    reasonable care and skill, 3.2.3.2
    utmost good faith, 3.2.3.1
Companies
  form of accountancy practices, and, 2.1.3
Company secretaries
  disqualification, 7.4.2
  generally, 7.4.1
Computers
  sale of accountancy practices, and, 2.4.1.5

Conflicts of interest
  fiduciary duties to client, and,
  3.2.3.3
Consumer credit licences
  membership of professional
  bodies, and, 1.2.3.2
Contracts
  sale of accountancy practices, and,
  2.4.1.2
Contracts with clients
  absence of written terms of
  engagement, 3.1.2.1
  exclusion clauses, 3.1.2.3
  implied terms
    compliance with professional
    conduct rules, 3.1.2.2.3
    reasonable care and skill,
    3.1.2.2.1
    time to complete work,
    3.1.2.2.2
  introduction, 3.1.1
  letter of engagement
    generally, 3.1.2
    sample, Precedent 1
  terms, 3.1.2.2
  unfair contract terms, 3.1.2.3
Contractual liability
  claims against accountants, and,
  4.1.2
Contributory negligence
  claims against accountants, and,
  4.1.3.2
  claims against auditors, and,
  6.1.3.2
Counsel, instruction of
  BarDIRECT scheme, 8.2.1, 8.2.2

Damages
  claims against accountants, and,
  4.1.6
  claims against auditors, and, 6.1.4
De facto directors, 7.3.1
De jure directors, 7.3.1
Defamation, 1.4
Direct professional access
  BarDIRECT scheme, 8.2.2
  generally, 8.2.1
Directors
  disqualification
    'cut-throat' defences, 7.3.3
    generally, 7.3.1
    vulnerability of accountants,
    7.3.2
    meaning, 7.3.1
    limited liability partnerships, and,
    2.1.2.6
Disciplinary proceedings
  admissible evidence, 9.1.5
  appeals, 9.1.7
  binding decisions, 9.1.2
  CIPFA, and, 9.1.9
  contractual relationship with
  professional body, 9.1.1
  courts, and
    enforcement powers, 9.3.1
    human rights, 9.2.2
    judicial review of disciplinary
    decision, 9.3.2
    stay of proceedings, 9.3.3
  hearings, 9.1.6
  human rights
    enforcement by courts, 9.2.2
    generally, 9.2.1
    hearings, and, 9.1.6
  investigation of complaints, 9.1.4
  judicial review of decision, 9.3.2
  misconduct, 9.1.3
  role of Accountancy Investigation
  and Discipline Board, 9.1.8
  stay of proceedings, 9.3.3
Disclosure
  revenue investigations, and
    other powers to compel, 1.3.3
    statutory power, 1.3.1
    "tax accountants", 1.3.2
  sale of accountancy practices, and,
  2.4.2
Discrimination
  partnerships, and, 2.1.1.6
Disqualification of directors
  'cut-throat' defences, 7.3.3
  "director", 7.3.1
  generally, 7.3.1
  limited liability partnerships, and,
  2.1.2.6
  vulnerability of accountants, 7.3.2
Dissolution
  goodwill, and, 2.5.3

partnerships, and, 2.1.1.2
Dormant companies
    audits, and
        exceptions, 5.1.2
        generally, 5.1.1
Employees
    sale of accountancy practices, and, 2.4.1.6
Employment of accountants
    checklist, Annex 3
    fit and proper enquiries, Annex 4
Engagement letters
    absence of written terms, 3.1.2.1
    exclusion clauses, 3.1.2.3
    generally, 3.1.2
    implied terms
        compliance with professional conduct rules, 3.1.2.2.3
        reasonable care and skill, 3.1.2.2.1
        time to complete work, 3.1.2.2.2
    introduction, 3.1.1
    terms, 3.1.2.2
    unfair contract terms, 3.1.2.3
Exclusion clauses
    claims against accountants, and, 4.1.8
    claims against auditors, and, 6.1.6—6.1.7
    contracts with clients, and, 3.1.2.3
Expert adjudicators, 8.4
Expert witnesses
    checklist for instruction, Annex 5
    checklist for report, Annex 6
    duties, 8.3.4
    generally, 8.3.1
    immunity from suit, 8.3.5
    privileges and limitations, 8.3.2
    qualification, 8.3.3
Fiduciary duties
    client, to
        conflicts of interest, 3.2.3.3
        introduction, 3.2.1
        obedience, 3.2.3.2
        reasonable care and skill, 3.2.3.2
        utmost good faith, 3.2.3.1

    employer, to, 3.2.2
    nature, 3.2.3
Financial Reporting Standards (FRS), 6.2.2
Financial services
    authorised public accountants, 7.2.5
    chartered accountants, 7.2.6
    chartered certified accountants, 7.2.4
    designated professional bodies, 7.2.1
    incidental to professional services, 7.2.1
    "investment", 7.2.2
    "investment business", 7.2.3
    mainstream investment business, 7.2.1
    regulatory framework, 7.2.1
    unauthorised conduct of investment business, 7.2.1
Fit and proper enquiries
    checklist, Annex 4
Furniture
    sale of accountancy practices, and, 2.4.1.5
Goodwill
    dissolution, on, 2.5.3
    nature, 3.5.1
    ownership, 2.5.2
    protection, 2.5.2
    sale, 2.5.4
    sale of accountancy practices, and, 2.4.1.1
Human rights
    disciplinary proceedings, and
        enforcement by courts, 9.2.2
        generally, 9.2.1
        hearings, and, 9.1.6
Implied terms
    contracts with clients, and
        compliance with professional conduct rules, 3.1.2.2.3
        reasonable care and skill, 3.1.2.2.1
        time to complete work, 3.1.2.2.2

Incorporated executive accountants
  licensing, 1.2.5.5
  marketing, 2.3.2.3
Incorporated financial accountants
  licensing, 1.2.5.8
  marketing, 2.3.2.6
Incorporated societies of accountants
  And see Professional bodies
  generally, 1.1.4
  history, 1.1.5
Insolvency practitioners
  authorisation to act, 7.1.4
  disqualification from acting, 7.1.3
  licence to act
    generally, 7.1.1
    recognised professional bodies, 7.1.2
Institute of Chartered Accountants (ICA) *And see* Professional bodies
  generally, 1.1.4
  history, 1.1.5
  investment business, 7.2.6
  licensing, 1.2.5.1
  marketing, 2.3.2.1
  misuse of name, 1.2.3
  mutual recognition of qualifications, 10.1.2
  name of accountancy practices, 2.2.4.1
  status of membership, 1.2.1
Institute of Cost and Executive Accountants (ICEA)
  And see Professional bodies
  generally, 1.1.4
  licensing, 1.2.5.5
  marketing, 2.3.2.3
Institute of Financial Accountants (IFA) *And see* Professional bodies
  generally, 1.1.4
  history, 1.1.5
  licensing, 1.2.5.8
  misuse of name, 1.2.3
  status of membership, 1.2.1
Instruction of counsel
  BarDIRECT scheme, 8.2.2
  generally, 8.2.1
Insurance companies
  audits, and, 5.1.1.3
  claims against auditors, and, 6.1.9

Intellectual property rights
  sale of accountancy practices, and, 2.4.1.7
International accountants
  licensing, 1.2.5.7
  marketing, 2.3.2.5
  name of accountancy practices, 2.2.4.4
International accounting standards (IAS), 6.2.4
International financial reporting standards (IFRS), 6.2.4
International practice
  mutual recognition of accountants
    designated authorities, 10.1.2
    generally, 10.1.1
    rights arising, 10.1.3
  mutual recognition of auditors
    Companies Act 2006, and, 10.2.3
    generally, 10.21
    rights arising, 10.2.2
Investment business
  authorised public accountants, 7.2.5
  chartered accountants, 7.2.6
  chartered certified accountants, 7.2.4
  designated professional bodies, 7.2.1
  incidental to professional services, 7.2.1
  "investment", 7.2.2
  mainstream investment business, 7.2.1
  meaning, 7.2.3
  regulatory framework, 7.2.1
  unauthorised conduct of investment business, 7.2.1

Judicial review
  disciplinary proceedings, and, 9.3.2
Leases
  sale of accountancy practices, and, 2.4.1.4
Legal professional privilege
  generally, 8.5.1
  limits, 8.5.2

Letters of engagement
  absence of written terms, 3.1.2.1
  exclusion clauses, 3.1.2.3
  generally, 3.1.2
  implied terms
    compliance with professional conduct rules, 3.1.2.2.3
    reasonable care and skill, 3.1.2.2.1
    time to complete work, 3.1.2.2.2
  introduction, 3.1.1
  sample, Precedent 1
  terms, 3.1.2.2
  unfair contract terms, 3.1.2.3
Liability for negligence
  limited liability partnerships, 2.1.2.7
Licensing of accountants
  authorised public accountants, 1.2.5.3
  chartered accountants, 1.2.5.1
  chartered certified accountants, 1.2.5.2
  chartered management accountants, 1.2.5.4
  chartered public finance accountants, 1.2.5.6
  incorporated executive accountants, 1.2.5.5
  incorporated financial accountants, 1.2.5.8
  international accountants, 1.2.5.7
  introduction, 1.2.5
Limitation period
  claims against accountants, and, 4.1.7
  claims against auditors, and, 6.1.5
Limited companies
  form of accountancy practices, and, 2.1.3
Limited liability partnerships
  agreements, 2.1.2.2
  audit, 2.1.2.8
  bankruptcy, and, 2.1.2.6
  designated members, 2.1.2.5
  disqualification of directors, and, 2.1.2.6
  introduction, 2.1.2
  legal nature, 2.1.2.1
  liability for negligence, 2.1.2.7
  membership, 2.1.2.4—2.1.2.6
  name, 2.1.2.3
  restrictions on membership, 2.1.2.6
Litigation
  expert adjudicators, 8.4
  expert witnesses
    duties, 8.3.4
    generally, 8.3.1
    immunity from suit, 8.3.5
    privileges and limitations, 8.3.2
    qualification, 8.3.3
  instruction of Counsel
    BarDIRECT scheme, 8.2.2
    generally, 8.2.1
  legal professional privilege
    generally, 8.5.1
    limits, 8.5.2
  rights of audience
    Commissioners, before, 8.1.5
    general position, 8.1.1
    membership of professional bodies, and, 1.2.3.1
    powers of court, 8.1.4
    professional risks, 8.1.2
    small claims, 8.1.3
Marketing by accountants
  general freedom, 2.3
  investment business, 2.3.1
  professional qualifications on freedom
    chartered accountants, 2.3.2.1
    chartered certified accountants, 2.3.2.2
    chartered management accountants, 2.3.2.7
    chartered public finance accountants, 2.3.2.4
    incorporated executive accountants, 2.3.2.3
    incorporated financial accountants, 2.3.2.6
    international accountants, 2.3.2.5
    introduction, 2.3.2

statutory qualifications on freedom, 2.3.1
Misconduct
  disciplinary proceedings, and, 9.1.3
Mutual recognition
  accountants, of
    designated authorities, 10.1.2
    generally, 10.1.1
    rights arising, 10.1.3
  auditors, of
    Companies Act 2006, and, 10.2.3
    generally, 10.21
    rights arising, 10.2.2

Name of accountancy practices
  common law restrictions, 2.2.3
  generally, 2.2.1
  passing off, and, 2.2.3
  professional restrictions
    authorised public accountants, 2.2.4.3
    chartered accountants, 2.2.4.1
    chartered certified accountants, 2.2.4.2
    chartered management accountants, 2.2.4.5
    international accountants, 2.2.4.4
    introduction, 2.2.4
  statutory restrictions, 2.2.2
Negligence
  claims against accountants, and
    "Bolam" test, 4.1.3.1
    contributory negligence, 4.1.3.2
    exclusion clauses, 4.1.8
    generally, 4.1.3.1
    introduction, 4.1.3
    limitation period, 4.1.7
    negligent misstatements, 4.1.3.1
  claims against auditors, and
    contribution, 6.1.3.3
    contributory negligence, 6.1.3.2
    generally, 6.1.3.1
    introduction, 6.1.3

Obedience
  fiduciary duties to client, and, 3.2.3.2
Office equipment
  sale of accountancy practices, and, 2.4.1.5
Partnerships
  checklist for deed, Annex 1
  consequences of relationship, 2.1.1.3
  creation, 2.1.1.1
  discrimination, 2.1.1.6
  dissolution, 2.1.1.2
  introduction, 2.1.1
  large partnerships, 2.1.1.5
  mixed practices, 2.1.1.4
  remuneration, 2.1.1.1
  sex discrimination, 2.1.1.6
Precedents
  annual general meetings
    notice, Precedent 24
  appointment of auditors
    board resolution, Precedent 22
    notice preventing, Precedent 28
    ordinary resln, Precedent 23
  auditors liability limitation agreement
    resolution, Precedent 32
  disciplinary proceedings
    model grounds of appeal, Precedent 21
  dissolution of accountancy partnership
    claim form, Precedents 19
    particulars of claim, Precedent 20
  injunction to release papers
    application notice, Precedent 15
    claim form, Precedents 16
    draft minutes of order, Precedent 18
    witness statement, Precedent 17
  late preparation of accounts
    defence and counterclaim, Precedent 5
    reply and defence to counterclaim, Precedent 6

laying accounts before general meeting
   resolution, Precedent 31
negligent audit
   claim form, Precedent 12
   defence, Precedent 14
   particulars of claim, Precedent 13
negligent tax claim
   claim form, Precedent 9
   defence, Precedent 11
   letter of claim, Precedent 7
   particulars of claim, Precedent 10
   pre-action protocol letter, Precedent 8
non-appointment of auditors
   dormant companies, Precedent 30
re-appointment of auditors
   resolution, Precedent 25
removal of auditors
   resolution, Precedent 29
resignation by auditors
   letter, Precedent 26
termination of appointment of auditors
   ordinary resolution, Precedent 27
unpaid accountancy fees
   claim form, Precedent 3
   particulars of claim, Precedent 4
Premises
   sale of accountancy practices, and, 2.4.1.4
Privilege
   generally, 8.5.1
   limits, 8.5.2
Professional bodies
   basis of regulation
      consequences of membership, 1.2.3
      generally, 1.2.1
      misuse of name of body, 1.2.3
   consequences of membership
      consumer credit licences, 1.2.3.2
      generally, 1.2.3
      rights of audience, 1.2.3.1
   generally, 1.1.4
   history, 1.1.5
   licensing
      authorised public accountants, 1.2.5.3
      chartered accountants, 1.2.5.1
      chartered certified accountants, 1.2.5.2
      chartered management accountants, 1.2.5.4
      chartered public finance accountants, 1.2.5.6
      incorporated executive accountants, 1.2.5.5
      incorporated financial accountants, 1.2.5.8
      international accountants, 1.2.5.7
      introduction, 1.2.5
   misuse of name, 1.2.3
   relationship with membership, 1.2.4
Professional conduct rules
   implied terms, and, 3.1.2.2.3
Professional negligence
   "Bolam" test, 4.1.3.1
   contributory negligence, 4.1.3.2
   damages, 4.1.6
   exclusion clauses, 4.1.8
   generally, 4.1.3.1
   introduction, 4.1.3
   limitation period, 4.1.7
   negligent misstatements, 4.1.3.1

Reasonable care and skill
   fiduciary duties to client, and, 3.2.3.2
   implied terms, and, 3.1.2.2.1
Reporting accountants
   abolition, 5.5.5
   eligibility for appointment, 5.5.2
   membership of specified bodies, 5.5.2—5.5.3
   report, 5.5.4
   role, 5.5.1
   statutory framework, 5.5.1
Revenue investigations
   tax accountants
      definition, 1.3.2
      other powers to compel disclosure, 1.3.3
      statutory power, 1.3.1

Rights of audience
  Commissioners, before, 8.1.5
  general position, 8.1.1
  membership of professional bodies, and, 1.2.3.1
  powers of court, 8.1.4
  professional risks, 8.1.2
  small claims, 8.1.3
Sale of accountancy practices
  assets and liabilities, 2.4.1
  "block of fees", 2.4.1.1
  book debts, 2.4.1.3
  cash in hand, 2.4.1.3
  caveat emptor, and, 2.4.2
  checklist for agreement, Annex 2
  client list, 2.4.1.1
  computers, 2.4.1.5
  contracts, 2.4.1.2
  disclosure letter, 2.4.2
  employees, 2.4.1.6
  furniture, 2.4.1.5
  goodwill, 2.4.1.1
  heads of agreement, Precedent 2
  intellectual prop rights, 2.4.1.7
  introduction, 2.4
  leases, 2.4.1.4
  office equipment, 2.4.1.5
  premises, 2.4.1.4
  tenancies, 2.4.1.4
  warranties, 2.4.2
  work in progress, 2.4.1.3
Sex discrimination
  partnerships, and, 2.1.1.6
Shadow directors, 7.3.1
Small companies
  audits, and
    exceptions, 5.1.2
    generally, 5.1.1
Statement of circumstances
  termination of auditors' appointment, and, 5.3.5
Statements of Auditing Standards (SAS), 6.2.3
Statements of Standard Accounting Practice (SSAP), 6.21
Statutory auditor, 5.18

"Tax accountants"
  revenue investigations
    definition, 1.3.2
    other powers to compel disclosure, 1.3.3
    statutory power, 1.3.11
Tenancies
  sale of accountancy practices, and, 2.4.1.4
Time to complete work
  implied terms, and, 3.1.2.2.2
Tortious liability
  claims against accountants, and
    "Bolam" test, 4.1.3.1
    contributory negligence, 4.1.3.2
    generally, 4.1.3.1
    introduction, 4.1.3
    negligent misstatements, 4.1.3.1
  claims against auditors, and
    contribution, 6.1.3.3
    contributory negligence, 6.1.3.2
    generally, 6.1.3.1
    introduction, 6.1.3
Trainee accountants
  relationships
    accountancy firm, with, 1.5.2
    professional body, with, 1.5.1
  status, 1.5.1—1.5.2
True and fair view
  duties of auditors, and, 5.4.4

Unfair contract terms
  contracts with clients, and, 3.1.2.3
Utmost good faith
  fiduciary duties to client, and, 3.2.3.1

Warranties, sale of accountancy practices, and, 2.4.2
Warranty of authority
  claims against accountants, and, 4.1.5
Work in progress
  sale of accountancy practices, and, 2.4.1.3